The Brave Sons of Skye

[Scotland]

Containing the Military Records
(Compiled from Authentic Sources) of the
Leading Officers, Non-Commissioned Officers, and
Private Soldiers Whom "Eilean A Cheo" Has Produced

with 100 Portraits

Na laoich nach robh meata,
Ri aodann a' bhatail,
Nach aomadh gu taise,
Ri caismeachd an namh;
Cha 'n 'eil raon agus machair,
Air 'n do sgaoil iad am bratach,
Nach d' fhàg iad an eachdraidh
Gun mhasladh do 'n àl.
—*Niall MacLeoid*

Lieut. Col. John MacInnes, V.D.
5th Volunteer Battalion (Princess Louise's) Argyll and Sutherland Highlanders

HERITAGE BOOKS
2010

HERITAGE BOOKS
AN IMPRINT OF HERITAGE BOOKS, INC.

Books, CDs, and more—Worldwide

For our listing of thousands of titles see our website
at
www.HeritageBooks.com

A Facsimile Reprint
Published 2010 by
HERITAGE BOOKS, INC.
Publishing Division
100 Railroad Ave. #104
Westminster, Maryland 21157

Originally published
Eyre and Spottiswoode,
Government, Legal, and General Publishers,
London: East Harding Street, E.C.
Norman MacLeod: Edinburgh
1899

— Publisher's Notice —
In reprints such as this, it is often not possible to remove blemishes from the original. We feel the contents of this book warrant its reissue despite these blemishes and hope you will agree and read it with pleasure.

International Standard Book Numbers
Paperbound: 978-0-7884-1769-6
Clothbound: 978-0-7884-8520-6

TO MY WIFE
AND CHILDREN

PREFACE.

MY researches (which began several years ago) regarding "The Brave Sons of Skye," having now come to a close, it only remains for me to offer, once more, my warmest thanks to those ladies and gentlemen who have so cordially helped me in my work, and without whose enthusiastic assistance this book would never have seen daylight. Much of the military history of the Island of Skye has undoubtedly been lost for ever; but, while we deplore this loss, we have reason to be proud of the noble heritage of valorous deeds—some of which are still unique in the annals of war—that has come down to us from the "brave and the true" of our kith and kin. Let this fact be remembered for ever, to the credit of the people of Skye, that, in the many official records (and they lie not, neither do they screen the worthless) which were searched in the course of this inquiry, only three cases of alleged misconduct against Skyemen came to light, and that, after due investigation, all the three charges broke down, and the individuals concerned were "honourably acquitted."

To the following ladies I feel under a deep obligation for the kind help and encouragement which they have given to me, viz.: The Lady MacDonald of the Isles; The Honourable Mrs. Abdy, London; Lady MacLeod, Glasgow; Miss MacKinnon (of Kyle), Edinburgh; the late Mrs. MacLeod-Clerk of Kilmallie; Mrs. Ann MacDonald, late of Eigg, now of Glasgow; Miss F. Tolmie, Oban; Miss Maggie M. Elder, late of Knock, Sleat; Miss Scobie, Keoldale, Sutherlandshire; Miss Cameron, of Dunvegan House, Dunedin, New Zealand; Mrs. Watson, Alness, Ross-shire; and Mrs. MacKenzie,* of Park House, Inverness, widow of "the

---

* Mrs. MacKenzie, in giving me permission to make quotations from her late husband's most valuable works, said, in the handsomest manner: "I shall be pleased for you to make "any extracts you like from my late husband's works, providing you acknowledge them "either in the preface or in the footnotes."

Clan Historian"—a man whose name will be revered by Highlanders in all future ages.

My grateful acknowledgments are also due to the gentlemen now named for the valuable aid which they have afforded to me, viz.:—MacLeod of MacLeod; General E. F. Chapman, C.B., commanding the North British District; General Lyttelton-Annesley, of Templemere, Weybridge; Admiral Norman MacLeod, of the Dutch Royal Navy; Lieutenant-General Sir R. C. Stewart, K.C.B., of the Indian Army; the late Lieutenant-General Sir Henry Lynedoch-Gardiner, K.C.V.O.; the late Surgeon-General W. C. MacLean, C.B., Southampton; Colonel Lionel D. MacKinnon, Tovil Court, Maidstone; Colonel Walter Henry MacKinnon, Grenadier Guards, Assistant-Adjutant-General, Horse Guards, London; Colonel Cunliffe Martin, C.B., Cheltenham; Colonel Hannay, Argyll and Sutherland Highlanders; Colonel Burnley-Campbell of Ormidale, Argyllshire; Colonel E. P. Campbell, younger, of South Hall, Argyllshire; Major John MacRae-Gilstrap of Ballimore, Argyllshire; Major Lewis MacFarlane, Lochgoilhead, Argyllshire; Captain W. M. Campbell of Glendaruel, The Black Watch; Captain Stewart of Ensay; Captain Norman MacLeod of Dalvey; Captain George B. MacQueen of Dundas Castle, Queensferry; Major John Wolrige-Gordon, Argyll and Sutherland Highlanders; Captain Malcolm MacDonald of Tormore, Sleat; Lieutenant John MacLeod, late of the 4th King's Own Royals; Lieutenant John MacCaskill, The Queen's Own Corps of Guides; Lieutenant Bernard Fletcher of Dunans, Argyllshire; The Reverend John Walker-Macintyre, Kilmodan, Argyllshire; The Reverend Roderick Charles MacLeod of MacLeod, Mitford Vicarage, Morpeth; The Reverend Donald D. MacKinnon, Speldhurst Rectory, Tunbridge Wells; The Reverend D. J. MacDonald of Killean and Kilchenzie, Argyllshire; The Reverend W. H. MacLeod, Minister of Buchanan; The Reverend Alexander Cameron, Minister of Sleat, Skye; Dr. Alexander Morrison, Larkhall; Mr. Alexander MacDonald of Balranald; Mr. Cameron, Banker, Stranraer (brother of the late talented Historian of Skye); Mr. John Mackay, Editor of "The Celtic Monthly;" Mr. Miles MacInnes, ex-M.P. for Hexham; Mr. Norman D. MacDonald, Advocate, Edinburgh; the late Mr. Roderick MacLeod, Merchant, Edinburgh; Mr. Samuel Nicolson, Secretary, Glasgow Skye Association; my relative, Mr. Norman MacLeod, Bookseller, Edinburgh; my brother-in-law,

Mr. James Brown, Greenock; and my cousin, Mr. John MacKinnon, Cruard, Isleornsay, Skye.

And I wish with particular gratitude to mention the names of those ladies and gentlemen who have been most closely associated with me in my task, and whose unwearied exertions in helping me during my inquiries have been beyond all praise. Lady MacLeod, late of Wardie, Edinburgh, now of London; Miss Susan M. Martin, of Glendale, Skye; Miss Janet MacAlister, of Portobello; Miss Flora D. MacKinnon, of Duisdale House, Sleat; and Mrs. D. Gordon (daughter of Major-General Coll MacLeod), have in the kindest manner given to me most useful information about, and several portraits of, their distinguished relatives respectively—the MacDonalds of Scalpay, the MacAlisters of Skye, the MacKinnons of Strath, the MacLeods of Arnisdale, and others. The late Surgeon-General Sir W. A. MacKinnon, K.C.B., was able (owing to his eminent official position) to expedite materially my researches at the War Office, the India Office, and the Public Records Office. Dr. Keith Norman MacDonald[*] of Ord; Mr. A. R. MacDonald, younger, of Waternish; Colonel Alexander MacDonald of Portree; Colonel D. W. MacKinnon, Edinburgh; Captain R. M. Livingstone MacDonald of Flodigarry; and Mr. Alexander R. Forbes, of the General Register House, Edinburgh, have rendered most important service to this work by their indefatigable zeal and enthusiasm, as well as by their accurate and extensive knowledge of Highland history, especially that of the people of Skye.

To my second cousin, Mr. James Kennedy, Greenock (an accomplished German and Dutch scholar), for his accurate translation from Dutch into English of the military records of the Netherlands branch of the Gesto MacLeods, I feel much indebted, as I do also to Sergeant-Instructor William MacPhail, of the Argyll and Sutherland Highlanders, for the perfectly satisfactory manner in which he has photographed for me many of the miniature portraits and other likenesses of "The Brave Sons of Skye."

The officials at the War Office, the India Office, and at the depôts of various regiments of the British Army, have, with uniform kindness and courtesy, furnished to me many valuable extracts from public records;

---

[*] The author of "The Gesto Collection of Highland Music": the best of the kind ever published.

and to all those gentlemen I now beg, publicly, to tender my heartiest thanks.

It may be mentioned, in conclusion, that a special effort was made to gather information regarding the military careers of the many non-commissioned officers and private soldiers whom "Eilean a Cheo" has produced, and the war medals which they had gained. With this object in view, a printed circular was sent (as a last resource) to each of the 48 school districts into which the island is divided, but the result was somewhat disappointing. As has been already stated, many of the records have been lost, and most of the medals seem to have disappeared with the gallant men who wore them.

It may not be inappropriate if, at this stage, some reference is made to, and reliable information given about, a subject which has occupied a good share of public attention in Scotland—especially in the Highlands—for some time past, viz., "Recruiting, and the Advantages of the Army at the present day."

Recruits for infantry of the line may now enlist for three years' service with the colours and nine years' service in the reserve; or, if they prefer it, for seven years in the one and five years in the other; but the period of colour service can be extended to the regulation limit at any time. The rates of pay are the same as those which have hitherto been in force, but efficient soldiers who are nineteen years of age or upwards, receive additional pay of threepence a day, which may be increased further by good-conduct pay of from one penny to fourpence a day, as well as extra duty pay, varying from threepence to two shillings a day.

The ordinary daily pay of private soldiers varies from one shilling to one shilling and ninepence, and of non-commissioned officers from one shilling and threepence to six shillings, according to rank and branch of the service. A private soldier receives without payment a daily ration of three-quarters of a pound of good meat and one pound of bread. Vegetables and groceries are provided for by a stoppage from his pay of threepence or threepence-halfpenny a day. On active service a fuller ration, including vegetables and groceries, is issued free. After deducting all stoppages, however, a well-conducted soldier has, at his own disposal, about five shillings a week. Gratuities varying from £2 to £12, according to length of service, are paid to men passing from the colours to the reserve. Soldiers serving in the reserve are paid fourpence or sixpence a day according to the class in which they are placed.

If a soldier stays in the army for twenty-one years, and serves for at least three years as a non-commissioned officer, he earns a pension for life varying from £22 to £50, according to his rank and service as a non-commissioned officer. If he becomes a warrant officer he can earn a pension of £80 a year.

A soldier may, if he qualifies himself for it, rise to be a commissioned officer. There are at the present time in the army over seven hundred officers who enlisted as private soldiers.

With the view of affording Government employment to deserving soldiers, the Postmaster-General has decided that certain vacancies among provincial letter carriers, and the auxiliary postmen in London, are in future to be offered to discharged soldiers and Army Reserve men. Work is also provided for many old soldiers in the Royal Arsenal, the Royal Army Clothing Department, the Army Ordnance Department, the Customs, and other Government Departments, as well as in the Police forces, Railway Companies, Corps of Commissionaires, and otherwise through agencies established for the purpose at the headquarters of all regimental districts, and by means of the National Association for the Employment of Reserve and Discharged Soldiers whose chief office is in London, but of which numerous branch offices have been established in other large towns.

Schools.

Schools for the education of non-commissioned officers and men are established in nearly all military stations, with a view to enable men who are desirous of promotion to obtain the qualifying certificate of education. The schools are under the control of the generals commanding districts, and are managed and conducted by experienced schoolmasters. There are no charges for tuition, and books and all the necessary materials are supplied free. During the daytime the schools are used for the education — free — of soldiers' children and the children of pensioners in the employment of the Crown.

PREFACE.

Regimental Institutes.

In every unit there is a Regimental Institute, formed for the exclusive benefit and convenience of the troops, and with the following objects :—
To supply them with good articles at reasonable prices, without in any way interfering with their right to resort to any other shops or markets, and to organize and maintain the means available for their recreation and amusement.

The Regimental Institute is divided into two branches :—
- (1.) Refreshment department, which includes the canteen, grocery shop, and coffee room.
- (2.) Recreation department, which embraces the library, recreation-room, skittle alley, shooting gallery, cricket, football, sports, theatricals, &c., &c.

Libraries.

Libraries are established in all military stations. Their object is to afford to the troops the means, within the barracks, of employing their leisure hours usefully.

The books embrace every subject, including light literature, sciences, languages, travels, adventures, &c., &c.

Recreation Rooms.

Recreation rooms are established with the same object as libraries.

When the construction of barracks affords it, there are two rooms. One is used as a recreation room, the other as a room for games. Usually in the latter a coffee bar is placed, where the soldier can obtain refreshments of almost every description, at nearly the cost price of the articles.

Writing materials are also supplied and every facility given to the men to spend their leisure moments in a profitable manner. The rooms are well furnished, lighted, warmed, and supplied with every necessary.

JOHN MACINNES.

LIST OF ORIGINAL SUBSCRIBERS.

ABDY, Hon. Mrs. A. V.; 10, Lowndes Square, London, S.W.
ADAM, Frank, Esq., Glen Nevis Estate, Raven Mountain, Banjoewangie, Java.
ALLAN, Colin, Esq., J.P., Dunedin, New Zealand.
ANDERSON, Daniel, Esq.; Solicitor, Dunoon.
ANDERSON, J. N.; Provost and Solicitor, Stornoway.
ANNESLEY-LYTTELTON, Lieutenant-General Arthur; Weybridge, Surrey. 3 copies.

BENNETT, Alex. J., Esq.; Solicitor, Struan Lodge, Kirn.
BINNIE, James, Esq.; Inspector of Schools, Belmont, Kilmalcolm, Renfrewshire.
BLACK, Miss; Ardentraive, Colintraive, Kyles of Bute.
BLACK, Archibald, Esq.; Farmer, Balliemenach, Strachur, Argyllshire.
BLACK, George H., Esq.; Solicitor, Greenock.
BLACKIE, W. B., Esq.; 6, Belgrove Court, Edinburgh.
BLAIR, Mr. Campbell; Manchester.
BORLAND BROTHERS, Messrs. J. and J.; Clothiers, 109, St. Vincent Street, Glasgow.
BOYD, John, Esq.; H.M. Inspector of Schools, Mount Blow, Pollockshields, Glasgow.
BROWN, Archibald, Esq.; Merchant, 10, Brisbane Street, Greenock.
BROWN, James, Esq.; Collector of Water Rates, 32, Ardgowan Street, Greenock.
BROWN, William, Esq.; Publisher, Edinburgh.
BUCHANAN, Donald, Esq.; Farmer, Achanelait, Glendaruel, Greenock.
BUCHANAN, Duncan, Esq.; Auchenbreck, Colintraive, Argyllshire.
BURGESS, A., Esq.; Banker, Gairloch, Ross-shire.

CAMERON, Mrs.; Dunain House, Inverness.
CAMERON, Rev. D. A.; The Manse, South Knapdale, Ardrishaig, Argyll.
CAMERON, Rev. A.; Manse of Sleat, Broadford, Skye.
CAMERON, Ewan, Esq.; of Rutherford, Midlothian.

List of Original Subscribers.

CAMERON, Captain Ewen Donald Charles, Royal Artillery.
CAMERON, Captain K. N.; President, Mess Committee, 2nd Argyll and Sutherland Highlanders, Bareilly, Bengal.
CAMERON, P., Esq.; "Corriechollie," Edinburgh.
CAMPBELL, Alastair, Esq.; of Kilmartin.
CAMPBELL, Lord Archibald; Coombe Hill Farm, Kingston-on-Thames.
CAMPBELL, Archibald, Esq.; Rothesay.
CAMPBELL, Mrs. Burnley; Ormidale, Colintraive, Argyllshire.
CAMPBELL, Rev. D. M.; The Manse, Cumlodden, Inveraray.
CAMPBELL, Lieut.-Colonel D.; South Hall, Colintraive, Argyllshire.
CAMPBELL, Lieut.-Colonel E. P., junr.; of South Hall, Fourmerkland. 4 copies.
CAMPBELL, Lieut.-Colonel H. Burnley; Ormidale, Colintraive, Argyllshire.
CAMPBELL, Mrs. Lamont; Copsewood, Tighnabruaich, Argyllshire.
CAMPBELL, Malcolm, Esq.; 25, Regent Street, Greenock.
CAMPBELL, J., Esq.; Broadford, Skye.
CAMPBELL, J., Esq.; of Kilberry.
CAMPBELL, Captain Wm.; Port Glasgow.
CHISHOLM, A., Esq.; Hope Street, Anderston, Glasgow.
CLARK, R. Ingham, Esq.; 59, Portland Place, W.
COATES, M. Lindsay, Esq.; Rackheath Park, Norwich.
COLQUHOUN, Sir James, Bart.; Lord Lieutenant of Dumbartonshire. 3 copies.
CONNAL, William, Esq.; 19, Park Circus, Glasgow.
COWAN, George, Esq.; Tournaveen, Edinburgh.
CUMMING, W. Skeoch, Esq.; Edinburgh.
CURRIE, James, Esq.; Shipowner, Trinity Cottage, Edinburgh.

DALTON, Joseph, Esq.; Manager, Kames Gunpowder Works, by Tighnabruaich.
DARROCH, Captain D.; Argyll and Sutherland Highlanders, Chaubattia, India.
DAVIES, Leyshon, Esq.; Kames Gunpowder Works, by Tighnabruaich.
DAVY, G. B., J.P., Notts.; Spean Lodge, Spean Bridge.
DEWAR, Dr.; Portree.
DOWNIE, Surgeon-Lieutenant-Colonel Kenneth MacKenzie; 3, Lansdowne Crescent, Edinburgh.

ELLISON, Captain Ralph Carr, Royal Dragoons, Hedgeley, Alnwick.

List of Original Subscribers.

FLETCHER, B., Esq.; of Dunans, Colintraive, Argyllshire.
FORBES, A. R., Esq.; Edinburgh.

GILSTRAP, Major John MacRae; of Ballimore, Otter Ferry, Argyllshire. 6 copies.
GLASS, Charles, Esq.; 122, North Street, St. Andrews, Fife.
GORDON, Major J. W.; Churchill House, Kilmainham, Dublin.
GORDON, Mrs. D. T.; Orchard Leigh, Paignton, South Devon.
GORE, R. C.; Captain, Argyll and Sutherland Highlanders, Dunoon.
GRANT, Rev. Neil; Glendale, Skye.
GREIG, S., Esq., W.S.; 134, George Street, Edinburgh.

HENDERSON, George, Esq., Ph.D.; Edinburgh.

JENKINSON, Rev. Arthur; The Manse, Innellan, Argyllshire.
JOHNSTON, David, Esq.; Sub-Inspector of Schools, Tintagel, Dalry.

KENNEDY, James; Master Mariner, 11, Albert Place, Rothesay.
KENNEDY, Neil, Esq.; Merchant, Armadale, Skye. 2 copies.

LAURIE, Colonel Robert Peter, C.B.; Hardres Court, Canterbury.
LIVINGSTON, John, Esq.; Shipbuilder, Port Glasgow.
LOWE, W. H. Dick, Esq.; Solicitor, Supreme Courts, 7, Sandford Street, Portobello, Edinburgh.

MACALISTER OF GLENBAR, Major, C.B.
MACASKILL, Allan, Esq.; Ullinish, Skye.
MACASKILL, John, Esq.; Grangetown Hotel, Yorks.
MACCALLUM, Major D.; East Cliff, Campbeltown, Argyllshire.
MACCASKILL, John, Esq.; Drynoch, Skye.
MACCASKILL, John Malcolm, Esq.; New Zealand.
MACDONALD, Colonel Alexander, V.D.; Portree, Isle of Skye. 4 copies.
MACDONALD, Alexander, Esq.; 7, Hope Street, Greenock.
MACDONALD, Alexander, Esq., M.A.; H.M. Inspector of Schools, 14, Carmichael Place, Langside, Glasgow.
MACDONALD, Allan Reginald, Esq.; Waternish, Isle of Skye.
MACDONALD, Rev. A. J.; Minister of Killearnan.
MACDONALD, A. R., Esq.; Ord, Skye.
MACDONALD, C. Neil; Second Lieutenant, Argyll and Sutherland Highlanders.

MacDonald, C. R., Esq., M.D., Ayr.
MacDonald, D., Esq.; of Lynedale, Skye.
MacDonald, D., Esq.; 19, MacAlpine Street, Glasgow.
MacDonald, Rev. D. J.; The Manse of Killean, Muasdale, Kintyre.
MacDonald, H. L., Esq.; of Dunach, Oban.
MacDonald, Harry, Esq.; Indigo Planter, Viewfield, Portree, Isle of Skye.
MacDonald, The Right Honourable J. H. A.; Lord Justice Clerk of Scotland.
MacDonald, Keith Norman, M.D.; 21, Clarendon Crescent, Edinburgh. 2 copies.
MacDonald, Lachlan, Esq.; of Skaebost, Skye.
MacDonald, Malcolm N., Esq.; Skirinish, Skaebost Bridge, Isle of Skye.
MacDonald, Lieutenant J. R. Moreton; Largie Castle, Tayinloane, Argyllshire.
MacDonald, Neil, Esq.; Quarry Bay Refinery, Hong Kong.
MacDonald, Roderick, M.B., C.M.; East Street, Ipswich, Queensland, Australia.
MacDonald, Captain Ranald Livingston; 3rd Seaforth Highlanders, Flodigarry, Staffin, Skye. 4 copies.
MacDonald, Ronald, Esq.; Solicitor, Portree, Isle of Skye.
MacDonald, Surgeon-Major T. R.; 7, Strathearn Place, Edinburgh.
MacDonald, William, Esq.; Publisher, Edinburgh.
MacDougall, Major S.; of Lunga, Ardfearn, Argyllshire.
MacEwan, Wm. C., Esq., W.S.; Edinburgh.
MacFarlane, Lewis; Captain and Hon. Major, 5th V. B. Argyll and Sutherland Highlanders, Invermay, Douglas Pier, Lochgoil.
MacFarlane, Parlane, Esq.; Faslane, Dumbartonshire.
MacGilp, Rev. Alexander, B.D.; Free Church Manse, Kilmodan, Colintraive, by Greenock.
MacGregor, Alexander, Esq. (Messrs. Arthur & Co.); Glasgow.
McGregor, D. R., Esq., J.P.; Duntulm, Hawthorn, Victoria.
McInnes, Rev. A., B.D.; North Knapdale.
MacInnes, Colin, Esq.; Farmer, Dunrostan.
MacInnes, H., Esq.; Middlesboro'. 3 copies.
MacInnes, Ian L., Esq., M.B., Ch.B.; Great Stuart Street, Edinburgh.
MacInnes, John; Lieutenant-Colonel, 5th Vol. Batt. (P. L.) Argyll and Sutherland Highlanders, Glendaruel, Greenock. 10 copies.
MacInnes, John, Esq.; Merchant, Onich.
MacInnes, M., Esq.; Hotel, Tongue.
McInnes, Malcolm, Esq., M.A., LL.B., Edinburgh.

List of Original Subscribers.

MacInnes, Miles, J.P., D.L.; Rickerby, Carlisle.
MacIntosh, Captain James; 8, Ardgowan Street, Greenock.
MacIntyre, Mrs.; 40B, George Square, Edinburgh.
McIntyre, Rev. Alexander Æneas; Shieldaig, Lochcarron, Ross-shire.
MacIntyre, Duncan, Esq.; 26, Albany Street, Edinburgh.
MacIver, Mrs.; 94, Kensington Park Road, W. 2 copies.
MacKay, John, Esq., Ass. Inst. C.E., and J.P.; Reay House, Hereford. 2 copies.
MacKenzie, A., Esq.; Glasgow.
McKenzie, Rev. John F.; The Manse, Gigha, by Greenock.
MacKenzie, J., Esq., junr.; Dunvegan, Skye.
MacKenzie, M. J., Esq.; The School House, Lochcarron, Ross-shire.
MacKenzie, William, Esq.; Secretary to the Crofters' Commission.
MacKinnon, Miss; Duisdale House, Broadford, Skye.
MacKinnon, Alexander D.; Lieutenant, 1st Volunteer Battalion Q. O. Cameron Highlanders, Portree.
MacKinnon, Alexander K., Esq.; 12, Fopstone Road, South Kensington, S.W.
McKinnon, Angus, Esq.; Commercial Traveller, Edinburgh.
MacKinnon, Donald, Esq.; 6, East Shaw Street, Greenock.
MacKinnon, Donald, Esq.; 16, Strand, Calcutta.
MacKinnon, James, Esq.; 32, Ardgowan Street, Greenock.
MacKinnon, John, Esq.; Ballnakill, Clachan, Argyllshire.
MacKinnon, Lieutenant-Colonel L. D.; Dochgarroch Lodge, Inverness.
Mackinnon, Neil, Esq.; Commercial Traveller, Edinburgh.
MacKintosh, Dr. C. Fraser; of Drummond, Inverness, 18, Pont Street, S.W.
Mackintosh, D. A. S., Esq.; Bertohill House, Shettleston, Glasgow.
MacLachlan, D., Esq.; Solicitor and Bank Agent, Portree, Skye.
McLachlan, Rev. Hugh; Ardchattan Manse, Taynuilt, Argyllshire. 4 copies.
MacLean, Magnus, Esq., M.A., D.Sc., F.R.S.E., &c.; Lecturer on Physics, The University, Glasgow.
MacLellan, Miss; Rockwood, Killin.
MacLeod, A., Esq.; Bo'ness.
McLeod, A., Esq.; Superintendent of Public Parks and Gardens, Edinburgh.
MacLeod, Alex. S., Esq.; Manila.
MacLeod, A. W., Esq.; Glasgow.

MacLeod, Angus, Esq.; 25, Regent Street, Greenock.
MacLeod, Captain Angus, R.N.; H.M. Ship "Pembroke," Chatham. 3 copies.
MacLeod, Bannatyne, Esq.; Barrister-at-Law, Indian Civil Service.
MacLeod, Fred T.; Edinburgh.
MacLeod, J., Esq.; Letterwalton, Ledaig, Argyllshire.
MacLeod, John, Esq.; Alvanley Terrace, Edinburgh.
MacLeod, John M., Esq.; 4, Park Circus Place, Glasgow.
MacLeod, John N., Esq.; of Kintarbert and Glen Saddell, Argyll.
MacLeod, Hugh, Esq.; Solicitor, 87, St. Vincent Street, Glasgow.
MacLeod, Captain N.; Dalvey, Forres.
MacLeod, N., Esq.; Tarskavaig, Skye.
MacLeod, Neil, Esq.; The Skye Bard.
MacLeod, Rev. Norman, M.A.; Free Church Manse, Portree, Skye.
MacLeod, Admiral Norman; Ryswyk, Holland.
MacLeod, Norman, Esq.; Bookseller, 25, George IV. Bridge, Edinburgh.
MacLeod of MacLeod; The Bungalow, Horsham, Sussex.
Macleod of Macleod, Reginald, Esq., C.B.; Granton House. 2 copies.
MacLeod, Rev. R. C., of MacLeod; Mitford Vicarage, Morpeth.
MacLeod, R. C., Esq.; Secretary to Edinburgh Clan MacLeod Society.
MacLeod, Roderick, Esq.; Hill Bank, Edinburgh.
MacLeod, William Bowman, Esq., L.D.S.Edin., F.R.S.E.; 16, George Square, Edinburgh.
MacNaughton, Walter; Quartermaster-Sergeant (retired), 5th Volunteer Battalion Argyll and Sutherland Highlanders.
McNeill, D., Esq.; Secretary of the Bank of Scotland, Edinburgh.
MacNicol, Mrs., of Garvie; Glasgow.
MacNicol, John, Esq.; of Messrs. Robert Simpson & Sons, Glasgow.
MacNiven and Wallace, Messrs.; Booksellers, Edinburgh.
Macpherson, A. M., Esq.; Glasgow.
McQueen, George Bliss; (late) Captain, 60th Rifles and 51st Light Infantry, Dundas Castle, South Queensferry. 2 copies.
Macrae, Mrs.; 163, Sandyford Street, Glasgow.
Mactaggart, Dan; Major, 5th Volunteer Battalion Argyll and Sutherland Highlanders, Campbeltown.
Malcolm of Poltalloch, Lord, C.B.; Lochgilphead, Argyllshire. 2 copies.
Manson, William, Esq.; Proprietor of the Victoria Hotel, Lochgilphead.

MARSHALL, J. N., Esq., M.D.; 7, Battery Place, Rothesay, Bute.
MARTIN, Miss; Glendale, Dunvegan, Skye.
MARTIN, Rev. D. J., M.A.; Oban.
MARTIN, Lieutenant-Colonel M., R.E.; Upper Ostaig by Broadford, Isle of Skye. 2 copies.
MARTIN, Murdoch, Esq.; Glasgow.
MARTIN, Nicol, Esq.; Glendale, Dunvegan, Skye.
MATHESON, Angus, Esq.; 3, Chalmers Crescent, Edinburgh.
MELDRUM, Rev. A.; Logierait.
MENZIES, Captain D., Q.R.V.B.R.S.; Regent Terrace, Edinburgh.
MENZIES, R., Esq., S.S.C.; Royal Terrace, Edinburgh.
MITCHELL, Library; Glasgow.
MORRISON, Alexander C., M.B.C.M.; Kinloid House, Larkhall.
MORRISON, Hew, Esq.; Edinburgh Public Library.
MUNRO, William, Esq.; 13, Hamilton Street, Greenock.

NAPIER, Theodore, Esq.; Edinburgh.
NICOL, Donald N., M.P.
NICOLSON, Mr. Alexander; Butler, Monzie Castle, Perthshire.
NICOLSON, Alexander N., Esq.; 7, Cathcart Street, Greenock.
NICOLSON, Donald, Esq.; Bearsden, Glasgow.
NICOLSON, Mr. John; Warehouseman, Edinburgh.
NICOLSON, W.; Purser, S.S. Lochiel, Portree, Isle of Skye.

PURVES, Mrs. David; Belfast.

ROBERTSON, Alexander, Esq., C.C.; Yachtbuilder, Sand Bank.
ROBERTSON, Angus, Esq.; 11, Hill Street, Greenock.
ROSS, Alexander, Esq.; Merchant, 29, Major Street, Manchester.
ROSS, Andrew, Esq., S.S.C.; Edinburgh.
ROSS, Rector David, LL.D., J.P.; Training College, Glasgow.
RUSSELL, Rev. J. C., D.D.; Dunfillan, Dunoon.

SCOBIE, Miss; Keoldale, Durness, Lairg.
SKENE, Lawrence J.; Captain, 1st Vol. Batt. Queen's Own, Cameron Highlanders, Portree.
SMITH, Mrs. Jervis; Brocksford Hall, Doveridge, Derby.

SMITHE, Major P. B.; Bangalore, Madras.
SOMERSET, H. G. the Duchess of; Maiden Bradley, Bath.
SOMERVILLE, John, Esq.; 11, Regent Terrace, Edinburgh.
STALEY, Mrs. A. E.; 6, Dudley Road, New Brighton, Cheshire.
STEWART, Andrew, Esq.; Lochview, Burnside, Rutherglen.
STUART, Captain John; The Black Watch, Perth.

THOM, Allan Gilmour, Esq.; Younger of Canna.
THOMSON, P. L., Esq.; of Strathaird, Skye.
TOLMIE, Rev. A. M. C., M.A.; Southend, Kintyre.
TOLMIE, Donald, Esq.; New Zealand.
TOLMIE, Hugh MacAskill, Esq.; New Zealand.
TWEEDIE, Mrs.; Denholm, Polmont.

WALKER, Alexander, Esq.; Rosscairn, Kirn, Argyllshire.
WATT, Rev. L. Maclean, Turriff.
WHYTE, Duncan C., Esq.; Farmer, Crossaig, Kintyre. 2 copies.
WILKIE, Daniel, Esq.; Architect, 27, Queen's Square, Strathbungo, Glasgow.
WILLIAMSON, John, Esq.; Steamboat Owner, 7, Bridge Wharf, Glasgow.
WILSON, D. Macfarlane, Esq.; Dunira, Hunter's Quay.

INDEX.

	Page
Bethune, Angus ("The Fair")	166
Bethune, Angus ("The Strong")	166
Bethune, Ferquhard ("Brave and Quiet")	166
Bethune, John	166
Bethune, John, The Black Watch	166
Bethune, The Reverend John, Royal Highland Emigrant Regiment	167
Campbell, Colonel Charles, of Strond	125
Campbell, Lieutenant Donald, of Strond, Royal Navy	125
Campbell, Private Donald, Sleat	226
Chisholm, Dr. Stewart	170
Chisholm, Captain MacRa	170
Chisholm, Loudon	170
Elder, Major-General Sir George, K.C.B.	219–224
Elder, Lieutenant-Colonel Alexander MacDonald	224
Elder, Commander Benjamin John	224
Fraser, Private James, Sleat	226
Gardiner, Sir Henry Lynedoch, K.C.V.O., C.B.	194–196
Gilstrap, Major John MacRae, The Black Watch	170
Grant, Superintending Surgeon John	168
Lindsay, General Sir Alexander	171
MacAlister, Major-General Keith	68
MacAlister, Colonel Norman	68
MacAlister, Colonel Matthew	69
MacAlister, Colonel John	69
MacBeth, Sergeant John, Cameron Highlanders	225
MacCaskill, Major-General William, of Rù-an-Dùnain	156
MacCaskill, Captain Kenneth, of Rù-an-Dùnain	156–157
MacCaskill, Major-General Sir John, K.C.B., and K.H.	157–160
MacCaskill, Colonel John C.	160
MacCaskill, Lieutenant Charles	160
MacCaskill, Major William	160
MacCaskill, Lieutenant John, The Queen's Own Corps of Guides	160
MacCrimmon, Major, of Glenelg	161
MacCrimmon, Captain Norman	161
MacCrimmon, Captain Peter, of Borreraig	161
MacCrimmon, Captain Donald	161
MacCrimmon, Lieutenant Donald, The Black Watch	161

	Page
MacDonald, Hugh, I. of Sleat	3
MacDonald, Donald Gruamach, IV. of Sleat, Domhnull Gruamach MacDhomhnuill Ghallaich	3
MacDonald, Donald Gorm, V. of Sleat	4
MacDonald, Donald Gormson, VI. of Sleat	5
MacDonald, Donald Gorm Mòr, VII. of Sleat	5
MacDonald, Sir James, eighth Baron and first Baronet of Sleat	6
MacDonald, Sir James, ninth Baron and second Baronet of Sleat	6
MacDonald, Sir Donald, tenth Baron and third Baronet of Sleat	6
MacDonald, Sir Donald, eleventh Baron and fourth Baronet of Sleat—Donald of the Wars—Domhnull a Chogaidh	6
MacDonald, Sir Donald, twelfth Baron and fifth Baronet of Sleat	7
MacDonald, Captain Donald Roy, of Knockow	7
MacDonald, James, of Heiskeir	7
MacDonald, Captain Francis, Royal Navy	7
MacDonald, Captain Sir Archibald Keppel, Baronet	7
MacDonald's Highlanders, 76th Regiment of (Highland) Foot	12
MacDonald, Lieutenant-General Sir Godfrey MacDonald Bosville, third Lord MacDonald	12–13
MacDonald, Captain the Honourable Archibald	13
MacDonald, Lieutenant-Colonel the Honourable James, 1st Guards	13
MacDonald, Ensign the Honourable William	13
MacDonald, General the Honourable James William Bosville, C.B.	14
MacDonald, Lieutenant the Honourable William Bosville	14
MacDonald, "Donald Herrach"	15
MacDonald, Ronald MacDhomhnuill Herraich	15
MacDonald, Lieutenant-Colonel Alexander, of Lynedale, IX. of Balranald	15
MacDonald, Major James, of Lynedale, Deputy-Paymaster, Chatham	15
MacDonald, James, I. of Kingsburgh	15
MacDonald, Donald, III. of Kingsburgh, "Domhnull Mac Iain 'Ic Sheumais"	15
MacDonald, Alexander, IV. of Kingsburgh	16
MacDonald, Donald, V. of Kingsburgh	16
MacDonald, Alexander, VI. of Kingsburgh	16
MacDonald, Flora	16–20
MacDonald, Captain Allan, VII. of Kingsburgh—Flora MacDonald's husband	17–20
MacDonald, Captain Charles, VIII. of Kingsburgh	24–27
MacDonald, Lieutenant Alexander, of Kingsburgh	28
MacDonald, Captain Ranald, of Kingsburgh	29
MacDonald, Captain James, of Flodigarry	30
MacDonald, Lieutenant-Colonel John, F.R.S., &c., of Kingsburgh	31–32
MacDonald, Captain Hugh, of Armadale	18
MacDonald, Major Donald, 84th, The Royal Highland Emigrants	22
MacDonald, Captain Alexander, of Skaebost	22
MacDonald, Captain Kenneth, of Skaebost	22
MacDonald, Lieutenant-Colonel James Somerled, of Flodigarry	35
MacDonald, Captain Allan Ranald, of Flodigarry	42

Index.

	Page
MacDonald, Major-General William Pitt, of Kingsburgh	44
MacDonald, Lieutenant-General Sir John (of Scalpay), G.C.B., Adjutant-General to the Forces	44-47
MacDonald, Lieutenant-General Alexander, C.B., of Scalpay	47-49
MacDonald, Archibald, K.H., of Scalpay	49
MacDonald, General John A. M., C.B., of Scalpay	49-50
MacDonald, Major-General Norman, of Scalpay	50
MacDonald, Brigadier-General the Right Honourable J. H. A., C.B., of Scalpay	51-52
MacDonald, Lieutenant Ranald Hume, R.E., of Scalpay	52
MacDonald, Captain Donald, of Ostaig	53
MacDonald, Colonel Donald, III. of Castleton	53
MacDonald, Major Alexander, of Castleton	53
MacDonald, Captain William, of Castleton	53
MacDonald, Lieutenant Donald, 67th Regiment	54
MacDonald, John, M.D., F.R.S., Inspector-General of Hospitals and Fleets	54
MacDonald, Captain Donald, I. of Tormore	54
MacDonald, Captain Roderick, of Tormore	54
MacDonald, Mr. Malcolm Henry Somerled, of Tormore, Royal Navy	54
MacDonald, William and James, of Vallay	54
MacDonald, Lieutenant-General Donald, of Knock, in Sleat, Colonel of the 55th Regiment	55-62
MacDonald, Captain John, Breakish, Strath	62
MacDonald, Captain Ronald, of Belfinlay	63
MacDonald, Major Allan, of Waternish	63-65
MacDonald, Captain Allan, of Waternish	65
MacDonald, Dr. Alexander, "An Doctair Ruadh"	65
MacDonald, Captain Alexander	65
MacDonald, Captain Ronald	65
MacDonald, Captain John	65
MacDonald, Lieutenant Keith, R.N.	66
MacDonald, Lieutenant Charles, of Ord	66
MacDonald, Lachlan, of Skaebost	66
MacDonald, Dr. Keith Norman, of Ord	66
MacDonald, Lieutenant Charles Neil, Argyll and Sutherland Highlanders	66
MacDonald, Private Hugh, Sleat	74
MacDonald, Marshal	66
MacDonald, Colonel Charles Williamson, V.D.	66
MacDonald, Colonel Alexander, V.D.	66
MacDonald, Surgeon-Major Thomas Rankin	67
MacGilvray, Private Alexander, Sleat	226
MacInnes, General John	73
MacInnes, Private Neil	74
MacInnes, Private	74
MacIntosh, Private John, Isleornsay	225
MacIntyre, Private Murdoch, Sleat	226
MacIvors	129

Index.

	Page
MacKenzie, Lieutenant Alexander, Royal Navy	162
MacKenzie, Donald, of Hartfield	171
MacKenzie, Captain William, Royal Navy	162
MacKenzie, Private Murdoch	227
MacKinnon, Major-General Henry	201–203
MacKinnon, General George Henry, C.B.	203
MacKinnon, Colonel Daniel	204–207
MacKinnon, Major-General Daniel Henry	207
MacKinnon, Lieutenant-Colonel Daniel Lionel	207–208
MacKinnon, Lieutenant-Colonel Lionel Dudley	208
MacKinnon, Surgeon-Major-General Sir William Alexander, K.C.B.	208–213
MacKinnon, Dr. Kenneth, of Corry	213
MacKinnon, Lieutenant-Colonel Charles Kenneth, of Corry	213–214
MacKinnon, Major Alexander, of Kyle	214
MacKinnon, Captain Neil, of Kyle	214–215
MacKinnon, Captain Donald William, of Kyle	215
MacKinnon, Colonel Donald William, of Kyle	215
MacKinnon, Lieutenant-Colonel William Alexander, C.B., of Kyle	215–217
MacKinnon, Brigade-Surgeon-Lieutenant-Colonel H. W. A., D.S.O., Strath	217–218
MacKinnon, Colonel Walter Henry MacKinnon, Grenadier Guards, Strath	218
MacKinnon, Bombardier Peter	218–219
MacKinnon, Private Norman, Strath	219
MacLean, Major-General Archibald Neil, of Boreray and Drimnin	125
MacLean, Captain Roderick Norman, of Boreray and Drimnin	125
MacLean, Surgeon-General William Campbell, C.B., of Boreray and Drimnin	125–129
MacLean, Colonel Norman, C.B., of Dunhalin, Waternish	137
MacLean, Captain Donald, of Vatten	155–156
MacLean, Captain Malcolm (Calum Mac an Doctair)	167–168
MacLean, Captain, of Kilmaree, Strath	225
MacLeod, Sir Ruairidh Mòr	83–85
MacLeod, Major Alexander, of Lochbay	85
MacLeod, Captain Norman, Cyprus	85–88
MacLeod, Lieutenant-General Norman, XX. Chief	88–90
MacLeod, Lieutenant Norman, R.N.	91
MacLeod, Captain Norman Magnus, C.M.G., XXIII. Chief	94–95
MacLeod, Major John, X. of Gesto	95
MacLeod, Captain Neil, XI. of Gesto	95–96
MacLeod, Lieutenant Norman, Netherlands Branch	96
MacLeod, Colonel John, Netherlands Branch	96–97
MacLeod, Major-General Norman, Netherlands Branch	97
MacLeod, Lieutenant-General Norman, Netherlands Branch	97–98
MacLeod, Captain William Pasco, Netherlands Branch	98–99
MacLeod, Captain John Van Brienen, Netherlands Branch	99
MacLeod, Vice Admiral Norman, Netherlands Branch	99–100
MacLeod, Lieutenant-Colonel Edward Donald Henry, Netherlands Branch	100–101

Index.

	Page
MacLeod, Major Rudolph, Netherlands Branch	101
MacLeod, Sergeant-Major Daniel; Captain John; Captain Angus; Lieutenant William; Ensign Donald; Ensign James; Dr. William; Ensign John—all of the Dutch Service	102
MacLeod, Tormod, of Meidle	103
MacLeod, Alexander and William, of Meidle	103
MacLeod, Tormod, III. of Glendale	103
MacLeod, Colonel Norman, IV. of Glendale	103
MacLeod, Colonel John, V. of Glendale	103
MacLeod, Captain John, of Glendale	103
MacLeod, Captain William, of Glendale	103
MacLeod, Roderick, of Glendale	103
MacLeod, John, VII. of Glendale	103
MacLeod, Captain Kenneth, of Glendale	103
MacLeod, Major-General William, of Arnisdale	103–104
MacLeod, Major-General Coll, of Arnisdale	104–105
MacLeod, Lieutenant Coll, of Arnisdale	105
MacLeod, Lieutenant-Colonel William, of Arnisdale, 59th Regiment	105–106
MacLeod, Lieutenant-Colonel Alexander, C.B., of Arnisdale, 59th Regiment	107–110
MacLeod, Superintending-Surgeon Bannatyne William, M.D., C.B., IX. of Glendale	111
MacLeod, Lieutenant Donald, of Glendale, The Royal Scots	111–112
MacLeod, Major Roderick, of Bailemeanach	112
MacLeod, Captain Alexander, of Bailemeanach and Stein	112–113
MacLeod, Donald Glas, of Drynoch	113
MacLeod, Alexander, of Drynoch	113
MacLeod, Lieutenant-Colonel Norman Chester	113–115
MacLeod, Major-General William Edmonstone, of Drynoch	115
MacLeod, Major Donald, of Drynoch	115
MacLeod, Captain Norman, of Drynoch	115
MacLeod, Major Alexander, of Drynoch	115
MacLeod, Captain John, of Drynoch	115
MacLeod, Captain and Paymaster Martin, of Drynoch	115–116
MacLeod, Midshipman Roderick William Keir, of Drynoch	116
MacLeod, Lieutenant Donald MacDonald, of Drynoch	116
MacLeod, Lieutenant Forbes Brodie, of Drynoch	116
MacLeod, Lieutenant-Colonel James Farquharson, C.M.G., of Drynoch	116–117
MacLeod, Sir Roderick, of Talisker	117–118
MacLeod, Captain Donald, of Talisker	118
MacLeod, Captain John, of Talisker	118
MacLeod, Major-General Roderick Bannatyne, of Talisker	118
MacLeod, Captain Roderick William, of Talisker	118
MacLeod, Colonel John, of Talisker	118–119
MacLeod, Lieutenant Colonel Magnus, of Talisker	119
MacLeod, Captain Norman, of Talisker	119
MacLeod, Sir Norman, of Bernera	119–120
MacLeod, Lieutenant John, of Bernera	120

Index.

	Page
MacLeod, Donald, of Bernera ("The Old Trojan")	120–121
MacLeod, Lieutenant-General Sir John, C.B., K.C.H., of Bernera	121
MacLeod, Lieutenant-General Sir Charles, K.C.B., of Bernera	122–123
MacLeod, General Sir Alexander, C.B., of Bernera	123–124
MacLeod, Captain Norman, of Hamer	129
MacLeod, Lieutenant John, of Hamer	129
MacLeod, Captain William, of Hamer	129
MacLeod, Major-General Norman, C.B., of Gillen, Waternish	130–132
MacLeod, Captain Arthur Lyttelton	132
(MacLeod), Lieutenant-General Lyttelton-Annesley	133
MacLeod, Captain Norman, of Bracadale, East India Service	133–134
MacLeod, Captain Angus, Royal Navy	134–136
MacLeod, Major-General William Comperus, of the ancient Borline Family	137–139
MacLeod, Major-General Donald James Sim, C.B., D.S.O.	139
MacLeod, Captain John, of Claigean	140
MacLeod, Colonel Donald, of Claigean	140
MacLeod, Colonel Alexander, of Grishornish	140
MacLeod, General Sir Donald, K.C.B., of Bharkasaig	140–141
MacLeod, Captain John, "The Veteran"	141
MacLeod, Sergeant Donald, of Ulinish	141–144
MacLeod, Lieutenant Roderick, of Ulinish	144
MacLeod, Major Norman, of Ulinish	144
MacLeod, Major Alexander, of Dalvey	144
MacLeod, Captain Norman, of Dalvey	144
MacLeod, Captain Norman, of Bernisdale	144
MacLeod, Dr. Donald, of Bernisdale, Inspector-General of Hospitals	144–145
MacLeod, Lieutenant Roderick, of Bernisdale	145
MacLeod, Captain Norman, of Orbost	145
MacLeod, Colonel Donald, of Colbost	146
MacLeod, Major-General Donald, of Colbost	146–147
MacLeod, Major-General Alexander, of Colbost	147–148
MacLeod, Captain Donald, of Colbost	148–149
MacLeod, Lieutenant John, of Colbost	149
MacLeod, Alexander, of Minginish	149
MacLeod, Lieutenant Norman, of Ferinlea	149
MacLeod, Captain Alexander, of Ose	149
MacLeod, Captain Roderick, of Ose	149
MacLeod, Captain Donald, of Swordale	150
MacLeod, Surgeon-Major Sir George H. B., Knight, of Swordale	150–152
MacLeod, Captain John Norman, of Swordale, Indian Medical Service	152
MacLeod, Dr. Murdoch, of Ebost	152
MacLeod, Brigade-Surgeon-Lieutenant-Colonel Kenneth, of Ebost	153
MacLeod, Private John, The Black Watch	153
MacLeod, Private Norman, The Black Watch (The Soldier-Catechist)	153–154
MacLeod, Private Murdoch, Aird of Sleat	154
MacLeod, John, Royal Navy	154
MacLeod, Private Murdoch	154

Index.

	Page
MacLeod, Private Donald, 74th Regiment	154
MacLeod, Private Donald, Strath	155
MacLeod, John Garbh, of Raasay	169
MacLeod, Malcolm, VIII. of Raasay	169
MacLeod, Captain Malcolm, of Eyre	169
MacLeod, The Reverend Malcolm, of Raasay	169
MacLeod, Dr. Roderick, of Snizort	169–170
MacLeod, John, IX. of Raasay	170
MacLeod, Colonel James, of Raasay	170
MacLeod, Captain Malcolm, of Raasay	170
MacLeod, John, XI. of Raasay	171
MacLeod, Captain Norman, of Rigg	171
MacLeod, Captain John, of Ollach	171
MacLeod, Lieutenant John, of Eyre, Royal Navy	172
MacLeod, Colonel John, of Colbecks	171
MacLeod, Lieutenant-General Sir John, G.C.H., Royal Artillery, Raasay Family	173–179
MacLeod, Lieutenant-Colonel Charles, 43rd Regiment, Raasay Family	179–191
MacLeod, Colonel George, C.B., Royal Engineers, Raasay Family	192–193
MacLeod, Captain James, Raasay Family	193
MacLeod, Colonel Sir Henry, Knight, Raasay Family	194
MacLeod, General Harry, Royal Artillery, Madras, Raasay Family	196–197
MacLeod, Major Neil, Royal Artillery, Raasay Family	197–201
MacLure, Private William, Sleat	226
MacNabb, Sir Donald Campbell, K.C.I.E., C.I.E.	171
MacNabb, John Campbell Erskine	171
MacPherson, Private Alexander, Sleat	226
MacPherson, Private Angus	227
MacPherson, Private Angus, Sleat	226
MacPherson, Private Donald, Sleat	226
MacPherson, Private Malcolm, Sleat	226
MacPherson, Private Malcolm, List of Names supplied by him	226
MacPherson, Lance-Corporal Alexander, Sleat	227
MacQueen, Major John Donald, K.H.	70–71
MacQueen, Lieutenant John Archibald	71–72
MacQueen, Captain George Bliss	72
MacQueen, Malcolm	72
MacQueen, Colonel Potter	72
MacQueen, Captain John	72
MacQueen, Captain Henry	72
MacQueen, Private "Wallace"	229
MacRa, Colonel Sir John, K.C.H.	172–173
MacRae, Major Colin	170
MacRae, Dr. Duncan, Deputy-Inspector-General of Hospitals	170
MacRae, Lieutenant Colin, The Black Watch	170
MacSween, Henry Davidson	171
MacSween, Hastings	171
MacSween, Sergeant Archibald	225

Index.

	Page
Martin, Lieutenant Angus	74
Martin, Lieutenant Angus, R.A.	75
Martin, Lieutenant Angus	77
Martin, Colonel Cunliffe, C.B.	75-76
Martin, Sir James Ranald, Knight and C.B.	74
Martin, Major James Ranald	75
Martin, Major-General John	75
Martin, Cornet Norman Alexander	76-77
Martin, Colonel Martin, R.E.	77
Martin, Simon Nicolson	75
Matheson, Private Donald	230
Morrison, Dr. Alexander, Inspector-General of Hospitals	162-164
Morrison, Captain, of Sgianaidean	164
Munro, Major-General Andrew Aldcorn, C.I.E.	81
Nicolson, Lieutenant George Elder	165
Nicolson, Captain James	165
Nicolson, Lieutenant Malcolm	165
Nicolson, Captain Samuel	165
Nicolson, Private Donald, Sleat	226
Nicolson, Private James, Sleat	226
Nicolson, Corporal John, The Black Watch	228
Nicolson, Corporal John, List of Names furnished by him	227-228
Nicolson, Private Malcolm ("Calum Na Rightaig")	229
Nicolson, Private Murdoch	228
Ramsay, Lieutenant A., Royal Artillery	94
Ramsay, Lieutenant D.	94
Ramsay, Major William Norman, R.H.A.	91-94
Regiment of the Isles, Fencibles, Local Militia, and Volunteers	81-82
Robertson, Private Hugh, Sleat	227
Ross, Major Thomas, Royal Artillery	171
Schubrick, General	171
Smith, Colonel Christopher Webb	171
Stewart, Field-Marshal Sir Donald Martin, Bart., G.C.B., &c.	77-80
Stewart, Colonel Norman Robert	80
Stewart, Captain Donald, C.M.G.	80-81
Stewart, Captain Donald	164
Stewart, Captain William, of Ensay	168
Tarrington, General	171
Tolmie, Captain Kenneth	161-162
Tolmie, Dr. William	162

The Brave Sons of Skye.

"Truly its inhabitants are a wondrous people."
An article on Skye in "The Inverness Journal."

INTRODUCTORY CHAPTER.

TERRITORIALLY considered the Isle of Skye does not occupy a high place among the islands of the world, occupying only some 700 square miles of the earth's surface, yet wherever the Gaelic language is spoken and Skye mentioned it is almost invariably referred to as "the Island" ("An t.-Eilean") *par excellence*.

Tradition tells us of the heroine, Princess Sgàthach, who dwelt at Dùn-Sgàthaich in Sleat (so named after herself), where she presided over the most notable military college of that dim and distant time. Skilful of thrust, cunning of fence, and matchless in the use of the "gath-bolg" were the pupils of the royal school of Dùn-Sgàthaich; but first and foremost among them all was the mighty chief of Skye, Cuchullin, who led a party of his countrymen against the Romans.

Be the many marvellous tales regarding Skye's heroes and heroines of prehistoric times true or not, a spirit of warlike enterprise has existed in the island from the earliest period of which we have any authentic record, and has been fostered by passing events (involving the strife of arms) century after century up to the present day. But it is with the share that "the Brave Sons of Skye" took in Britain's great wars in foreign lands that this work more particularly deals.

William Pitt (afterwards Earl of Chatham), addressing the House of Commons, said: "I have sought for merit wherever it could be found. It is my boast that I
" was the first Minister who looked for it, and found it in the mountains of the north.
" I called it forth, and drew into your service a hardy and intrepid race of men; men
" who, when left by your jealousy, became a prey to the artifices of your enemies,
" and had gone nigh to have overturned the State in the war before last. These men
" in the last war were brought to combat on your side; they served with fidelity,
" as they fought with valour in every quarter of the globe."

"The Island of Mist" made a noble response to the patriotic appeal of the great Minister. We have it on the authority of a former Adjutant-General of the Forces[1]

---

[1] Manuscript received from the late Mrs. MacLeod-Clerk of Kilmallie, daughter of the Reverend Dr. Norman MacLeod, Caraide Nan Gaidheal.

that, in the 40 years preceding 1837, Skye had furnished for the public service 21 Lieutenant-Generals and Major-Generals, 45 Lieutenant-Colonels, 600 Majors, Captains, and subalterns, 10,000 private soldiers, 120 pipers, four Governors of British Colonies, one Governor-General of India, and one Adjutant-General of the British army. It has also been stated on the same testimony that 1,600 Skyemen fought in the British ranks at the battle of Waterloo.

"They have had representatives in every Peninsular and Indian battlefield. Of the miniatures kept in every family more than one half are soldiers, and several have attained to no mean rank. . . . And in other services the Islesman has drawn his sword. Marshal MacDonald had Hebridian blood in his veins. . . . The tartans waved through the smoke of every British battle, and there were no such desperate bayonet charges as those which rushed to the yell of the bag-pipe. At the close of the last and the beginning of the present century half the farms in Skye were rented by half-pay officers. The Army List was to the island what the Post Office Directory is to London."[1]

---

[1] Alexander Smith's "A Summer in Skye."

THE MACDONALDS OF SLEAT, Etc.

> "Clann Domhnuill a chruadail
> "Choisinn buaidh anns na blàraibh."
>
> "Clann Domhnuill tha mi 'g ràite,
> "'N sàr chinneadh urramach,
> "'S tric a fhuair 'sna blàraibh,
> "Air nàmhaid buaidh iomanach,
> "Iad feara tapuidh dàna
> "Cho làn do nimh ghuineadeach,
> "Ri nathraichean an t-sleibhe,
> "Le 'n geur-lannaibh fulangach."
>
>   Alasdair Mac Mhaighstir Alasdair.

HUGH MACDONALD, I. of Sleat (after whom the MacDonalds of Sleat are called "Clann Uisdean"), was a brother of John, last Lord of the Isles, and ancestor of the present Lord MacDonald. In 1460 this Hugh, accompanied by William MacLeod of Harris and "the young gentlemen of the Isles," made a raid into the Orkney Islands (after the fashion of those times) and ravaged the country, returning home with their galleys loaded with spoil, but not without a fierce fight for it, in which the Orcadians were totally routed and their Earl was killed.

Donald Gruamach, IV. of Sleat's (Domhnull Gruamach MacDhomhnuill Ghallaich) reign was a turbulent one. "During the life of this chief the usual feuds "and slaughters continued rampant in the Isles, but they did not extend to the rest "of the kingdom."[1]

Next to MacDonald of Islay (who appears to have been at that time the acknowledged head of the whole clan), Donald Gruamach was the most prominent chieftain of his race in his own day, and as such took a leading part in the warlike proceedings of the Clan Donald. Donald the Grim despised the peaceful art of the clerk. In his day the sword was more powerful than the pen; and when, along with certain other chiefs, "Donald Ilis of Slate" signed a bond of offence and defence (at Inverness, on the 30th of April, 1527) it was with his "hand at the pen, guided by Sir William Munro, Notary Public."[1]

According to Mr. Fraser Mackintosh, it is from this Donald Gruamach Lord MacDonald has derived the Gaelic patronymic of "MacDhomhnuill na 'n Eilean."[2]

Donald Gruamach died in 1534.

---

[1] Mackenzie's "History of the MacDonalds."   [2] Invernessiana.

Donald Gorm MacDonald, V. of Sleat, son of Donald Gruamach, IV. of Sleat, " claimed for his family and in his own person the ancient honours of his ancestors, " the Lordship of the Isles and the Earldom of Ross."[1]

Donald Gorm, having married the heiress of the Siol Torquil MacLeods, led that warlike clan as well as his own immediate followers into Troternish, which had been seized by the MacLeods of Dunvegan, and which he laid waste. It was after this raid that the chiefs of Sleat left Dunsgathaich and took up their abode in the Castle of Duntulm.

For opposing his claim to the Lordship of the Isles and the Earldom of Ross, Donald Gorm next resolved to be revenged upon Mackenzie of Kintail, whose lands of Kinlochewe were accordingly ravaged, and whose Castle of Eileandonan was besieged by the Islesmen.[1] "Exposing himself rashly under the walls of the castle, the chief " of Sleat received a wound in the foot from an arrow shot by the constable, which " proved fatal; for, not observing that the arrow was barbed, the enraged chief pulled " it hastily out of the wound, by which an artery was severed, and the medical skill " of his followers could devise no means of checking the effusion of blood which " necessarily followed." Thus perished, in 1539, the first Donald Gorm, at a spot on an islet near Eileandonan Castle, which is still known as "Larach Tigh Mhic Dhomhnuill."

Donald Gormson MacDonald, VI. of Sleat, "was a minor of tender years when his father died."[2]

A notable event in the history of the Western Isles at this time was the visit of King James V. (with an armed expedition), which took place in 1540, in order to overawe the turbulent inhabitants of those regions. It was then, and in honour of the Royal advent, that the capital of Skye exchanged its ancient name (Loch Choluim Chille—Saint Columba's Loch) for the more modern one which it now bears—Portree—Port an Righ—the King's Port.

It may be mentioned, in passing, that the Royal visitor greatly admired the stronghold of Duntulm, which had then, as we have already seen, become the principal residence of the MacDonalds of Sleat.

The King proceeded on his voyage, receiving as he went along the homage of the Western chiefs, who, however, soon found themselves prisoners and not guests on board His Majesty's ships. And, as if to add bitterness to their captivity, the fleet was sent with them (to bring them to Edinburgh) round the north of Scotland, passing their own territories, while the King himself landed at Dumbarton and went by the shorter route to the capital.

These harsh measures on the part of the King bore the fruit of rebellion by-and-by.

In 1543 Donald Dubh of Islay, who had been for nearly forty years in captivity, managed to escape; and, not long after that event, the other island chiefs were

---

[1] Mackenzie's "History of the MacDonalds."

[2] Mackenzie's "History of the MacDonalds," and Cameron's "History and Traditions of the Isle of Skye."

set at liberty—a well-meant but ill-timed act of clemency. "Almost immediately "after this liberation Donald Dubh assembled an army of 1,800 men, invaded Argyll's "territories, slew many of his followers, and carried away a large number of his "cattle with a great quantity of other plunder."[1]

In the summer of the following year the Earls of Huntly and Argyll were ordered to proceed, by land and by sea, "to the utter extermination of the Clanranald, "Donald Gormson (the heir of Sleat), and of MacLeod of Lewis, and their associates "who had failed to present hostages for their good conduct."[1] "It is a far cry to Lochowe," but still farther to Loch Coiruisk; and it is not surprising to learn that their Lordships "met with little success."

The MacDonalds of Sleat supported the MacLeods of Lewis in their desperate struggles with the MacKenzies of Kintail. At length the feud was terminated by an agreement made, in 1569, by the chiefs of Sleat and Kintail.[1]

Donald Gormson died in 1585.

Donald Gorm Mòr MacDonald, VII. of Sleat, eldest son of Donald Gormson, "immediately on his accession became involved in serious disputes with his neighbours, "the MacLeans, through the treachery of his nephew, Uisdean MacGhilleaspuig "Chlèirich. Donald Gorm went with his retinue, in 1585, to pay a complimentary "visit to his relative Angus MacDonald of Dunyvaig, in Islay, and was forced, by "stress of weather, to take shelter in the island of Jura, on a part of it belonging "then to MacLean of Duart. At the same time Uisdean MacGhilleaspuig Chlèirich "and a son of Donald Herrach were also driven into a neighbouring creek for shelter, "and they by night carried off a number of cattle from MacLean's lands, and took "to sea in the expectation that Donald Gorm and his party would be blamed by "the MacLeans for the robbery."[1] And that was exactly what took place. The MacLeans naturally supposed that the "creach" had been raised by the strangers whom they found on the ground. On the following night accordingly they (with superior numbers) attacked the unsuspecting MacDonalds, sixty of whom were killed, their chief escaping the same fate because he happened that night to sleep on board his galley.

The heather was now fairly on fire. The Clan Donald and their allies were roused to fury at what they believed to have been an act of unprovoked treachery as well as a gross breach of Highland hospitality on the part of the MacLeans. "Violent measures "of retaliation were immediately resorted to. . . . . . The feud was carried on "in true Highland fashion, and ended in Donald Gorm and others being taken prisoners "by the MacLeans." The Government now interfered, the prisoners were released, and peace was for the time being restored.[1]

Not many years afterwards (in 1601) a violent feud began between the two great clans of Skye—the MacDonalds of Sleat and the MacLeods of Dunvegan—which, after "much bloodshed and various desolating inroads," culminated in "the Desperate Battle" ("Am Blàr Fuathasach")—better known as the battle of Ben Coolin—in which

---

[1] Mackenzie's "History of the MacDonalds."

both clans fought, of course, with the greatest bravery, and in which the MacLeods were overthrown. "The Privy Council now interfered to prevent further mischief, "and ever afterwards these clans refrained from open hostility, and submitted their "disputes to the decision of the laws."[1]

Donald Gorm Mòr died in December, 1616, and was succeeded by his nephew, Sir Donald MacDonald, eighth Baron and first Baronet of Sleat, who died in October, 1643, and whose eldest son and successor was Sir James MacDonald,[2] ninth Baron, and second Baronet of Sleat, joined the Marquis of Montrose in 1645, and many of the Skye chief's followers fought in the Royal cause at the battle of Inverlochy of that year (which was so disastrous to the Clan Campbell, 1,500 of whom were killed there), and at the battle of Worcester, in 1651, where the Royalists were defeated and hundreds of Skyemen fell.

After the defeat of the King's forces at Worcester, Sir James retired to Skye, "where he lived with great circumspection."[1] He died on the 8th of December, 1678, and was succeeded by his eldest son,

Sir Donald MacDonald, tenth Baron and third Baronet, who took up arms under Viscount Dundee, in 1689; but, having been taken seriously ill in Lochaber, was obliged to return home. Sir Donald died on the 5th of February, 1695, and his successor was his eldest son, Donald of the Wars—Domhnull a Chogaidh (so called from the part which he took in the Jacobite risings of 1689 and 1715).

Sir Donald MacDonald, eleventh Baron and fourth Baronet.

Sir Donald fought with great bravery at the head of his clan in the battle of Killiecrankie, on the 27th of July, 1689, where, in addition to many of his clansmen, there fell five of his cousins-german (including Alexander MacDonald of Kingsburgh and James MacDonald of Capisdale); but he himself escaped and returned to the Isles with the survivors of his followers.[1]

Sir Donald was one of the Highland chiefs who supported the Earl of Mar in the 'Fifteen, and, along with the Earl of Seaforth and some other Jacobite chiefs, at the head of 3,000 men, attacked and defeated a large Government force at Alness in Ross-shire. Domhnull a Chogaidh afterwards joined the Earl of Mar at Perth. Then followed the battle of Sheriffmuir, which took place on Sunday, the 13th of November, 1715, and was the last fight in which the MacDonalds of Sleat, as a clan, took part.

In the hottest part of the contest the Clan Donald exhibited the ancient valour of the race. "The clans, led on by Sir Donald MacDonald's two brothers (James and "William), Glengarry, Captain of Clanranald, Sir John MacLean, Campbell of "Glenlyon, and others, made a most furious attack; so that, in seven or eight

---

[1] Mackenzie's "History of the MacDonalds."
[2] The avenger of the Keppoch murders, Archibald MacDonald (Gilleaspuig Ruadh MacDhomhnuill, "an Ciaran Mabach"), the accomplished scholar, poet, and soldier, was a brother of this Sir James.

"minutes, we could neither perceive the form of a squadron nor battalion of the "enemy before us. We drove the main body and left of the enemy in this manner "for half a mile, killing and taking prisoners all that we could overtake." Thus spoke an eye-witness of the battle of Sheriffmuir.

The battle of Sheriffmuir (although only a drawn one) put an end to the campaign of 1715. The clans were willing enough to continue the contest, but the Earl of Mar was irresolute and still more so was his Master the Chevalier. "Sir Donald, seeing "this, left them, and returned with his followers (numbering about a thousand "able-bodied warriors) to the Isle of Skye, where he continued for some time at their "head. Ultimately he allowed them to disperse; and, for his share in the rising, was "attainted by Act of Parliament, and his estates were forfeited to the Crown."[1]

Donald of the Wars died in 1718, and was succeeded by his only son,

Sir Donald MacDonald, twelfth Baron and fifth Baronet, who, however, owing to the forfeiture, never possessed the estates. This chief (said to have been the last of his family, who was born in the ancient Castle of Duntulm) died, unmarried, in 1720, and the succession passed to his uncle, James MacDonald of Oronsay.[1]

The MacDonalds of Sleat took no part, as a clan, in the rising of 1745. The only gentlemen of note among Sir Alexander MacDonald's followers who openly espoused the cause of the Young Chevalier were Captain Donald Roy MacDonald of Knockow in Skye, and James MacDonald of Heiskeir in North Uist. Captain Roy MacDonald, at the outset, joined the MacDonalds of Keppoch, but, after the battle of Falkirk, was appointed a Captain in Clanranald's regiment, in which he gallantly fought at Culloden, where he was wounded in the foot, and "having travelled home to Skye hastily in this "state, his wound took a long time to heal." Having made a sham surrender of his arms (inferior weapons which he had purchased for the purpose!), he was allowed considerable freedom of action of which he made good use in helping the Royal fugitive to escape from his enemies.

Captain Francis MacDonald, of the Royal Navy, son of Sir Archibald MacDonald, Baronet (the eminent English judge), died in the West Indies on the 20th of June, 1804, in the twentieth year of his age.

Captain Sir Archibald Keppel MacDonald, Baronet, of East Sheen, Surrey, grandson of the first Baronet of the same name and branch, served in the Scots Fusilier Guards (now the Scots Guards), from which he retired in 1849. He acted for a time as Equerry to His Royal Highness the Duke of Sussex.

The 76th Regiment of (Highland) Foot or MacDonald's Highlanders.

Sir Alexander MacDonald, sixteenth Baron, ninth Baronet, and first Lord MacDonald of Sleat, was appointed an Ensign in the Coldstream Guards in May, 1761. In December, 1777, letters of service were granted to his Lordship, empowering him to

---

[1] Mackenzie's "History of the MacDonalds."

raise a regiment in the Highlands, of which he was offered the command. This honour, however, he declined, but on his recommendation it was conferred upon Major John MacDonell, of Lochgarry. A fine body of men, numbering 1,086, was soon embodied as the 76th Regiment of (Highland) Foot or MacDonald's Highlanders.[1]

The 76th remained for twelve months in Fort George, undergoing training by Major Donaldson, an officer who was admirably qualified to command a body of young Highlanders, being a native of the Highlands himself, and having served for nineteen years as captain and adjutant in the 42nd Regiment.

In March, 1779, the corps was removed to Perth, where they were reviewed on the 10th of that month by General Skene. Being complete in number, and in a high state of discipline, they were marched to Burntisland, whence they embarked for New York, under the command of Major Lord Berriedale, and arrived at their destination in the month of August.[2]

On the arrival of the regiment in America the flank companies were attached to the battalion of that description. The rest of the corps remained between New York and Staten Island till February, 1781, when they embarked with a detachment of the army, commanded by Major-General Phillips, for Virginia, the light company being in the second battalion of light infantry, formed a part of the army. The Grenadiers remained at New York. This year, Major Lord Berriedale (having on the decease of his father become Earl of Caithness, and been severely wounded at the siege of Charlestown) returned to Scotland. The command of the regiment then devolved on the Honourable Major Needham, afterwards Lord Killmorey, who had purchased Major Donaldson's commission. "The detachment landed at Portsmouth in Virginia, in
" March, and joined the troops under Brigadier-General Arnold. In May, they
" formed a junction with the army under Lord Cornwallis. When the soldiers of
" the 76th found themselves with an army which had been engaged in the most
" incessant and fatiguing marches, through difficult and hostile countries, they
" appeared to look down on themselves as having done nothing which could enable
" them to return to their country and friends with that reputation which their
" countrymen and brother soldiers had acquired. And they were often heard
" murmuring among themselves, lamenting their lot, and expressing the strongest
" desire to distinguish themselves. This was particularly observable, and their regrets
" greatly heightened when they were visited by men of Fraser's Highlanders, who had
" been in so many actions to the southward. However, the MacDonalds soon got the
" opportunity which they had so much desired, and the spirit with which they availed
" themselves of it showed that no more was wanting to prove that they were good
" and brave soldiers. On this occasion [at St. James's Island] they were fortunate in
" being in the brigade of Colonel Thomas Dundas,[3] whose spirited example would have
" animated any soldier; but in this instance no excitement was necessary. On the

---

[1] Mackenzie's "History of the Macdonalds."
[2] General David Stewart's "Military Annals of the Highland Regiments."
[3] General David Stewart's "Military Annals of the Highland Regiments, History of the Highlands, Highland Clans, Highland Regiments, &c."

"evening of the 6th July the Marquis de la Fayette, eager to signalise himself in the
"cause of his new friends, and ignorant of the full strength of those he was about to
"attack, pushed forward a strong corps, forced the picquets (twenty men of the 76th
"and ten men of the 80th Regiments), who made an admirable resistance, and drew up
"in front of the British line. A smart engagement immediately ensued, the weight of
"which was sustained by the left of Colonel Dundas's brigade, consisting of the 76th
"and 80th, both young regiments; and it so happened that, while the right of the line
"was covered with woods, they were drawn up in an open field and exposed to the
"attack of La Fayette with a chosen body of troops. They made their début in a
"very gallant style: the 76th being on the left, and Lord Cornwallis, coming up in rear
"of the regiment, gave the word to charge, which was immediately repeated by the
"Highlanders, who rushed forward with their usual impetuosity, and decided the
"matter in an instant. The enemy were completely routed, leaving their cannon
"and three hundred men killed and wounded behind them. The conduct of Colonel
"Dundas and his brigade was noticed with great approbation, and it was also remarked
"that the Americans on this occasion exhibited more than their usual bravery and
"skill under their gallant French commander. After this action four hundred men
"of the 76th were employed as mounted infantry, attached to Tarleton's Legion, and,
"having made several forced marches (far more fatiguing to these Highlanders than
"if they performed them on foot), they returned to the army, heartily tired of their
"new mode of travelling. No other service was destined for the 76th until the siege
"and surrender of Yorktown in 1781.[1]

"After this unhappy surrender the 76th was marched, in detachments, as prisoners to different parts of Virginia; and, although many tempting offers were made to induce them to become subjects of the American Government, not a single Highlander allowed himself to be seduced from the duty which he had engaged to discharge to his King and country. Their conduct in quarters stood a trial of six years, and during that period there were only four instances of corporal punishment inflicted on the Highlanders of the regiment (more than seven hundred and fifty in number), and these were for military offences. Thefts and other crimes, implying moral turpitude, were unknown.

"The regiment was disbanded in March, 1784, at Stirling Castle."

The Stations of the 76th, as given in an old Station List, were:—

    1778, North Britain.

    1779, Coast of the Atlantic, America.

    1780 ,,   ,,   ,,

    1781, Virginia.

    1782 ,,

    1783, New York.[2]

---

[1] General David Stewart's "Military Annals of the Highland Regiments."
[2] War Office Records.

The following is a list of the officers of the corps (copied from the Army List, issued 4th June, 1779,[1] with the dates of their commissions):—

Rank.	Name.	Rank in the Regiment.	Rank in the Army.
Lieutenant-Colonel Commanding	John MacDonald	25th Dec. 1777.	29th Aug. 1777.
Major	Alexander Donaldson	19th ,, ,,	
	John Lord Berriedale	29th ,, ,,	
Captains	John Macdonald	26th ,, ,,	
	John Bruce	27th ,, ,,	
	James Fraser	28th ,, ,,	
	John Macdonald	29th ,, ,,	
	William Cunningham	30th ,, ,,	
	A. Mont. Cunningham	31st ,, ,,	
	Charles Cameron	1st Jan. 1778.	
Captain-Lieutenant and Captain	Samuel Graham	9th April 1779.	
Lieutenants	Alexander MacDonald	26th Dec. 1777.	
	Alexander Mackenzie	27th ,, ,,	
	Allan MacDonald	28th ,, ,,	
	John Shaw	29th ,, ,,	
	Alexander MacDonald	30th ,, ,,	
	Angus Martin	31st ,, ,,	
	Charles Alex. Macrae	1st Jan. 1778.	
	David Barclay	2nd ,, ,,	
	Æneas MacDonell	3rd ,, ,,	
	John Stuart	4th ,, ,,	
	Angus MacDonald	5th ,, ,,	
	Colin Lamont	6th ,, ,,	
	Donald MacDonald	7th ,, ,,	
	Charles Robertson	8th ,, ,,	
	Donald MacQueen	9th ,, ,,	
	Evan Cameron	10th ,, ,,	
	John Mackinnon	11th ,, ,,	
	John Trail	12th ,, ,,	
	Patrick MacLachlan	13th ,, ,,	
	Hugh Rose	14th ,, ,,	
	Angus MacLean	9th April 1779.	

[1] The number of the regiment does not appear in the Army List issued in 1778.

List of officers continued:—

Rank.	Name.	Rank in the Regiment.	Army.
Ensigns	Colin MacDonald	26th Dec. 1777.	
	Wm. Wemyss	27th ,, ,,	
	Simon MacDonald	28th ,, ,,	
	James MacDonald	29th ,, ,,	
	Robert H. MacColme	30th ,, ,,	
	James Bruce	31st ,, ,,	
	Wm. Mackay	15th Oct. 1778.	
	Duncan MacDonald	9th April 1779.	
Chaplain	James MacDonald	25th Dec. 1777.	
Adjutant	William Mackay	,, ,, ,,	
Quarter-Master	David Barclay	,, ,, ,,	
Surgeon	Hamilton MacLure	,, ,, ,,	
Agents	Messrs. Bisshopp and Brummell, Vine Street.		

The following changes took place in the commissioned ranks during the existence of the regiment[1]:—

Captain John MacDonald (2) retired on the 9th of November, 1779, and his place was taken by Captain Alexander MacDonald.

Lieutenant Evan Cameron resigned on the 29th of September, 1779, and Lieutenant Simon MacDonald came in his room.

Ensign Simon MacDonald was replaced by Ensign Colin MacDonald on the 2nd of September, 1779.

Major Alexander Donaldson left, and was succeeded by Major Francis Needham (on the 10th of August, 1780), who came from the 17th Dragoons.

Captain John MacDonald retired on the 6th of September, 1780, his post having been taken by Captain David Barclay, who was himself succeeded by Lieutenant William Wemyss, shortly afterwards.

Lieutenant John MacKinnon made room for Lieutenant James MacDonald on the 9th of September, 1780.

On the 10th of November, 1780, Ensign James Bruce was promoted in the 70th Regiment, and the vacancy thus caused was filled up by Ensign Ronald MacDonald.

On the 1st of April, 1781, Lieutenant John Shaw was appointed Adjutant in place of Lieutenant William Mackay.

On April 6th, 1780, Sergeant Stuart was promoted to the rank of Quarter-Master, in room of Captain David Barclay.

Captain John Shaw took the place of Captain Charles Cameron on the 31st December, 1781, and Lieutenant John Grant succeeded to the vacant post.

On April 1st, 1781, Captain John Shaw was appointed Adjutant in place of Captain William Mackay, who was promoted.

---

[1] War Office Records.

In the Army List issued on the 31st of March, 1784, Lieutenant-Colonel John MacDonell is shown on the list of Colonels, with the date of 20th November, 1782, and "late 76th Foot" against his name. The Earl of Caithness also appears in the list of Lieutenant-Colonels.

The Honourable Francis Needham joined the 1st Life Guards as Captain and Lieutenant-Colonel on the 2nd of April, 1783; rank in the Army, 20th of February, 1783.

Charles Hastings is shown in the list of Lieutenant-Colonels at the same time. The other officers appear to have retired on the disbandment of the regiment.

The late Surgeon-General Sir W. A. MacKinnon, writing on the 2nd of August, 1897, said—

"I am sorry to tell you that not much information is to be obtained from the Public Record Office. I got a friend, who is much interested in your work, to go to that office on two occasions. He finds the information is very meagre, and is in most cases limited to muster rolls and pay sheets, and there is nothing in the nature of records of service. My friend found that the muster rolls of the 76th contained many officers' names of MacDonalds, MacKinnons, and one or two privates of the name of Myles MacInnes. I have no doubt Skye must have given these names."

The present 76th Regiment was raised in 1787 for service in India, to which place it went shortly after organisation; but its records do not go farther back than that year, and, beyond its number, it seems to have no link joining it with the old 76th, or MacDonald's Highlanders.

Lieutenant-General Sir Godfrey MacDonald Bosville, eighteenth Baron, eleventh Baronet, and third Lord MacDonald of Sleat, second son of Sir Alexander MacDonald, sixteenth Baron, and Elizabeth Diana, eldest daughter of Godfrey Bosville of Gunthwaite, county of York, was born on the 14th of October, 1775. He was appointed Ensign in the Kelso Regiment on the 28th of August, 1794; transferred to the 60th Foot on the 30th of November, 1795; appointed Lieutenant in the 70th Foot on the 12th of March, 1796; Captain in the 86th Foot on the 9th of November, 1796, in the 23rd Foot 25th April, 1797; Major in the 55th Foot on the 13th of November, 1801; Lieutenant-Colonel of the 24th Foot on the 28th of April, 1802; Captain and Lieutenant-Colonel in the 1st Foot Guards on the 11th of February, 1808; Colonel-Brevet on the 4th of June, 1811; Major-General on the 4th of June, 1814; and Lieutenant-General on the 22nd of July, 1830.[1] Lord MacDonald married on the 15th of October, 1803, Louisa Maria, daughter of Farley Edsir, and had issue. His Lordship (then Captain the Honourable Godfrey MacDonald Bosville) was present with the 23rd Regiment at the landing of the British troops in Holland on the morning of the 27th of August, 1799, where he was wounded.[2][3]

---

[1] War Office Records.

[2] Regimental Depot Records.

[3] The corps principally engaged were the reserve consisting of the 23rd and 55th Regiments, under the command of Colonel (afterwards Lieutenant-General) Donald MacDonald of Knock in Sleat, who, as well as the fine troops whom he led, "behaved on this occasion with the greatest ardour and gallantry."

THE MACDONALDS OF SLEAT, ETC.

Lieutenant-General GODFREY, third Lord MACDONALD.

(From Miniature lent by Lady MacDonald,
Armadale Castle, Skye.)

General the Honourable JAMES W. B. MACDONALD, C.B.

(From his niece, the Honourable Mrs. Abdy,
London.)

Mr. MALCOLM HENRY SOMERLED MACDONALD,
Royal Navy.

(From his father, Captain Malcolm MacDonald of Tormore.)

In June, 1802, the 24th Regiment, under the command of Major Kelly, marched from Hilsea Barracks to Liverpool, where, in the month of December, Lieutenant-Colonel the Honourable Godfrey MacDonald joined them, and assumed the command, vice Lieutenant-Colonel John Randall-Faster, who retired from the service.

The 1st Battalion of the 24th Foot,[1] 500 strong, Lieutenant-Colonel the Honourable Godfrey MacDonald Bosville in command, marched from Woodbridge to Portsmouth in April; and on the 5th of May, 1805, embarked for Cork to join the expeditionary force, under Sir Eyre Coote, K.C.B., which was intended for service in the West Indies; but Villeneuve, fearing Nelson's pursuit, returned to France, and the expedition was thus rendered unnecessary.

The troops, including the 1st Battalion of the 24th Regiment, sailed from Cork on the 27th of September 1805, and, after a long delay, refitting and purchasing horses at San Salvador (Bahia, Brazil), arrived off Table Bay, in South Africa, on the 4th of January, 1806. In the battle which ensued, the 24th, under Lieutenant-Colonel the Honourable Godfrey MacDonald Bosville, with the 59th and 83rd Foot, formed the right column of attack. The Grenadiers of the 24th particularly distinguished themselves in dislodging a considerable force of the enemy's horse and riflemen, which was hovering on the British right flank.[1]

In his despatch relating to the operations at the Cape of Good Hope, dated 12th January, 1806, General Sir David Baird described the gallant conduct of the 24th as "a brilliant achievement."

In 1807, Lieutenant-Colonel the Honourable Godfrey MacDonald Bosville returned home. In the following year he exchanged into the Grenadier Guards, and saw no more active service.

His Lordship died on the 18th of October, 1832.[2]

Captain the Honourable Archibald MacDonald, of the Prince of Wales's Own Regiment of Light Dragoons, was the third son of Alexander first Lord MacDonald. He married Janet, eldest daughter of Duncan Campbell of Ardneave, Argyllshire, with issue.[3]

Lieutenant-Colonel the Honourable James MacDonald, 1st Guards, a younger brother of Lieutenant-General Sir Godfrey MacDonald Bosville, Lord MacDonald, was born on the 29th of January, 1783.

He joined the 3rd Battalion of the Guards as an Ensign on the 29th of December, 1799; was promoted to the rank of Lieutenant and Captain on the 17th of December, 1802; and to that of Captain and Lieutenant-Colonel in the 2nd Battalion on the 7th of April, 1813.

He took part in the expedition to Sicily in 1806, fought at Corunna in 1809, and was killed at Bergen-op-Zoom in 1814.[2]

He was not married.

Another brother was Ensign the Honourable William MacDonald, who was born in 1789.[3]

---

[1] Regimental Depôt Records.   [2] War Office Records.
[3] Mackenzie's "History of the MacDonalds."

General the Honourable James William Bosville MacDonald, C.B., third son of Lieutenant-General Sir Godfrey MacDonald Bosville, Lord MacDonald, was born on the 31st of October, 1810. He was appointed Ensign in the 81st Foot on the 1st of October, 1829; Ensign in the 1st Life Guards on the 16th of February, 1831; Lieutenant on the 24th of January, 1834; Captain on the 24th of June, 1837; Captain unattached on the 30th of December, 1842; Major-Brevet on the 19th of October, 1849; Major unattached on the 12th of December, 1854; Lieutenant-Colonel Brevet on the same date; Colonel Brevet on the 1st of April, 1860; Major-General on the 6th of March, 1868; Lieutenant-General on the 1st of October, 1877; Colonel of the 21st Hussars on the 1st of July, 1880; removed to retired pay on the 31st of October, 1880; and was granted the honorary rank of General on the 1st of July, 1881.

He served on the Staff as Aide-de-Camp to the Colonel on the Staff in the Ionian Islands from the 20th of April, 1843, to the 7th of April, 1845; to the General Officer commanding the Dublin District[1] from the 1st of October, 1846, to the 31st of March, 1852; to the General Officer commanding the cavalry brigade at Chobham from the 14th of June, 1853, to the 20th of August, 1853; to the Inspector-General of Cavalry at the headquarters of the Army, from the 1st of April, 1852, to the 24th of February, 1854; to a Lieutenant-General commanding a division in the Crimea, from the 26th of February, 1854, to November, 1854; and acted as private secretary to the General Officer Commanding-in-Chief the Forces at the headquarters of the army (His Royal Highness the Duke of Cambridge) from the 15th of July, 1856, to the date of his death.

He was present at the battle of Alma (where his horse was shot under him), at the battle of Balaklava, at the sortie of the 26th of October, 1854, at the battle of Inkerman (where his horse was shot), and at the siege of Sebastopol. His name was mentioned in despatches in the "London Gazette" of the 10th of October and 2nd of December, 1854. He received the Crimean War medal with four clasps, the brevet rank of Lieutenant-Colonel[1]; was made a Companion of the Bath on the 5th of July, 1855; Knight of the French Legion of Honour; got the fifth class of the Turkish Order of the Medjidie; the Turkish medal, and was granted a reward for distinguished service.[1]

General MacDonald married on the 26th of September, 1859, Elizabeth Nina, daughter of Joseph Henry, third Lord Wallscourt, and left issue.

He died at St. Leonard's-on-Sea on the 4th of January, 1882.

Lieutenant the Honourable William Bosville MacDonald, fourth son of Lieutenant-General Sir Godfrey MacDonald Bosville, Lord MacDonald, was born on the 27th of September, 1817. He entered the army as an Ensign in the 93rd Highlanders on the 23rd of October, 1835; was promoted to the rank of Lieutenant on the 1st of June, 1838, and retired in the following year. He died, unmarried, on the 11th of May, 1847.[2]

---

[1] War Office Records.   [2] Regimental Depôt Records.

THE MACDONALDS OF BALRANALD.

The MacDonalds of Balranald are descended from Donald MacDonald, "Donald Herrach," who was a son of Hugh, I. of Sleat, and who was remarkable for his great personal strength. Donald Herrach's "single blow seldom left work for two."

Ronald MacDhomhnuill Herraich went to Ireland, where he distinguished himself in the wars carried on in the northern provinces of that country by the Antrim family; but, having been severely wounded, he returned to his native country, and afterwards lived at Griminish.

Lieutenant-Colonel Alexander MacDonald of Lynedale, IX. of Balranald, was a captain in the Bengal Artillery, from which he retired in consequence of ill-health. He afterwards raised, and became Lieutenant-Colonel of, the 2nd Isle of Skye Regiment of Volunteers, numbering 510 men, most of whom, when the Militia were disbanded, joined the Glengarry Fencibles, or Caledonian Rangers. He had three sons in the army, viz., Captain Alexander MacDonald of the 16th Bengal Native Infantry, who died in India, unmarried, and John Robertson MacDonald, who served in the 38th, 39th, and 16th Regiments successively, and who afterwards lived at Rodill in Harris, and married Mary, daughter of Captain MacRae, of the Inverinate family.[1]

Major James MacDonald, brother of Lieutenant-Colonel Alexander MacDonald of Lynedale and IX. of Balranald, had nine sons, three of whom attained distinction in the army, and all of whom died unmarried.[1] The youngest son, John, died in the Crimea. Major James MacDonald was, in his later years, Deputy Paymaster at Chatham.

THE MACDONALDS OF KINGSBURGH AND FLODIGARRY.[2]

"We were entertained with the usual hospitality by Mr. MacDonald and his lady, Flora MacDonald, a name that will be mentioned in history; and, if courage and fidelity be virtues, mentioned with honour. She is a woman of middle stature, soft features, gentle manners, and elegant presence."[3]

The first of this family was James MacDonald, second son of Donald Gruamach MacDonald, fourth Baron of Sleat. This James lived in very turbulent times, and took a prominent part in the various disputes between the MacDonalds of Sleat and the MacLeods, during the reigns of James V. and Queen Mary.[1]

Donald MacDonald, III. of Kingsburgh, commonly known as " Domhnull MacIain 'Ic Sheumais," was a distinguished warrior. A man of unsurpassed courage and

---

[1] Mackenzie's "History of the MacDonalds."
[2] From notes prepared by Captain R. M. Livingston-MacDonald of Flodigarry.
[3] Dr. Samuel Johnson's "Tour to the Hebrides."

enormous bodily strength, he commanded the MacDonalds of Skye in three set battles against the MacLeods and MacLeans. In each case he came off victorious against much larger forces than his own.[1]

Alexander MacDonald, IV. of Kingsburgh, was a great loyalist, joined the Marquis of Montrose, and was engaged in all his battles. He was one of Sir Donald MacDonald's five cousins who were killed at the battle of Killiecrankie.[1]

Donald MacDonald, V. of Kingsburgh, was one of the bravest men of his day, who, with his father, joined Viscount Dundee at the time of the Revolution, was present at the battle of Killiecrankie, and fought afterwards at the battle of Sheriffmuir. His son was Alexander MacDonald, VI. of Kingsburgh, who, having entertained Prince Charles at his house in Skye, and assisted him in making his escape, was apprehended by order of the Duke of Cumberland, and sent as a prisoner to the Castle of Edinburgh, where he was closely confined for about twelve months.

The following extract from a letter written by Captain R. M. Livingston-MacDonald of Flodigarry (a great-great-grandson of the celebrated Flora MacDonald, being descended from Captain James MacDonald of Flodigarry, the fourth son of the heroine), dated 4th March, 1898, cannot fail to be interesting:—

"In the notes *re* Captain Allan, Kingsburgh, I have given you some information which, as far as I am aware, has never appeared in any notice that has ever been written.

"In MacGregor's 'Life of Flora MacDonald,' it is stated that the ship in which Flora MacDonald sailed on her *return to Scotland* was attacked by a French privateer. That was not the case, as I have it on the authority of many relatives, one of whom is the daughter of the young man, Ensign Kenneth MacDonald, that it was on the voyage *out* the ship was attacked. This young man was with his regiment (the Royal Highland Emigrant Regiment) when Flora MacDonald *recrossed* the Atlantic.

"MacGregor also states that Flora MacDonald, in 1779, left her husband a prisoner in Halifax Jail. This is quite incorrect. There is abundant proof to show that Captain Allan was liberated in 1777, and was stationed in New York, both in that year and in 1778.

"MacGregor also states 'that when peace was eventually restored Flora's husband was liberated from Halifax Jail.' This statement is as erroneous as the others, for Captain Allan was serving with his regiment in Nova Scotia and Cape Breton during the last three years of the war. I have examined, in the Public Record Office in London, the muster rolls of the regiment during these years, and have found Captain Allan's signature on all the muster rolls of his company. I can quite understand how MacGregor fell into these mistakes. Letters from Captain Allan in 1780 and 1781 to his wife were dated from *Halifax*, and MacGregor took it for granted that it was *Halifax, Virginia!*"

---

[1] Mackenzie's "History of the MacDonalds."

THE MACDONALDS OF KINGSBURGH AND FLODIGARRY.

ALLAN MACDONALD, VII. of Kingsburgh,
Captain 84th Regiment (Royal Highland Emigrants),
Husband of the celebrated Flora MacDonald.

Captain CHARLES MACDONALD, VIII. of Kingsburgh,
eldest son of Captain Allan MacDonald.

Captain JAMES MACDONALD,
fourth son of Captain Allan MacDonald of Kingsburgh.

Lieutenant-Colonel JOHN MACDONALD,
fifth son of Captain Allan MacDonald of Kingsburgh.

Lieutenant-Colonel JAMES SOMERLED MACDONALD OF FLODIGARRY,
eldest son of Captain James MacDonald of Kingsburgh.

Captain ALEXANDER MACDONALD OF KNOCKOW, in Skye,
a nephew of Captain Allan MacDonald, VII. of Kingsburgh,
on his father's side, and of Major Roderick MacLeod of
Bailemeanach on his mother's side. Captain ALEXANDER
MACDONALD died in early life in the West Indies.

(From Mrs. MacRae, Glasgow.)

(From Copies of Miniature Portraits lent by Captain R. M. Livingston-MacDonald of Flodigarry.)

Allan MacDonald, VII. of Kingsburgh, was the eldest son of Alexander MacDonald, VI. of Kingsburgh, by his wife Florence MacDonald of Castleton.

With reference to Alexander MacDonald, one of his contemporaries—Douglas—writes of him in his Baronage as "a man of great integrity, probity, and honour, and "has long been one of the principal managers of his chief's affairs, having been first "appointed into that station by old Sir Donald, was continued by his son, young Sir "Donald, by Sir James, whose son, Sir Alexander, left him one of the tutors to his "sons, the late Sir James, and the present Sir Alexander, and has always acquitted "himself with great fidelity and an unspotted character."

Besides Allan, "Old Kingsburgh," as he was familiarly called, had other two children, a son James, who subsequently became factor for his chief, and a daughter Ann, who married Ronald MacAlister of Strathaird.

Allan's childhood was spent at Kingsburgh.

He was a particular favourite of his chief, Sir James MacDonald, who undertook to educate him, and for that purpose Allan was sent to school in Edinburgh, where he remained some years.

On his education being completed he returned home to assist his father in the multifarious duties of his post as Chamberlain.

Much of the rent in those days was paid in kind—sheep, cattle, &c.—and Allan, being considered a good judge of farm stock, was entrusted with the task of valuing the cattle, and taking delivery of the same on behalf of his chief.

The cattle were then collected by drovers from the various districts of the MacDonald Estate (which at that time comprised the half of Skye and the whole of North Uist), and brought to Kyle-Rhea, where they swam them across the ferry, thence driven to Falkirk, and sold at the trysts periodically held there.

Vast herds, numbering many hundreds at a time, were annually driven to Falkirk in this way by drovers; and Allan, on whom rested the responsibility of ensuring a good sale for the cattle at the trysts, was locally designated "Ailean na mìle mart," or "Allan of the thousand kine."

About the year 1734 the lands of Flodigarry, falling vacant through the death of John Martin, whose ancestors had lived there for generations, Alexander MacDonald invested himself with these lands, deeming them to be suitable for the raising of a good class of Highland cattle.

Shortly afterwards he handed over Flodigarry to Allan, who, having arrived at man's estate, took up his residence there.

He had grown up a singularly handsome man, with powerful frame, and was ever foremost in all daring and athletic feats.

He specially excelled in wrestling, though on one particular occasion, under somewhat unfair circumstances, he was worsted.

A wrestling match took place between him and Martin of the Bealach in a building near Kilmuir Manse. After several bouts, in which Martin was thrown, Allan had the misfortune to stumble over a "caber" which was lying on the floor, and was thus easily thrown by his opponent. Martin, elated at his victory over so formidable an antagonist, declined to risk another round, preferring to rest on his not too-well-won laurels.

Allan showed no resentment, but his henchman, a bard, who was at the time of the encounter absent in Edinburgh, on having the details of the match related to him, and conceiving that Allan's fame as a wrestler had suffered an injustice at Martin's hands, composed, in his indignation, a song, which became popular and widely known, entitled "Ailein duinn nach till thu an taobh so."

Early in the summer of 1745, Flora MacDonald (of subsequent historic fame) came to Monkstadt—the MacDonald's principal seat, and a few miles distant from Flodigarry—with Lady Margaret MacDonald, through whose services she had for some years been placed at a boarding school in Edinburgh.

Allan MacDonald, who had on former occasions met this young lady at Monkstadt and elsewhere, and with whom he seemed to be much *épris* now, on her return from the south, found that the attraction on his part had developed, and a mutual attachment was formed.

Neither of the young couple being at that time in a position to marry no engagement was made, but in the hope of their prospects brightening a tacit understanding existed between them.

In June, 1745, Flora proceeded to her brother's house at Milton (South Uist), which was her home, and remained there till the following year, when the stirring events took place in which she played so conspicuous a part.

At the time of Flora's arrival at Monkstadt with the young Chevalier, Allan was at his own home at Flodigarry, and it was not till the end of 1747, when she was liberated from her imprisonment in the Tower of London, that he had the felicity of again meeting the object of his affections. This meeting took place at a ball at Monkstadt, given in honour of Flora's return by Sir Alexander and Lady Margaret. The prospect of their union still seemed most remote, for old Kingsburgh's affairs had become wofully embarrassed during his enforced absence from Skye, he having been imprisoned in Edinburgh Castle for a twelvemonth for affording one night's hospitality to the fugitive Prince. He, therefore, was unable to make any settlement on his son.

In the course of three years (by 1750) matters were so far righted as to enable them to formally announce their engagement, and on the 6th November of that year their marriage took place at Flora's stepfather's[1] house at Armadale. The following notice of which appeared in the "Scots Magazine" of that month:—
" November 6th at Armadale, Sleat, Allan Macdonald, eldest son of Alexander
" MacDonald of Kingsburgh, married to Miss Flora MacDonald, daughter of Ranald

---

[1] Captain Hugh MacDonald, Armadale, Sleat, who was in Uist commanding a party of Militia at the time of Flora's departure from that island. He was a Jacobite at heart, and furnished the heroine with a passport for herself and "Betty Burke," and the whole crew of the boat, to enable them to cross the Minch to Skye. Hugh was one of the most powerful men of his clan, and hardly ever met his equal in wrestling and other feats of strength. He was blind of an eye, hence he was known as Uisdean Cam. He was seventh in descent from Domhnull Gorm Mòr of Sleat.

" MacDonald of Milton, deceased. This is the young lady who aided the escape
" of the young Chevalier."

The home-coming of Allan and his bride to Flodigarry was marked by great rejoicings and festivities, which were kept up for the best part of a week. They new settled down at Flodigarry, and here all their children were born. Their eldest son—born 22nd October, 1751—they called after the unfortunate Prince for whom so many members of their family had risked their all.

Their elder daughter—born 18th February, 1754—was named Ann, after Allan's sister, Mrs. MacAlister of Strathaird.

Their second and third sons, Alexander and Ranald—born 1755 and 1756—were called after their paternal and maternal grandfathers respectively. Allan named his fourth son—born November, 1757—James, out of regard for his late chief, through whose generosity he had received a liberal education in Edinburgh.

Their youngest son John and younger daughter Fanny were born respectively in October, 1759, and May, 1766.

On the 13th February, 1772, Alexander MacDonald, who had become frail and infirm, passed away at the advanced age of eighty-three. Shortly afterwards Allan, who had spent twenty-two years of undisturbed domestic happiness at Flodigarry, removed with his family to Kingsburgh.

In July of the same year Pennant, in the course of his celebrated tour throughout Scotland, visited Kingsburgh. His host presented him with an ancient urn and a Druidical charm-bead or serpent-stone, which gifts, together with his visit, are expatiated upon in his account of the tour.

In the autumn of the following year Kingsburgh was visited by other two celebrated men—Doctor Samuel Johnson and his biographer, Boswell.

The latter describes Allan Macdonald as being one who "was completely the
" figure of a gallant Highlander, exhibiting the graceful mien and manly looks
" which our popular Scotch song has justly attributed to that character.

"He had his tartan plaid thrown around him, a large blue bonnet with a knot
" of black ribbon like a cockade, a brown short coat, a tartan waistcoat with gold
" buttons, a bluish philibeg, and tartan hose. He had jet black hair tied behind,
" and was a large stately man with a steady, sensible countenance."

The learned Doctor not only had the gratification of sleeping in the bed in which Prince Charles had slept, but also between the identical sheets.

After Johnson's departure from Kingsburgh, a slip of paper was found in his bedroom on which was written: "Quantum cedat virtutibus aurum"—"With virtue weighed what worthless trash is gold."

Owing to the general depression which prevailed throughout the West Highlands in the early Seventies, many families of social position were obliged to emigrate to the North American Colonies.

A large number of these families settled in North Carolina.

Allan MacDonald, finding himself in no better plight than his neighbours, decided to follow his fellow countrymen.

Accordingly, Kingsburgh—the home of his family for over two centuries—was given up, and in August, 1774, his wife and family, with the exception of his eldest son, Charles, and his youngest son, John, sailed with him in the ship "Baliol" from Campbeltown, Kintyre, for Wilmington, near the mouth of Cape Fear River, in North Carolina.

Their passage was marked by an untoward incident.

The "Baliol" was attacked by a French privateer, and a desperate struggle ensued.

Flora MacDonald, who on a former memorable occasion had been under fire, refused to go below, but remained on deck in view of her husband and sons, who, along with the other passengers, were in the thick of the fight.

With words of encouragement she inspired the defenders, and finally the privateer was beaten off.

During the scuffle her left arm was broken, but luckily one of the passengers, a young Skyeman, Kenneth MacDonald, who had some knowledge of surgery, was able to set it.

This young man had for some time studied surgery in Glasgow with a view to entering the medical profession, but finding his studies uncongenial he determined to emigrate and join his eldest brother, Donald MacDonald, in North Carolina.

On the emigrants' arrival at Wilmington they were enthusiastically received by their countrymen, numerous festivities were held in their honour, the fame of Allan MacDonald's heroic wife intensifying the joyousness of the welcome.

From Wilmington they proceeded some hundred miles further up the Cape Fear River to Cross Creek, the capital of the Highland settlement, in the vicinity of which Allan purposed to purchase land and make a home. At Cross Creek the emigrants were again received with unbounded enthusiasm by all the settlers, many of whom were clan and kinsfolk from the Hebrides.

They resided there for about six months, during which time Anne, the elder daughter, married Major Alexander MacLeod, a Skyeman, who subsequently settled at Lochbay, Skye.

From Cross Creek the family removed to Cameron's Hill, Cumberland, where they remained for six months, whilst Allan went to the western and outlying part of the colony in quest of land, which he duly purchased, and called the place Killiegray. They had barely settled in their new home when the War of Independence broke out. At the time of Allan's arrival, in 1774, at Wilmington, the quarrel between the Home Government and the American colonists, was becoming very serious, and during 1775 matters reached a crisis.

On the 14th April, 1775, a skirmish took place at Lexington, and after the Second Congress the battle of Bunker's Hill was fought on the following 17th June between General Gage's forces and the insurgents.

On the 12th of June, General Gage issued an order to Lieutenant-Colonel Allan MacLean (son of Torloisk), residing in Canada, empowering him to raise a regiment of Highland emigrants in two battalions, ten companies in each, the whole corps to be clothed, armed, and accoutred in like manner with His Majesty's Royal Highland Regiment (Black Watch), and to be called "the Royal Highland Emigrants."

He further empowered him "to rendezvous at Lake Champlain, the officers' "commissions to date from 14th June, 1775."

This order was duly carried out. Two battalions were raised, Lieutenant-Colonel MacLean being appointed Commandant of the 1st Battalion, and Major Small, a native of Strathardle, Perthshire—a man most popular amongst the Highlanders—was appointed Commandant of the 2nd Battalion.

The uniform was the same as that of the Black Watch. The sporrans, however, were made of racoons' instead of badgers' skins.

The officers wore the broadsword and dirk, and the men a half-basket sword.

It was arranged that the companies were to be raised throughout the Highland settlements in North America. The necessity of this step was obvious. The insurrection soon spread to North Carolina, and Martin, the Governor of that Colony, was obliged to retire on board a British Government vessel at the mouth of Cape Fear River, owing to a serious disturbance which took place on 1st June at his house in Newburn regarding some pieces of old cannon which he had mounted there. Martin, placing great reliance on the loyalty of the Highland emigrants in North Carolina, conceived the idea of immediately enlisting their services and sympathies in the Royal cause; and, though on board ship, was by no means inactive in his endeavours to carry out this scheme. During the autumn he was in constant correspondence with General Gage on the subject, and indirectly with Lieutenant-Colonel Allan MacLean and Major Small, which correspondence resulted in his co-operation with them in raising men for their newly-formed regiment. To aid him in this respect, Martin applied to Allan MacDonald, of whom he had formed a high opinion, and whom he knew to be most popular and held in great esteem by all classes of Highlanders throughout the colony.

Allan MacDonald readily fell in with Martin's plans, and loyally undertook to further his efforts. Through Martin's influence Allan MacDonald was presented with his commission as Captain of the 6th Company in the 2nd Battalion (Major Small's), whose headquarters were fixed at Halifax, Nova Scotia.

Martin also secured commissions in the same battalion for various Skyemen, including one of Allan MacDonald's sons (Alexander), Donald and Kenneth MacDonald afore mentioned, the former being appointed Lieutenant, whilst Kenneth MacDonald received his commission as Ensign.

Allan MacDonald was appointed recruiting officer for the regiment in the colony, and for his services in this post he subsequently received the sum of £677.

The wisdom of Martin's step in selecting him was soon apparent, for the Highlanders, as much through their personal devotion to the recruiting officer as through their loyalty to the Royal cause, speedily enrolled themselves in the new regiment. By January, 1776, as many recruits were raised as were deemed sufficient to bring up the strength of the regiment, and forthwith arrangements were made for their conveyance to headquarters.

Major Donald MacDonald and Captain Donald MacLeod, both of the 1st Battalion, were despatched from Canada to conduct the force to Halifax, Nova Scotia.

Major MacDonald, being an old and tried soldier, was invested with the chief command, whilst to Captain Allan MacDonald was allotted the post of Brigade Major. They received orders to march from Cross Creek to Brunswick, a town at the mouth of Cape Fear River, there to embark for Halifax, whither General Gage had retired, awaiting reinforcements from England.

In February, 1776, amidst an outburst of loyal enthusiasm, the Highlanders, 1,500 in number, left Cross Creek, and proceeded on their march to Brunswick.

All went well till, on the evening of the 27th February, they reached Moore's Creek, where they had to force their way through a narrow and dangerous defile, and to cross a bridge defended by cannon, and by a force of insurgents double their numbers; but the officers in command, being aware that the Americans entertained a dread of the broadsword from experience of its effects in the last war, determined to attempt the post sword in hand, and pushed forward to the attack at nightfall.

On reaching the bridge they found, to their dismay, that the Americans had removed several of the planks, and that in consequence only a few men could cross at a time. Nothing daunted, they persevered in the attempt, Major MacDonald and the Brigade Major leading the attack.

When a considerable number of the Royal Highland Emigrants had crossed the bridge the insurgents rushed from an ambush and assailed them.

A hand-to-hand fight followed, in which the Royal Highland Emigrants displayed their wonted valour. The enemy advancing in overwhelming numbers, the commander gave orders to retire across the bridge.

Owing, however, to the darkness of the night his orders were misunderstood, for those of the regiment who had as yet not crossed the bridge continued to reinforce, thereby blocking their comrades' retreat.

A terrible *mêlée* ensued on the bridge, the advance party of the Royal Highland Emigrants, with their faces to the foe, being pressed by their comrades in the rear, found themselves in a desperate plight.

Many of them fell into the water and were drowned. The remainder were either killed or taken prisoners. Those of them who did not cross the bridge escaped under cover of the darkness, and succeeded in reaching Brunswick, from whence, in due course, they joined the regiment at Halifax.

Of the officers who crossed the bridge, Captain Donald MacLeod, after a gallant stand, was killed.

Major Donald MacDonald and Captain Allan MacDonald (both of whom showed signal bravery) were, along with Lieutenant Alexander Macdonald, son of the latter, and Ensign Kenneth Macdonald, taken prisoners. So ended the brief but heroic engagement at Moore's Creek.

By the strange irony of fate, these officers, instead of finding themselves at Halifax, Nova Scotia, found themselves incarcerated as prisoners of war in the jail at Halifax, Virginia.

Ensign Kenneth Macdonald effected his escape from prison in the spring of 1777, forthwith joining the regiment, and on the 25th August, 1778, was promoted to Lieutenant.

Captain Allan Macdonald and his son were retained till the autumn of 1777, when, an exchange of prisoners taking place, they were liberated.

They made their way to New York, where they reported themselves to General Howe, the Commander-in-Chief.

Instead of General Howe ordering Captain Allan to join his regiment, he gave him the temporary command of a company of provincials at New York, which post he held till the end of 1778, when he finally reached Halifax, the headquarters of his regiment. In the summer of 1778, General Howe was recalled to England, and Sir Henry Clinton appointed Commander in his place.

By the end of 1778, the Royal Highland Emigrants were numbered the 84th, and placed on the same footing as the home regiments, Sir Henry Clinton being appointed Colonel-in-Chief.

During his stay at Halifax, in 1776, General Clinton was so favourably impressed with the efficiency of the 2nd Battalion of the Royal Highland Emigrants that he drafted five of the companies into his own army at New York.

Five companies—the 6th Company, Captain Allan's, being one of them—were thus left in Nova Scotia along with other troops to guard that province against the attacks of the French Admiral Estaing, who was during the summer of 1778 and 1779 cruising about the Canadian Coast with a view to regaining for France her lost provinces.

During that period these five companies were actively engaged in repelling many harassing attacks of parties from French and American men-of-war and privateers. By the fall of Yorktown in October, 1781, the campaign was virtually over, but they remained in Nova Scotia during the fag end of the war till peace was declared in 1783.

For the greater part of these years Captain Allan Macdonald, with his company, was stationed at Halifax, as was also that of the Colonel Commandant; but in 1782, he was despatched with it to Spanish River, Cape Breton, there to guard the entrance of Sidney Harbour.

In the summer of 1783 he returned to Halifax, and in October of that year the regiment was disbanded, the officers being placed on half pay. Captain Allan, along with the other Captains of the 2nd Battalion, received from Government, in recognition of their services, a grant of land extending to 5,000 acres at a small town, Douglas, in the vicinity of Halifax.

As his wife and daughters had returned to Scotland in 1779, he determined to follow them, and so, though he took possession of the land, he never actually settled there. Shortly after the disbanding of the regiment he returned to Scotland. In view of his return, through the kind influence of Lady Margaret MacDonald, who had never ceased to be a firm friend of the family, Kingsburgh was left untenanted, and thither he repaired on his arrival at Portree in the spring of 1784.

For six years he resided at Kingsburgh, with nothing to mar the happiness of his life, till March 1790, when he was bereft of his beloved wife, who died suddenly, after a short illness.

In the September of the same year his younger daughter, Fanny, married Lieutenant Donald MacDonald, his faithful subaltern who had faced with him many dangers and endured many trials.

Left alone—for his entire family were now married—he sorely felt the loss of his wife.

In the beginning of the autumn of 1792, he was seized with a serious illness to which he succumbed on the 20th September.

He was laid to rest beside his wife, in the Kingsburgh burying-ground, at Kilmuir churchyard.

> Lann sgaiteach de smior cruadhach air,
> 'San truaill bu dreachmhor duàlanan :
> Cha stad e 'm feòil a 'm buailear e,
> Gu 'n ruig e smuais na 'n cnàmh.
> Oran do Chaiptein Ailean Chinsborg, le Iain MacCodrum.

Captain Charles MacDonald, VIII. of Kingsburgh.

Captain Charles MacDonald, the eldest son of Captain Allan MacDonald of Kingsburgh, was born at Flodigarry on the 22nd October, 1751. His childhood and youth were spent at Flodigarry, where he was educated under tutors.

When in his teens Charles MacDonald went to Bombay, having procured an appointment in the East India Company's Service; but promotion just at that time being slow he became disheartened, resigned his commission, and returned to England in the end of 1775.

In taking this step he was hasty, for his youngest brother, some years afterwards, mentions in a letter to his mother—"that though his (Charles') case in India was hard, "if he had remained, by the great promotion which took place a few years ago, he "would have been now near a majority in my corps; but there is a fatality in a man's "life not to be avoided." In March, 1776, Charles MacDonald wrote to Colonel MacLean, of the 1st Battalion Royal Highland Emigrants, informing him that he had obtained a commission in that regiment through Major Small, the Commandant of the 2nd Battalion. Shortly afterwards he sailed for Halifax, and, on reaching that place in the beginning of May, he again wrote to Colonel MacLean informing him of his arrival.

On the 16th of the same month he was gazetted to the 2nd Battalion Royal Highland Emigrants as Lieutenant.

From May, 1776, to the end of 1778, owing to Major Small's enforced absence in England and New York, for many months at a time, the command of that battalion devolved upon Captain Alexander MacDonald, an officer who had seen much service during the French Canadian War.

Captain Alexander MacDonald gave Charles MacDonald the command of his father's (Captain Allan's) company, the duties in connection with which he performed to the satisfaction of his commanding officer.

Captain Alexander MacDonald, writing to Captain Allan MacDonald, refers to his son in the following terms :—" Charles is a fine young fellow, for whom I have the " sincerest regard. He is sensible and very clever." Charles MacDonald's principal duty lay in patrolling the country with detachments of his company searching for spies and repelling attacks of armed parties from the New England States. One of the most notable of these attacks took place at River St. John's, which divides Nova Scotia from New England. An armed party of New Englanders arrived there to rebuild and occupy a disused fort, thereby to overawe and check the Nova Scotians.

The Royal Highland Emigrants and a detachment of marines were despatched to dislodge the invaders, and after a smart encounter, with some killed and wounded on both sides, the New Englanders were routed, and "ran with the greatest precipitation to their boats."

Charles MacDonald, wishing to see warfare waged on a larger scale than in Nova Scotia, determined to exchange out of the Royal Highland Emigrants into some regiment fighting in Clinton's army to the southward.

Accordingly he was gazetted out of the Royal Highland Emigrants on 24th November, 1779, and in that month quitted Halifax for New York.

On his arrival there he exchanged into the 19th Foot, which regiment was daily expected to arrive from Ireland, and was to serve under Clinton in the intended attack upon Charleston and the Southern Provinces.

The date of Charles MacDonald's exchange was not notified in the Gazette till 8th March, 1780.

Clinton with his army sailed from New York for South Carolina on the 26th December, 1779; and as the 19th Foot had not at that time arrived from Ireland, Charles MacDonald got the command of a troop of horse in Tarlton's British Legion, which corps formed part of Clinton's army.

The British Legion, consisting of cavalry, infantry, and mounted infantry, did yeoman service throughout the campaign of 1780-81. The fleet conveying the army encountered terrific storms, during which all the cavalry horses perished.

After their arrival in South Carolina two months elapsed before the legion cavalry was equipped with the requisite number of horses, which were of inferior quality to boot, and it was not till the end of March that the corps succeeded in joining the main army encamped before Charleston.

From that time till the fall of Charleston (12th May) the legion cavalry was employed in the vicinity of that town in beating off the enemy's forces moving to the relief of the beleaguered town.

On the 16th April, at Monk's Corner, a large force of Americans was surprised and completely routed, four hundred horses—an invaluable prize for the cavalry—arms, clothing, &c., falling into the hands of the victors.

Shortly afterwards, at Tenen's Ferry, another smart engagement took place in which a superior American force was "most spiritedly charged and defeated," the cavalry only losing two men and four horses. With regard to both these engagements Clinton writes in his despatches: "I have to give the greatest praise to Lieutenant-Colonel Tarlton and the cavalry for their conduct, bravery, and eminent services."

Shortly after the surrender of Charleston, Clinton returned to New York, and the command of the army was given to Lord Cornwallis.

On the 27th May Tarlton and the legion were despatched in pursuit of General Buford, whom they, after a singularly rapid march, overtook at Wacsaw. There on the 29th May a sanguinary fight ensued, in which one hundred American officers and men were killed and two hundred taken prisoners. With reference to the behaviour of the legion in this pursuit and fight, Clinton mentions in his despatches that their "celerity in performing a march of near a hundred miles in two days was equal to the "ardour with which they attacked the enemy."

Regarding the same, Tarlton reports to Lord Cornwallis: "It is above my ability "to say anything in commendation of the bravery and exertion of officers and men. "I leave their merit to your Lordship's consideration."

A few days after this fight the legion rejoined Lord Cornwallis's army at Camden.

On the 16th August the battle of Camden was fought, which resulted in a victory for the British arms.

The infantry first forced the Americans to give way in all quarters, and then Lord Cornwallis "ordered the cavalry to complete the rout, which was performed with their "usual promptitude and gallantry."

Lord Cornwallis states that on this occasion "the capacity and vigour of "Lieutenant-Colonel Tarlton at the head of the cavalry deserve my highest com-"mendations." To complete this victory the legion were despatched on the following morning in pursuit of General Sumpter, whom they overtook at noon of the 18th at Catawba Falls.

The infantry and cavalry were formed into line, and with a general shout advanced to the charge.

Before the Americans could recover from their consternation the action was decided in favour of the legion. Sumpter's force was totally destroyed or dispersed, and one hundred and fifty were killed on the spot.

After three days' rest the legion returned to the main army, when their services were awarded the approbation of Lord Cornwallis and the acclamations of their fellow soldiers. "This action was too brilliant to need any comment of mine," wrote Lord Cornwallis.

No action of much importance took place till the 20th November, when at Blackstock an American force was defeated—Sumpter, the general in command, being dangerously wounded, and three of their colonels killed, while upwards of one hundred officers and men were killed, wounded, or taken prisoners.

In this action Tarlton "commends much the good behaviour of officers and men under his command." On the 17th January, 1781, the legion suffered a defeat at Cowpens. The cavalry, however, "having had time to recollect themselves, and "becoming animated by the bravery of their leader, who had so often led them to

" victory, charged and repulsed Colonel Washington's Horse, retook the baggage of
" the corps, and cut to pieces the detachment who had taken possession of it."

Thus, in a measure, the cavalry retrieved the honour of the legion. A fortnight later, on the 1st February, the fighting fame of the legion was restored at the affair at Tarrants, where "at a proper distance Tarlton ordered his soldiers to advance and
" *remember the Cowpens.*"

"Animated by this reproach a furious onset ensued. They broke through the centre with irresistible velocity, killed nearly fifty on the spot, wounded many in the pursuit, and dispersed five hundred of the enemy."

At the battle of Guildford, on the 15th March, the legion's appearance "contributed
" much to a speedy termination of the action," which resulted in a British victory.

In the beginning of May, Tarlton with the legion was despatched to make an attempt on Halifax, Virginia, which attempt was successfully carried out, the enemy " routed with confusion and loss," and Halifax taken.

In the beginning of June, they captured Charlotteville, where an American Assembly was sitting.

Seven members of Assembly were taken prisoners.

During July, they occupied themselves in destroying the enemy's stores throughout Virginia.

In August, Lord Cornwallis with his army entered Yorktown and Gloucester, there to await reinforcements from New York.

During September, the infantry and artillery were employed in constructing defences, while the legion were equally active in collecting forage and cattle for the use of the army. The combined French and American armies, under Rochambeau and Washington, appeared before Yorktown and Gloucester in the end of September, while the French fleet blockaded the harbour, thereby cutting off the means of assistance from New York.

On the siege commencing, the legion moved into Gloucester, where they remained till Lord Cornwallis capitulated on the 19th October.

Shortly after the capitulation the soldiers of the legion were sent to quarters in Virginia, but the officers, amongst whom was Captain Charles MacDonald, proceeded on parole to New York.

In May, 1783, the soldiers of the legion were released from their various places of imprisonment and conveyed to New York.

In August, an order was issued providing for the reduction of the legion.

This order was duly carried out in the following October at Halifax, Nova Scotia, whither officers and men were brought in transports. The officers retained their rank and retired on half-pay.

In the beginning of 1784, Captain Charles MacDonald returned to Scotland, and forthwith proceeded to Skye, where he determined to make his home. In 1787, he married Isabella, second daughter of Captain James MacDonald, Aird, at which place he and his wife resided till September, 1792, when, on his father's death, he removed to Kingsburgh.

His tenure of Kingsburgh was but a short one.

Captain Charles MacDonald died on the 2nd March, 1795, in the forty-fourth year of his age, survived by his widow, without issue.

At his funeral, in Kilmuir churchyard, Lord MacDonald remarked :—"There lies the most finished gentleman of my family and name."

Lieutenant Alexander MacDonald, 84th Royal Highland Emigrant Regiment.

Lieutenant Alexander MacDonald, the second son of Captain Allan MacDonald of Kingsburgh, was born at Flodigarry on the 21st February, 1755. His youth was passed in Skye, and when nineteen years of age he accompanied his family to North Carolina.

In June, 1775, he was gazetted to the Royal Highland Emigrants, and materially assisted his father in raising recruits for their regiment. Alexander MacDonald marched out with the force which in February, 1776, left Cross Creek to join the main body of the regiment in Nova Scotia, and he took part in the gallant but disastrous stand which that force made against the insurgents at Moore's Creek.

At that engagement he was taken prisoner along with his father, and confined in Halifax Jail till the summer of 1777, when they were both liberated and permitted to proceed to New York.

Lieutenant Alexander MacDonald remained at New York for about a twelvemonth, drilling provincial recruits, and it was not till the summer of 1778 that he joined his own regiment at Fort Edward, Nova Scotia. He took part in the various exploits in which his regiment was engaged throughout that province.

Captain Alexander MacDonald, the Commandant, took much interest in his young Lieutenant, and entrusted him with despatches on missions of importance to the heads of the army in North America.

Not being satisfied with the drafting of the companies which took place in 1780, Lieutenant MacDonald resigned his commission, and after a service of five and a half years was gazetted out of the regiment on the 6th November of that year.

In the following year he obtained an appointment on board a Government vessel, and shortly afterwards, much to the distress of his relatives, he went amissing.

Regarding him his mother writes in July, 1781, to Lady Mackenzie, of Delvine : " I have heard nothing since I left you about my son Sandy, which, you may be sure, " gives me much uneasiness."

In July, 1782, his mother again writes to Lady Mackenzie : " As for my son Sandy, " who was amissing, I had accounts of his being carried to Lisbon, but nothing certain, " which I look upon as a hearsay, but the kindness of Providence is still to be looked " upon.

" I have no reason to complain, as God has been pleased to spare his father and " the rest."

It was supposed that, in the autumn of 1782, Lieutenant Alexander MacDonald succeeded in joining his brother Captain Ranald, on board the " Ville de Paris," at one of the American ports, and with him perished in that vessel, which foundered on her voyage to England.

Captain Ranald MacDonald, Royal Marines.

Captain Ranald MacDonald, the third son of Captain Allan MacDonald of Kingsburgh was born at Flodigarry on the 16th August, 1756. He proceeded to North Carolina with his family in 1774.

On the 26th July, 1775, Ranald MacDonald was gazetted as Lieutenant to the Royal Marines, and joined a detachment of that branch of the service stationed at Halifax. From 1775 till 1780 this detachment was actively engaged in beating off parties of New Englanders, who were constantly harassing the Province of Nova Scotia. A notable encounter took place in July, 1777, between his marines and a force of New Englanders at River St. John's, where the latter were signally defeated.

In December, 1777, Captain Alexander MacDonald, Commandant of the Royal Highland Emigrants, writes to Captain Allan MacDonald :—" Your son Ranald is a fine " young fellow, and will make an excellent officer if he lives."

In January, 1778, the same officer again writes :—" Ranald is already in a good " corps and pretty far advanced, and probably may have a chance of a company before " this work is over."

In September, 1779, Ranald MacDonald was promoted to Captain-Lieutenant, and in the following year to Captain.

On the arrival of Rodney's fleet in American waters, Captain Ranald, with his detachment of marines, was placed on board one of the men-of-war belonging to the fleet.

At the battle of Eustati (12th April, 1782), " which of all other victories immortalised " the name of Rodney," Captain Ranald MacDonald and his men fought on board the " Princessa," a ship of 70 guns, commanded by Rear Admiral Drake.

The " Princessa " began the battle, and as she was ranged alongside her opponent a desperate fight ensued, in which Captain Ranald was wounded. The contest ended at sunset, when the Count de Grasse surrendered with his flagship, the " Ville de Paris."

This historic ship was presented by the citizens of Paris to Louis XIV., and was reckoned the most magnificent man-of-war afloat at that time.

Captain Ranald and some other officers were put on board the " Ville de Paris " in charge of the prisoners and treasure.

The prize ships were ordered to be brought over to England.

In the month of September, when half-way across the Atlantic, these ships encountered a terrific storm, which lasted several days; and during the night of the 14th of that month the " Ville de Paris," owing to her battered condition, foundered.

Every soul on board perished.

Flora MacDonald was deeply affected at the loss of her son under such peculiarly sad circumstances, and she wore till the end of her days a handsome memorial ring containing a small lock of his hair, over which was inscribed, " Ranald MacDonald, lost in the Ville de Paris."

CAPTAIN JAMES MACDONALD, FLODIGARRY.

Captain James MacDonald, Flodigarry, the fourth son of Captain Allan MacDonald of Kingsburgh, was born at Flodigarry on the 30th November, 1757.

He was educated partly at home under tutors, and partly at the Portree Public School.

When seventeen years of age, on his voyage to America, he received his *baptême de feu* on board the emigrant ship "Baliol," when she was attacked by a French privateer.

When, in 1776, his father and three elder brothers entered the service of the King James was left in North Carolina to look after his father's newly-purchased property, Killiegray, and to protect his mother and young sister, who otherwise would have been subject to insults and molestation by the rebels.

During his mother's stay at Killiegray, he jealously but tactfully guarded her welfare, though on one occasion she herself was forced to show "her spirited behaviour " when brought before the Committee of Rascals in North Carolina."

In 1779, Flora MacDonald and her daughter returned to Scotland; and the rebels, having seized and confiscated Killiegray, James repaired to New York, where he was given a commission as Lieutenant in Tarlton's British Legion.

James MacDonald "served with distinction" in the legion from the time of its arrival in South Carolina (1779) till the surrender of Yorktown in October, 1781, and was present in the enterprises and actions in which that dashing corps showed such unflagging energy and unceasing bravery.

At the battle of Camden, where the legion as usual distinguished themselves, James MacDonald was severely wounded.

It is needless to recapitulate the various doings of the British legion, as they are related in the notice of Captain Charles MacDonald's military career.

After the surrender of Yorktown, James MacDonald proceeded on parole to New York, where he remained till peace was declared.

On the reduction of the legion taking place in October, 1783, James Macdonald retired on half-pay with the rank of Captain.

On his return to Scotland, in 1784, Captain James MacDonald lived for some time at Dunvegan Castle (with his brother-in-law, Major MacLeod), who with his wife and family, during MacLeod's absence in India, occupied the Castle. Major MacLeod was engaged for several years in raising recruits for the various Highland regiments and Fencibles; and in this duty he was ably assisted by Captain MacDonald.

In 1788, through the kind influence of Lady Margaret MacDonald, he obtained the lands of Flodigarry, which once more became his home, and where he lived to the end of his days.

In 1791, he married Emily, daughter of James MacDonald, of Skaebost, by whom he had a family of three sons (James, Allan, and John) and three daughters (Jessie, Flora, and Charlotte).

On the death of his eldest brother, Captain Charles MacDonald, who died childless, Captain James MacDonald became the head of the Kingsburgh family; therefore had he taken up his residence there, he would have been MacDonald, IX. of Kingsburgh ; but he never assumed that designation, as Flodigarry continued to be his residence.

Captain James kept up the reputation of Flodigarry, which his father had laid as a high-class Highland cattle farm, "the big Flodigarry heifers" being ever eagerly sought for by cattle-dealers, who, at market times, used to proceed miles out of Portree to meet them.

Like his father, he was foremost in Highland athletic feats, and on his return home fought his battles over again on the "Camanachd" field.

Many celebrated "Camanachd" matches took place between his team from Flodigarry and that of Captain Somerled MacDonald, at Sartle.

Captain James MacDonald was extremely popular amongst his countrymen, on account of his genial and affable disposition, and in local song and story was familiarly designated "Seumas Ruadh Mac Ailein."

In the summer of 1807, after brief illnesses, he and his wife died at Flodigarry within a week of one another.

Caprain James was laid to rest in the Kingsburgh burying ground at Kilmuir churchyard.

Of Captain James MacDonald's family, Flora and Charlotte predeceased their parents. John died in boyhood. Jessie [1] married Ninian Jeffrey, Lochcarron, Captain, Ross-shire Militia. James and Allan entered the East India Company's Service.

Lieutenant-Colonel John MacDonald, F.R.S., &c., youngest son of Allan MacDonald of Kingsburgh and the celebrated Flora MacDonald, was born at Flodigarry, in the Island of Skye, on the 30th of October, 1759. John MacDonald was sent at an early age to the Grammar School at Portree and afterwards to the High School of Edinburgh. He did not in after life forget the scenes of his younger days, and some time previously to his death he invested a sum of money for the purpose of giving a medal to the dux of the third class of the High School of Edinburgh, and another sum for the purchase of a book for the head boy of the school at Portree, thus evincing his gratitude to those institutions in which he had imbibed the principles and improved the talents which carried him through life with credit to himself, utility to his country, and the approbation of all within his sphere of action.[2]

He was originally intended for the law, but being of an ardent and enterprising disposition was anxious for a more active life and coveted the profession of a soldier. In the year 1780 his wishes were gratified by obtaining, through the influence of Sir John MacPherson, a cadetship in the service of the East India Company on the Bombay establishment. He was at first attached to the Infantry, but, in consequence

---

[1] Her son, Captain George Jeffrey, greatly distinguished himself under Sir de Lacy Evans at the battle of Venta Hill on the 5th of May 1836, when he had to be carried off the field with three bullets in his body. He served afterwards through the Sikh War of 1848-49, was present at the siege and storming of Mooltan, and at the closing battle of Goojerat.—Mackenzie's "History of the MacDonalds."

[2] Memoir of Lieutenant-Colonel John MacDonald, F.R.S., &c. London : Printed by J. L. Cox and Son, Great Queen Street, 1831.

of his knowledge of fortification, was transferred to the Engineers. In September, 1782, he received the appointment of Ensign in the Corps of Engineers on the Bengal establishment through the interest of his cousin, Colonel Murray, and was ordered on duty to Bencoolen, where he arrived in November following. In 1783 he was made assistant engineer, and was directed by the Governor and Council to survey the Dutch settlements in the northern parts of Sumatra, which were to be immediately restored to the Prince of Orange.[1]

Though the season of the year was adverse to the undertaking, and notwithstanding that he was at the time suffering from the effects of a severe illness, yet so zealous was he in the discharge of his professional duties that he performed this arduous task in a tropical climate with the most consummate skill and scientific accuracy in the short space of four months. So satisfied were the Government with the manner in which he had performed his duty on that occasion that they recommended him to the Court of Directors of the East India Company " as a young officer of great merit and highly worthy of encouragement ; " and the Governor-General in Council bestowed upon him in the year 1784 (although he was only an ensign) the brevet rank of captain while employed in service in the Island of Sumatra, as a special mark of their favour and approbation.[1]

Shortly afterwards, owing to his special acquaintance with the science of projectiles, he received the additional appointment of Commandant of Artillery on that station. Colonel MacDonald was employed in 1786, by direction of the Governor-General of Bengal, to survey the harbour and roadstead of Bencoolen, but before he had completed the survey of Pulo Bay and Rat Island he was recalled to Calcutta by Lord Cornwallis, and ordered to return by Penang for the purpose of surveying that valuable island then just ceded to the British Government by the Queen of Queedah. On his arrival there he found Captain (afterwards General) Kidd employed on that service, and he consequently proceeded direct to Calcutta. Here, however, he did not remain long, his knowledge of the language, manners, and habits of the people recommending him to the Governor-General as a fit person to be sent to Bencoolen to superintend the military and civil works in operation there, and to complete the survey of the port and other parts of the west coast of Sumatra. He accordingly returned thither in 1788, and continued on this duty till the year 1796, when, having suffered much from his laborious professional avocations and the pestilential climate of the island, he returned to Europe on furlough, where he arrived in January, 1798, after an absence of nearly seventeen years, the greater part of which was spent in a place proverbial for its insalubrity.

While at Bencoolen he took observations on the diurnal variation of the magnetic needle, and so anxious was he to obtain every possible information on this very interesting subject that (at considerable expense to himself) he went to the Island of St. Helena, where he remained for some months making similar observations. The results of his labours were submitted to the Royal Society, and were deemed by

---

[1] Memoir of Lieutenant-Colonel John MacDonald, F.R.S., &c. London : Printed by J. L. Cox and Son, Great Queen Street, 1831.

them worthy of being given to the scientific world. Immediately on his return to England he was elected a Fellow of the Society.[1]

Ever active in the discharge of the duties of his profession, he accepted (with the permission of the East India Company) the post of Captain in the Royal Edinburgh Volunteer Artillery, which had been offered to him in a season of alarm and danger, though he was far from being restored to health. On resigning this appointment, in consequence of being appointed Major in Lord MacDonald's Regiment of the Isles, the gentlemen under his command presented him with a superb sword as a mark of their affection and esteem. While in command of this fine corps (composed of gentlemen of Edinburgh) he wrote, with the approbation of Sir Ralph Abercromby, a treatise on "Some Practical and Theoretical Parts of Artillery."

In June, 1800, he was made Lieutenant-Colonel of the Royal Clan Alpine Regiment, and proceeded with that corps on duty to Ireland, where it continued until the peace of Amiens, when the regiment was disbanded, and he returned with his family to London.[1]

At the beginning of the year 1804 Mr. Pitt, having in a very complimentary manner selected him to be one of his field officers in the Cinque Ports Volunteers, he removed with his family from London to Dover in March of that year. He had not been there many hours before, unasked, he embarked in an open boat and reconnoitred the harbour of Boulogne with a view to obtain information as to the state of preparation for the threatened French invasion of this country. The results of his observations (which he made at great personal hazard) on this and various other occasions he communicated to the Prime Minister (at his own desire), by whom they were considered of the utmost importance.

Colonel MacDonald remained at Dover until the Volunteers, having been greatly reduced in numbers, no longer required a field officer of his rank.

Colonel MacDonald was a voluminous writer on military and scientific subjects. The following are some of the works he had translated and published, viz. :—" Rules " and Regulations of the Field Exercise and Manœuvres of the French Infantry;" "An " Essay on the Principle and Origin of Sovereign Power;" "The Experienced Officer, " &c."; " Instructions for the Conduct of Infantry on Actual Service," and "The " Formation and Manœuvres of Infantry, by the Chevalier Duteil."

He was also the author of several original works, all displaying talents and extensive acquirements. His knowledge of music was unusually refined, as appears by his "Treatise on the Violoncello," and also that on " The Harmonic System of Stringed Instruments," the merits of which two works had been acknowledged by the most eminent musical professors of his day.[1]

As for rewards he met with but few beyond honorary marks of distinction and the self-approbation of having done his duty. A Chairman of the East India Company justly remarked that Colonel MacDonald was " one of those destined to labour for others more than for himself." He received from the King of the Netherlands a gold

---

[1] Memoir of Lieutenant-Colonel John MacDonald, F.R.S., &c. London : Printed by J. L. Cox and Sons, Great Queen Street, 1831.

snuff-box, and from the King of Prussia a gold medal. Colonel MacDonald died at Exeter on the 16th of August, 1831, and is buried in the cathedral there. A provincial newspaper, referring to the Colonel's death, said:—"The activity of his mind and the "benevolence of his heart would not permit him to remain an indifferent spectator "of events daily passing around him, and he was in consequence one of the first to "step forward upon all occasions of national or local interest, as well as to assist in "ameliorating individual or general calamity."[1]

The following is the inscription on the monument erected to the memory of Colonel John MacDonald in Exeter Cathedral:—

Sacred to the memory of
John MacDonald, Esq., F.R.S. and F.A.S.,
Fifth son of Captain Allan MacDonald, of the 84th Regiment,
And of Flora MacDonald.
Obit 16th August, 1831.
Aged 72 years.
Beloved by the poor for his benevolence.
Firm in moral rectitude.
In integrity sincere.
He departed this life revered and lamented.
Christianity having to deplore the loss of a disciple
Who admired and venerated her principles and enforced by constant practice
her benevolent and charitable admonitions.

Colonel MacDonald's family consisted of seven sons and two daughters—

Robert, a Major in the Indian Army;
John, a Captain in the Indian Army;
Allan, died young;
William Pitt, Major-General in the Indian Army;
Charles Edward, in the Indian Civil Service;
James, a Captain in the Indian Army;
Reginald, Lieutenant, 17th Lancers;
Flora, married Edward Wylde, R.N.;
Henrietta, who married Benjamin Cuff Greenhill, of Knowle Hall, Somerset

NOTES.

Colonel John MacDonald, of Somerlands, Exeter, youngest son of Captain Allan MacDonald, Kingsburgh.

During a conversation with George IV. on Jacobite subjects the King remarked to Colonel MacDonald, "I shall always look upon your mother as having been the saviour of a member of my family."

---

[1] Memoir of Lieutenant-Colonel John MacDonald, F.R.S., &c. London: Printed by J. L. Cox and Sons, Great Queen Street, 1831.

Once in conversation with Sir Walter Scott to a query of the Colonel's as to Flora MacIvor of Waverley, the novelist replied :—"I do not know but what I had "your mother in my mind when I portrayed the character of Flora MacIvor."

LIEUTENANT-COLONEL JAMES SOMERLED MACDONALD OF FLODIGARRY, 45TH MADRAS NATIVE INFANTRY.

Lieutenant-Colonel James Somerled MacDonald, the eldest son of Captain James MacDonald, was born at Flodigarry on the 29th May, 1792. He was educated at Flodigarry under tutors and afterwards at Inverness Academy. On his leaving school he resolved to enter the army, and in the following year, through the influence of his uncle, Lieutenant-Colonel MacDonald, Exeter, a cadetship was promised him in the East India Company's service.

In view of this James MacDonald entrusted the management of Flodigarry to his relative, Lachlan Mackinnon of Corry, and in the autumn of 1810 sailed for Calcutta, where he arrived in the December of that year.

On the nomination of Sir Thomas Metcalf, and on the recommendation of his uncle afore-mentioned, James MacDonald received, on the 15th January, 1811, his commission as Ensign on the Madras Establishment. He proceeded to Madras in the end of February, and on the 11th March was posted to the 25th Madras Native Infantry. It may be interesting to relate that, for the first twelvemonths of his residence in Madras, Ensign MacDonald shared quarters with a son of the poet Burns, who was an officer in another Madras regiment.

In the beginning of 1812 the 25th Native Infantry was moved to Lanjan, where it remained till January, 1813.

In February, 1813, the 25th was ordered to return to Madras, and after long halts and tedious marches through a country infested with the hostile Pindarries, the regiment reached its destination in the following July. In September, 1813, James MacDonald was promoted to Lieutenant, and in the beginning of 1814 was appointed to the Military Institution at Madras for the purpose of studying Hindustanee, surveying, &c.

To this he refers in a letter to his only surviving sister, Miss MacDonald, Flodigarry :—"I have been appointed to the Military Institution at this Presidency. "This was effected through the interest of Sir Robert Abercromby, the Governor, who "uniformly behaved to me with the most disinterested kindness. He recommended "me strongly to some of the heads of departments, and I expect to be well provided "for in the course of a few years."

At Madras Institution Lieutenant MacDonald found himself surrounded by numerous fellow Highlanders, amongst whom great enthusiasm prevailed for all matters Celtic, and a Highland Society was formed by these young officers. With reference to this, in a letter to his sister, he mentions : "The Governor-General, Sir Robert Aber- "cromby, is President of a branch of the Highland Society here. He has paid me a "great deal of attention, and at his suggestion I was elected an honorary member of "the society for the memory of my old grandmother ! A son of the poet Burns was "also made an honorary member at the same time. This is the young man with whom

"I wrote you I lived for the first year after my arrival in this country. He and I have "always been on the most intimate terms, and I regret very much that we should be "in different corps." In August, 1815, James MacDonald passed the examinations in Hindustanee, and for his high proficiency therein obtained an honorary degree and a reward of £200. He next turned his attention to Persian and surveying, and remained at the institution prosecuting his studies till December, 1815, when, despite the fact of the outlying provinces being still subject to the inroads of the Pindarries, all the officers of the institution were sent to Guntoor for practical surveying.

In this outing what befell Lieutenant MacDonald and his brother officers can best be related in an extract of a letter to his sister.

"I remained at my studies in the institution until the month of December, 1815, when we all went out to put in practice our knowledge of trigonometrical surveying into the neighbourhood of Guntoor and the banks of the Kistnah. Reports of the expected approach of the Pindarries were in general circulation, but as I was within 40 miles of two brigades I unfortunately disbelieved them, and continued surveying till the 11th March, 1816, when, as I was taking a few angles with the theodolite on the top of a little hill, my servant pointed out some horsemen armed with swords and spears.

"I turned the glass of the theodolite towards them, and to my consternation made them out to be Pindarries advancing towards me.

"I told my servants to provide for themselves, and mounting my horse set off at full speed for Guntoor, distant eight miles. Being better mounted than the Pindarries I gained ground on those pursuing me, but had the ill-luck on nearing Guntoor to hear a heavy firing there, by which I knew that they were attacking the town.

"Thus enemies in front and in rear, my horse jaded, what could I do? I determined to make for Guntoor at all hazards. I therefore spurred my horse towards the Collector's office, but I had not gone far when those in front came down in hundreds, surrounded me, unhorsed me, stripped me to the skin, and had the kindness to give me one spear and three sabre wounds.

"However, they all turned out slight, and a month afterwards I was as well as ever, and, what is lucky, none of them have spoiled my beauty! The spear wound is on the collar-bone, which saved my life, and the sabre wounds are on the back of my neck.

"Well, here I was, naked, fatigued, bleeding, thirsty, angry with my own imbecile Government for permitting, and with the Pindarries for inflicting, such indignities and suffering.

"The wounds bled so much I determined to make for Guntoor again, and either be killed or get to the surgeon, but I thought the former more certain. I walked through them for some time unmolested, but as I came near the Collector's office I saw five or six killed by its fire.

"The remnant of this party on seeing me, galloped up, and when they were just going to give me the *coup de grâce*, they were perceived by three or four Sepoys at the corner of the Collector's office, who very judiciously fired at us all (!) in order, if possible, to save me.

"None of us, friend or foe, were knocked over. However, they took to their heels, and I took to mine, but in opposite directions, as you may well imagine.

"On entering the Collector's office I found two serjeants, who were at Guntoor by accident, defending the house with twenty-five Sepoys against 400 Pindarries. The doctor had hardly dressed the wounds when I began to fire away like a devil, and I killed five or six of them before I satisfied my revenge.

"This was a most miraculous escape, as I am the only officer the Pindarries have ever spared."

In this adventure Lieutenant MacDonald lost all his baggage, clothing, and his father's gold watch.

For his pluck shown he subsequently received a handsome pecuniary reward from Government.

Letter continued :—

"The institution was abolished by an order from the Court of Directors shortly after my return to the Presidency. Finding there was nothing to be got, I took a furlough of four months to Bengal.

"Accordingly I arrived there in the month of September, 1816, and after a good deal of difficulty got admitted to the Civil College, Fort William, Calcutta, as a student.

"Government gave me quarters in the Writer's Buildings.

"I paid a good deal of attention to the Oriental languages, and in June, 1817, and December of the same year I obtained degrees of honour and gold medals in Arabic, Persian, Hindustanee, and Maharatta.

"In January, 1818, I ran up into the Governor-General's camp, in the neighbourhood of Gwalior, by dawk, and went 900 miles in ten days. I was not out of my palki twelve hours in all, during the whole of the ten days.

"Lord Hastings, the Governor-General, behaved very handsomely, much more than my most sanguine hopes could have anticipated.

"He issued a general order directing me to join Sir John Malcolm, and gave me a letter for him.

"I crossed Central India with a detachment sufficiently strong to prevent our becoming the prey of the wandering bands of predatory horse with which this unfortunate country is still infested.

"I joined Sir John Malcolm at Oojein on the 24th March, 1818, and on the same day, in consequence of the letter from Lord Hastings, was appointed Assistant Quartermaster-General to Sir John's division, which situation I kept for six days, when this situation—Assistant to the Political Agent at Bhopaul—falling vacant, I succeeded.

"It is a new appointment, made in consequence of the Pindarry War. I shall give you an abstract of the war, and of the great political changes which India has undergone within the last few months. Ever since the wars for the succession on the death of Aurumgzèbe, and since the dismemberment of the Mogul Empire, Central India has been the scene of wars, tumults, and contests between the different Maharatta States that rose up on the ruins of the Moguls.

"In consequence of this state large bands of predatory horse rose up under enterprising soldiers of fortune, who used to be hired by the different adverse parties in their contests.

"The men of ability and address among those chiefs founded principalities and independent states. Scindia, Holkar, and, more recently, Ameer Khan may be given as instances; but the smaller fry, the less considerable, were obliged, when they could not be hired, to plunder, burn, and destroy, and they latterly had systemised their proceedings to such a degree as to levy money from the villages and districts that were unable to defend themselves, exactly similar to 'the blackmail' in Scotland.

"These pests of India had in latter years multiplied so exceedingly, and had extended their ravages so far and wide, that they at last touched the sacred boundaries of John Company; and it was in one of their first and most successful expeditions that they did me the favour to leave their marks upon me.

"The extirpation of these hell-hounds, whose habits were violent and cruel in the extreme, became incumbent on the British, as the most powerful and leading Power in the East.

"But the regular empires and states derived frequent assistance from these freebooters, particularly Scindia and Holkar.

"It was accordingly likely that we should be involved with all the predatory Powers.

"Large armies were assembled at the three Presidencies.

"They advanced from all sides to Malwa (where I am now), the chief haunt of the Omdarahs.

"As was foreseen, the Peishwa and the Rajah of Nagpoor broke out most insidiously, and without warning attacked the Residents at their different capitals.

"There happened to be only two battalions at Poonah and the like strength at Nagpoor, but they repulsed and defeated, after great carnage, armies twenty-five times their strength.

"The action at Nagpoor was particularly brilliant, but was a touch-and-go affair. The battalion to which the two MacDonalds, sons of the Sheriff of Skye, belong was there, and distinguished itself very much.

"Neither of them was touched, though there was great slaughter among the officers.

"The result of the war is, that the Rajah of Nagpoor is a prisoner in our camp. The Peishwa lost his crown and country, but is not yet mastered or caught.

"The army of the Holkar was defeated and dispersed in a very gallant manner at the Ludpoor, about sixty miles from this place—Bhopaul. In short, we are pencilling and dividing India as to us seems fit.

"I, as one of the Corps Diplomatique, have the negotiations, &c., which take place all over India within my reach."

Lieutenant MacDonald continued to reside at Bhopaul till October, 1822, when owing to ill-health he was obliged to resign his appointment and go on furlough to England, where he arrived in the beginning of 1823.

After his arrival in London he was much consulted by the India Office authorities as to the political and military affairs in the native states of the Madras Presidency, and for some months he was engaged in compiling a work relative thereto.

In the end of 1823, after an absence of thirteen years, Lieutenant MacDonald returned to Flodigarry, where he resided for some time.

His only sister afore-mentioned had by this time married Ninian Jeffrey, Captain in the Ross-shire Militia, and was settled at Attadale, Lochcarron.

With his sister he remained on a visit of some months, returning to London in the spring of 1824, when he received promotion as Captain.

During the summer of 1824 a controversy arose between Lord MacDonald of the Isles and Glengarry as to the chiefship, &c. of the clan, and in course of the correspondence between the two chiefs Glengarry used language which his opponent considered unjustifiable and requiring explanation, if not redress.

Lord MacDonald deputed Captain James MacDonald, as being an intimate friend and representative of his senior cadet family—the MacDonalds of Kingsburgh, Captain MacDonald being X. of that designation—to act for him as his second in this delicate matter. Captain James strenuously but tactfully supported his chief throughout the whole controversy, which was no easy task when dealing with a man of Glengarry's fiery nature.[1]

Matters came to a crisis in September, 1824, shortly after the northern meeting, at which all parties were present. On the 3rd October Lord MacDonald handed over the correspondence to Captain James, who on the same evening and again on the following morning called upon Glengarry. Glengarry did not appear to be in a humour to be reasoned with, and after some conversation of an altercatory nature, Captain James took his leave, perceiving that evidently the affair would end seriously, and that Glengarry would send his seconds to arrange a meeting. The same evening at a dinner party at Lord MacDonald's, Colonel D'Este was introduced to Captain James as Glengarry's "friend."

Colonel D'Este then repeated to Captain MacDonald the explanation or apology that he had been authorised to make on the part of Glengarry, "That Glengarry had " not the remotest intention of hurting Lord MacDonald's feelings or giving him " personal offence, and he regretted he was so understood." This apology was accepted by Captain MacDonald, and, after both seconds agreeing that the correspondence should be kept private, the affair ended. Captain MacDonald proceeded with Lord MacDonald to Armadale, and from thence to Flodigarry.

In the end of November the dispute broke out afresh, in consequence of Glengarry having published part of the correspondence in the newspapers. Captain James was again to the fore as second to his chief, and was obliged, in the beginning of December, to send his own version of the affair to the public prints, a long notice of which appeared in the "Caledonian Mercury."

Again it was feared that a meeting would have to be arranged, but through the tact of Captain MacDonald that unpleasant contingency was happily avoided, and so in time the matter dropped. In recognition of his loyal services, Lord MacDonald presented his second with a complete Highland costume of Somerled MacDonald tartan, with ornaments.

In this costume Captain MacDonald appeared at a Levée held by George IV., at St. James's Palace, in the spring of 1825. Captain MacDonald's furlough being up in May, 1825, he succeeded in having it extended for a twelvemonth, with a view to his obtaining, through the India Office, a diplomatic appointment at one of the native states.

---

[1] Glengarry, after a former northern meeting, killed in a duel Lieutenant Norman MacLeod, a first cousin of Captain James MacDonald.

In the summer of 1825, whilst in London, Captain MacDonald, as heir to his grandfather, Captain Allan MacDonald of Kingsburgh, attempted to establish his claim to the grant of land in Nova Scotia, which his grandfather had received from Government for his services rendered throughout the American War of Independence (*vide* notice Captain Allan MacDonald).

However, after much inquiry and correspondence, he could make nothing of it, as the land had been forfeited to Government owing to the non-residence of the grantees.

After a farewell visit to Flodigarry, and to his friends in the Highlands, Captain James MacDonald sailed for India in September, 1826.

Not having been successful in obtaining a diplomatic appointment, on his arrival at Madras he was posted to the 45th Madras Native Infantry. In August, 1827, he was appointed Brigade-Major in Malabar and Canara, which post he held for seven years. The Napoleonic wars over, cattle farming in the Highlands was carried on under very unremunerative conditions, and, after battling with falling prices for thirteen years, on the advice of his agent, Lachlan Mackinnon of Corry, Captain James, with much reluctance, gave up Flodigarry at the Whitsuntide term of 1828.

In the beginning of 1834 the Coorg war broke out, and in March of that year Captain MacDonald was appointed Deputy-Assistant-Adjutant-General to the 3rd or western column of the field force fighting in Coorg.

Colonel Fowler commanding the column writes on the 7th April, 1834, to the Secretary of State for India:—"To Captain James MacDonald, Deputy-Assistant-Adjutant-General, who was most forward on all occasions, and to whose energy and exertions I am equally indebted with Captain Butterworth; as well on the evening of the 2nd, as on the attacks on the 3rd, Captain MacDonald led the light company and Grenadiers of the 32nd Regiment to take the last stockade in reverse.

"The ascent was steep and the enemy defended every tree.

"Captain MacDonald received the Rajah's vakeels, translated the letters, and contrived, without allowing the Rajah's title, to keep them in good humour and give us supplies."

The war over in September, 1834, and the force disbanded, Captain MacDonald was directed to rejoin his regiment, and resume his duty as Major of Brigade in Malabar and Canara.

In January, 1837, owing to the Colonel of the 45th Native Infantry having received an appointment in Palaveram, Captain MacDonald, as senior officer, got command of his regiment, which he held till June of the same year, when, the Mahratta translator having been removed from the army, "the Governor was pleased to appoint Captain MacDonald to that office."

In April, 1839, he was appointed to act as secretary to the College Board and Committee for Native Education at Madras.

In August of the same year he was promoted to Major.

In February, 1840, owing to ill-health, he was obliged to resign his appointments, and go on sick leave to the Neilgherry hills.

After some months' residence at the Neilgherries his health was somewhat restored, and he rejoined his regiment, of which he remained in command till September, 1842.

In that month his health again becamed impaired and he was forced to proceed to Europe on furlough.

In the beginning of 1843 he received his promotion as Lieutenant-Colonel.

In the spring and summer of 1843 he spent some months at Arcachon and Vichy vainly endeavouring to establish his health.

By August he reached London in fast failing health, and there, on the 28th of that month, he died, in the fifty-first year of his age.

Colonel MacDonald was buried in Kensal Green Cemetery, where a simple Roman cross of white marble marks his last resting-place.

Captain Allan Ranald MacDonald, Flodigarry, 4th Bengal Native Infantry.

Captain Allan Ranald MacDonald, the second son of Captain James MacDonald, was born at Flodigarry on the 22nd January, 1800.

His father and mother having died when he was only seven years of age, he was placed under the care of his relative, Lachlan Mackinnon of Corry, and brought up at Corry House.

At the age of twelve he was sent to Elgin Academy, returning to Corry during vacations.

His education completed in the beginning of 1818, Allan Ranald received a commission as Ensign in the East India Company's service, through the influence of his uncle, Colonel MacDonald, Exeter; and on his arrival in Calcutta in the March of that year he was posted to the 1st Bengal Native Infantry.

In the following October he was promoted to Lieutenant.

Having a natural aptitude for languages, Lieutenant Allan Ranald, on his arrival in India, applied himself to the study of Oriental languages, and after passing the necessary examinations therein, he was appointed in May, 1822, Interpreter and Quartermaster to his corps.

In March, 1825, he exchanged these appointments for that of Adjutant to his corps.

In January, 1829, Lieutenant MacDonald exchanged into the 4th Bengal Native Infantry, in which regiment he again acted as Interpreter and Quartermaster.

In August, 1831, he was promoted to Captain.

In December, 1833, Captain MacDonald was appointed to act as Deputy-Assistant-Adjutant-General of the Saugor Division, which post he held till September, 1834, when he was appointed A.D.C. to Brigadier-General Smith, Commandant of that division.

On the 17th February, 1835, Captain MacDonald was directed to act as Deputy-Judge-Advocate-General to the same division.

In 1836 he married Leila, elder daughter of Brigadier-General Smith.

In December, 1837, Captain MacDonald was appointed Brigade-Major to the Oude Auxiliary Force, which was employed in quelling risings of the natives in that province.

In a letter dated 10th April, 1838, the Governor-General, Lord Auckland, states that "Captain MacDonald was marked as eminently possessing the necessary "qualifications for this duty, and he was designated by Lieutenant-Colonel Anquetal "as the officer whom he would himself select, and upon whom he could best depend "for efficient co-operation."

In July, 1839, the Governor-General writes "of the favourable testimony borne "by Brigadier Anquetal to Captain MacDonald's zeal and efficiency as Major of "Brigade to the Oude Auxiliary Force."

In December, 1839, the troubles in Oude being over, the Auxiliary Force was abolished, and Captain MacDonald was given command of the Bundlecund Legion, which command he held till May, 1841.

At that date he was appointed Commandant of the Oude Native Infantry.

Captain MacDonald, while in command of this force, was taken suddenly ill at Lucknow in the end of December, 1841, and on the 2nd January, 1842, he died, in the forty-second year of his age, survived by his widow and three children—a son and two daughters.

"Captain Allan Ranald MacDonald was a man of great ability, and may be honourably mentioned amongst those officers who in the early decades of the present century so materially helped to build up and consolidate our Indian Empire."

He was beloved alike by the officers and men of his corps, and they, out of regard and affection for their commandant, erected a handsome monument over his grave.

Captain MacDonald's widow survived him till February, 1896, when she died at her residence, Clarence House, Windsor.

Of his three children, his son Reginald Somerled held an appointment in the Colonial Office for many years.

He married Zela, daughter of Sir William Grove, and died in 1874, leaving two daughters, Flora, who married Captain Duff Baker, R.A., and Leila, who married Hubert Crackanthorpe.

Of Captain MacDonald's two daughters, Ellen died young, and Leila Flora, who was remarkable for her great beauty, married Marshal Canrobert.

The Maréchale Canrobert died in 1889, leaving three children—Marcel, Lieutenant in the Regiment of Spahis; Claire, married to Henri de Navacelle, Lieutenant de Vaisseau; and Louis, who died in 1894. Marshal Canrobert died in 1895.

Lieutenant-Colonel John MacDonald, son of Allan MacDonald of Kingsburgh and Flora MacDonald, had five sons in the military service, viz.:—Major Robert MacDonald, Captain John MacDonald, Major-General William Pitt MacDonald, Captain James MacDonald, all in the Indian Army; and Lieutenant Reginald MacDonald, in the 17th Lancers.[1]

Major-General William Pitt MacDonald was appointed as an Ensign in the 21st Native Infantry Regiment on the 6th of April, 1820; Lieutenant on the 10th of

---

[1] Mackenzie's "History of the Macdonalds."

January, 1822; Captain on the 9th of November, 1831; Major on the 6th of October, 1851, and subsequently he reached the rank of a general officer.

In his examination in Hindustanee on the 4th of May, 1829, Lieutenant MacDonald was reported to have made " first-class progress, and on the 21st of May in the following " year he passed a creditable examination in that language, and was recommended to " continue his studies for the reward." [1]

In reporting the capture of one of the fugitive Kemedy rebel chiefs in May, 1833, Major Baxter said " the clue of information, it is due to Captain MacDonald to say, was " obtained by him which led to the Subidar's success during Captain MacDonald's " absence on duty at Polcondan." The enemy having taken confidence from their success in the attack upon Major Baxter, Mr. Russell, the Commissioner, in a demi-official letter, wrote :—" If a detachment comes from Vizanagrum, pray take care that " it is under an officer junior to MacDonald, as it is an advantage to me to correspond " with a man who knows Kemedy and its politics." Accordingly Captain MacDonald was appointed on the 13th of January, 1834, to act as a staff officer to the field detachment under Major Nash's command, with regard to which appointment Brigadier-General Taylor said :—" Captain MacDonald has been selected by Major Nash for the " above situation from his local knowledge, zeal, and activity in the service while " under the command of the late Major Baxter, and his general character as an " officer, and I must beg to bear my testimony to the latter from my own continued " observation."

On the restoration of tranquillity in the district, General Taylor reported that Major Nash spoke of the conduct of his " Brigade-Major, Captain MacDonald, in terms " of high encomium ;" and the General himself added that he had much reason to be pleased with him in his situation of Deputy-Judge-Advocate-General on the trials of the rebels that had been brought forward:—" Captain MacDonald is an officer of much " promise, and well deserving of further employment," concluded the report, and in a General Order, dated 1st July, 1834, it is stated : " that the Governor-General has " observed with pleasure the approbation expressed by Brigadier-General Taylor of the " services of Captain MacDonald as Brigade-Major, and officiating Deputy-Judge-" Advocate-General with the force lately employed in the Ganjam District. In " consideration of the peculiar and difficult duty he has had to perform, and of his " having been indefatigable in his exertions to fulfil it, the Governor-General in " Council forwards his case [1] for the consideration of the Supreme Government."

In December, 1835, Captain MacDonald was directed to join the 3rd Light Infantry, and to do duty with the detachment in the Ganjam District, where he was appointed as Judge-Advocate to conduct such trials as might be held there as well as at Vizagapatam.

On the 21st of January, 1836, he took charge of the Judge-Advocate-General's Department of the Goomsoor Field Force. On the restoration of peace in the Ganjam he again received the approbation of the Governor-General in Council, the Commissioner

---

[1] India Office Records.

(the Honourable Mr. Russell) having reported that Captain MacDonald had "conducted "with great ability the trials under military law."

General William Pitt MacDonald (then a Captain) was employed as a Deputy-Paymaster to the Madras troops which served with the Eastern Expedition on the Yang-tse-Kiang River (under a General Order dated 5th November, 1844), for which he received the China War medal.[1]

THE MACDONALDS OF SCALPAY.

Lieutenant-General Sir John MacDonald, G.C.B., Adjutant-General to the Forces, a son of Norman MacDonald of Scalpay by Susannah MacAlister, his wife, was appointed an Ensign in the 89th Foot on the 15th of April, 1795; Lieutenant on the 2nd of February, 1796; Captain on the 22nd of October, 1802; Major in the 99th Foot on the 28th of February, 1805; Major, half-pay, in the 10th West India Regiment on the 21st of March, 1805; Major in the 43rd Foot on the 20th of February, 1806; Lieutenant-Colonel in the 51st Foot on the 17th of March, 1808; Lieutenant-Colonel in the 90th Foot on the 21st of April, 1808; Lieutenant-Colonel in the 5th Garrison Battalion on the 16th of June, 1808; Lieutenant-Colonel, half-pay, in the 1st Garrison Battalion on the 11th of August, 1808; Colonel, Brevet, on the 4th of June, 1814; Major-General on the 27th of May, 1825; Lieutenant-General on the 28th of June, 1838; Colonel of the 67th Foot on the 25th of August, 1838; and Colonel of the 42nd Royal Highlanders (the Black Watch) on the 15th of January, 1844. He served as Deputy-Adjutant-General from the 14th of August, 1818, to the 26th of July, 1830, and Adjutant-General from the 27th of July, 1830, to the date of his death, which took place in London on the 28th of March, 1850.[2]

Sir John MacDonald[2] served with the 89th Regiment in Ireland during the Rebellion of 1798, and was present at the battles of Ross, Vinegar Hill, and other principal actions. In 1799 and 1800 he was at the siege of La Valetta and capture of Malta. He served in Egypt in the three following years, and was present in the action of the landing on the 8th of March, and also in the two other general actions fought on the 13th and 21st of March, 1801. In 1807 he was employed as Military Secretary to Lord Cathcart whilst his Lordship commanded the King's German Legion as a distinct army in Swedish Pomerania, as well as during the subsequent attack upon and capture of Copenhagen and the Danish Fleet. In 1809 he served in the Walcheren Expedition, and had charge of the Adjutant-General's department of the reserve commanded by Sir John Hope. In the following year he was employed as Deputy-Adjutant-General to the force allotted to the defence of Cadiz, under Lieutenant-General Graham (afterwards Lord Lynedoch), and was present at the battle of Barossa. In 1813 and 1814 he was employed in charge of the left wing of the Peninsular Army, and in that capacity was present in the actions of the 9th, 10th, 11th, and 12th of December, 1813, upon the Nive, and in the affairs which attended the closing of the blockade of Bayonne, and at the action brought on by the general sortie from that fortress. Sir John

---

[1] India Office Records.   [2] War Office Records.

THE MACDONALDS OF SCALPAY.

Lieutenant-General Sir JOHN MACDONALD, G.C.B., Adjutant-General to the Forces.

Lieutenant-General ALEXANDER MACDONALD, C.B. (The hero of "the brilliant feat of arms" (along with Norman Ramsay) at Fuentes d'Onor.)

(From Portraits lent by their grand-niece, Lady MacLeod of Wardie, Edinburgh, wife of the gallant Highlander and distinguished soldier, Lieutenant-General Sir J. C. MacLeod, G.C.B.)

received a medal for his services in Egypt, and a gold medal and one clasp for Barossa and the Nive.[1]

The following extract from "The British Army Despatch" of the time shows how highly popular the Adjutant-General was in the Army:—

"Rewards for military services. The 'Gazette' of Friday last contained the long expected announcement of the appointment of Lieutenant-General Lord Fitzroy James Henry Somerset, K.C.B., Colonel of the 53rd, and Lieutenant-General Sir John MacDonald, K.C.B., Colonel of the 42nd Highlanders, to be Knights Grand Cross of the Most Honourable Order of the Bath. These appointments, we are sure, will be received by the Army with great satisfaction. In the decoration of these distinguished officers the Army will recognise an honour conferred upon the whole service."

The following obituary notice of Lieutenant-General Sir John MacDonald, G.C.B., which appeared in "The British Army Despatch" of those days, speaks for itself:—

"It is with feelings of the sincerest regret that our Journal contains this day the announcement of the lamented decease of Lieutenant-General Sir John MacDonald, G.C.B., Colonel of the 42nd Highlanders and Adjutant-General to the British Army. It has often been our duty to record the loss to the service of many brave and estimable officers distinguished in the heroic annals of their country; but never since the establishment of this paper have we found ourselves before wholly incompetent to express in language strong enough the feelings of poignant regret which we now experience at the loss the soldier, the service, and the country have suffered in the death of Sir John MacDonald. After fifty-six years' faithful and gallant duty this distinguished officer has 'passed to that bourne from whence no traveller returns.' Sir John transacted business at the Adjutant-General's office on Monday. On Tuesday he was taken unwell with an attack of bronchitis. On Wednesday he rallied, but on Thursday, at eleven, in his eightieth year, he was summoned before his Maker. He had the week before attended, in health and spirits, the dinner given by the United Service Club to Lord Gough, and participated with enthusiasm in the reception given to the gallant hero of the Punjaub. Sir John held a position no less honourable than arduous; the whole of the correspondence relating to the arming and allotting of the troops, leave of absence, and discharging and transfer of soldiers, appointment or removal of general or other officers to or from the staff, the recruiting of the army, military regulations, and all subjects connected with the discipline, equipment, and efficiency of the army passed through the hands of the Adjutant-General. Nobly did that lamented officer perform those duties, and with candour and rectitude of purpose maintain that course of undeviating impartiality which secured for him the gratitude of the whole army. As a soldier Sir John excelled in gallantry on the field; as an officer his public duties were performed with zeal and dignity; as a gentleman he was ever ready to befriend the friendless, rebuke the tyrant, and shield the honourable from malice and injustice; as a parent he was all that a kind heart and noble nature could exhibit; and as a Christian he forgot not the 'fatherless and the widowed,' and he offered an example of the purest precept of our religion by 'doing as he would wish to be done by.' To the claimant upon his attention he was ever ready to give a

---

[1] War Office Records.

willing ear and a cheerful audience. When advice was wanted he offered it with frankness and urbanity. When his services were required to admonish the misdeeds of the oppressor and take the part of the oppressed he was ever ready; to the man of influence he acted with dignity, and to the child 'whose fortune was his sword' he offered the hand of friendship. It was never considered by him, in the multiplicity of his duties, beneath the high position he held to privately write, without the assistance of official routine, to advise or give timely caution to the subaltern. The despot has met from him a cold reception; and of the machinations of evil minds he often quietly gave warning to the unconscious victim. The hours that might have been spent in relaxation from duties so onerous have been often devoted in his closet to the correspondence suggested by his kind and generous nature. The set days for general levées at the Horse Guards were punctually kept by him, but the urgent necessity or business of the officer had ever with Sir John MacDonald an immediate audience, and the unobtrusive card of the ensign obtained as high a favour as that sought by the general. As a mediator between the high authorities he was not unwilling to act; and he ever as cheerfully pressed the claims of the humble as he would represent those of the noble. To officers in the service he acted as the high-minded gentleman, and when that service had been relinquished he still watched with interest the prosperity in life of those young officers whom he had befriended when serving under his orders. If the thoughtless needlessly transgressed in discipline, Sir John MacDonald was the first to influence himself on their behalf; and the same post which has caused a reprimand or an order of arrest has also borne with it a quiet, unobtrusive note from 'John MacDonald' to cheer up the drooping spirits of the careworn. The buzz of the smiling toady has ceased to give utterance to venom and spite when the poison has had conveyed with it an unerring antidote in the rapid caution of the kind-hearted Adjutant-General. It was but the other day we stood foremost to repel with scorn a cowardly attack upon the fame of the gallant soldier; and little did we then think that so soon would the object of malevolence be removed far from the chilling ingratitude of man. The loathing words of abuse must now fall coldly on the ear of the detractor. The good old Adjutant-General is to be envied, but not his traducer. We speak advisedly when we say the service has sustained a loss which it is impossible to remedy. His position can never be filled as it has been. Discipline may be coldly maintained, but that which renders an obedience to discipline a pleasure will long seek in vain for an Adjutant-General such as has passed from us. The spirit which maintained the system at the Horse Guards so long in a state of perfection is no longer present to guide its destinies. New blood may be introduced, but not better; new ideas may claim precedence, but not so sound as those which for so many years guided the authorities at the head-quarters of the British Army. Sir John MacDonald has passed away from us, and the soldier offers his tribute of regret. Let his name still be cherished as a household word embodying justice, rectitude, and humanity; let his memory be revered and engraven on the hearts of the brave and loyal. A faithful champion of our monarchical institutions, let his honoured ashes rest in a tomb worthy of his name; let the sepulchre rites record the regret of the nation at his loss; and though no royal dignities remain to be proclaimed by the Garter King-at-Arms, yet the scroll of chivalric deeds will form an escutcheon as lasting and honourable to the patriot's heart as the 'style' of more sacred memory. One of the bravest knights of Peninsular heroism passed to the tomb when the helmet and pennon of Sir John MacDonald lowered to the summons of a higher order. But the 'body is buried in peace and the name lives evermore.'"

LIEUTENANT-GENERAL ALEXANDER MACDONALD, C.B., ROYAL ARTILLERY.

This brilliant soldier (a son of Norman MacDonald of Scalpay and Susannah MacAlister, his wife) was born in the Island of Skye on the 10th of November, 1786, and entered the army at the age of seventeen years and one month. He was commissioned as a Second Lieutenant in the Royal Artillery on the 3rd of December, 1803; First Lieutenant on the 1st of May, 1804; Second Captain on the 1st of October, 1812; Brevet-Major in the army on the 18th of June, 1815; Brevet-Lieutenant-Colonel in the army on the 21st of June, 1817; Captain in the Royal Artillery on the 12th of December, 1826; Brevet-Colonel in the army on the 10th of January, 1837; Lieutenant-Colonel in the Royal Artillery on the 13th of August, 1840; Major-General in the army on the 9th of November, 1846; and Lieutenant-General in the army on the 20th of June, 1854.[1]

Alexander MacDonald was a soldier born, and a soldier he would be in spite of fate. It is said that at first more than one obstacle was put in his way to prevent his going to the army, but eventually he gained his object. He first saw active service at the Cape of Good Hope in the expeditionary force which was sent there in 1805, under General Sir David Baird. The expedition reached its destination on the 5th of January, 1806. The campaign was sharp and short. On the 8th of January Sir David Baird attacked the Dutch army, and on the 18th of the same month he received the surrender of the colony.

In the same year Lieutenant MacDonald proceeded from the Cape of Good Hope to Buenos Ayres (in the expedition commanded by General Beresford), where he was twice severely wounded, and named in the official despatches[1] for his gallant conduct.

Alexander MacDonald served in the campaigns of 1809, 1810, 1811, 1812, 1813, and 1814; in the Peninsula and in France as a subaltern in Ross's troop; at Waterloo as Second Captain of Major Norman Ramsay's superb troop of Royal Horse Artillery, where he was severely wounded,[2] and where he had the proud distinction of his troop being singled out for praise by Napoleon (the great master of artillery tactics), who asked one of his staff " what officer was in charge of that battery of Horse Artillery, " as he worked it and rushed it about so well"; and at the capture of Paris in 1815, under His Grace the Duke of Wellington. In the course of the campaigns just mentioned he was engaged at the Battles of the Coa and Busaco in 1810; in the affairs

---

[1] War Office Records.

[2] The story goes that it was a soldier from Broadford, in Skye, of the name of MacKinnon or MacInnes (who in his younger days had been a herd-boy at Scalpay) that found the wounded Captain and had him carried off the field in a plaid. It was their first meeting, strange to say, since they had been "boys together." It is also said that Captain MacDonald's sword was lost when he was being taken to the hospital, but afterwards found and placed in the Museum at Waterloo along with other relics of the ever-memorable battle, where the owner himself, seeing it some time after, recognised it, and wanted to repurchase it, but the authorities of the Museum would not give it to him.

of Redinha, Pombal, Condetia, and Foss de Roos in 1811; at the battles of Fuentes d'Onor and Salamanca, and at the affair of San Munios in 1812. In 1813 he was present at the battle of Vittoria, the siege of San Sebastian, and the battle of the Pyrenees. In 1814 he took part in the affairs of the Garve Dolloron and Ayres, and in the battle of Toulouse. He was mentioned in public orders and in Lord Hill's despatch for the affair of Ayres. General MacDonald received the Peninsular War medal with eight clasps, the Waterloo medal, the high military Order of St. Anne of Russia, was made a Companion of the Bath,[1] and Governor of Honduras.

"At the battle of Busaco" (so runs the official record) "the guns under his " command rendered most important service."[1]

He was Subaltern of Captain Norman Ramsay's celebrated troop of Royal Horse Artillery at the battle of Fuentes d'Onor, which was fought on the 5th of May, 1811, and took part in "the brilliant feat of arms" (as Napier well describes it) which was performed on that memorable occasion—an achievement which is still unique in character, and probably for the soldierly qualities (in the face of a most serious crisis) of prompt decision, instant action, resolute leading, and superb discipline, intelligent and effective, combined with valour that knew no fear, will never be excelled. Napier, in a passage of graphic beauty, thus depicts the scene: "After " one shock in which the enemy were partially checked . . . . . . the cavalry " withdrew behind the Light Division. Houston's people being thus entirely exposed " were charged strongly, and Captain Norman Ramsay's Horse Artillery was cut off " and surrounded. The Light Division instantly threw itself into squares,[2] but the main " body of the French horsemen were upon the 7th Division ere a like formation could " be effected. Nevertheless the troops stood firm. Immediately after this a great " commotion was observed amongst the French squadrons. Men and officers closed " in confusion towards one point, where a thick dust was rising, and where loud cries " and the sparkling of blades and flashing of pistols indicated some extraordinary " occurrence. Suddenly the multitude was violently agitated. An English shout " arose, the mass was rent asunder, and Norman Ramsay burst forth at the head of his " battery, his horses breathing fire and stretching like greyhounds along the plain, his " guns bounding like things of no weight, and the mounted gunners, in close and " compact order, protecting the rear."[2]

That was truly "a brilliant feat of arms." It was "magnificent," and at the same time it was "war."

The battle of Vittoria (so disastrous to the French arms) was fought on the 21st of June, 1813. The enemy left much of their baggage on the field of battle, and succeeded in taking only two of their field guns out of action. On the 25th of June MacDonald "came up with the retreating enemy and succeeded in dismounting one of " the only two guns which they had extricated from the field of Vittoria."[1]

The siege of San Sebastian was begun in the beginning of July, 1813. On the 24th of that month General Sir Thomas Graham (afterwards Lord Lynedoch) attempted to take the fortress (then one of the strongest in Europe) by storm, but was repulsed

---

[1] War Office Records.
[2] From Napier's "History of the Peninsular War," by kind permission of Messrs. George Routledge and Sons, Limited.

THE MACDONALDS OF SCALPAY.

Colonel ARCHIBALD MACDONALD, K.H.
(From Miss Susan M. Martin, of Glendale, Skye.)

Captain DONALD MACDONALD, Ostaig.
(From Miss Flora D. MacKinnon, Duisdale, Skye.)

General JOHN A. M. MACDONALD, C.B.

with a loss of 2,000 men; and on the 27th he was compelled to raise the siege. It was renewed, however, after the defeat of Soult at the foot of the Pyrenees on the 28th and 29th, and in repeated assaults the British suffered severely. There were many brave men in that besieging army, but to General Alexander MacDonald of Scalpay (then Captain) fell the honour of showing the way into San Sebastian. "One dark "night during the siege of San Sebastian he forded the River Urumea and made a "reconnaissance under the enemy's batteries. By this daring act it was made known "that the river was fordable."[1] On the 31st of August Sir Thomas Graham became master of the most important works at a loss of 3,000 men, and on the 9th of September the citadel surrendered.

General MacDonald married Susanna (sister of Brigadier-General Strangways and niece of the Earl of Ilchester). He died at Aix-la-Chapelle on the 31st day of May, 1856.

Colonel Archibald MacDonald, K.H., a son of Norman MacDonald of Scalpay and Susannah MacAlister, his wife, joined the army as an Ensign in the 89th Foot on the 24th of June, 1795; was promoted to the rank of Lieutenant on the 29th of May, 1796; to that of Captain on the 14th of February, 1803; was transferred to the 45th Foot on the 13th of October, 1808; to the 1st West India Regiment on the 27th of June, 1811; to the 3rd (afterwards the 1st) Garrison Battalion on the 21st of January, 1813; made Lieutenant-Colonel, Brevet, on the 25th of November of the same year; Major on half-pay in the 1st Garrison Battalion on the 24th of September, 1817; Inspecting Field Officer of the Guards' Recruiting District on the 18th of June, 1825; was Major of a Brigade from the 25th of February, 1806, to the 24th of December, 1809; Assistant Adjutant-General in England, and on particular service from the 25th of September, 1813, to the 24th of March, 1817; went out with Lord Combermere (the famous Peninsular cavalry officer, better known as Sir Stapleton Cotton), and served as Adjutant-General in the East Indies from the 2nd of June, 1825, to the time of his death, which took place at Bengal on the 24th of November, 1827.[1]

Colonel MacDonald served in the disastrous Walcheren Expedition in 1809, and throughout the Peninsular War, for the greater part of the time on the Staff, and in recognition of his meritorious services he was created a Knight of the Hanoverian Order of the Guelphs.

General John A. M. MacDonald, C.B., Indian Staff Corps, son of Colonel Archibald MacDonald, K.H., of Scalpay, was appointed as an Ensign on the 21st of February, 1843; Lieutenant on the 15th of December, 1847; Captain on the 18th of June, 1857; Major on the 24th of March, 1858; Lieutenant-Colonel on the 29th of April, 1866; Colonel on the 23rd of February, 1874; Major-General on the 19th of September, 1855; Lieutenant-General on the 12th of January, 1889; and General on the 1st of April, 1894.

---

[1] War Office Records.

General MacDonald served as Deputy-Quarter-Master-General to the headquarters of the Persian Expeditionary Force in 1857, for which he received a medal and clasp. He acted in the same capacity with the Indian Field Force in the same year; and was present at the capture of Dhar, and Mundisore, and in the action at Gurraria.

General MacDonald was appointed Assistant-Quarter-Master-General to Sir Hugh Rose, and served in that capacity throughout the Central India campaign; was present at the capture of Rhatghur; in the action of Barodia; at the relief of Saugor; at the capture of Gorrakota; in the action at the Pass of Muddenpore; at the battle of Betwa (where his horse was killed); at the siege and storming of Jhansi; in the actions of Koonch and Mutra; at the battle of Galowlee, and at the capture of Calpee. For his services in this campaign he was made a Brevet-Major, and received a medal and clasp. After the termination of the Central Indian campaign he served as Assistant-Quarter-Master-General with the field columns operating south of the Nerbudda, under the command of Sir Hugh Rose, and on the conclusion of these operations he was appointed Assistant-Quarter-Master-General of the Rajpootana Field Force; but was subsequently transferred to the Poona Division, which appointment he held until he was promoted to be Deputy-Quarter-Master-General at Bombay, and head of the Transport Department. Afterwards he was appointed Deputy Secretary, and finally Secretary, to the Government, in charge of the Military Departments.

General MacDonald was granted a Good Service Pension in 1881, and was placed on the unemployed and supernumerary list in 1892.

Major-General Norman MacDonald (son of Matthew Norman MacDonald Hume of Ninewells, and grandson of Norman MacDonald of Scalpay by his wife, Susannah MacAlister), entered the army as an Ensign in the 39th Foot on the 14th of May, 1852; was promoted to the rank of Lieutenant on the 24th of June, 1853; to that of Captain on the 27th of July, 1855; placed on half-pay on the 10th of November, 1857; transferred to the 5th Foot on the 23rd of October, 1857; made Brevet-Major on the 30th of April, 1875; Major in the same corps on the 5th of October, 1872; Lieutenant-Colonel, Brevet, on the 1st of October, 1877; removed to half-pay on the 5th of October, 1879; appointed Lieutenant-Colonel of the Northumberland Fusiliers (5th Foot) on the 1st of July, 1881; Colonel in the army on the 1st of October, 1881; placed on half-pay on the 22nd of February, 1886; and on retired pay on the 2nd of September of the following year, with the honorary rank of Major-General.

General MacDonald served in the Crimean Campaign of 1854–55; was present at the siege and fall of Sebastopol, at the assaults on the Redan on the 18th of June and 8th of September, 1855; was mentioned in despatches,[1] received the British war medal with a clasp for the Crimean campaign, and also the Turkish medal and the 5th class of the Order of the Medjidie.

General Macdonald (then a Captain) acted as Assistant Military Secretary on the Staff in Mauritius from the 17th of April, 1859, to the 4th of June, 1862. He died at Ayr on the 17th of September, 1892.[1]

---

[1] War Office Records.

THE MACDONALDS OF SCALPAY.

Major-General NORMAN MACDONALD.
(From his niece, Lady MacLeod.)

Brigadier-General J. H. A. MACDONALD, C.B., V.D.
("The Heaven-born Soldier.")

(From his son, Mr. Norman D. MacDonald.)

Lieutenant RANALD HUME MACDONALD,
Royal Engineers.

(From his brother, Mr. Norman D. MacDonald.)

THE MACDONALDS OF SCALPAY.

Brigadier-General the Right Honourable J. H. A. MacDonald, C.B., V.D. (son of Matthew Norman MacDonald Hume of Ninewells, by his second wife, Grace, daughter of Sir John Hay, of Smithfield and Haystoune, Baronet, and grandson of Norman MacDonald of Scalpay), was born on the 27th of December, 1836. His great-grandmother was a sister of Allan MacDonald of Kingsburgh, husband of the celebrated Flora MacDonald.

It need hardly be asserted that General MacDonald ("the heaven-born soldier," a soubriquet by which he has been generally known since 1862, when it was bestowed upon him at a review by General Walker, then Commander-in-Chief in Scotland, because of the masterly manner in which on that occasion he handled his battalion) has come of a warlike race. Many members of his family have served their Sovereign and country well in all parts of the world, as may be seen elsewhere in this work. His father's seven brothers were all soldiers, three of whom rose to great distinction, viz. :— Lieutenant-General Sir John MacDonald, G.C.B., Adjutant-General of the British Army ; Lieutenant-General Alexander MacDonald, C.B. ; and Colonel Archibald MacDonald, K.H.

In March of the year 1859, General Macdonald joined the Advocate's company of the Queen's Edinburgh Rifle Volunteer Brigade as a private, became a Sergeant in August, Lieutenant in November, and Captain in December. At the Royal Review of 1860, his company (No. 13) was specially complimented for its smartness and efficiency by the General Commanding in Scotland. He was promoted to the rank of Major in 1861, Lieutenant-Colonel in 1864, and to that of Colonel in 1886, in which year he was made a Companion of the Bath, in recognition of his meritorious services in the Volunteer force.[1]

General MacDonald was the first Volunteer officer who received the rank of Brigadier-General. His brigade numbers about 2,500 of all ranks, is in the highest state of efficiency, and is completely equipped with flag-signallers, mounted troop, cyclist troop, telegraph troop, regimental transport waggons, and three bands.

In 1872, General Macdonald (then a Lieutenant-Colonel) commanded a provisional battalion at the great manœuvures on Salisbury Plains, and received special commendation for his work on that occasion from his superior officers. He has acted as Assistant-Adjutant-General for several years to Major-General the Honourable W. H. A. Fielding at Aldershot when the Volunteers are assembled there, and also frequently as umpire, and on one occasion as Chief of the Staff on a Divisional Field Day.

General MacDonald is the author of several standard works dealing with military subjects, and is the inventor of a portable field telegraph for the use of armies in the field.

"If I were asked" (said Lord Wolseley at a public banquet in London not long ago) "at the present moment to point out any particular officer who I thought had " left his stamp on the subject of drilling, I would point to an officer in a high position,

---

[1] War Office Records.

"who has now command of a brigade in the Volunteers, and who, I may also add, is a "very important judge in Scotland."

Referring to Brigadier-General MacDonald, Lord Wolseley said on another occasion (when addressing the Philosophical Institution in Edinburgh):—"He is a very old friend "—may I say an old comrade of mine—because not only have we worked together on "the same lines with regard to the army, but I have for some years had the honour "of being the Colonel of the regiment with which his name has been so long identified. " . . . . I cannot sit down without telling you, his fellow-citizens, and his "fellow-countrymen, how much the British Army owes him for what he has done for "it in teaching us to get rid of our old-fashioned and obsolete modes of drilling, and "adopting those clear lines that he laid down for drilling his volunteers."

General MacDonald married, in 1864, Adelaide Jeannette, daughter of Major Doran of Ely House, Wexford, who died in 1870.

Lieutenant Ranald Hume MacDonald, Royal Engineers (a son of "the heaven-born soldier," Brigadier-General the Right Honourable J. H. A. MacDonald, C.B., V.D., commanding the Forth Volunteer Brigade), distinguished himself in the Chitral in May, 1898, by an act of gallantry which forcibly reminds one of the daring spirit of adventure which characterised General Alexander MacDonald of Scalpay in Peninsular days. Colonel J. Davidson, commanding the Chitral Relieved Force, in a column order dated Camp, Dir, 18th May, 1898, says:—"The officer commanding the Chitral "Relieved Force desires to place on record the gallant conduct of Lieutenant "MacDonald, R.E.; No. 3409, Lance-Naik Habib Khan; No. 4871, Sapper "Seikh Abdul Samand; No. 4872, Sapper Khalan Kahan of No. 6 Company, Bengal "Sappers and Miners, on the summit of Lowarai Pass on the 16th of May, 1898, in "rescuing from an avalanche, in which they had been embedded for four hours in soft "snow, Sepoy Karmdad, 27th P.I., and the corpses of Jemadar Madho Khan, "Havildar Ali Shah, and Sepoy Kashim Ali. When Lieutenant MacDonald set the "example to his men by himself tunnelling through an accumulation of soft snow, "20 feet deep, he was cautioned by Chitralis snow experts to leave the task, as he "would be certainly embedded in the snow, and the party would only share the fate "of the men of the 27th P.I. Lieutenant Macdonald, however, regardless of con-"sequences, and at the risk of his life, continued digging, and succeeded in rescuing "alive one of the four men. Whilst the party were digging it was nearly embedded "in one of several avalanches which fell during the day. The conduct of all concerned "reflects the greatest credit on the corps. The matter will be represented to army "headquarters for the information of His Excellency the Commander-in-Chief in "India." And Major Barton, Commandant of the Bengal Sappers and Miners, in publishing the foregoing order, adds:—"He also wishes to thank Lieutenant "MacDonald and the three sappers for the gallant way they have added to the "reputation of the corps."

Lieutenant Macdonald and his comrades have received the Royal Albert Medal in recognition of their gallantry.

Captain Donald MacDonald of Ostaig, Sleat, a son of Archibald, and a nephew of Norman MacDonald of Scalpay, was appointed an Ensign in the 42nd Foot on the 8th of April, 1801; Lieutenant on the 9th of July, 1803; Captain on the 25th of January, 1810; put on half-pay on the 27th of May, 1819; transferred to the 27th Foot on the 26th of April, 1833; and he retired from the service by the sale of his commission on the 10th of May of the same year.

Captain MacDonald served with the Royal Highlanders during the Peninsular War; was wounded at the action of Fuentes d'Onor on the 3rd of May, 1811, where he helped, by his gallantry, to win for the regimental colour the battle-honour of that name. He was also wounded at the battle of Quatre Bras on the 16th of June, 1815. Seriously it would seem, because in one regimental return he is shown as having "died of wounds received at Waterloo." In this engagement, so desperate were the charges of the enemy's lancers and cuirassiers, as well as the fire of their artillery and infantry, that in a few minutes the command of the Black Watch had changed hands four times, and before the end of the day it had lost its commanding officer, two other officers, two sergeants, and 40 rank and file killed, and 243 of all ranks wounded. In recognition of his gallant services, Captain MacDonald got the Waterloo medal, as well as the Peninsular War medal with four clasps.

After the conclusion of peace, Captain MacDonald acted for a time as Barrack Master at Dumbarton Castle. He died at Musselburgh on the 24th of September, 1865, at the age of eighty-two.[1]

Captain MacDonald's brother William was also in the army and saw a great deal of active service.

THE MACDONALDS OF CASTLETON, Etc.

The founder of this branch of the Clan Donald[2] was Donald, second son of Sir Donald MacDonald, eighth Baron and first Baronet of Sleat. This Donald of Castleton and his son John II. of that house fought with distinction in the civil wars of their time, the latter under Viscount Dundee at the battle of Killiecrankie in 1689, at which five gallant cousins of the chief of Sleat "fell together, with the tutor of MacDonald of Largie and his sons."

Colonel Donald MacDonald, III. of Castleton, began his military career as Captain of one of the independent companies raised in Skye in 1745, and was afterwards transferred to the Imperial army, in which he rose to the rank of Colonel. His successor, John MacDonald, IV. of Castleton, Sheriff Substitute in Skye, had three sons in the army, viz.:—Major Alexander MacDonald, and Captains John and William MacDonald, the first and last named of whom "greatly distinguished themselves at the battle of Nagpoor" (which was a particularly brilliant affair), and escaped unhurt, although there was a great slaughter among the officers. Both died (in the East Indies) without issue, as did also the other son, who died at Skerrinish in 1833, when the male

---

[1] War Office Records.   [2] Mackenzie's "History of the MacDonalds."

representation of the family reverted to that of Roderick MacIain of Camuscross, in Sleat.

Lieutenant Donald MacDonald, of the 67th Regiment, was a son of Donald, grandson in the direct line of Roderick MacIain of Camuscross.[1]

John MacDonald, M.D., F.R.S., Inspector-General of Hospitals and Fleets, was a son of James MacDonald, who was third in descent from Roderick MacIain.

Captain Donald MacDonald, I. of Tormore, in Sleat, a son of Roderick MacIain, received a Lieutenant's commission in "the MacDonald Highlanders" on the 7th of January, 1778, and when on his way to the American War of Independence was killed in a duel by Captain Alexander Fraser, of Culduthel.

Captain Roderick MacDonald, of the 21st Regiment (the Royal Scots Fusiliers), a son of Captain Donald MacDonald, I. of Tormore, is said to have served in Egypt under Sir Ralph Abercromby, and subsequently in Spain (where Godfrey, the eldest member of his family, was born) "in the same regiment as Lord MacDonald," his daughter, Miss Eliza MacDonald, says, probably with the 23rd or 24th Regiment, in both of which his Lordship (who was an intimate friend of Captain MacDonald) held commissions. As we have seen already, Lord MacDonald did not serve either in Egypt or in the Peninsula; neither did the Fusiliers, apparently, but the other two regiments took part in both these campaigns.

Mr. Malcolm Henry Somerled MacDonald, a son of Captain Malcolm MacDonald, of the Behar Light Horse Volunteers, and a grandson of Alexander MacDonald, II. of Tormore, is an officer in the Royal Navy.

William MacDonald (from whom are descended the MacDonalds of Vallay) and James MacDonald, sons of Sir Donald MacDonald, third Baronet of Sleat, led their clan at the battle of Sheriffmuir, in 1715, the last occasion on which the MacDonalds of Sleat fought as a clan. The Clan Donald occupied the post of honour on the right, as was their due, and so impetuous was their charge that in a few minutes they scattered in all directions the infantry opposed to them—veterans who had been trained in the Duke of Marlborough's campaigns, and General Witham's cavalry, who ought to have protected the defeated infantry, fled in panic from the field of battle without striking a blow.

William MacDonald, above referred to, married Catherine, daughter of Sir Ewen Cameron of Lochiel, by whom he had a numerous family.[1] Their two sons, Captain James MacDonald of Aird in Troternish, Skye, and Captain John MacDonald of Kirkibost, in North Uist, each brought a company of 100 men to Inverness, on the side of the Government, in 1745.

---

[1] Mackenzie's "History of the MacDonalds."

Major Alexander MacDonald, III. of Vallay, served in the army, and his son, Alexander, was an officer in the Royal Navy.

Lieutenant-General Donald MacDonald, Colonel of the 55th Regiment, son of Major Allan MacDonald [1] of Knock, in Sleat, and Sibella, daughter of the famous Donald MacLeod of Bernera, "the Old Trojan," was gazetted as Ensign in the 55th Foot on the 17th of September, 1773; Lieutenant on the 8th of September, 1775; Captain on the 24th of July, 1779; Major on the 26th of October, 1793; Lieutenant-Colonel on the 14th of December, 1793; Colonel, Brevet, on the 26th of January, 1797; Major-General on the 25th of September, 1803; Colonel of the Cape Regiment on the 30th of October, 1806; Lieutenant-General on the 25th of July, 1810; and Colonel of the 55th Foot on the 20th of March, 1811.

General MacDonald was Governor of Fort William from 1805 to the time of his death, which took place on the 7th of October, 1812.[2]

[3] In the beginning of the year 1793, the 55th Regiment was quartered at Londonderry and Coleraine, and from there it embarked and joined the army in Holland, where it greatly distinguished itself in the campaigns of that and the two following years under the command of His Royal Highness the Duke of York. In a divisional order, dated 20th May, 1794, General White said:—"To Lieutenant-Colonel "MacDonald, who led on the 55th Regiment with such marked propriety and "discipline to support the attack on the front, his best and distinguished thanks "are due."

His Royal Highness, in his despatch dated Nimeguen, November 6th, 1794, said:—"The sortie made by the garrison of Nimeguen on the night of the 4th instant "was conducted under the orders of General De Burgh, assisted by General "Wammerstein. The troops employed in this service were detachments from the 8th, "27th, 28th, 55th, 63rd, and 78th of British infantry, with the 7th and 16th of light "cavalry, and a party of Dutch and Hanoverian troops, forming altogether a corps "of 3,000 men. It is impossible yet to ascertain who gave the information, but it is "certain that the French knew of our intention and were prepared to receive us. "General De Burgh headed the detachments against the enemy's entrenchments and "attacked them in their trenches, where they were chin-deep. A terrible carnage "ensued on both sides. The French made a very obstinate resistance, but were at "length obliged to give way to the superior gallantry of our troops, who mounted "their works with fixed bayonets, and in the end completely destroyed them. From "the nature of the service the detachment under General De Burgh, which performed "prodigies of valour, suffered most, and the loss is very considerable.[3]

In October, 1795, the regiment embarked at Portsmouth with the expedition to the West Indies under General Sir Ralph Abercromby; but, in consequence of storms and

---

[1] Miss Mary MacDonald (daughter of Captain Kenneth MacDonald of the old Skaebost family, referred to in another part of this work) says that Major Allan MacDonald had another son, Forbes MacDonald, who was an officer in the army, and died of wounds which he received at the storming of Seringapatam.
[2] War Office Records. [3] Regimental Depôt Records.

disasters encountered at sea, which repeatedly rendered it necessary for the fleet to put back, they did not finally sail from England till the 14th of February, and reached Barbadoes on the 14th of March, 1796. On the 15th of April a small force was sent to attack Demerara and Berbice, and preparations were made for effecting a landing with the remainder of the troops on the Island of St. Lucia. Admiral Christian, who commanded the fleet, having arrived on the 22nd of that month, the expedition immediately sailed, and on the 26th appeared off St. Lucia. The troops had previously been told off into divisions and brigades, on which occasion Lieutenant-Colonel MacDonald, who had distinguished himself in the command of the regiment, under His Royal Highness the Duke of York, received a high mark of approbation[1] in being, when only a field officer, appointed to command the reserve of the army, consisting of 18 Grenadier companies, and the Royal Highland Regiment. Dispositions were made for landing in four divisions at Longueville Bay, Pigeon Island, Chock Bay, and Anee-la-iaze. Major-General Campbell commanded the disembarkation at Longueville Bay, directing Brigadier-General Moore to land in a small bay close under Pigeon Island. This service was easily accomplished, and on the 27th the different divisions moved forward from their landing places to close in upon Morne Fortuna, the principal post upon the island. Before this place could be fully invested it was necessary to take possession of Morne Chaliot, a strong and commanding position overlooking the principal approach. An attack was accordingly made on two different points by detachments under Brigadier-Generals Moore and the Honourable John Hope.[1]

The former commenced its march at midnight, and, an hour after, the latter followed by a less circuitous route. Through the mistake of the guides, General Moore's division fell in with the advanced guard of the enemy, nearly two hours sooner than was expected. Finding himself discovered, he resolved to make an immediate attack; and being well seconded by his troops, he pushed forward, and, after a short but smart resistance, carried the post, the enemy flying with such precipitation that they could not be intercepted by General Hope, who arrived exactly at the appointed time. On the following day General Moore occupied Morne Duchassaux, and Major-General Morshead, moving forward from Anee-la-iaze, Morne Fortuna was thus completely invested, but not without resistance on the part of the enemy, who attacked the advanced post of Lieutenant-Colonel MacDonald's Grenadiers with such force and vivacity that several officers and nearly fifty of the Grenadiers were killed and wounded before the assailants were repulsed.[1] In order to dispossess the enemy from the batteries which they had erected on the cul-de-sac, Major-General Morshead's division was ordered to advance against two batteries on the left, while Brigadier-General Hope, with five companies of the 42nd Highlanders, the light company of the 57th Regiment, and a detachment of Malcolm's Rangers, supported by the 55th Regiment, was to attack the battery of Seoke, close to the works of Morne Fortuna. These quickly drove the enemy from the battery, but the other divisions, under Brigadier-General Perryn and Colonel Reiddle, meeting with some unexpected obstruction, the intended service was not accomplished; and it became necessary for

---

[1] Regimental Depôt Records.

General Hope's detachment to retire from the battery which they had carried with so much gallantry. This was not effected without the loss of some officers and men killed and wounded, a loss trifling, however, in comparison with that sustained by the other divisions.[1] From the steep and rugged nature of the ground, the greatest difficulty was experienced in bringing the guns into position; and, notwithstanding the zeal and strenuous exertions of the seamen who assisted in dragging them across the ravines and up to the acclivities of rocks and mountains, it was not till the 14th of May that the first battery was ready to open fire.

On the night of the 17th a regiment (the 31st) was ordered to take possession of a fortified ridge under the principal fortress. The attempt failed, and the regiment was forced to retire with great loss; but the Grenadiers under Colonel MacDonald, who had pushed forward to their support, compelled the enemy to retreat in their turn. A continued fire was now kept up for six days between the battery and the fort. At length, on the 24th, the 27th Regiment pushed forward,[1] and after a brisk engagement formed a lodgment at two different points within 500 yards of the garrison. The enemy immediately sallied out with all their disposable force to drive them back, but were repulsed, and they retreated within the fort. This was their last attempt. They demanded a suspension of hostilities, which was granted, and a capitulation and surrender of the whole island followed, in consequence of which the enemy marched out on the 26th and became prisoners of war. The loss sustained in these operations was two field officers, three captains, five subalterns, and 184 non-commissioned officers and rank and file killed; four field officers, twelve captains, fifteen subalterns, and 523 non-commissioned officers and rank and file missing.

A striking and melancholy instance now occurred of the influence of the mind on bodily health,[1] and of the effect of mental activity in preventing disease. During the above operations, which, from the nature of the country and climate, were extremely harassing, the troops continued remarkably healthy; but immediately after the cessation of hostilities they began to droop. The sudden transition from incessant bodily and mental activity to a state of repose produced the most disastrous effects on the health of the troops, and reduced many of the regiments in the course of a few days to half their original strength. After the fall of the fort the 55th Regiment was employed with the 31st, 44th, and 48th Regiments, under Brigadier-General Moore, in reducing some considerable bodies of the enemy who had taken refuge in the woods and refused to surrender conformably to the capitulation, and, continuing actively employed on this service, did not at first suffer so much from the climate as some of the others.[1]

At the end of one year, however, during which the regiment formed part of the garrison of the island, three-fourths of its number were carried off. The 31st Regiment was almost annihilated. After losing twenty-two officers, the remainder were ordered to Barbadoes. The few men that remained active in the other two corps were drafted into the 55th Regiment. The General himself was at length attacked by the prevailing

---

[1] Regimental Depôt Records.

sickness, but he determined to remain in the active performance of his duty, and was only carried on board ship when he became insensible.

The following are interesting extracts from General Orders issued by Sir Ralph Abercromby:—

"Headquarters, St. Lucia,
"2nd May, 1796.

"Yesterday the enemy attacked the advanced post, commanded by Lieutenant-Colonel MacDonald, of the 55th Regiment, but were repulsed with considerable loss,[1] though I am sorry to say that we had several officers and forty or fifty men killed and wounded."

"St. Lucia, May 4th, 1796.

"To render the success more secure, Brigadier-General Hope was detached from the side of Morne Chaliot with 350 men of the 42nd Regiment, the light company of the 57th Regiment, and part of Malcolm's Corps on the night of the 2nd May, supported by the 55th Regiment, which was posted at Terranas."

"St. Lucia, May 22nd, 1796.

"For this purpose, on the night of the 17th instant, the 31st, happening to be the nearest regiment at hand, was ordered to march immediately after it was dark to take possession of the Vizie, where the enemy had not apparently more than from 150 to 200 men. The first part of the attack succeeded to our wish, a battery of three 18-pounders, which was feebly defended, was seized, the guns spiked, and thrown over the precipice. There remained on the summit of the hill one large gun and a field-piece, of which the regiment was ordered to take possession. Unfortunately the guide was wounded, and the troops became uncertain of the right approach to the hill. While in this situation the enemy's grape-shot took effect to such a degree as to induce Lieutenant-Colonel Hay to order the regiment to retreat, which it did with considerable loss. Lieutenant-Colonel MacDonald handsomely advanced with part of the Grenadiers (55th Regiment) to cover the retreat of the 31st Regiment, which he accomplished."

"St. Lucia, 31st May, 1796.

"Upon the evening of the 24th the enemy desired a suspension of arms until noon the next day, which was granted till 8 in the morning. A capitulation of the whole island ensued . . . . . . On the 26th the garrison, to the number of 2,000, marched out and laid down their arms, and are become prisoners of war. Pigeon Island is in our possession.[1] . . . . . .

". . . . It is but justice to the troops to say that they have undergone an uncommon share of fatigue with cheerfulness, and in several instances have given proof of the greatest intrepidity.

"(Signed)   R. ABERCROMBY,
"Lt.-General."

In 1797 the 55th Regiment returned to England and was stationed at Chatham; in 1798 at Horsham Barracks, and in 1799 at Guernsey.

---

[1] Regimental Depôt Records.

Although weak, the regiment, consisting of only twenty-six officers, three staff, and 443 non-commissioned officers and private soldiers, was ordered (it was thought at the particular request of Sir Ralph Abercromby) to form part of the expedition to Holland, under His Royal Highness the Duke of York, and embarked accordingly at Deal on the 13th of August, 1799. It landed at the Helder at daybreak on the morning of the 27th, and, with the 23rd Regiment, formed the reserve under the command of Colonel MacDonald. The 55th Regiment behaved on this occasion with the greatest ardour and gallantry, and Major Lumsden (afterwards killed in the action of the 2nd of October, who commanded it on both days) particularly distinguished himself by his coolness, zeal, and activity, as did also Colonel MacDonald (under whom they had so frequently fought before) for the skill and judgment with which he led on the reserve to the attack, and who, though painfully wounded in the arm at an early part of the action, would not quit the field until the enemy were finally driven from their strong entrenchments in the sands.[1] On that night the 55th Regiment lay upon their arms, expecting by daylight in the morning to be again attacked. The enemy, however, had retreated during the night. The action of the 27th had lasted from five o'clock in the morning till three o'clock in the afternoon, but by the courage and perseverance of the British troops the enemy was fairly worn out and obliged to retire in the evening to a position two leagues in rear.[1]

The following is an extract from a despatch from Lieutenant-General Sir Ralph Abercromby, dated 11th September, 1799:—

"Yesterday morning at daybreak the enemy commenced an attack on our centre and right from St. Martin's to Pettew in three columns, and apparently with the whole force. . . . . They were, however, everywhere repulsed, owing to the strength of our position, and the determined courage of the troops . . . . . Colonel MacDonald with the reserve pursued them for some time and quickened their retreat."

His Royal Highness the Duke of York, having landed with the remainder of the troops, had concerted arrangements for an attack upon the whole of the enemy's position at Alkmaer on the morning of the 19th of September, in consequence of which the army moved forward in four columns on the previous evening. The 55th Regiment, at the head of the reserve, led the left column under Sir Ralph Abercromby, marched towards Hoorn, the distance to which was twenty miles, and the march, from the state of the roads, was a most harassing one. The regiment came up close to the gates at about three o'clock in the morning, without being perceived; and the town was summoned to surrender, which it did in half an hour afterwards—six officers and 200 men of the enemy being taken prisoners by the 55th Regiment.

In consequence, however, of the (partly) unexpected obstacles which presented themselves to the advance of the 2nd and 3rd columns on the right (the country they had to pass over being intersected by innumerable wet ditches and canals—the bridges

---

[1] Regimental Depôt Records.

[2] Sir Ralph Abercromby, in his despatch referring to this action, said:—"The corps principally engaged were the reserve under Colonel MacDonald, consisting of the 23rd and 55th Regiments. Colonel MacDonald who commanded the reserve, and who was much engaged during the course of the day, though wounded, did not quit the field."

over which had been destroyed), the strong position occupied by the enemy, and the determined opposition offered by him to the attacks of these columns, but principally owing to the misconduct of some Russians acting as auxiliaries, who, after driving the enemy back as far as Bergen, gave themselves up to plunder, and were, while so employed, attacked, thrown into confusion, and defeated. The whole plan of operations was thus unfortunately disconcerted, and the army was obliged to retire to its former position.[1]

"Blar na H-Olaind."
"Air mios deireannach an fhoghair,
"An dara latha 'smath mo chuimhne,
"Ghluais na Breatunnaich bho 'n fhaiche,
"Dh 'ionnsuidh tachairt ris na naimhdean,
"Thug Abercrombaidh taobh na mara
"Dhiubh le 'n canain 'smi ga 'n cluinntinn ;
"Bha fòirneadh aig Moore gu daingeann,
"Cumail aingil ris na Frangaich."

Alasdair Mac-Ionmhuinn.

The following extracts from two despatches sent home by Field-Marshal His Royal Highness the Duke of York—the first dated at headquarters at Zyper Sluys, 4th October, and the second at Alkmaer 6th October, 1799—refer to the famous battle of the 2nd of October, in which the 55th Regiment bore so distinguished a part, and when it had the good fortune to be successfully opposed to the best troops of the French army—the post of honour having been (from the well-known gallantry of the two regiments forming the reserve) assigned to them :—" The necessary previous arrange-
" ments having been made, the attack was commenced on the whole of the enemy's
" line on the morning of the 2nd, and I have now the happiness to inform you
" that, after a severe and obstinate action, which lasted from six in the morning till
" the same hour at night, the distinguished valour of His Majesty's and the Russian
" troops prevailed throughout ; and the enemy, being entirely defeated, retired in
" the night from the positions which he occupied." [2]

"Alkmaer, 6th October, 1779.

"The combined attacks were made in four columns. The first on the right under General Sir R. Abercromby. . . . . Its advanced guard composed of the reserve under Colonel MacDonald—viz., the 1st Battalion of Grenadiers of the Line, 1st Battalion Light Infantry of the Line, 23rd and 55th Regiments of Infantry—drove the enemy from the Campe and from the sand-hills above the village, and continued its march upon the ridge of those hills inclining a little to the left. Part of Major-General's Coote's brigade in connection with Colonel MacDonald's corps drove the enemy from the sand-hills to the right and front of the Russian column. . . . . . . Colonel MacDonald's corps had moved considerably to the right with a view to connect itself with the right column, and continued warmly engaged with the enemy, who were in very large forces in the sand-hills. The extension of General Dundas's line had now brought its right very near to the reserve, who had been advancing rapidly notwithstanding the great resistance they had experienced. . . . .

---

[1] Regimental Depôt Records.

[2] Return of killed and wounded of the 55th Regiment in the battle of the 2nd of October, 1799:—One Major (Lumsden) and two rank and file killed; one subaltern, one sergeant, one drummer, and sixteen rank and file wounded.

Colonel MacDonald distinguished himself by his usual spirit and activity in the command of the reserve."[1]

The exhausted state of the troops, from the almost unparalleled difficulties and fatigues which they had encountered, prevented the Commander-in-Chief from taking full advantage of the enemy's retreat on the 2nd of October.

The following extract refers to the action which took place in front of Boccum[1] on the 6th of October, 1799:—

"Alkmaer, 7th October, 1799.

"The column of Russian troops under the command of Major-General D'Ossen, in endeavouring to gain a height in front of their intended advanced post at Boccum (which was material to the security of that point), was vigorously opposed, and afterwards attacked by a strong body of the enemy, which obliged General Sir R. Abercromby to move up in support with the reserve of his corps. The enemy on their part advanced their whole force, and the action became general, and was maintained with great obstinacy on both sides until night, when the enemy retired, leaving us masters of the field of battle. The conflict has, as I am concerned to state, been as severe, and has been attended with as serious a loss (in proportion to the number engaged), as any of those which have been fought by the brave troops composing the army since their arrival in Holland. The gallantry which they displayed, and the perseverance with which they supported the fatigues of the day, rival their former exertions. To General Sir R. Abercromby . . . . . . as also to Colonel MacDonald, my warmest acknowledgments are due for their spirited and judicious exertions during this affair."[1]

The 55th Regiment had two Lieutenants and ten rank and file wounded in this action.

In consequence of strong reinforcements being received by the enemy, the state of the weather and the roads, and the want of the necessary supplies,[1] it became necessary, in the first instance, to withdraw the troops from the advanced positions they had taken up, and ultimately to re-embark them for England.

On the 4th of June, 1801, while stationed at Guernsey, the 55th Regiment was presented with a pair of colours, on which occasion Colonel MacDonald made the following spirited speech:—

"Officers and soldiers,—I have the honour to present a pair of new colours, provided by the liberality of our Colonel conformably to general orders, in consequence of that happy and important event, the union of Great Britain and Ireland, which has cemented in bonds of amity and affection three brave and free nations, and formed them into one kingdom.

"This day is well adapted to the presentation, it being the anniversary of the birth of our most gracious and beloved Sovereign and Master, whose reign has been pre-eminently distinguished by his watching with paternal regard and anxious solicitude over the interests of his subjects, their happiness constituting his chiefest care.

"I need not, in addressing my brother officers and soldiers, expatiate on the honour attending on the attachment to and the preservation of the colours.

---

[1] Regimental Depôt Records.

"The fair fame acquired in three wars and nearly thirty actions with the enemy sufficiently impresses on all the value of a well-earned reputation long and justly enjoyed by the 55th Regiment. Much less will I offend against their feelings by making mention of the disgrace and mortification which would destroy a soldier's peace of mind in the loss of colours to the enemy, that being a misfortune of which we have hitherto been ignorant, and to which, I trust with confidence, the 55th Regiment will during its existence remain a stranger.

"In the appropriate service which encircles the number of the Regiment—entwining, as if they grew from one stem, the Rose, the Thistle, and the Shamrock, emblems of three sister nations—let brother officers and soldiers of the three countries contemplate a symbol of harmony, concord, and unanimity of the corps.

"Receive these new colours in the name of General Tottenham, our Colonel, from the hands of the oldest soldier of the regiment—from me, your Lieutenant-Colonel, who is well acquainted with your merits."[1]

Captain John MacDonald of Breakish, in the Parish of Strath.

Nothing seems now to be known regarding this officer, what family he belonged to, or what branch of the service he was in, beyond the fact recorded by Alexander Smith (in his "Summer in Skye"), who quoted Dr. Brown's "History of the Highlands," that Captain MacDonald was a perfect mine of Highland poetical lore. This is the quotation referred to:—"Captain John MacDonald is a native of the Island "of Skye, who declared, upon oath, that he could repeat, when a boy between fifteen "and sixteen years of age (about the year 1740), from one to two hundred Gaelic "poems, differing in length and in number of verses, and that he learned them from an "old man about eighty years of age, who sang them for years to his father when he "went to bed at night, and in the spring and winter before he rose in the morning."

THE MACDONALDS OF SKAEBOST.

Three brothers belonging to the old Skaebost family—Captains James, Donald, and Kenneth MacDonald—all served in the 84th Royal Highland Emigrant Regiment (a corps composed largely of gentlemen who had emigrated with their families from Skye to Canada a few years before the outbreak of the American War of Independence) during the campaign in America, and had the misfortune to be taken prisoners by the enemy.

Captain James MacDonald died in prison, and after that sad event his widow and his mother returned to Skye, as also did Captain Donald MacDonald with his wife, when he was released from confinement at the close of the war. Captain Kenneth MacDonald, however, having got a grant of land, remained in America until he was sixty years of age, and then he came home to Skye (in company with the celebrated Flora MacDonald) and married a daughter of an old Skye family, the Nicolsons of

---

[1] Regimental Depôt Records.

THE MACDONALDS OF BELFINLAY AND WATERNISH.

Captain RONALD MACDONALD OF BELFINLAY.
(In the Uniform of a Captain of Prince Charlie's Army, 1745.)

Major ALLAN MACDONALD OF WATERNISH.
(In the Uniform of the 55th Regiment.)

Captain ALLAN MACDONALD OF WATERNISH.
(In the Uniform of the 99th Regiment.)

Major ALLAN MACDONALD OF WATERNISH.

(From Portraits given by Mr. A. R. MacDonald, Younger, of Waternish.)

Scorrabreck. Captain Kenneth MacDonald left two daughters, one of whom (Mary) was living in October, 1897, wonderfully strong in mind and body, although she was then ninety-seven years of age.

THE MACDONALDS OF WATERNISH.

Captain Ronald MacDonald of Belfinlay served in the Highland Army in the '45, was wounded in both legs at the battle of Culloden, and barbarously treated afterwards by the Red-coats of the Duke of Cumberland. Belfinlay died prematurely from the effects of his wounds and of the cruel treatment he had received. He was succeeded by his son Allan, who was then a child. Of Captain MacDonald Mr. Fraser-Mackintosh says in his interesting "Antiquarian Notes," "Take Belfinlay, which sent out in the " 'Forty-five' one of the bravest of the warlike race of Clan Donald."

Major Allan MacDonald of Waternish.

Allan MacDonald of Belfinlay (a son of the gallant Belfinlay of the "Forty-five") married Jane, eldest daughter of Lachlan Mackinnon, VI. of Corry (the great-grandfather of the present Duchess of Somerset, and the entertainer of Pennant, Dr. Johnson, and Boswell). They had a son Allan, who, having a predilection for the profession of arms, entered the army as an Ensign in the 55th Regiment on the 5th of November, 1799, through the influence of Sir John MacPherson, Governor-General of Bengal, a connection of the family. Mr. MacDonald proceeded shortly afterwards with his regiment to the West Indies, where he served with distinction. He was promoted to the rank of Lieutenant on the 5th of October, 1800, and to that of Captain on the 22nd of January, 1808. In the year 1808 Captain MacDonald took part in the expedition under Major-General Carmichael against the Island of St. Domingo, and on the termination of hostilities had the honour conferred upon him of being placed in temporary command of the 2nd West India Regiment (owing to the indisposition of the senior officer of that corps) then under orders for Providence. Captain MacDonald also served in the campaign in the Netherlands in the years 1813 and 1814, and distinguished himself at the storming of Bergen-op-Zoom, where he was second in command as Captain of Grenadiers of the 55th Regiment, Major Frederick having relinquished the command only a few days before, because of illness. There were only two Captains (MacDonald and another) with the right wing of the regiment in the town of Bergen-op-Zoom, and it was by them that the several charges upon the ramparts were conducted, of which Major-General Cooke, in a letter to Sir Thomas Graham, spoke in the highest terms. Major Frederick (as soon as he heard of the result of the attack) also sent MacDonald a very nice letter of thanks. In this unfortunate assault Captain MacDonald was wounded, but he never applied for nor received the allowance which was graciously granted by His Majesty to officers who had been wounded in action with the enemy.

The following is an interesting account of the attack written at the time :—" On " the night of the 8th of March the British besieging army, under the command of Sir

"Thomas Graham (afterwards Lord Lynedoch), before the strong and important fortress "of Bergen-op-Zoom, attempted to take that place by storm. The troops advanced in "four columns to the attack; the first column, consisting of 1,000 men of the Brigade "of Guards, under Colonel Lord Proby; the second, 1,200 men, under the command "of Lieutenant-Colonel Morrice, 69th Foot; the third, 650 men, under the command "of Lieutenant-Colonel Henry, 21st Foot; and the fourth, 1,100 men, under the "command of Brigadier-Generals Gore and Carleton. After the most desperate efforts "and the most gallant conduct, two of the columns established themselves upon the "ramparts of the place, but the others were completely unsuccessful, and were driven "back with prodigious loss. Above two-thirds of the whole of the force engaged "were either killed, wounded, or taken prisoners. Nothing could exceed the bravery "of the British troops; but by some means or other the Governor had become "acquainted with their design to attack the fortress, and was therefore completely "prepared for them."

It was also stated (though not officially) that General Graham had been offered some assistance from the inhabitants of the place, which was the reason that he attempted to attack one of the strongest fortresses in Europe with the small force at his disposal, and in the manner in which the assault was carried out; but that this offer of help was made merely to lead the British troops to certain destruction. The failure of the attack was severely felt by the gallant general who commanded the army. In his despatch of the 10th of March, 1814, he said: "Though it is impossible not to feel "the disappointment of our failure in the attack, I can only think at present with the "deepest regret of the loss of so many of my gallant comrades." The troops under the command of Sir Thomas Graham, however, did excellent service at Hoogstraten and at Antwerp, at which places they fought with their usual bravery in assisting a division of the Prussian army, under the command of General Bulow. At the former place the enemy was compelled to relinquish the field of battle with the loss of twelve or fourteen cannon and at least 3,000 men, including 300 prisoners; and from his position in front of Antwerp the enemy was driven into Antwerp by the valour of the British soldiers with considerable loss.

At Bergen-op-Zoom Captain MacDonald got his foot entangled in some débris in the confusion of the fight, and, being unable to extricate himself, was hanging by one leg in a perilous condition, when fortunately he was discovered and rescued by one of his own men (a MacDonald from Belfinlay), who with true Highland devotion appears to have kept as close as possible to his master when in action.

On the 18th of December, 1817, Captain MacDonald was promoted to the majority of his old corps, and, not long afterwards, he married Flora, daughter of Peter Nicolson of Ardmore, and granddaughter of Anne of Kingsburgh, who, when a little girl of seven years, on seeing Prince Charlie taken into the house by old Kingsburgh, ran up to her mother's bedside and told her, with many expressions of childish surprise, that her father had brought home "the most odd, muckle, ill-shaken-up wife" she had ever seen, "and brought her into the hall too!"

THE MACDONALDS OF ORD IN SLEAT.
THE MACDONALDS OF PORTREE AND TREASLANE.

Captain ALEXANDER MACDONALD.
(From his nephew, Dr. Keith Norman MacDonald of Ord.)

Surgeon-Major THOMAS RANKIN MACDONALD
OF PORTREE AND TREASLANE, Indian Medical Service.
(From his sister, Mrs. MacLaren, Edinburgh.)

Lieutenant CHARLES MACDONALD OF ORD.
(From his son, Dr. Keith Norman MacDonald.)

In 1820, Major MacDonald went with his regiment to Ireland, and in the following year he (being then senior Major of the 55th) was anxious to succeed to the command by the purchase of the Lieutenant-Colonelcy, on the understanding that Lieutenant-Colonel Frederick was desirous of retiring from the service by the sale of his commission. But having fallen into bad health, and the regiment having received orders to go to the Cape, Major MacDonald was prevailed upon to leave the service, which he did by selling his commission on the 24th of October, 1821, after a varied military career of twenty-one years, during which his conduct and zeal were such as to gain for him "the favourable estimation of many general officers of the most distinguished rank and merit." He always afterwards regretted having left the army.

In 1833, Major MacDonald purchased the fine estate of Waternish from Lord Glenelg, and in the following year he sold his Clan Ranald property. He then took up his residence at the former place, where he resided till his death in May, 1855.

Major MacDonald was a typical Highlander, tall, handsome, and well proportioned; such as one would stop to look at among a thousand.

Captain Allan MacDonald of Waternish, son of Major Allan MacDonald, joined the 99th Regiment in 1848, and served with it in Tasmania and Australia. He was one of the officers who were sent out to the latter colony in charge of a batch of convicts, in the last convict vessel which left British waters. After the death of his father Captain MacDonald returned to this country, and in 1857, retiring from the army, took up his abode in his fine Highland home.

THE MACDONALDS OF ORD, IN SLEAT.
(MacEachainn MacDonalds.)

The first of this branch of the great Clan Donald who settled in the Island of Skye was Dr. Alexander MacDonald of Gillen, in Sleat—An Doctair Ruadh, or the Red Doctor—whose father, Charles MacEachainn MacDonald of Kinloid and Keppoch, in Arisaig, armourer to the Clan Ranald of the 'Forty-five, was a staunch Jacobite, and, along with 120 Arisaig MacDonalds, joined the Highland army under the Young Chevalier. For his devotion to the Stuart cause generally, but more particularly for having broken the gates of Carlisle during the siege of that place by the Highlanders, Charles MacDonald was outlawed, but was never caught, having hidden in a cave in Ardnamurchan for seven years, by the end of which time the search for "rebels" had considerably slackened or ceased altogether. He married Marcella, daughter of Alexander MacDonald of Dalilea, who also had been "out" with "bonnie Prince Charlie." Their son, the Red Doctor (a military surgeon who served in Ireland in the Rebellion of 1798 with the Glengarry Fencibles), married Margaret, daughter of Ranald MacAlister of Strathaird, in Skye, by whom he had five sons, who all took to the profession of arms, viz., Captain Alexander MacDonald (of whom it has been said that "he was the handsomest man that ever crossed the line"), Captain Ronald MacDonald, and Captain John MacDonald (all three of whom were in the employment of the East India Company and did much gallant service in the old Indian wars),

Lieutenant Keith MacDonald of the Royal Navy, who married a daughter of Colonel Norman MacAlister, and assumed the surname of MacAlister (of Inistrynich, in Argyllshire) after his marriage; and Lieutenant Charles MacDonald of Ord, in Sleat, an officer of the Glengarry Fencibles, and afterwards of the 7th West India Regiment, with the former of which he was employed in Ireland in quelling the rebellion of 1798, where he witnessed many scenes of cruelty and bloodshed, and where he had the honour of carrying the colours of his corps in Dublin Castle.

Lieutenant Charles MacDonald married Ann, daughter of Captain Neil MacLeod, XI. of Gesto, who was celebrated for his marvellous knowledge of bagpipe music. Their son, Mr. Lachlan MacDonald of Skaebost, in Skye ("the best landlord in the Highlands"), an indigo planter in India, fully justified his Celtic birth by his undaunted behaviour during the Indian Mutiny. He was for a time the only European residing in one of the disturbed districts, but he completely awed the mutineers around him, frustrated their plans, and subsequently served with a field force, the Behar Light Horse. During a part of that critical period his brother, Mr. Neil MacDonald (afterwards Laird of Dunach, in Argyllshire), was associated with him and shared his anxiety, and they used to keep their horses saddled day and night in the stables to be ready for instant action. Dr. Keith Norman MacDonald, another brother, went out to India in 1863, and immediately after his arrival there joined the Behar Light Horse. Even then, so unsettled was the country in some parts, owing to bands of Dacoits prowling about, that he had often to sleep with a rifle by his side and a revolver under his pillow.

Lieutenant Charles Neil MacDonald, of the 1st Battalion of the Argyll and Sutherland Highlanders, is a son of Mr. Neil MacDonald of Dunach.

To the same branch of the Clan MacDonald belonged Marshal MacDonald of France, Duke of Tarentum, one of the most illustrious soldiers of the First Empire.

Colonel Charles MacDonald Williamson, V.D., the capable commanding officer of "the Glasgow Highlanders," is descended (on his mother's side) from the MacEachainn MacDonalds.

THE MACDONALDS OF PORTREE AND TREASLANE.

Colonel Alexander MacDonald, V.D., of Portree, Isle of Skye, commanding the 1st Volunteer Battalion of the Queen's Own Cameron Highlanders, eldest son of the late Harry MacDonald of Treaslane by his wife, Johanna Campbell, daughter of Dr. Alexander McLeod (the revered Doctair Bàn), was born on the 3rd of April, 1840, and has for many years been probably the most prominent, enthusiastic, and capable volunteer officer in the north of Scotland. Colonel MacDonald is a keen student of military subjects, and has, as a Captain, passed through the School of Instruction at Wellington Barracks, London, and as a Field Officer through that of Aldershot, gaining on both occasions the higher proficiency certificate. In addition to this he holds a certificate for having passed in tactics in the scope of study laid down for Captains of the army before promotion to the rank of Major, and he has received the Volunteer Decoration for long and efficient service, having joined as an Ensign on

THE MACALISTERS OF SKYE.

Major-General KEITH MACALISTER.

(From Mr. A. R. MacDonald, Younger, of Waternish.)

Colonel MATTHEW MACALISTER.

(From Miss Susan M. Martin, of Glendale.)

Colonel NORMAN MACALISTER.

(From Miss Susan M. Martin, of Glendale.)

the 20th of July, 1867, and passed through the intermediate grades, reaching his present rank on the 22nd of July, 1896.

Surgeon-Major Thomas Rankin MacDonald, Indian Medical Service, brother of Colonel Alexander MacDonald, V.D., above mentioned, was born at Portree in the year 1853, and was educated in the Parish School there, continuing his studies at the Edinburgh Academy and University, graduating in medicine at the latter institution in 1876, and at the same time becoming a Licentiate of the Royal College of Surgeons of the same city. Before engaging in practice at Broughty Ferry, near Dundee, Dr. MacDonald visited Vienna in pursuit of a varied professional experience; but, having found the life of a country medical man to be too contracted a sphere for his energies, he determined to join the Indian Medical Service, into which he passed in 1879, afterwards passing through the usual probationary course at the Army Medical School at Netley. The Afghan War was then going on, and, after the repulse of the British Forces at Maiwand River, reinforcements were hurried out to India, which Dr. MacDonald was ordered to join. He accordingly left Skye in August, 1880, for Portsmouth, where he embarked on Her Majesty's ship "Jumna," which had the Rifle Brigade, amongst other troops, on board. At Aden the news was received that the honour of the British arms had been retrieved after the affair of Maiwand by the troops on the spot, so that the prospect of seeing active service by the passengers of the "Jumna" seemed to be remote. Dr. MacDonald, however, was lucky. At Bombay he received orders to proceed to Peshawur on the North-West frontier of India, from whence he was instructed to go up the Khyber Pass, which he frequently traversed in medical charge of sick, and for nearly two years he was attached to the 45th Sikhs and 28th Punjab Native Infantry at and around Peshawur. From that station he went to Lucknow, where he was posted to the 11th Native Infantry, and while there he volunteered for the Egyptian Campaign of 1882, when Arabi Pasha's rebellion broke out. Permission having been obtained, he was sent in medical charge of a wing of the 7th Bengal Infantry. In Egypt Dr. MacDonald was present in the famous night march on Tel-el-Kebir, at the brilliant battle of the same name which followed, and at the subsequent occupation of Cairo, for which he received a medal and clasp, together with the Khedive's bronze star. Having returned to India and resumed his duties at Lucknow, he was before long transferred to Calcutta, and whilst serving there was one of eight Indian medical officers who were sent to Egypt to cope with the severe outbreak of cholera which occurred there in 1884, receiving for his services the special thanks of the Egyptian Government through Lord Cromer. On his return to India again Dr. MacDonald entered civil employment under Government, and held various appointments in Bengal, Burma, and the Central Provinces. In 1892 he was promoted to the rank of Surgeon-Major.

THE MACALISTERS.

The MacAlisters (as their name implies) trace their origin to Alasdair, or Alexander, a son of Angus Mòr of the Clan Donald.

Major-General Keith MacAlister, of the Madras Cavalry (the eldest of three soldier brothers and Indian heroes of the olden time), son of Ronald MacAlister of Glenbarr and Cour, in Argyllshire, and Anne, daughter of Alexander MacDonald of Kingsburgh, was born at Skerrinish in the Isle of Skye. He was appointed a Cadet in 1777; Cornet on the 13th of May, 1778; Captain on the 1st of June, 1796; Lieutenant-Colonel on the 4th of September, 1799; Colonel on the 25th of October, 1809; and Major-General on the 1st of January, 1812.[1]

General MacAlister served with great distinction in the Indian wars, especially at the storming and capture of Seringapatam, and was one of the avengers of the cruel imprisonment of his own brother (Colonel Matthew MacAlister) and his companions in misfortune. In the course of his service General MacAlister took a prominent part in organising the Madras Light Cavalry, which many competent judges called "the crack regiments of India."

He died at Torrisdale, in Argyllshire, on the 9th of March, 1820, at the age of seventy-four.

Colonel Norman MacAlister, son of Ronald MacAlister of Glenbarr and Cour, in Argyllshire, and Anne, daughter of Alexander MacDonald of Kingsburgh, was born at Skerrinish, in the Isle of Skye. After having "endured much suffering, and fought "with matchless valour on behalf of the British Crown," he rose to the rank of Colonel in the service of the East India Company, and was appointed to the honourable and responsible post of Governor of Penang or Prince of Wales Island.

Colonel MacAlister was lost at sea on board the East Indiaman "Ocean" on the voyage home in 1812.

Colonel Matthew MacAlister, son of Ronald MacAlister of Glenbarr and Cour, in Argyllshire, and Anne, daughter of Alexander MacDonald of Kingsburgh, was born at Skerrinish, in the Island of Skye, entered the service of the East India Company, and rose to the rank of Colonel.[2] He was one of the very unfortunate officers of Lieutenant-Colonel Baillie's detachment that was cut off on the 10th of September, 1780, by Hyder Ali. Having been reinforced by Colonel Fletcher with a detachment of about 1,000 men, "the army, under the command of Colonels Fletcher and Baillie, "and Captain Baird, marched in column. Suddenly, whilst in a narrow defile, a battery "of twelve guns opened upon them, and, loaded with grape-shot, poured it in upon "their right flank. The British faced about, another battery opened immediately "upon their rear. They had no choice but to advance. Other batteries met them here "likewise, and in less than half an hour fifty-seven pieces of cannon, brought to bear on "them at all points, penetrated into every part of the British line. . . . . Captain "Baird and his Grenadiers fought with the greatest heroism, surrounded and attacked "on all sides by 25,000 cavalry, by thirty regiments of Sepoy Infantry, besides Hyder's "European Corps and a numerous artillery playing upon them from all quarters "within grape-shot distance. The little army, so unexpectedly assailed, had only

---

[1] India Office Records.
[2] He was a Major in 1796, as is shown by an inscription on his miniature portrait, viz.:—"Major MacAlister, Bombay, 1796."

"ten pieces of cannon, but these made such havoc among the enemy that, after a
"doubtful contest of three hours, from six to nine in the morning, victory began to
"declare for the British. The flower of the Mysore cavalry, after many bloody
"repulses, were at length entirely defeated with great slaughter, and the right wing,
"composed of Hyder's best forces, was thrown into disorder. . . . . Hyder
"himself was about to give orders for retreat, when, by some unhappy accident, the
"tumbrils which contained the ammunition suddenly blew up in the centre of the
"Brirish lines. One whole face of their column was thus entirely laid open, many
"men perished. The whole of the artillery as well as the ammunition was destroyed.
"Tippo Saib instantly seized the moment of advantage, fell with the utmost rapidity,
"at the head of the Mogul and Carnatic horse, into the broken square. This
"attack by the enemy's cavalry being immediately seconded by the French corps,
"and by the first line of infantry determined at once the fate of the unfortunate
"British army. After successive prodigies of valour, the brave Sepoys were, almost
"to a man, cut to pieces. Colonels Baillie and Fletcher, assisted by Captain Baird,
"rallied the Europeans under the whole fire of the immense artillery of the enemy,
"and formed a new square on a little eminence, where, with swords and bayonets
"only, they resisted and repulsed the myriads of the enemy in thirteen different attacks,
"until at length they were fairly borne down and trampled upon, many of them
"continuing to fight under the very legs of the horses and elephants. The British
"loss in this engagement, called the battle of Perimbancum, amounted to about
"4,000 Sepoys and about 600 Europeans."[1] In consequence of nine wounds which he
received on that day (two of which were thought to be mortal), MacAlister was left
for dead upon the field of battle for nearly a whole day among a heap of slain.
However, it was discovered that his life was not extinct, and so he was carried to
Hyder Alli's camp, and, in a most miraculous manner, escaped death. He was
mangled in such a shocking manner as to soften the very heart of Hyder Alli himself,
before whom he was carried, perfectly naked, and terribly disfigured by his wounds;
and although Colonel Baillie and the other officers, who were badly wounded, were left
sitting upon the ground for some hours near Hyder, yet he ordered MacAlister's
wounds to be first and instantly dressed by his own surgeons. Colonel MacAlister
suffered a painful and cruel imprisonment for nearly four years (1780-1784), along with
Sir David Baird, loaded with heavy chains (nine lbs. in weight), in the prison of
Seringapatam. Notwithstanding his sufferings, Colonel MacAlister lived till 1829.[2]

Colonel John MacAlister, son of Alexander MacAlister of Strathaird, and nephew of General Keith, and Colonels Norman and Matthew MacAlister, was born at Strathaird, Skye, joined the East India Company's service, and rose to the rank of

---

[1] Anderson's "Scottish Nation."

[2] Mr. A. R. MacDonald, younger, of Waternish, says:—"There were two other brothers of the "MacAlisters, Charles and James, in the East India Company's service. Both of them died in India. Of "the latter I know absolutely nothing, but of the former the following notification of his death appeared in "the Scots Magazine, 1791:—'April, 1790, near Vizagapatam, Lieutenant Charles MacAlister, Commander of "'a Revenue Battalion in the East India Company's service.'"

Colonel. He died in India, leaving enough of money to enable his father to buy the estate of Strathaird from Charles MacKinnon.

THE MACQUEENS.

The MacQueens are a sept of the Clan MacDonald. This was acknowledged by Lord MacDonald, in 1778, when he offered a commission in the 76th Regiment to Donald MacQueen, younger, of Corrybrough. They derive their name probably from "Conn of the Hundred Battles—Clann Chuinn Cheud Chathaich."

Major John Donald MacQueen, K.H., 74th Highlanders, son of the Rev. Mr. MacQueen, minister of the parish of Applecross, and grandson of the famous Celtic scholar and divine, the Rev. Dr. Donald MacQueen[1] of Kilmuir, in Skye, was born at Applecross, in Ross-shire, on the 4th of May, 1786. He was appointed as an Ensign in the 74th Regiment on the 14th of July, 1800; and, as a Captain in the same corps, he served in the Peninsula in Picton's division from 1810 to the end of the war in 1814. He fought in *nine* battles, besides various minor affairs; was five times severely wounded, and received more than one less serious wound. He was present at the battle of Busaco, the retreat to the lines of Torres Vedras, the actions of Pombal, Redinha, Casal Novo, Foz d'Aronse, and Sabugal; in the battles of Fuentes d'Onor (where he was severely wounded) and Salamanca; the capture of Madrid and Retiro; the affairs in the retreat from Madrid to Portugal; in the battle of Vittoria (where he was three times wounded); the Pyrenees on the 27th, 28th, and 30th July, 1813; Nivelle, Nive, Orthes; in the actions of the Bijorree and Tarbes; and in the battle of Toulouse (where he was severely wounded through the lungs). Major MacQueen received the silver war medal with nine clasps; retired in 1834; was nominated a Knight of the Royal Hanoverian Guelphic Order in 1835; was appointed a Military Knight of Windsor; and died shortly after at Windsor in 1836.

[2] The 74th received particular praise from both Lieutenant-General Picton and Major-General Brisbane, commanding the division and brigade respectively, for its alacrity in advancing and charging through the village of Arinez. This was a very brilliant affair, and was one in which the 74th was most particularly engaged. The right wing, under Captain MacQueen, went off at double quick, and drove the enemy outside the village, when they again formed up in line opposite their pursuers. The French, however, soon after fled, leaving behind them a battery of seven guns.[2]

MacQueen's own account of the battle is exceedingly graphic. "At Vittoria," he says, "I had the command of three companies for the purpose of driving " the French out of the village of Arinez, where they were strongly posted. We " charged through the village, and the enemy retired in great confusion. Lieu- " tenants Alves and Ewing commanded the companies which accompanied me. I

---

[1] It was of this clergyman that Dr. Samuel Johnson said:—"This is a critical man, sir; there must be great " vigour of mind to make him cultivate learning so much."

[2] Scottish Highlands, Highland Clans, and Highland Regiments.

Major John Donald MacQueen, K.H.
(From his son, Captain George Bliss MacQueen.)

General John MacInnes.
(From his son, Mr. Miles MacInnes, ex-M.P. for Hexham.)

"received three wounds that day, but remained with the regiment during the whole
"action, and next day I was sent to the rear with the other wounded. Davis
"(Lieutenant) carried the colours that day, and it was one of the finest things you
"could conceive to see the 74th advancing in line, with the enemy in front, on very
"broken ground full of ravines as regularly and in as good a line as if on parade.
"This is in a great measure to be attributed to Davis, whose coolness and gallantry
"were conspicuous. Whenever we got to the broken ground he, with the colours,
"was first on the bank, and stood there until the regiment formed on his right
"and left." [1]

Adjutant Alves says in his Journal that in this advance upon the village of Arinez he came upon Captain MacQueen, as he thought, badly wounded. Alves ordered two of the Grenadiers to lift MacQueen, and lay him behind a bank, out of the reach of the firing, and there leave him. About an hour afterwards, however, Alves was very much astonished to see the indomitable Captain at the head of his company, the shot that had struck him in the breast having probably been a spent one which did not do him much injury.

The following incident in which Captain MacQueen was concerned at Toulouse (where, it may be remembered, he was severely wounded in the lungs) is worth narrating. When left for dead on the field of battle, and his regiment had moved on, a soldier—his foster-brother, named John Gillanders, whom he had taken with him from his native parish as a recruit—missed his Captain and hurried back through a heavy fire, searched for and found him, and carried him to the rear. There were few places for shelter, and the faithful soldier, loaded with his almost insensible burden, pushed his way into a house which was filled with officers, and called out for a bed. In the room was a bed, and on it lay a wounded officer. He heard the entreaty of the soldier, and saw the desperate condition of the officer he carried, and at once exclaimed, "That poor fellow needs the bed more than I do," rose and gave it up. That officer was the gallant Sir Thomas Brisbane.[1]

Major MacQueen was for some years Barrack-Master at Dundee and Perth. As we have seen, he was in almost every battle fought during the Peninsular War, and seldom came out without a wound, and yet he became Major of his regiment only in 1830, six years before his death.

Lieutenant John Archibald MacQueen, son of Major Donald John MacQueen, K.H., served in the 1st Battalion of the 60th Rifles[2] during the second siege operations at Mooltan, including the siege and storming of the town, and the capture of the citadel of Mooltan. He was afterwards present at the battle of Goojerat (for which he received a medal); took part in the pursuit of the Sikh army under Rajah Shere

---

[1] Scottish Highlands, Highland Clans, and Highland Regiments.

[2] It is very much to be regretted that the regimental records of the 1st Battalion of the 60th Rifles have recently been lost in the unfortunate wreck of the "Warren Hastings." The regiment is greatly to be congratulated, however, upon the splendid discipline which it showed on that unfortunate occasion. The military records of Lieutenant John Archibald MacQueen and Captain George Bliss MacQueen, as given in this work, have suffered in fulness owing to the accident to which reference has been made.

Sing until its final surrender at Rawal Pindee; in the occupation of Attock and Peshawur, and the expulsion of the Afghan force under the Ameer Dost Mahomed beyond the Khyber Pass. He also served in the expedition against the Afridis in the Kohat Pass in February 1850.

Lieutenant MacQueen died in India in 1852.[1]

Captain George Bliss MacQueen, son of Major Donald John MacQueen, K.H., received the rank of Second Lieutenant (without purchase) in the 1st Battalion of the 60th Rifles, on the 9th of March, 1849; that of Lieutenant (without purchase) in the 2nd Battalion of the same corps on the 23rd of December, 1853; was transferred to the 1st Battalion (on the same date), and in it he got his commission as Captain (without purchase) on the 19th of June, 1857; exchanged into the 51st Light Infantry Regiment on the 23rd of October, 1860; and retired by the sale of his commission on the 6th of July, 1870. He was engaged with the mutineers near Cawnpore on the 26th and 27th of November, 1857, and commanded a company of the 34th Regiment (to which corps he was then attached for duty) at the defence of Cawnpore from the 26th of November, 1857, to the 1st December, 1858; but he served with the 1st Battalion of the 60th Rifles in the campaign in Rohilcund in 1858; in the actions of Bugawalla and Nuggina; the relief of Moradabad; the action on the Dojura; the assault and capture of Bareilly; the attack and bombardment of Shahjehanpore; the defeat of the rebels and relief of the garrison; the capture of the fort of Bunnai; the pursuit of the enemy to the left bank of the Goomtee; the destruction of the fort of Mohamdee; the attack on, and capture of, Shahabad, and in the action of Bunkagong. He took part in the Oude campaign, including the action of Rissalpore and the attack and capture of Fort Mittowlie, where he succeeded to the command of the 1st Battalion.[2]

In recognition of his gallant services Captain MacQueen received the Indian Mutiny medal.

Malcolm MacQueen, of the MacQueens of Skye, fell at the battle of Culloden in 1746 (when gallantly fighting for bonnie Prince Charlie), and in consequence of the part which he took in the rising his estates were forfeited. His son (also called Malcolm) was born in England after the battle. He became a medical man, and married Maria Potter, grand-daughter of the Archbishop of Canterbury. They had two sons, Colonel Potter MacQueen, who in early life served in a cavalry regiment, but afterwards commanded the Bedfordshire Yeomanry Cavalry, for which county he sat for fifteen years as member of Parliament. His brother, Captain John MacQueen, of the Life Guards, received his first commission from His Majesty King George IV.

Captain Henry MacQueen, of the 31st Madras Light Infantry, youngest son of Colonel Potter MacQueen, died at Agra, while serving with his regiment, at the early age of twenty-six.

---

[1] This and other quotations from "Hart's Army List" are given by kind permission of the proprietors.
[2] Hart's Army Lists of 1852 and 1863, and Regimental Depôt Records.

Captain Henry MacQueen was a direct descendant, on his mother's side, from Lord Astley, "who commanded the Foot in the Civil Wars in the reign of Charles the First."

THE MACINNESES.

The MacInneses, Cinel Angus, or Clann Aonghais, are of common origin with the Clan MacDonald, and derive their name from Angus, who was one of the "three powerfuls of Dalriada."

General John MacInnes, eldest son of Miles MacInnes and his wife, Grace Grant, daughter of the Reverend William Grant, for many years minister of the parish of Kilmonivaig, was born at Camuscross, in the parish of Sleat, Isle of Skye, on the 1st of August, 1779. His father died in 1785, and John MacInnes was admitted to the service of the Honourable East India Company on the 23rd of November, 1799. He soon applied himself to the study of Oriental languages, and, owing to his proficiency, was often enabled to hold good Staff appointments where a competent knowledge of these languages was essential.

MacInnes received the rank of Lieutenant in the 20th Native Infantry Regiment on the 4th of March; 1800, was appointed Persian Interpreter to the Commanding Officer and Assistant to the Commissioners for the affairs of Cuttack on the 21st of June, 1804; promoted to the rank of Captain on the 19th of May, 1808; Aide-de-Camp to the Governor of Prince of Wales Island on the 1st of May, 1812; appointed a member of the committee established for superintending all public buildings, fortifications, and public roads in that island on the 10th of March, 1813; despatched with communications from the Government to the King of Acheen on the 13th of December, 1813; promoted to the rank of Major on the 3rd of June, 1816; to that of Lieutenant-Colonel on the 26th of August, 1822; appointed to the temporary command of the local corps and troops at Fort Marlborough, by the Lieutenant-Governor, on the 7th of October, 1822; to the command of the Light Brigade of Infantry of the South-East Division on the 4th of June, 1825; and to the temporary command of the Arracan force, with the rank of Brigadier, on the 30th of December, 1825. He is informed (on his appointment) that "the Governor-General, fully " confiding in his judgment, zeal, intelligence, and discretion, has nominated him to the " temporary command of the South-Eastern Division of the army"; appointed to the command of the same division on the 9th of January, 1826; promoted to the rank of Colonel on the 5th of June, 1829; and to that of Major-General on the 28th of June, 1838. He was a full general at the time of his death, which took place on the 12th of March, 1859.[1]

General MacInnes was twice married. By his second wife, Miss Anna Sophia Reynolds, he had three children, and the eldest of these, Miles MacInnes of Rickerby, near Carlisle, was for several years Member of Parliament for Hexham Division of Northumberland.

---
[1] India Office Records.

General MacInnes lived during the later years of his life at Fern Lodge, Hampstead, near London, where he was much occupied with scientific, philanthropic, and religious pursuits.

Private Hugh MacDonald, Camuscross, Sleat, served in the 42nd Highlanders during the Peninsular War, and was present at the battle of Corunna and other engagements, for which he received the Peninsular War Medal.

Private Neil MacInnes, parish of Strath, is said to have seen much active service, but in what regiment it appears to be impossible now to ascertain.

Private MacInnes, Strathaird, joined the 42nd Highlanders and fought in its ranks in the Crimean campaign.

THE MARTINS OF BEALLACH AND DUNTULM.

The Martins of Beallach and Duntulm are one of the old families of Skye, being a sept of the Clan MacDonald.

Lieutenant Angus Martin (a son of Donald Martin of Beallach and Duntulm, and an uncle of Sir Ranald Martin, Knight and C.B.) joined the 76th Regiment of (Highland) Foot as a Lieutenant on the 31st of December, 1777, and served with it in the American War of Independence. He appears to have retired from the service on the disbandment of the regiment in March, 1784.

Sir James Ranald Martin, Knight and C.B., F.R.S. (son of the Reverend Donald Martin, minister of the parish of Kilmuir, in Skye, and Mary, elder daughter of Norman MacDonald of Scalpay), was born at Kilmuir in 1796. He was offered a combatant's commission in the 42nd Highlanders by his uncle, Lieutenant-General Sir John MacDonald, G.C.B., Adjutant-General of the British Army, which, however, he was obliged (for private reasons) to decline—much to his regret—and to go to India as a military surgeon, where, through the influence of his cousin, the Marchioness of Hastings, he was attached to the cavalry body-guard of her husband, who was then Governor-General of India, with which force Dr. Martin served through the first Burmese war in 1825, under Sir Archibald Campbell.

Sir Ranald Martin was an able writer on tropical diseases and kindred subjects, and was one of the earliest advocates of sanitary reform in the army in India.

A true and loyal Highlander himself, he sent six of his sons into the army, all gallant soldiers, while another son (although only a civilian) fought in the Indian Mutiny with the bravery of his race; and nothing gave Sir Ranald more genuine pleasure than to give a helping hand to a kinsman or to a countryman when an opportunity of doing so presented itself. For his various eminent services he received the Cross of the Order of the Bath and the honour of knighthood.

Sir Ranald Martin married, in 1826, Jane Maria, third daughter of Colonel Paton, C.B. He died in 1874.

THE MARTINS OF BEALLACH AND DUNTULM.

Lieutenant ANGUS MARTIN.
(In the Uniform of the old 76th Regiment of (Highland) Foot, or MacDonald's Highlanders.)
(From the 76th Regiment.)

Colonel CUNLIFFE MARTIN, C.B.
(From a photograph given by himself.)

Sir JAMES RANALD MARTIN, Knight and C.B.
(From his daughter, Miss Anne M. Martin.)

Lieutenant Angus Martin, Royal Artillery (a brother of Sir James Ranald Martin, Knight and C.B.), was wounded at the battle of Waterloo. When recovering from his wounds he resided for a time with General Count Maurin, who had himself been wounded on the same day when commanding a brigade of cuirassiers under Napoleon Bonaparte. General Maurin had (when a prisoner of war in England previously) married a cousin of Lieutenant Martin, Jane, daughter of Martin Martin of Beallach.

Lieutenant Martin died at Woolwich (and was buried there) about the year 1818.

Simon Nicolson Martin (second son of Sir James Ranald Martin, Knight and C.B.), an Indian Judge, was caught in Lucknow by the rebels in 1857–58; fought as a volunteer during the siege, was wounded, and received the Indian Mutiny medal with a clasp for the "Defence of Lucknow."

Major James Ranald Martin, Bengal Artillery (third son of Sir James Ranald Martin, Knight and C.B.), served in India throughout the Mutiny. He died in New Zealand.

Major-General John Martin (fourth son of Sir James Ranald Martin, Knight and C.B.) was an infantry officer, who fought in the Indian Mutiny (for which he got a medal); was for a time second in command of the Gwalior Regiment of Native Infantry, and after some service in the Army Pay Department retired with the rank of Major-General.

Colonel Cunliffe Martin, C.B. (fifth son of Sir James Ranald Martin, Knight and C.B.), was born on the 3rd of February, 1834. He was appointed to the Bengal Light Cavalry on the 20th of November, 1851, and in 1852 was transferred to the 1st Bengal Light Cavalry at Cawnpore. He was officiating second in command and Adjutant of the Governor-General's body-guard in 1854–55, and in the latter year was employed with it in the suppression of the Southal rebellion, after which he rejoined the 1st Bengal Light Cavalry in the capacity of Interpreter and Quartermaster. The regiment formed part of a column, under Brigadier-General Wheeler, which marched from Cawnpore to Lucknow, in 1856, to annex the Province of Oude.

In 1857, Martin went to Mhow, in Central India, and was appointed Adjutant. On the 1st of July of that year the regiment mutinied, killing its commanding officer, Major Harris, and after that event Lieutenant Martin was attached to the 14th Light Dragoons, and served with it at the siege and capture of Dhar (in October, 1857), on the day of the investment of which he greatly distinguished himself while leading D Troop of Captain Barrett's squadron. A native leader of the enemy's horse (a powerful swordsman) singled him out for personal combat. The challenge was at once accepted, and the native leader fell.

Colonel Martin was also present with the 14th Light Dragoons in the action of Mundisore on the 22nd of November, 1857, where he was severely wounded in charging and putting out of action a battery of six guns (protected by 250 matchlock men), which he took with twenty men, for which he was recommended for the Victoria Cross, mentioned in despatches, and received a medal and clasp for Central India.

Unfortunately, the letter sent by Major Gall (who then commanded the left wing of the 14th Light Dragoons), which was strongly endorsed by Brigadier-General (afterwards Sir Charles) Stewart, recommending Lieutenant Martin for the distinction of the Victoria Cross never reached Bombay, the post having been cut off by the mutineers, who at that time surrounded the Central India Field Force. In 1859, Sir Ranald Martin submitted his son's case (through the Adjutant-General of the Bombay army) for the favourable consideration of Lord Clyde, who was then Commander-in-Chief in India; but the result was a refusal, practically on the singular ground that the act of gallantry performed by Lieutenant Martin was one "in which the men under his command equally shared." If this principle had been carried out all along, several officers who could be mentioned would still be without Victoria Crosses. But "the war-bred Sir Colin," like smaller men, had strong prejudices; and we have it now, on the authority of Sir W. H. Russell, the veteran War Correspondent of the "The Times," that "Sir " Colin Campbell regarded the institution of the Victoria Cross with strong dislike. It " was, according to his views, a mischievous innovation." [1]

After the suppression of the Indian Mutiny, Martin was appointed Adjutant of the newly-raised 1st Bengal European Light Cavalry, the present 19th Hussars, and in 1860 he was promoted to the command of the 2nd Central India Horse. In 1867, he served as Aide-de-Camp to Brigadier-General Donald Martin Stewart (now Field-Marshal Sir Donald Martin Stewart, G.C.B., &c.) commanding the Bengal Brigade in the expedition sent to Abyssinia, and was attached to the 12th Bengal Cavalry at the capture of Magdala, having daringly ridden (attended by only one servant, a syce) through a hostile country from Zulla to within a few miles of the capital. For the Abyssinian Expedition Colonel's Martin's name was mentioned in despatches, and he received a medal.

Colonel Martin was promoted to be commandant of the Central India Horse, and Political Agent in Western Malwa in 1877. He served in command of the Central India Horse in Afghanistan in 1880; in the Besud and Khama Valleys Expedition under Brigadier-General J. Doran, C.B., for which he was mentioned in despatches; took part in the march from Kabul [2] to Kandahar under Sir Frederick Roberts, and was present at the action of Kandahar on the 1st of September, 1880. For these services he got a medal and clasp, the bronze star, and the Companionship of the Bath.

Colonel Martin is one of the "mighty hunters" of India, having been present at the death of about 200 tigers, besides other big game, including a savage "man-eater," which was the pest of a wide tract of country for several years, and the lion that figures in Mr. Rowland Ward's well-known group called "The Struggle."

Colonel Martin retired from the army in 1889.

Cornet Norman Alexander Martin, seventh son of Sir James Ranald Martin, Knight and C.B., served in the Indian Native Cavalry. At the time of the outbreak of the Mutiny he was an Aide-de-Camp, and threw up his post to rejoin his troop of the

---

[1] *See* "The Army and Navy Gazette" of the 8th of January, 1898.

[2] One day, during these operations, Colonel Martin pluckily swam the River Kabul four times when in flood with his whole regiment.

Field Marshal Sir DONALD MARTIN STEWART, Baronet, G.C.B., &c.
(From his daughter, Mrs. Murphy.)

7th Bengal Cavalry, which soon mutinied. Young Martin could have escaped, but stopped to rescue his Captain (Jack Staples), a fat, clumsy man, who had lost his horse in trying to mount. The gallant youth got his unwieldy comrade up behind him, but, owing to the double burden which the horse was carrying, the two officers were ridden down and shot. This happened close to Cawnpore in 1857, and thus passed away a chivalrous and promising soldier at the early age of nineteen.

Lieutenant Angus Martin, eighth son of Sir James Ranald Martin, Knight and C.B., joined the Native Indian Infantry, but got attached to the 97th Foot, with which he served in India during the Mutiny, and for his services there received a medal. He died in 1897.

Colonel Martin Martin, Royal Engineers, ninth son of Sir James Ranald Martin, Knight and C.B., when serving in India as a Lieutenant participated in the thanks of the Government of that country, along with the 2nd Company of Bengal Sappers, then under his command, for successful bridging operations across the Jumna, in a threatened overflow of that river, in 1872-73, and while employed during the famine in Madras, in 1877, he was thanked by the Government of that Presidency for a rapid march which he made when in command of a portion of "O" Field Battery, 1st Bengal Royal Artillery, and for the demolition, by gunpowder, of the weir of the Red Hills Lakes, which were then bursting their dams and threatening a serious flood, which might have swept into the city of Madras. He served in the Afghan Campaigns of 1878, 1879, and 1880 with General Sir Frederick Roberts and General Donald Martin Stewart, including the march from Kandahar to Kabul, and the action of Ahmed Kheyl. He also took part in the Zhob Valley Campaign of 1884.

While in command of the troops at Port Royal, Jamaica, in 1890-93, Major Martin was one of those who received the thanks of the War Office for the judicious disposal of the large grant of money which had been made by Government to put that fortress in a state of defence. During this period most of the forts were rebuilt, and almost wholly re-armed with the most modern artillery, while a native garrison was raised to obviate the employment of Europeans in such a fever-stricken spot, it being a remarkable fact that yellow fever does not usually attack negroes, or even those mixed breeds who have some negro blood in their veins. Jamaica is not a fortress of the first importance at present, but it might become so if ever the Panama or the Nicaragua Canal were completed. A thoughtful paper by Colonel Martin, entitled "Cover, Screen, and Illusion," extracts from which appeared in "The Army and Navy Gazette" in October, 1896, was very favourably received and commented upon at the time in military circles.

Field-Marshal Sir Donald Martin Stewart,[1] Baronet, G.C.B., G.C.S.I., C.I.E., Indian Staff Corps, Governor of Chelsea Hospital (son of Captain Robert Stewart of

---

[1] To the same branch of the Stewart family—viz., the Stewarts of Kincardine—belonged the famous soldier-poet of the '45, Colonel John Roy Stewart, and likewise Lieutenant-General Sir John Stewart, the hero of Maida. Sir Donald Stewart is also connected with the MacLeods of Drynoch through the marriage of his ancestor, Bailie Stewart of Inverness (a noted Jacobite), with Anne, daughter of Norman MacLeod, IV. of Drynoch.

the Perthshire Militia, and Flora, daughter of the Reverend Donald Martin, Minister of the parish of Kilmuir, in Skye, by his wife, Mary, daughter of Norman MacDonald of Scalpay), was born on the 1st of May, 1824, and was educated partly at one of the old parochial schools of Scotland (of which he himself said, in one of his public speeches, he had "a grateful and affectionate recollection") and partly at Aberdeen, where he distinguished himself in classics.

In 1897, Sir Donald Stewart presided at the annual dinner of the Inverness-shire Association, in London, and in the course of a speech said :—" I am an old Inverness-"shire man ; I am a Skyeman, and I believe that my relations still living in the Isle "of Skye number, at least, 3,000 ! At all events I have never yet met a Skyeman "who did not inform me that he was a cousin, more or less removed !"

Donald Martin Stewart began his brilliant military career in India. Having been nominated at the recommendation of his relative, Lieutenant-General Sir John MacDonald, G.C.B., Adjutant-General of the British Army, he was appointed an Ensign on the 12th of October, 1840 ; posted to the 9th Native Infantry Regiment, at Secrole, Benares, on the 5th of March, 1841 ; promoted to the rank of Lieutenant on the 3rd of January, 1844 ; appointed Adjutant to his corps on the 5th of March, 1845 ; and before the end of the following year had acquired " a competent knowledge of Hindustanee." General Kennedy in an inspection report, dated 23rd December, 1847, said :—" Lieutenant Stewart is in an eminent degree qualified for his duties as Adjutant, "and the high state of discipline in which the 9th Native Infantry Regiment is in "reflects the greatest credit on Major Smith and his Adjutant."

On the 29th of July, 1848, Lieutenant Stewart, having been found duly qualified, was allowed to resign the adjutancy and to take up instead the duties of Interpreter and Quartermaster to his corps. He was appointed to act as Brigade-Major at Peshawur on the 23rd of January, 1854,[1] and on the 24th of the following June received the rank of Captain. In the same year he was engaged in the operations against the Momunds, for which he was mentioned in Brigadier-General Cotton's despatches in the following terms :—" He is a very able officer and competent to all his duties . . . . Captain "Murray, who is absent at this moment, and Captain Stewart are two very superior "officers, and particularly distinguished themselves in the action with the enemy near "Mitchnee . . . . Captain Stewart is now second in command, and ably supports "his commanding officer."

Acting as Deputy-Assistant-Adjutant-General of the Delhi Field Force, Captain Stewart served at the siege and storming of that city in 1857 ; was thanked by General Reed for his services, as well as by General Wilson, who said :—" To that experienced "officer . . . . and his gallant and energetic coadjutor, Captain D. M. Stewart, "Deputy-Assistant-Adjutant-General, who have conducted the duties of this important "department much to my satisfaction, I am greatly indebted for the assistance they "have afforded me."[1]

Captain Stewart's perilous ride out of the beleaguered city of Agra, through the enemy's lines, with despatches to Alleyghur and Delhi was one of the most daring feats

---

[1] India Office Records.

done by any soldier during the Indian Mutiny, and would, doubtless, have secured for him the Victoria Cross, if rewards were then as common as they are nowadays.

On the 30th December, 1857, Captain Stewart was made Second Assistant-Adjutant-General of the Army, Brevet-Major on the 19th of January following, and Deputy-Adjutant-General in India in February, 1863.[1]

Colonel Stewart was selected by General Sir William Mansfield, Commander-in-Chief in India, to organise and equip a brigade of all arms of Bengal troops for service in the Abyssinian Expedition of 1868. Captain Frederick Roberts, V.C. (now Lord Roberts), was the Assistant-Quarter-Master-General of the brigade, and it was under his careful supervision that the transport vessels were selected in the port of Calcutta, and their sanitary condition (including cubical space) thoroughly tested. The brigade carried its own land transport, so that on its arrival at Zulla, the port of debarkation, it could have taken the field at once without any further assistance. No force was ever more perfectly equipped; but on its arrival at Zulla the brigade was broken up, Brigadier-General Stewart remaining in command there until he was relieved (by General Russell from Aden) and ordered to take command at Senafe, the first station on the high tableland, where he remained till the object of the expedition was accomplished, and then he returned to India.

For his services in the Abyssinian Expedition Brigadier-General Stewart received a medal, and was made a Companion of the Bath.

General Stewart was appointed to the command of the Peshawar District in July, 1869;[1] Chief Commissioner of the Adaman and Nicobar Islands in 1871, and transferred to the command of the Lahore District in 1876. He commanded the Kandahar and South Afghanistan force from 1878 to 1880 at Kabul; and in North Afghanistan from the latter year till the withdrawal of our troops from that country, for which important services he received the thanks of both Houses of Parliament; was created a K.C.B., a G.C.B., a Baronet, and got a medal with a clasp.[1]

In December, 1879, General Sir Frederick Roberts was overpowered by Mahomed Jan, and beleaguered in Sherpur. The advance of Sir Charles Gough, and the difficulty of keeping the Afghan Highlanders together, relieved him partially; but the country around was so unsettled that he could not move far from the shelter of the walls. In April, 1880, Sir Donald Stewart moved from Kandahar to Kabul to relieve Sir Frederick Roberts, and to strengthen his position in the north—a more difficult and dangerous march[2] even than the one which Roberts afterwards made the reverse way, because Stewart had to make a road as he went along (smoothing all the difficult places, including the formidable Zambaruk Pass) and taking guns and waggons on wheels over the whole of it; the country was comparatively unknown, not having been traversed till then since the first Afghan War in 1839–42; the whole of the forage was hidden and the people of the country bitterly hostile; and, finally, he met and defeated a superior force (on the 19th of April) near Ghazni, at Ahmed Kheyl.

---

[1] India Office Records.
[2] It is said that the reason why this march is not so well known as the other is that Stewart gave the "specials" the slip.

The Battle of Ahmed Kheyl.[1]

"Sir Donald Stewart, knowing the efficacy of taking the initiative, formed front (to a flank) and was preparing to deliver an attack with his leading brigade, when the enemy suddenly burst upon him and compelled him to take up a defensive position. . . . . . It was the General's intention to advance to the attack, but at 9 a.m., before his dispositions were fully developed, the whole crest of the curved line of hills, held by the enemy, was observed to be swarming with men along a front of nearly two miles. Scarcely had the guns opened fire, when from the enemy's position rushed out successive waves of swordsmen on foot stretching out beyond either flank and seeming to envelope the British force. . . . . . After an hour's gallant and strenuous exertion to break the British line the efforts of the enemy began to fail under the murderous fire. The onslaught was checked, hesitated, and died away—the entire body dispersing broadcast over the country, completely defeated and scattered. The enemy left 1,000 dead on the field, and their total loss amounted to about 3,000. The British loss was only 141, including killed and wounded."

Sir Donald Stewart was appointed Military Member of the Governor-General's Council in 1880, Commander-in-Chief in India, and Extraordinary Member of the Governor-General's Council in 1881; Member of the Council of India in 1885 (reappointed for a further period of five years in December, 1895); received the bâton of a Field Marshal in May, 1894; was appointed a Member of the Royal Commission on Indian Expenditure, and Governor of Chelsea Hospital in 1895.[2]

Sir W. H. Russell, writing in "The Army and Navy Gazette," regarding the Diamond Jubilee procession in June, 1897, said:—"If the people had known Sir Donald "Stewart, the valiant soldier of the Mutiny, the successful Commander-in-Chief who "had contributed so largely to the settlement of the North-West frontier by his "military skill, or had identified his comrade on his right, Sir Linthorn Simmons ". . . . . they would have given hand and voice to record their sense of the "merits of two soldiers, whose careers, widely different in a degree, were most "meritorious."

Sir Donald Stewart married, in 1847, Marina, daughter of Commander T. D. Dabine, Royal Navy, with issue.

Colonel Norman Robert Stewart, son of Field-Marshal Sir Donald Martin Stewart, Bart., G.C.B., &c., saw active service both in Afghanistan and in Egypt.

Captain Donald Stewart, C.M.G., son of Field-Marshal Sir Donald Martin Stewart, Bart., G.C.B., &c., took part, along with the 92nd Highlanders, in the march from Kabul to Kandahar, and was present at the battle of Kabul, where he was wounded. He also served with the 75th Highlanders in Egypt in 1885, but afterwards left the

---

[1] From Major G. J. Younghusband's "Indian Frontier War," by kind permission of Messrs. Kegan Paul, Trench, Trübner, and Company, Limited, London.
[2] India Office Records.

service, and is now (in 1898) British Resident at Kumasi, after having been employed in the police service along with the last Ashanti Expedition. For his great zeal and devotion to duty in Africa, Captain Stewart was made a Companion of the Order of St. Michael and St. George in 1898.

Major-General Andrew Aldcorn Munro, C.I.E., J.P. (whose mother was Anne, daughter of the Rev. Donald Martin, minister of Kilmuir, in Skye, and sister of Sir James Ranald Martin, Knight and C.B.), entered the Bengal Army in 1846, and obtained his Lieutenant's commission three years later. He served in the Punjab campaign of 1848-49 (for which he got a medal), and in the Southal campaign of 1855-56; was promoted to the rank of Captain in 1860; took part in the Umbeyla campaign in 1863 with the Euzofzaie Field Force, under Brigadier-General Chamberlain, for which he obtained a medal with clasp; was Commissioner of the Punjab, and Deputy Commissioner of the frontier districts of Peshawur, Hazara, Dera, Ghazi Khan, Kohat, Bannu, and Dera Ismail Khan, from 1855 to 1880. He was promoted to be Major in 1866; appointed officiating Commander of the Multan Division in 1871, and made a Lieutenant-Colonel in the following year. He served as Commander of the Derajat Division from 1871 to 1880, and commanded the Dour Valley Expedition in 1872. He got the rank of Colonel in 1877, and that of Major-General in 1881, when he retired on full pay as a Colonel of the Bengal Staff Corps.

General Munro married, in 1867, Janet Victoria, daughter of General Sir R. H. Cunliffe, Bart., with issue a son (Ranald) and a daughter (Annabel). The General died at his residence, Woodside, Frant, Sussex, on the 2nd of February, 1898, aged seventy-two. He was an enthusiastic Highlander, and spoke, read, and wrote the Gaelic language with perfect ease.

NOTES.

The Regiment of the Isles, the Fencibles, and the Local Militia.

The Regiment of the Isles (552 strong), raised by Lord MacDonald, chiefly on his own estates, was embodied at Inverness on the 4th of June, 1799. All the men were in the prime of life, their average age being twenty-two, and their conduct was most exemplary in camp and quarters. The only duty of an active nature which fell to their lot during their short period of service was restoring order among the sailors of Whitehaven, who had taken up a threatening attitude towards their employers, the shipowners. This unpleasant task the Highlanders were enabled to perform "without force, and more by "the respect in which the regiment was held, and the imposing appearance of the men "when drawn up ready to act, than by violence."[1]

The corps was reduced at Fort George in July, 1802.

---

[1] General Stewart of Garth's "Annals of the Highland Regiments."

A regiment of Local Militia, consisting of 500 men, was formed in the Island of Skye in 1811.

"There are so many old soldiers settled in Skye, receiving pensions for wounds and length of service, that the circulation of so much ready money is no small advantage to their native isles. The Collectors of Excise, who usually pay these pensions, sometimes find their collections of duties too small to meet the military payments at their half-yearly collections. While so many soldiers returned home to enjoy their country's rewards for their services, I have access to know that an equal number settled in other parts of the kingdom after their discharge."—General Stewart of Garth.

THE SKYE VOLUNTEERS.

In the year 1803,[1] two regiments of Volunteers were formed in Skye. The command of the 1st Regiment (which numbered 507 men) was given to Lieutenant-Colonel James MacLeod of Raasay, and that of the 2nd Corps (whose strength was 510 men) was bestowed upon Lieutenant-Colonel Alexander MacDonald of Lynedale.

A meeting of the officers was held at Portree on the 16th of November, at which, in addition to the two Lieutenant-Colonels and the two Majors (Major Alexander MacDonald of Mugstot and Major John Campbell of Kingsburgh), Norman MacDonald of Scalpay and Lachlan MacKinnon of Corry were present. Twenty alarm posts were fixed upon, at which arrangements were made to convey signals either by day or by night, and "upon the first intelligence of the landing of an enemy" the one battalion was to muster at Sconser, and the other at Portree, ready, of course, to take the field at a moment's notice. The services of these patriots were not required, as it afterwards turned out, Nelson's victory at Trafalgar in 1805 having upset Napoleon's plans for the invasion of Great Britain; but doubtless many of the men would have found their way into the regular army when the Peninsular War began in 1808.

At the present day there is only one Volunteer company in the whole of the Island; but, if the cry of "the Empire in danger" arose again, the men of Skye would be found equal to the emergency as in the days of yore.

---

[1] Cameron's "History and Traditions of the Isle of Skye."

THE MACLEODS OF SKYE AND THEIR CONNECTIONS.

(MACLEOD OF MACLEOD AND HIS CLAN.)

" Agus t-òlachd as t-uaisle,
" Cha bu shuarach ri leanmhuinn ;
" Dh-fhuil dìreach rìgh Lochluinn,
" B 'e sid toiseach do sheanachais.
" Tha do chairdeas so-iarraidh,
" Ris gach Iarla tha 'n Albuinn ;
" 'S ri uaislean na h-Eireann,
" Cha bhreug, ach sgeul dearbht 'e.
   " I h-urabh o, &c.

" 'S ri uaislean na h-Eireann,
" Cha bhreug, ach sgeul dearbht 'e,
" A mhic an fhir chliutaich,
" Bha gu fiughantach ainmeil,
" Thug barrachd an gliocas,
" Air gach Ridir bha 'n Albuinn ;
" Ann an cogadh 'san sio'-chainnt,
" 'S ann an dioladh an airgeid.
   " I h-urabh o, &c.

" Ann an cogadh 's an sio'-chainnt,
" 'S ann an dioladh an airgeid ;
" 'S beag an t-ionghnadh do mhac-sa,
" Bhidh gu beachdail, mòr, meanmnach,
" Bhidh gu fiughant', fial, farsuinn,
" O 'n a ghlachd sibh mar shealbh e ;
" Clann Ruairidh n 'am bratach,
" 'Se mo chreach-sa na dh-fhalbh dhiu."
   " I h-urabh o, &c."
     Mairi Nighean Alasdair Ruaidh.

" 'S tric a dhearbh iad bho 'n uair sin,
" Ann an cathan 's an cruadal,
" Gu 'm bheil gaisgeadh nach fuaraich,
" Ann an dualchas Chloinn Leoid."
     Niall MacLeoid.

Sir Ruairidh Mòr MacLeod—designated Mòr, or Great, "not so much from his "size or stature of his body, which was not remarkably large, as from the strength of "his parts"[1]—was undoubtedly the most notable warrior of the race of Leod up to his own day. A Highland chief of the first rank and of the best type of those times— daring and impetuous even beyond the verge of rashness, but noble-spirited, generous,

---

[1] Mackenzie's "History of the MacLeods."

and given to hospitality that knew no bounds, Rory Mòr's soul was thoroughly imbued with the turbulent spirit of the age in which he lived.

In the year 1594, the Chief of Dunvegan crossed over to the north of Ireland with 500 of his clansmen, and there took part in Red Hugh O'Connell's rebellion against the rule of Queen Elizabeth of England, for which incursion he incurred the displeasure of his own Sovereign, the Scottish King James the Sixth ; but, having made due submission, he was again received into the Royal favour. And when, two years later, he was ordered by the King, on two days' notice, to appear at Islay with all his followers, "under pain of treason and forfeiture," Rory Mòr, while remonstrating against the unreasonableness of the Royal command, offered to prove his loyalty in characteristic fashion. He said :—"Whom your Grace or my Lord Crowner will command in your
" Highness's name to pass on, either by sword or fire, I shall do the same on any
" your Grace may command me to fight hand in hand in your Grace's sight, I shall
" prove my pith on him." It does not appear, however, that the Scottish Solomon took advantage of this handsome offer, but we find, not long afterwards, Rory Mòr proving his pith on a personal enemy, " Sir Roderick MacKenzie of Coigeach, Tutor
" of Kintail, who purposely insulted him, and whom he knocked down in the presence
" of the Privy Council, an offence which was at that time punishable by death ;
" but MacLeod managed to effect his escape, and soon after arrived safely in the
" Isles."[1]

Donald Gorm Mòr MacDonald of Sleat married Margaret, eldest sister of Rory Mòr. For some reason or other the marriage was not a happy one. The story goes that the lady was blind of an eye, and that on account of this blemish (unnoticed by the lover's eyes) her husband sent her home, "air each cam 's le gille cam," on a one-eyed horse led by a one-eyed lad, thus adding insult to injury. Be this as it may, MacDonald divorced his wife, and (as if still further to exasperate MacLeod) married soon afterwards Mary, a sister of MacLeod's mortal enemy, the Tutor of Kintail. Matters had now come to a crisis. Rory Mòr was furious, " assembled his vassals, and
" carried fire and sword into MacDonald's lands of Troternish. The MacDonalds, in
" revenge, invaded Harris, which they laid waste. The MacLeods then made a foray
" upon MacDonald's estate of North Uist under their chief, who sent his kinsman,
" Donald Glas of Drynoch with forty men to lay waste the land . . . .
" Donald Glas and his men were met by a celebrated warrior of the Clan Donald,
" Donald MacIain 'Ic Sheumais of the Kingsburgh family, who had only twelve men
" in his party. The MacLeods were routed, and their leader, Donald Glas, was killed.
" These incursions were carried on with so much inveteracy that both clans were
" brought to the brink of ruin."[1] Then followed "the Desperate Battle" ("Am Blàr Fuathasach"), which was fought in the year 1601 on the shoulder of one of the Coolin Hills, hence it is frequently spoken of as "the Battle of Benquillin." " After a fierce
" and obstinate combat, in which both clans fought with great bravery, the MacLeods
" were overthrown."[1] This was the last battle fought between the two clans. Ever after that day " they submitted their disputes to the decision of the law."

---

[1] Mackenzie's " History of the MacLeods."

THE MACLEODS OF DUNVEGAN.

Lieutenant-General NORMAN MACLEOD OF MACLEOD, XX. Chief.
(From Raeburn Portrait at Dunvegan Castle.)

Captain NORMAN MAGNUS MACLEOD OF MACLEOD, C.M.G., the present and XXIII. Chief.

Major ALEXANDER MACLEOD OF LOCHBAY.
(From Captain R. M. Livingston-MacDonald of Flodigarry.)

Captain NORMAN MACLEOD (Cyprus).
(From the Rev. D. J. MacDonald of Killean and Kilchenzie.)

Rory Mòr died in the year 1626 at the Chanonry of Ross, and his remains were interred in the aisle of Fortrose Cathedral, where his tomb with its inscription can still be seen. Never has the grief of a whole clan been more fittingly expressed than when Patrick Mòr MacCrimmon, refusing to be comforted, "lifted on him his pipes," and, turning his back upon the halls of his dead chief, hied him home to Borreraig, composing as he went along his matchless lament for Ruairidh Mòr MacLeod.

The MacLeods of Dunvegan as a clan kept aloof from the three Jacobite risings of 1689, 1715, and 1745.

Major Alexander MacLeod of Lochbay and Stein was an illegitimate son of Norman MacLeod, XIX. Chief of MacLeod, and a brother or half brother of Captain Norman MacLeod (Cyprus). Major MacLeod served with distinction in the American War of Independence, and also, it is said, at the storming of Seringapatam, as well as, subsequently, in some of the European wars. He married Ann, daughter of Allan MacDonald of Kingsburgh and the celebrated Flora Macdonald.

Their two sons, Allan and Norman, followed the profession of arms. The former was killed in the Peninsular War, and the latter fell by the hand of Glengarry in a duel at Fort George. The following is one verse of a song composed by Mrs. MacLeod for her young soldier son:—

> B' fhearr leam fhein
> Gu 'n tigeadh an t-sith,
> 'S gu faighinn gu 'n stri
> Mo ghille bho 'n "Champ."
>
> So a bhliadhna
> A shiaraidh buileach mi,
> 'S mi nach do bhuinig
> Air cogadh na Fraing.[1]

Mr. Knox (who visited Skye after Dr. Johnson), speaking of Dunvegan Castle, says:—"The Castle was inhabited at the time by Major Alexander MacLeod and "his lady, a daughter of the celebrated Flora Macdonald, who protected the Young "Pretender through all his hairbreadth escapes after the battle of Culloden."

Captain Norman MacLeod[2] (Cyprus) was born in Edinburgh about 1740. His father was Norman MacLeod, XIX. of Dunvegan, and his mother an Edinburgh lady, who loved the gallant Chief of MacLeod "not wisely, but too well." Young Norman was brought up in Glenelg, and received a good education. As a youth he went to the Island of Cyprus, where he lived for seven years. He held a good appointment there, and was on the way to preferment when he was recalled by his father, who had meanwhile purchased a commission for him in the army—first in the Black Watch (probably the 2nd Battalion), and afterwards in the 72nd Highlanders.

---

[1] The Reverend D. J. MacDonald's notes.

[2] Notes supplied to the Rev. D. J. MacDonald, minister of Killean and Kilchenzie, Argyllshire, by his aunt, Mrs. MacDonald, late of the Island of Eigg.

He served in America, where he was wounded, and had the reputation of being a brave and capable officer.

Captain MacLeod sold out shortly after returning to this country, having been induced to take this step in order that his nephew, Norman MacLeod, son of his brother, Major Alexander MacLeod of Stein, might get his commission.

Captain MacLeod married for his first wife Jessie, daughter of "MacLeod of Ellanriach," Glenelg. About a year after his marriage he and his wife accepted an invitation to visit their friends at Talisker; and a boat was engaged to convey them there. Along with Captain Macleod and his wife were his sister-in-law and Miss MacLeod, daughter of MacLeod of Bernera, who afterwards became the wife of Major Macdonald of Askernish, South Uist, known as "Seumas 'Og," a cadet of the Boisdale family. On reaching the shore, Miss MacLeod, Bernera, would on no account enter the boat. The event justified her fears. The boat struck on a sunken rock, split, and the occupants were thrown into the water. Captain MacLeod seized an oar, and endeavoured to get hold of his wife. Having succeeded, as he thought, he said: "Are you Jessie?" And the lady answered "Yes." They were for three-quarters of an hour in the water. At length his sister-in-law (for it was she, and not his wife, he was supporting, without his knowing it) said:—"I am not Jessie. "I am becoming exhausted. We shall certainly be drowned. Let me go." This, however, he refused to do, saying that it was now too late to undo what had been done. In the meantime the accident was observed from Talisker House; and, after some delay, a boat was launched, which reached them in time to save them all from drowning, but, alas! Captain MacLeod's young wife died from exhaustion that same night. For many years after her death he remained a widower. When well advanced in years, however, he married for his second wife Jessie, daughter of James MacDonald of Knockow, son of Alexander Macdonald, the worthy bailie of Kingsburgh. Jessie Macdonald was twenty-two years of age when she married Captain MacLeod. She was a beautiful woman of middle height and dark-haired. Her mother was Margaret MacLeod, a sister of Major MacLeod, Bailemeanach.

Mrs. MacLeod (Cyprus) died at Keill, Eigg, in 1846, aged eighty-eight years, in the house of her granddaughter, Mrs. John MacDonald, from whose narration this information has been written down.

Captain MacLeod lived at Musselburgh for some time after his marriage, and he and his wife associated while there a good deal with his half-sister, Lady Pringle. He resided for about five years in Dunvegan Castle, where he had apartments. For a few years before his death, however, he lived near Dunvegan. His widow made her home at Stein for many years before removing to the Island of Eigg.

There were born to Captain MacLeod by his second wife one son, who died young, and four daughters, viz.:—

(1.) Elizabeth, who married the Reverend Roderick MacLean, minister of South Uist;
(2.) Margaret, who married Donald Calder, teacher in Troternish;
(3.) Alexandra, who married —— Cowan, Skye, and emigrated to America; and
(4.) Matilda.

The following incidents in the life of Captain MacLeod are worth recording. After an engagement in the American War he saw some Indians stripping a wounded man who was lying under a tree, and went to his rescue. The wounded man, recognising Captain MacLeod as he approached, offered some resistance to his tormentors. It proved to be Lieutenant MacLeod, son of Sheriff MacLeod of Ulinish. Captain MacLeod remained with him for some time, took his directions about his affairs, cut off a lock of his hair, and received from him a ring to convey to his sister. Thereafter the dying man said to him, "You can do nothing more for me. I am at " the point of death. You cannot remain here without great danger to yourself. " Go now." In the course of time Captain MacLeod came home, and being in Edinburgh he went to a jeweller's shop, and had some of the hair which he had cut off the head of his late comrade put into his ring. Receiving the ring, as he was setting out on his journey from Edinburgh to Inverness, and thence to Skye, he placed it on his finger. He was disappointed in not being able to secure a place in the mail coach from Edinburgh, but he bought a horse and rode all the way. In the course of his journey the ring was lost. How mortifying this was can be imagined. On returning to Edinburgh he bethought him to call at the jeweller's house on the slender chance of his having seen or heard anything of the ring. What was his astonishment when the jeweller said, "Here it is!" handing it to him. Not many days before a man had come into the shop offering the ring for sale, stating that he had picked it up. The jeweller, suspecting foul play, had the man arrested, and he was detained for forty-eight hours. Captain MacLeod's reappearance, however, set all unpleasant suspicions at rest. The ring, which had met with such strange adventures, was ultimately put into the possession of Mrs. MacQueen, Lieutenant MacLeod's sister.

In the course of the journey referred to, Captain MacLeod rode across Monadh Mòr Dhruim Uachdarach on his way from Inverness to Skye. When in the heart of that lonely region, out of a lurking-place sprang a savage-looking man with long shaggy hair and beard ; and, seizing Captain MacLeod's horse by the bridle, demanded "Money or life." In relating the story of this wild man of the waste, Captain MacLeod was wont to say that he never knew what fear was when in action, but confessed that a feeling of wholesome dread came over him as he found himself face to face with the fierce-looking robber on Monadh Mòr Dhruim Uachdarach. Taking his courage, however, in both hands, he replied : "I am sorry, my man, that " you have taken to this kind of life. You will not be much the better for all I " possess, for I am but a poor soldier lately returned from the war, and I have no more " money than is barely needful to defray the cost of my journey." Without pausing, he went on to tell about the campaign, relating story after story of adventure and battle—who had been distinguished here, and who had fallen there.

The robber, with his hand on the bridle all the time, listened intently. At length Captain Macleod, pulling out a little money, said :—"I regret this is all I can afford to give." The robber immediately let go the bridle saying, "I thank you, sir ; it is a long time since I heard so much news," and then disappeared.

Lieutenant-General Norman MacLeod of MacLeod, XX. Chief.

Norman MacLeod[1] was born at Brodie House, Nairnshire, the residence of his maternal grandfather on March 4th, 1754; was appointed Captain in the 71st Foot on the 7th of December, 1775; Major in the 73rd Foot on the 25th of September, 1778; Lieutenant-Colonel in the 42nd Foot on the 21st of March, 1780; Colonel, Brevet, on the 18th of November, 1790; Major-General on 3rd of October, 1794; and Lieutenant-General on the 1st of January, 1801.

MacLeod received a liberal education, was an accomplished linguist, a man of extensive reading and culture, and could wield the pen as well as the sword. It was of him that Pennant, who visited the Island of Skye in 1772, said :—" He feels for the " distress of his people, and, insensible of his own, instead of the trash of gold, is " laying up the treasure of warm affection and heartfelt gratitude."

In 1773, Dr. Johnson and his friend Boswell, when at Raasay, met the young chief there, of whom the Doctor said, " I have not met a young man who had more desire to learn, or who has learnt more."

In the year 1774, MacLeod determined to enter the army. His relative,[2] Colonel the Honourable Simon Fraser of Lovat, in 1757, raised a regiment of 1,460 men, who afterwards greatly distinguished themselves in the American wars. In 1775, Fraser got letters of service for raising another regiment of two battalions in the Highlands. Having very soon completed his task, he, in April, 1766, marched with a fine body of 2,340 men by way of Stirling and Glasgow to Greenock, whence they sailed for America. For this new 71st Regiment Norman MacLeod raised a company, and joined it with the rank of Captain. When he embarked for America he was accompanied by his young wife, Mary MacKenzie of Suddie; but on the passage they were both taken prisoners by the Americans. They were kindly treated, however, by General Washington. In a few years MacLeod returned to Britain, and was on the 21st March, 1780, made Lieutenant-Colonel of the 2nd Battalion of the 42nd Highlanders, raised by himself. This corps was, in 1786, formed into a separate regiment, designated the 73rd Foot, of which he was appointed Lieutenant-Colonel. In December, 1780, the newly-raised regiment embarked at Queensferry to join an expedition then fitting out for service abroad, but, owing to the transport " Myrtle,"[1] in which Colonel MacLeod sailed, having separated from the other vessels of the fleet, and in consequence of other adverse circumstances, he did not reach Madras till the 23rd day of May, 1782. In the absence of Colonel MacLeod, the command of the troops destined for active service against Tippoo Sahib devolved upon Colonel Humberston MacKenzie. The former, however, joined the force at Paniane on the 20th day of November, 1782, and immediately took command. Here he found himself surrounded by an enemy mustering 10,000 cavalry and 14,000 infantry, including two corps of Europeans under the French General Lally, while his own force had been reduced by sickness to 380

---

[1] War Office Records. Mackenzie's " History of the MacLeods." General Stewart of Garth's " History of the Highland Regiments."

[2] Colonel (afterwards General) Simon Fraser's grandmother was of the Dunvegan family.

Europeans and 2,200 Sepoys. Before the dawn of the 28th, the enemy made a furious attack on Colonel MacLeod's position, but were gallantly repulsed, Colonel MacLeod himself taking an active part in the fight, and he and the Highlanders greatly distinguishing themselves,[1] the enemy losing 2,000 men in dead, wounded, and prisoners, while the British loss was only eight officers and eighty-eight rank and file killed and wounded. Tippoo retreated after this decisive defeat towards Seringapatam. MacLeod was now ordered to Bombay to join the army under Brigadier-General Matthews, with whom he formed a junction at Cundapore on the 8th day of January, 1783. On the 23rd he moved forward to attack Bednore, meeting with considerable opposition by the way from the enemy, who had constructed a series of earthworks on the face of the mountains, which the invading British force had to ascend. These fieldworks were, however, soon taken possession of by the intrepid MacLeod at the head of the 42nd Highlanders and his Sepoys. On the 26th February, 1783, according to the official despatches: "The 42nd, led by Colonel MacLeod, and followed by a corps of "Sepoys, attacked these positions with the bayonet, and, pursuing like Highlanders, "were in the breastwork before the enemy were aware of it; 400 were bayonetted, "and the rest pursued to the wall of the fort."[1]

In this manner General Stewart of Garth says seven forts were attacked and taken in succession. The seventh, however, Hyder Gurr, so called from its pre-eminent strength, being formidably armed, presented greater difficulty, but it did not stand long against the undaunted bravery of the Highlanders, and the stronghold of Bednore was captured by MacLeod on the 27th of January, 1783. Hyder Gurr contained 8,000 stand of new arms, with a large quantity of powder, shot, and other military stores, as well as a vast amount of treasure.

General Matthews, who was hopelessly inefficient, having been superseded for flagrant conduct in connection with the disposal of the treasure found in the city, Colonel MacLeod was promoted to the post with the rank of Brigadier-General and Commander-in-Chief of the Malabar army. While on the way from Bombay to the army, with two other officers in the "Ranger," he fell in, off Geriah, with a Mahratta fleet of five vessels on the 7th of April, 1783. This fleet was not apprised of the peace which had previously been arranged, and MacLeod, instead of attempting an explanation, or submitting to be detained at Geriah for a few days, gave orders to resist the enemy. The "Ranger" was taken, but only after nearly every man on board was either killed or wounded. Among the latter was MacLeod himself. During Brigadier-General MacLeod's absence, the army was dispersed in small detachments all over the country, those in charge of it shamefully neglecting their duties. Tippoo soon took advantage of this unfortunate state of matters, suddenly appeared on the 9th of April, 1783, seized Bednore, laid siege to the fort, occupied the ghauts, cut off the garrison from all possibility of retreat, and on the 30th April its defenders capitulated, honourable terms being promised to them; but instead of these conditions being implemented, officers and men were placed in irons and marched off like felons to a dreadful imprisonment in the fortresses of Mysore.[1]

---

[1] War Office Records. Mackenzie's "History of the MacLeods." General Stewart of Garth's "Sketches."

The military authorities, having resolved to draft the men of the 2nd Battalion of the 42nd Regiment to other regiments, and to send the officers and non-commissioned officers home to Great Britain, MacLeod strongly urged, in a letter addressed to the Commander-in-Chief in India (Sir Eyre Coote, K.B.), that the proposed drafting should not take place. This spirited communication had the desired effect, and not only saved his own clansmen from being drafted into other corps, but prevented the battalion itself from being broken up. It was ordered by the King to be formed into a separate corps, and this arrangement was carried into effect at Dinapore, in Bengal, on the 18th of April, 1786, when General MacLeod rejoined his old corps and became one of its Lieutenant-Colonels.[1]

In one of his despatches addressed to the Sultan about this time General MacLeod pens the following spirited passage which explains itself. He says, "You, or your "interpreter, have said in your letter to me that I have lied, or made a mensonge. "Permit me to inform you, Prince, that this language is not good for you to give or "me to receive, and if I were alone with you in the desert you would not dare to "say these words to me. . . . . I tell you our customs, if you have "courage enough to meet me, take a hundred of your bravest men on foot, meet me "on the seashore, I will fight you, and a hundred men of mine will fight yours."[2][3]

Thus spoke the Highland chief, but Rory Mòr's successor does not appear to have had an opportunity given to him of "proving his pith" upon his adversary, the wily Tippoo having evidently shunned the combat.

General MacLeod[4] died at Guernsey in the year 1801. It was of him the poet Burns said—

"Chieftain MacLeod, a chieftain worth gowd,
"Though bred amang mountains of snow."

---

[1] War Office Records. Mackenzie's "History of the MacLeods." General Stewart of Garth's "Sketches."
[2] There are some old letters in Dunvegan Castle in which this bold challenge is referred to.
[3] Mackenzie's "History of the MacLeods."
[4] When MacLeod sailed for India with his men the following song was composed in his honour by a Skye bard of the name of Mac an Leigh, Livingstone, or Leech:—

(1) 'Se speireag na h-uaisle,
 A ghluais bh-uainn a null,
 'S leat urram gach cruadail,
 Is buaidh air gach cliu,
 Ged' nach robh thu ach leanabh,
 Bu smearail do shuil,
 'S ma philleas tu fallain
 Cha bhi d' fhearann gu 'n diu.

(2) 'S ann an cuideachd Mhic Leoid,
 Tha na h-òganaich ghrinn,
 Na seoid nach eil gealtach,
 'S na gaisgich nach crion,
 'N am nochdadh ri teine,
 Cha tig tiom' air na suinn,
 Tha mo dhùrachd gu brath
 'S gach blàr a dhol leibh.

Major WILLIAM NORMAN RAMSAY, Royal Horse Artillery.

The hero (along with Sandy MacDonald of Scalpay) of "the brilliant feat of arms" at Fuentes d'Onor.

(By permission, from the Portrait in the Royal Artillery Institution, Woolwich.)

Lieutenant Norman MacLeod, Royal Navy, eldest son of Lieutenant-General Norman MacLeod, XX. Chief, died young, having been lost at sea with his ship, the "Queen Charlotte."

NOTE.

The first colours of the 2nd Battalion of the 42nd Regiment, and a sword, which once had a jewelled hilt, and which belonged to Tippoo Sahib, are preserved in Dunvegan Castle.

Major William Norman Ramsay,[1] Royal Horse Artillery (eldest son of Captain David Ramsay, Royal Navy, of the Ramsays of Balmain, in Kincardineshire, and his wife, Mary, daughter of John MacLeod of MacLeod, and sister of General Norman

---

[1] From an interesting memoir by Major R. Holden, Royal United Service Institution, which he very kindly placed at the disposal of the author of this book by the hands of the late Surgeon-General Sir W. A. MacKinnon, K.C.B.

(3) 'S iomadh òganach deas,
Anns a' reisimeid ùir,
Gu 'n chùram an aitich,
Na màil air an cùl,
Ach claidheamh geur sgaiteach,
Na 'n aisnichean dlùth,
Bu bhòidheach a 'n "camp" sibh,
An am dol a' null.

(4) Bith' Frisealaich ann,
A tha teann anns an tòir
Agus Domhnullaich ghasda
Fo bhratach Mhic Leoid,
Le 'n taghadh "recruit,"
Nach sgrubadh an t-òl,
'S a thraigheadh na buideil,
'S nach tuiteadh bhon' bhòrd.

(5) 'S iomadh òganach cùl-fhionn,
'S a chùl ris an tir,
'O dhùthaich gu duthaich,
'Dol a null air an luing,
Le 'm breacannan boidheach
'Dol a chomhnuidh an righ,
'S a Righ! gu robh buinig
Air turuis sin dhuibh.

(6) Mo rùn na fir ùra
Le 'n ruisgear a phiob,
Le 'm meoirean g 'an gleusadh,
Gu 'm b' eibhinn sud dhuibh
'N am nochdadh na 'n armaibh,
Gu 'm b' fhearganta sibh,
'S 'nuair a gheibh sibh "calìbhir"
Bith' sibh dileas do 'n righ.*

---

* Notes supplied to the Rev. D. J. MacDonald, minister of Killean and Kilchenzie, Argyllshire, by his aunt, Mrs. Ann MacDonald, late of the Island of Eigg.

MacLeod, XX. Chief) was born in 1782; entered the Royal Military Academy as a cadet on the 17th of January, 1797; obtained his commission as Second Lieutenant in the Royal Artillery on the 27th of October, 1798; First Lieutenant on the 1st of August, 1800; Second Captain on the 24th of April, 1806; Brevet-Major on the 22nd November, and First Captain on the 17th of December, 1813.

Norman Ramsay (the name by which this most gallant and dashing officer, who was the beau-ideal of a Horse Artillery soldier, is generally known) first saw active service with one of the companies of Royal Artillery, under Lieutenant-Colonel Thomas Seward, in Sir James Pulteney's unsuccessful expedition to Ferrol in June, 1800; and in the following year he served in the Egyptian Campaign under Sir Ralph Abercromby, for which he received the Turkish medal. In 1809 he was posted to I Troop (now I Battery), Royal Horse Artillery, with which he went to Portugal, where he first came into prominence. He was present at the battle of Busaco in 1810, "where the Horse Artillery did excellent service in spite of the ignorance of "artillery tactics which Lord Wellington displayed," and in which action "immense "slaughter was inflicted on the enemy by the shrapnel shells thrown from Ross's guns, "aided by those of Norman Ramsay's troop."[1]

For its zeal and activity in covering the retreat of the British army on the famous lines of Torres Vedras in 1810, I Troop was specially thanked by Sir Stapleton Cotton, afterwards Lord Combermere; and when the army advanced again in the following year it greatly distinguished itself under Norman Ramsay in the affairs of Pombal, Redinha, Cazal Nova, Foz d'Aronze, and Sabugal, for which it was mentioned in Wellington's despatches of the 14th and 16th of March and 9th of April, 1811.

At the battle of Fuentes d'Onor, which was fought on the 5th of May, 1811, Norman Ramsay and Alexander MacDonald of Scalpay were the heroes of "the brilliant feat of arms" (that of charging and breaking through an overwhelming force of French cavalry by which they and their troop, or a part of it, had been cut off and surrounded), which is so graphically described by Napier in his "History of the Peninsular War":—"Suddenly a great commotion was observed among the French "squadrons; men and officers closed in confusion towards one point, where a thick "dust was rising, and where loud cries and the sparkling of blades and flashing of "pistols indicated some extraordinary occurrence. Suddenly the multitude was "violently agitated. An English shout arose, the mass was rent asunder, and Norman "Ramsay burst forth at the head of his battery, his horses breathing fire and "stretching like greyhounds along the plain, his guns bounding like things of no "weight, and the mounted gunners following close, with heads bent low and pointed "weapons, in desperate career."[2] From this day forward the name of Norman Ramsay represents all that is dashing and brilliant on the field of battle, and more than one artist has depicted on canvas his unique exploit at Fuentes d'Onor.

In 1812, I Troop took part in the battle of Salamanca, in the advance on, and retreat from, Burgos, as well as in the action of Venta de Pozo, in which it distinguished

---

[1] Major Holden's Memoir. [2] History of the Peninsular War.

itself, and for which Ramsay's name was mentioned in Lord Wellington's despatch of the 26th of October.

Norman Ramsay commanded his troop throughout the campaign of 1813. "At the battle of Vittoria on the 21st of June, 1813, the troop was attached to Lieutenant-General Sir Thomas Graham's corps, and contributed largely to the capture of Abechuco, by which the French army was cut off from the Bayonne road, its best line of retreat. In this battle, in which the services of the artillery generally were conspicuous, Norman Ramsay's daring and dash were again prominent; he rode a couple of 6-pounders over a hedge and ditch in order to get them up in time to act against the retreating enemy. Sir Augustus Frazer, in his letters, wrote: 'Bull's troop, which I have no hesitation in saying is much the best in this country, had, under Ramsay's command, been of unusual and unquestionable service.' But a sad misfortune shortly overtook poor Ramsay—a grief which never quitted him while he lived."[1] When in pursuit of the enemy after the battle Lord Wellington overtook him and ordered him to take his troop to a village near a cross road which joins the main roads leading to San Sebastian and Pamplona respectively, and there to await personal orders from his Lordship. At six o'clock next morning an Assistant-Quarter-Master-General arrived on the spot, and ordered him to join his brigade, to whom Ramsay said, "Am I to take this order as from Lord Wellington, for he gave me positive orders not to move without personal orders from himself?" to which the other officer replied, "The order is from Lord Wellington." This new order was then given in writing by the Assistant-Quarter-Master-General to Ramsay, who immediately left the ground with his troop, but he had not gone far when Lord Wellington arrived at the village, and not finding Ramsay there galloped after him and placed him under arrest. "Every effort was made by Sir Thomas Graham, Lord Fitzroy Somerset, and others to get the order cancelled; but Lord Wellington would listen to no reason or explanation, and omitted Ramsay's name in despatches. This act of injustice was much felt in the army, and occasioned general regret; for Norman Ramsay, by his personal character, his enthusiasm, bravery, and ability, was universally beloved by his brother officers and his men. . . . . . . The letters of his brother officers show the affection which was felt for him. . . . . If his troop distinguished itself they all rejoiced as if it had been their own; if he met with any grief they longed to share it; and if sorrow came upon themselves their first instinct was to confide it to him."[1] He was released from arrest, however, in July, 1813, and afterwards received the Peninsular gold medal for the battle of Vittoria; but "he was never the same man."

I Troop formed part of Lieutenant-General Sir John Hope's corps in the operations in the Pyrenees; at the battle of Nivelle "it repeatedly silenced the guns opposed to it"; and Norman Ramsay (who was twice wounded) was specially mentioned by Sir John Hope in his report of the actions on the Nive on the 10th and 12th of December. On the 17th of the same month Captain Ramsay was posted to No. 8 Company, 1st Battalion (now the 11th Field Battery, Royal Artillery), then serving in

---

[1] Major Holden's Memoir.

the West Indies; but was transferred early next year to K Troop (afterwards E Battery, A Brigade, which was reduced in March, 1882) at that time stationed in England. In the spring of 1815 Ramsay was removed to H Troop (now H Battery), Royal Horse Artillery, then forming part of Wellington's army in the Netherlands; and, to quote Sir Augustus Frazer's words, "was soon adored by his men; kind, "generous, and manly; he is more than the friend of his soldiers."

And now comes the closing scene of a great drama. "During the retreat from "Quatre Bras, Ramsay was wounded in the head, and wore a forage cap at Waterloo. "On the morning of that day, as he went into action at the head of his troop, it passed the "Head Quarters Staff. The Duke, who had not seen him since his arrival in Belgium, "accosted him cheerfully, saying something to the effect, 'Very good,' or 'Well done, "Ramsay.' The latter saluted profoundly . . . . but could not speak. In the "great fight Norman Ramsay's troop defended the key of the position and suffered "severely . . . . his battery was placed a little to the left rear of Hougomont, "and there before the end of the day it had lost four officers out of five. . . . . . "Many who knew Ramsay well said that the remembrance of his unjust treatment "led him to court unnecessary exposure throughout the day. . . . . . A bullet "passing through the snuff-box which he carried entered his heart, and he was where "sorrow and injustice are unknown."[1]

"During a momentary lull in the battle," wrote Sir Augustus Frazer (who afterwards erected a monument to the memory of his friend in the church at Waterloo), "I buried my friend Ramsay, from whose body I took the portrait of his wife, which "he always carried next his heart. Not a man assisted at the funeral who did not "shed tears. Hardly had I cut from his head the hair which I enclose, and laid his "yet warm body in the grave, when our convulsive sobs were stifled by the necessity "of returning to renew the struggle." The body was afterwards taken home and buried in the churchyard of Inveresk.

Norman Ramsay married his cousin, Mary, daughter of General Norman MacLeod, XX. Chief (by his first wife, Mary MacKenzie of Suddie), but she died soon after their marriage without issue.

Lieutenant A. Ramsay, Royal Artillery, a brother of Norman Ramsay, was killed at New Orleans on the 1st of January, 1815.

Lieutenant D. Ramsay, Royal Navy, another brother of Norman Ramsay, died in Jamaica on the 31st of July, 1815; so that in the short space of eight months Captain David Ramsay had to lament the loss of three gallant sons.[1]

Captain Norman Magnus MacLeod, C.M.G., the present Chief and XXIII. MacLeod of MacLeod, son of Norman MacLeod, XXII. Chief, was born on the 27th of July, 1839, and joined the 74th Highlanders in 1858. He went to India in 1860, and served as Aide-de-Camp to Sir Hope Grant, Commander-in-Chief of the

---

[1] Major Holden's Memoir.

THE MACLEODS OF GESTO.

Captain NEIL MACLEOD, XI. of Gesto.
(From his grandson, Dr. Keith Norman MacDonald of Ord.)

Colonel JOHN MACLEOD, Netherlands.
(From Admiral Norman MacLeod, of the Dutch Royal Navy.)

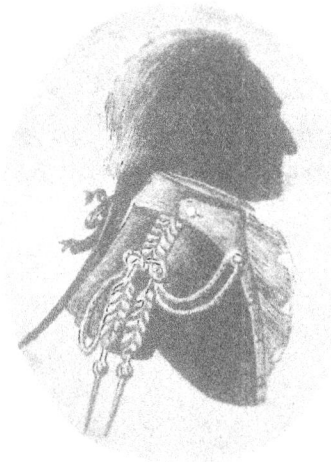

Major-General NORMAN MACLEOD, Netherlands.
(From Admiral Norman MacLeod.)

Captain JOHN VAN BRIENEN MACLEOD, Netherlands.
(From Admiral Norman MacLeod.)

Lieutenant-Colonel EDWARD DONALD HENRY MACLEOD, Netherlands.
(From Admiral Norman MacLeod.)

Major RUDOLPH MACLEOD, Netherlands.
(From Admiral Norman MacLeod.)

THE MACLEODS OF GESTO.

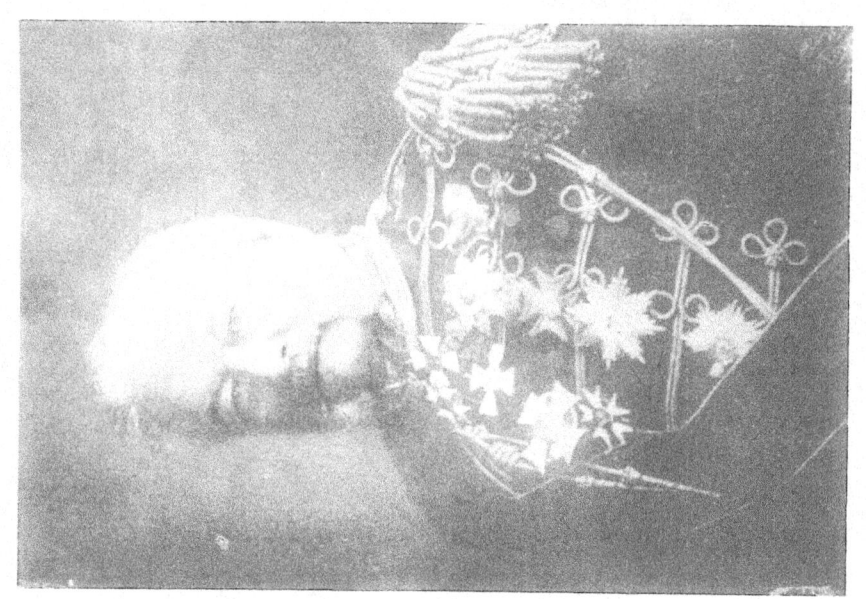

Lieutenant-General NORMAN MACLEOD, Netherlands.
(From Admiral MacLeod.)

Vice-Admiral NORMAN MACLEOD,
Dutch Royal Navy.

Madras Presidency from 1862 to 1865. After his return home from India MacLeod went with his regiment to Gibraltar in 1869, and to Malta in 1872, at the latter station acting as a Brigade-Major for a short time. He sold out in the end of 1872.

Captain MacLeod was employed in South Africa during the Zulu War as Political Agent in charge of the Swazie, Zulu, and Transvaal border. He raised, equipped, and afterwards led the Swazie army of 8,000 men in the successful attack on the Basuto Chief, Sekukuni, on which occasion so desperate was the fight that one man out of every ten of the Swazies fell. For these important and gallant services Captain MacLeod was created a Companion of the Order of Saint Michael and Saint George.

When MacLeod[1] was stationed at Gibraltar a soldier of the 74th Highlanders, seized with one of those fits of desperation which occasionally appear among men, who either think they are wronged, or who are bored to death by dreary exile ("fed up," as soldiers call it), took up his rifle and cartridges and, going into the barrack square, threatened to shoot any one who approached him. Captain MacLeod quietly walked up to the man, and saying "Let me look at your rifle," took it away from him. A less cool and popular officer would probably have been shot.

THE GESTO BRANCH.

The MacLeods of Gesto, whose patronymic is "Mac Mhic Thormoid," and who, it is said, can claim kinship with the Royal race of Bruce, as well as with that of Norway and Man, were the first that branched off from the main stem of the MacLeods of Dunvegan and Harris.

Major John MacLeod, X. of Gesto, was an officer of the Gordon Highlanders. He married Annabella, daughter of Neil MacKinnon of Borreraig, in Strath, son of Lachlan MacKinnon, Corry.[2]

Captain Neil MacLeod, XI. and last of Gesto, son of Major John MacLeod, X. of that house, and Annabella MacKinnon, his wife, was appointed as a Lieutenant in the 116th Regiment of Foot (then commanded by Colonel Alexander Campbell) on the 15th of February, 1794, and subsequently promoted to the rank of Captain.

According to the most reliable information now obtainable (from family records and other sources), Captain MacLeod served in Egypt under Sir Ralph Abercromby, and this statement was corroborated by Norman MacLeod, the well-known soldier-catechist, to whom reference is made elsewhere in this work, who used to say (speaking of Gesto and himself), "'Nuair a bha sinn anns an Eiphit," "When we were in Egypt." And there was kept among the family treasures at one time a

---

[1] Captain Charles Campbell, D.S.O., Royal Navy, now (1898) in command of Her Majesty's first-class battleship "Empress of India," is a cousin of the present MacLeod of MacLeod. Captain Campbell's father was John Campbell of Glensaddel, Argyllshire, and his mother, Harrietta Maria, daughter of John MacLeod, XXI. of MacLeod.

[2] Mackenzie's "History of the MacLeods."

copy of the Koran which Captain MacLeod had taken home from the land of the Pharaohs.

Gesto afterwards acted as a recruiting officer for the Highland regiments (especially the 2nd Battalion of the Black Watch), in which duty he met with much encouragement and success, owing to his personal popularity and family influence. His portrait was taken in the uniform of one of the Highland corps.

Captain MacLeod was a great authority[1] on Highland music; and, although he himself could not play the bagpipes, he knew almost all the piobaireachds ever composed, as well as their origin and history. In 1828, he published a small book containing twenty piobaireachds to illustrate the MacCrimmon system of pipe music, known as "Canntaireachd." Major-General MacLeod, a brother of Captain Neil MacLeod of Gesto, served in the Royal Artillery, and died at Woolwich.[1]

Donald MacLeod, third son of John MacLeod, VI. of Gesto, by his wife, Mary, daughter of Donald MacDonald, III. of Kingsburgh ("Domhnull MacIain 'Ic Sheumais"), the famous Skye warrior, married Isabella MacLennan, daughter of the Reverend Allan MacLennan, minister of Glenelg, and their third son Norman was an officer in the Dutch Scots Brigade.

Lieutenant Norman MacLeod, third son of Donald MacLeod and Isabella MacLennan, above referred to, was appointed as an Ensign in the company of Captain Cathcart in Hepburn's Regiment, in place of Angus MacLeod, who had retired, and Lieutenant in Douglas's regiment on the 3rd of December, 1709. In 1717 the regiments of Douglas and Wood were disbanded, and the officers who were not incorporated into other regiments were pensioned. Being recommended by the Princess of Anhalt-Bernburg to Baron Keppel, and by him to the Earl of Cadogan, Lieutenant MacLeod obtained an appointment, dated 3rd April, 1719, as a Lieutenant in a Company of Invalids in England, with which he was garrisoned successively at Tilbury Fort, Pendennis Castle, and Plymouth. He was married to Gertrude Schrassert. He died in London on the 6th of September, 1729.[2]

Colonel John MacLeod, son of Norman MacLeod and Gertrude Schrassert, was born in February, 1727.

He joined Lamy's regiment as a cadet in 1738; was appointed an Ensign in Captain Lockhart's company of Colyear's regiment on the 28th of April, 1741; Lieutenant on the 1st of March, 1745; Aide-de-Camp to Major-General Græme on the 5th of January, 1748; Captain on the 23rd of October, 1748; Second Under-Major on the 16th of February, 1749; Captain in Halkett's regiment on the 23rd of September, 1749; transferred to Gordon's regiment on the 8th of November, 1758; Major on the 24th of April, 1766, in the same corps; Lieutenant-Colonel of the same battalion on the 11th of April, 1774; Effective Major in Dundas's regiment on the 1st of February, 1776; and Colonel of the same corps on the 8th of July, 1779.

---

[1] Mackenzie's "History of the MacLeods."   [2] Dutch War Office Records.

In 1782 the Scotch regiments lost their nationality and were transformed into Dutch corps. Colonel John MacLeod then applied for his discharge, which having been obtained on the 17th of February, 1783, he went at once to England, getting a Lieutenant-Colonel's half-pay. He afterwards lived for some time in Scotland, and after that again in Holland. Having returned to England, Colonel MacLeod died at Chelsea on the 12th of December, 1804. His wife was Margaretha Arnolda van Brienen.[1]

Major-General Norman MacLeod, son of Colonel John MacLeod and Margaretha Arnolda van Brienen, was born on the 15th of June, 1755, at Elburg, in the province of Gelderland. He was appointed a cadet in Major-General Gordon's regiment on the 15th of June, 1765; Ensign on the 30th of March, 1769; Honorary Lieutenant on the 30th of March, 1775; Acting Lieutenant in Dundas's Regiment on the 30th of March, 1777; Honorary Captain on the 30th of March, 1781; Acting Captain on the 22nd of February, 1783; Major on the 10th of November, 1787; Lieutenant-Colonel in Bentink's regiment on the 15th of September, 1790; and, on his return from France, where he was detained as a prisoner of war, he received his discharge on the 11th of July, 1795. On the 30th of December, 1797, he obtained a Lieutenant's commission from His Royal Highness the Duke of York, in the 60th Regiment, in the service of His Majesty the King of Great Britain and Ireland, but was transferred to the Dutch service as Lieutenant-Colonel of Bentink's regiment in 1798; became Lieutenant-Colonel of the 1st Regiment of the Dutch troops[2] of His Serene Highness the Prince of Orange-Nassau; Lieutenant-Colonel of the 15th Battalion of the Infantry of the Line on the 15th of January, 1814; Colonel on the 8th of April, 1814; and (by Warrant of the Sovereign Prince, dated 31st of July, 1814) he was appointed Provincial Commander in Overyssel, with the rank of Major-General; pensioned by Royal Decree on the 21st of December, 1818; and died at Kampen on the 4th of December, 1837.

General MacLeod took part in the campaign of 1794; was taken prisoner at the siege of Nimeguen on the evacuation of the fortress by the French troops on the 7th of November, 1794; and participated in the blockade of the Helder in 1814.[2]

General MacLeod married on the 1st of June, 1809, Sarah Evans, a Welsh lady, by whom he had seven sons.

Lieutenant-General Norman MacLeod, son of Major-General Norman MacLeod and Sarah Evans, was born on the 16th of March, 1811, at Llanstephan, County of Caermarthen, Wales. He volunteered for the 7th Division of Infantry on the 7th of December, 1822; was appointed a cadet on the 31st of March, 1823; Honorary Corporal on the 1st of June, 1825; Honorary Sergeant on the 18th of October, 1826; Second Lieutenant, by Royal Warrant, on the 16th of August, 1829, as well as Battalion Adjutant of the Mobilized North Brabant Militia; First Lieutenant on the

---

[1] Colonel MacLeod's remains were interred (by special permission and command of His Royal Highness the Duke of York) in the burial ground of the Military College of Chelsea.
[2] Dutch War Office Records.

5th of June, 1832; Captain of the 3rd Class on the 28th of November, 1850; Corps Adjutant on the 4th of July, 1853; Captain of the 2nd Class on the 31st of March, 1854; honourably discharged from the Adjutancy and transferred to the Army Staff for service in the War Department on the 28th of March, 1855; Captain of the 1st Class on the 8th of April, 1856; was attached to the Inspector of Infantry on the 21st of May, 1857; on the 28th of May, 1857, satisfaction was expressed by Royal Warrant, with respect to the varied services which he had rendered to the War Department; he was appointed a Major on the 3rd of November, 1857;[1] transferred to the Regiment of Grenadiers and Riflemen on the 8th of May, 1858; appointed a Lieutenant-Colonel of the 3rd Regiment of Infantry on the 23rd of September, 1862; Colonel of the 4th Regiment on the 20th of April, 1866; transferred to the command of the Regiment of Grenadiers and Riflemen on the 20th of May, 1867; appointed to be Adjutant to His Majesty for service in Foreign Affairs on the 12th of September, 1868; made a Major-General on the 18th of March, 1871; promoted to be a Lieutenant-General on the 27th of February, 1874; and "was pensioned, with "thanks for the good and true services rendered by him during the period of his "long-continued military career," on the 8th of February, 1878.

General MacLeod died at the Hague on the 3rd of April, 1896.

Campaigns:—

On the occasion of the Insurrection in Belgium.
- In 1830, with the Mobilized Army.
- In 1831, participated in the Tiendaag campaign.
- In 1832, 1833, and 1834, in the Fortress of Gorinchem.

Decorations:—

The Metal Cross, 5th April, 1832; awarded, 6th December, 1844, the Badge of Honour (instituted for long service as officer in the service of the Netherlands); created a Knight of the Luxemburg Order of the Oaken Crown, 10th May, 1849; created a Commander of the Order of the Oaken Crown on the 27th of February, 1868; created a Knight of the Order of the Netherlands Lion on the 6th of October, 1872; permission granted to him to accept and wear the Insignia of Commander of the Legion of Honour, presented to him by the President of the French Republic on the 9th of February, 1873; permission granted to him to accept and wear the Decoration of the Grand Cross of the Order of the Red Eagle, presented to him by the Emperor of Germany on the 28th of September, 1877; created a Commander of the Order of the Netherlands Lion on the 18th of February, 1878; and permission granted to accept and wear the Grand Cross of the Order of Frederick, conferred upon him by His Majesty the King of Würtemberg on the 4th of July, 1882.

Captain William Pasco MacLeod, son of Major-General Norman MacLeod and Sarah Evans, was born at Abergevilly, in England, on the 29th of December, 1812. He was appointed a cadet in the 7th Infantry Division on the 25th of July, 1827; Honorary Corporal on the 9th of October, 1828; Honorary Petty Officer on the

---
[1] Dutch War Office Records.

1st of January, 1830; Second Lieutenant in the 14th Division of Infantry on the 17th of February, 1831; transferred in the same rank and seniority to the 2nd Battalion of Riflemen on the 18th of July, 1832; appointed First Lieutenant on the 7th of December, 1837; transferred to the army in the East Indies on the 3rd of March, 1843; embarked on board the ship "Louisa Maria" for the East Indies on the 7th of June, 1843; arrived at Batavia on the 1st of October, 1843; appointed Captain in the 4th Battalion on the 3rd of December, 1843; and died at Kedongkebo on the 22nd of September, 1846.

Captain MacLeod served as a Lieutenant with the Mobilized Army, on the occasion of the rebellion in Belgium in 1830–34, and received the Metal Cross on the 5th of April, 1832.[1]

Captain John van Brienen MacLeod, Royal Navy of the Netherlands, son of Major-General Norman MacLeod and Sarah Evans, was born at Kampen, Overyssel, on the 11th of February, 1825. He was appointed a cadet in the Royal Military Academy of the infantry branch of the service on the 10th of July, 1841; Second Lieutenant of the 5th of Regiment of Infantry on the 23rd of June, 1845; Battalion Adjutant on the 19th of October, 1852; First Lieutenant on the 1st of February, 1853; transferred to the General Disciplinary Depôt on the 14th of March, 1856; removed to the 4th Regiment of Infantry on the 9th of March, 1857; appointed Captain of the 3rd Class on the 26th of March, 1860; Captain of the 2nd Class on the 24th of July, 1862; Captain of the 1st Class on the 25th of April, 1866; and died in the camp at Milligen on the 14th of September, 1868.

On the 6th of December, 1860, Captain MacLeod was awarded the Honour Badge for long service as an officer in the navy of the Netherlands.[1]

Vice-Admiral Norman MacLeod,[2] son of Lieutenant-General Norman MacLeod and Jacomina Joanna Esser, was born at Bergen-op-Zoom, on the 18th of September, 1837. He entered the Royal Military Academy at Breda on the 1st of September, 1850; was appointed a midshipman of the First Class on the 1st of September, 1853; Lieutenant at sea of the Second Class on the 1st of January, 1856; Lieutenant at sea of the 1st Class on the 1st of July, 1866; Lieutenant-Captain at sea on the 16th of

---

[1] Dutch War Office Records.

[2] Not truer is the needle to the pole than the hearts of these gallant Gesto-Dutch MacLeods are to "the Island" of the Western Sea. This is shown by the following extract from a letter written by Admiral MacLeod to a relative (a lady) in Skye. He says:—"I cannot tell you how glad I am with this kind token of interest" [a letter] "from a relative, however unknown, in the dear little island which I have always considered as " my fatherland, although it is more than 150 years ago that my great-great-grandfather left it. If anything " can prove that 'blood is thicker than water,' I think this does."

Lieutenant-General MacLeod, writing to the same lady afterwards, says:—"I have not the pleasure of being " personally acquainted with you. I only know you by a letter which you had the kindness to write to my " son Norman, Captain [now Vice-Admiral] in the Royal Navy of the Netherlands. Your letter delighted me, " and struck me at once by your saying that your heart warmed at the name of MacLeod. So does mine " . . . . I have been to Scotland, but I fear I can never more see that country. I hope my sons will, and " that they and Donald, in proper time, will not fail to keep up the relations with the 'auld country.'"

November, 1875; Captain at sea on the 1st of June, 1882; Rear-Admiral on the 1st of May, 1890; and Vice-Admiral on the 10th of July, 1892.

On the 15th of September, 1853, Admiral MacLeod (then a midshipman) proceeded with the "Sea Hound" to the Mediterranean, where he remained from the 21st of March, 1855, to the 7th of December, 1859. From the 22nd of April, 1862, to the 28th of September, 1865, and from the 24th of March, 1872, to the 22nd of April, 1877, he served in the East Indies; and subsequently from the 22nd of July, 1882, to the 3rd of January, 1884. He afterwards held the important posts at home of Chief of the Department of Materiel, Superintendent[1] of Yards, and Director and Commandant of the Marine, with the command of the mouths of the Maas and other rivers; and, finally, Director and Commandant of the Marine at Amsterdam.

Admiral MacLeod's decorations and medals:—

He was appointed a Knight of the Order of the Oaken Crown on the 17th of July, 1882; awarded the Badge of Honour for important military services with the decoration "Atjeh, or Atcheen, 1873-75," and the Atjeh, or Atcheen, war medal; on the 18th of February, 1884, he was nominated a Knight of the Order of the Netherlands Lion; permission was granted to him to accept the Decorations of Knight of the Second Class, with the Star of the Crown of Prussia, on the 13th of November, 1891; on the 20th of October, 1892, he was created a Commander of the Order of Orange-Nassau; and he is entitled to wear the Badge of Honour for long service as an officer, with the Cypher XL. On the 1st of August, 1894, his name was placed on the Pension List; and at the same time thanks were tendered to him for the many good and important services which he had rendered to the State.[2]

Lieutenant-Colonel Edward Donald Henry MacLeod, son of Lieutenant-General Norman MacLeod and Jacomina Joanna Esser, was born on the 2nd of September, 1842, at Maastricht, Province of Limburg. He joined, as a volunteer, an instructional battalion on the 18th of August, 1858; was appointed Honorary Corporal on the 1st of March, 1859; transferred to the Regiment of Grenadiers and Riflemen on the 19th of August, 1859; made a Corporal on the 11th of October, 1859; Honorary Sergeant on the 1st April, and Sergeant on the 6th of October, 1860; Second Lieutenant in the 3rd Regiment of Infantry on the 23rd of December, 1862; First Lieutenant on the 30th of December, 1865; attached to the Battalion of Sappers and Miners from the 10th of April to the 6th of September, 1867; appointed Adjutant of a Battalion of Riflemen on the 17th of December, 1868; Captain of the Second Class on the 16th of July, 1868; ordered to join the Dutch Indian Army for five years from the 11th of November, 1884; arrived at Batavia on the 25th of October, 1885, but had to return home owing to ill-health in 1887;[3] appointed Major in the 4th Regiment of Infantry on the 2nd of September, 1890; Lieutenant-Colonel on the 24th of July, 1894; and transferred to the Regiment of Grenadiers and Riflemen on the 13th of September, 1895.

---

[1] Dutch Marine Department Records.   [2] Dutch Navy Records.
[3] Dutch War Office Records.

Decorations :—

Distinguished Service Badge, 6th December, 1878; created an officer of the Luxemburg Order of the Oaken Crown on the 12th of October, 1880; Medal of Honour for important military achievements in the military operations against Atjeh, or Atcheen, with the "Atjeh war medal, 1873-90"; and Cross of Honour of the Mecklenburg-Schwerin Order of the Griffin on the 15th of January, 1896.[1]

Major Rudolph MacLeod, son of Captain John Van Brienen MacLeod, Royal Navy of the Netherlands, and Dina Louisa, Baroness Sweerto de Landas, was born on the 1st of March, 1856, at Heukelom, South Holland. He joined an instructional battalion on the 15th of August, 1872; was appointed Honorary Corporal on the 1st of January, 1873; Honorary Sergeant on the 6th of March, 1874; Sergeant on the 21st of July, 1876; Second Lieutenant in the army in the East Indies on the 22nd of July, 1877; arrived at Batavia on the 27th of December, 1877, and was attached there successively to the 15th Battalion, 3rd Battalion, and the Garrison Battalion of Atjeh; promoted to the rank of First Lieutenant on the 16th of December, 1881, and, after serving in various battalions, was transferred as Adjutant to the 6th Battalion on the 11th of November, 1889; promoted to the rank of Captain on the 7th of April, 1892; and transferred to the Depôt of the 1st Battalion on the 9th of January, 1894.

In 1878, Captain MacLeod took part in the military operations in Toba, on the West Coast of Sumatra; and in the military operations against Atjeh, or Atcheen, in 1878-83 and 1890-92.[1] He was awarded the Badge of Honour,[2] for important military transactions, "1873-80, Atjeh"; and also the Badge of Honour for distinguished and long service as an officer.

NOTE.

Admiral Norman MacLeod, of the Royal Navy of the Netherlands, in a letter dated April 17th, 1898, says :—

"In this envelope I send you all the particulars about MacLeods that have served in Holland in the eighteenth century, at least as regards officers. There were also many non-commissioned officers and privates who are mentioned in the registers of the Scottish Church at Rotterdam, and many other Skyemen, of course; but I am sorry to say that I could not afford the time to investigate all that, even what I have collected has taken a good deal of time. I think the rest would be of little use, being only names without almost any possibility of tracing the men's descent."

The following names of officers and non-commissioned officers are taken from the list furnished by Admiral MacLeod; and, if these gallant men were not all Skyemen (for it seems to be impossible now to tell exactly whether they were or not), it is certain that they were Highlanders, hence they have been deemed worthy of mention in this place.

---

[1] Dutch War Office Records.

Sergeant-Major Daniel MacLeod was serving in 1702 in Colonel George Lauder's Regiment. At that time and in that service a sergeant-major was a staff officer, ranking next above a captain.

Captain John MacLeod was appointed a Lieutenant in Captain James Cunningham's company of Murray's Regiment; promoted to be a Captain-Lieutenant on the 1st of July, 1706; Captain in place of Andrew Munro, who had been killed in the trenches at Merin, and retired with a pension on the 17th of May, 1709.

Captain Angus MacLeod was received as a cadet into Portmore's Regiment, then commanded by Lieutenant-Colonel Hepburn. On the 10th of October, 1702, MacLeod was promoted to the rank of Ensign in Mowat's company; Lieutenant in Kennedy's Regiment on the 9th of August, 1708; Captain-Lieutenant in Keppel's Regiment on the 28th of November, 1709; and Captain in Douglas's Regiment on the 28th March, 1710, which appointment he held till the year 1717, when this and Wood's Corps were disbanded. He was married, and was living in London in 1729.

Lieutenant William MacLeod was appointed as an Ensign in Van Beest's company in Colyear's Regiment, and promoted to the rank of Lieutenant in the same company on the 28th of October, 1710.

Ensign Donald MacLeod entered Colyear's Regiment as a cadet, and was advanced to the rank of Ensign in the same corps on the 29th of January, 1711.

Ensign James MacLeod entered the service as a cadet in Cunningham's Regiment, was appointed as an Ensign in Captain Hugh MacKay's company on the 13th of August, 1731, and died in 1741.

Dr. William MacLeod was appointed surgeon in the 2nd Battalion of Marjoribanks' Regiment on the 5th of February, 1753.

Ensign John MacLeod was promoted from the rank of Sergeant to that of Ensign in the Regiment of Villegas (Captain MacKay's company) on the 11th of February, 1745, when twenty-four new companies were raised.

The following is an extract from the Church Registers in Rotterdam :—

On the 27th September, 1712, were married Duncan MacCloud, bachelor, son of the deceased Dugal MacCloud, from the Isle of Skie, and Elisabeth Jacobs Littlejohn, widow of the deceased William Forbes, Sergeant in Honeywood's Regt., who was killed at Douay, July 3rd, 1710.

Their children :—
        John, born Aug. 9th, 1713.
        Daniel, born Aug. 4th, 1715.
        Marion, born July 2nd, 1717.
        Matthew, born Feb. 9th, 1720.

THE MACLEODS OF ARNISDALE AND GLENDALE.

Major-General WILLIAM MACLEOD.
(From Mrs. D. Gordon.)

Major-General COLL MACLEOD.
(From his daughter, Mrs. D. Gordon.)

Lieutenant-Colonel WILLIAM MACLEOD.
(From Mrs. D. Gordon.)

Lieutenant COLL MACLEOD.

Major RODERICK MACLEOD OF BAILEMEANACH.
(From his great-great-grand-daughter, Mrs. MacRae, of Glasgow.)

On the 18th Dec., 1738, were married Daniel McLeod, son of Duncan and Helen Ross.

Their children:—

Daniel, baptized Sept. 17, 1738 (presented by Duncan MacLeod).
John, baptized Sept. 8th, 1741 (presented by John Ross).

THE MACLEODS OF MEIDLE, GLENDALE, DRYNOCH, BAILEMEANACH, VATTEN, ETC.

Tormod MacLeod,[1] the progenitor of the MacLeods of Meidle (Sliochd Iain 'Ic Thormoid) was killed at the head of his clan, when supporting Alexander, Lord of the Isles, in the battle which he and his followers fought against the forces of King James I. in Lochaber in 1429.

Two brothers of this family, William and Alexander, fell at the battle of Worcester in 1651, while (on the same occasion) a son of the latter—Alexander, a mere youth—was taken prisoner, but afterwards escaped.

Tormod MacLeod, III. of Glendale (a son of Alexander who escaped from the English prison after the battle of Worcester), having espoused the cause of James II., lost his life at the battle of the Boyne in 1690.

Colonel Norman MacLeod, IV. of Glendale, began his military career in the Spanish service, but joined the Jacobite rising of 1715, and was wounded at the battle of Sheriffmuir.

Colonel John MacLeod, V. of Glendale, served on the Continent under the Elector of Hesse-Cassel. One of his sons, Captain John MacLeod, of the Scots Brigade in Holland, was killed at the battle of Fontenoy in 1745, and another son—Captain William MacLeod, of the Black Watch—fell in a duel in Glasgow by the hands of a Colonel Beresford. Colonel MacLeod's grandson, Roderick, perished in the battle of Falkirk in 1746.

John MacLeod, VII. of Gendale, followed Prince Charlie in 1745, was wounded at the battle of Culloden, but afterwards received the Royal pardon, and emigrated to America, where he died. His son, Captain Kenneth MacLeod (of the British Army), was killed in the American War of Independence.[1]

Major-General William MacLeod, son of Donald MacLeod of Arnisdale, and grandson of Kenneth MacLeod of Scallasaig, fourth son of Tormod MacLeod, III. of Glendale, became an Ensign on the 21st of May, 1779; Lieutenant on the 21st of February, 1786; Captain on the 1st of June, 1786; Major on the 17th of June, 1800; Lieutenant-Colonel on the 21st of September, 1804; Colonel on the 4th of June, 1813; and Major-General on the 12th of August, 1819.[2] Young MacLeod arrived at Madras

---

[1] Mackenzie's "History of the MacLeods."   [2] War Office Records.

on the 17th January, 1780, and was appointed agent on the part of the East India Company for adjusting with Tippoo the boundaries of the two Powers on the Madras side. To show their appreciation of his services on that occasion the Court of Directors presented him with an additional allowance of money. The following extract is from a letter written by General Harris, and dated at Seringapatam on the 13th of May, 1799:—"Captain MacLeod, of the Intelligence Department, has been " employed in the management of the bazaars of the army, in the management " of the Brinjarries, and on a variety of services, not especially the duty of any " regularly-established officer, but which required a perfect knowledge of the customs of " India and the strictest integrity in the person charged with their execution. I have " on all such occasions given full confidence to Captain MacLeod, and his conduct has " shown him deserving of the trust." In a general order, dated 24th May, 1799, it is stated that "the Governor-General is also happy to concur in the honourable testimony " borne by the Commander-in-Chief to the merits of Captains Turing and MacLeod, " and directs that his thanks may be conveyed to those meritorious officers." Captain MacLeod was appointed Collector at Salem, Calcutta, on the 8th of August, 1799; and on the 13th of the same month the Government remarks regarding him " that this officer in the Intelligence Department with the army at Seringapatam " and in the management of the camp bazaar had manifested the strictest integrity and " a very extensive knowledge of the customs of India; and, the settlement of Salem " by him having been concluded, his zeal and able exertions are commended."[1] In a general order, dated 26th February, 1809, Lieutenant-Colonel MacLeod is mentioned favourably for the skill and gallantry displayed by him at Cotar and Magre Coil.

General MacLeod received the silver medal for his gallant services at Seringapatam. He died (unmarried) at Fulham on the 16th November, 1836.

Major-General Coll MacLeod,[1] son of Donald MacLeod of Arnisdale, and nephew of Major-General William MacLeod, was appointed Ensign on the 22nd of April, 1822; Lieutenant on the 1st of January, 1825; Captain on the 10th of February, 1827; Major on the 1st of March, 1851; Lieutenant-Colonel on the 1st of May, 1855; and in 1863 his name appeared on the list of retired officers as a Major-General.

Coll MacLeod arrived in India on the 6th of July, 1822, and on the 23rd of February, 1823, was posted to the 21st (now the 42nd) Native Infantry, of which regiment he was appointed Adjutant on the 17th of January, 1826.

In the inspection report of his corps, dated December, 1843, it is stated that " Captain MacLeod's conduct and character are strictly correct, and that he is well " acquainted with his duties, and performs them with zeal and ability." He was engaged in the operations on the Canton River; thanked for his services, and mentioned in despatches.[2] "Captains Stewart and MacLeod, commanding the flank " companies of the 42nd Madras Native Infantry, were frequently employed in the " more important operations, and evinced all the coolness and zeal which might be

---

[1] India Office Records.
[2] Major-General D'Aquilar's Despatch, "London Gazette," 25th June, 1847.

"expected from British officers." Having previously been favourably reported upon as a linguist, he was on the 7th April, 1849, appointed Quarter-Master and Interpreter to his corps. "His conduct and character unexceptionable. He is an intelligent and "zealous officer, and well acquainted with his military duties," according to the inspection report of his regiment, dated 31st January, 1851.

On the 9th of September, 1853, Major MacLeod was placed temporarily at the disposal of the Government of India with a view to his being employed as Commandant of the Koordah and Balasore Paik Companies.

On the 13th September, 1854, he was appointed to the charge of the bazaar and police at Jubbulpore, without prejudice to his regimental duties.[1] Major-General MacLeod died on the 20th of May, 1875.

Lieutenant Coll MacLeod, son of Major-General Coll MacLeod, was appointed Ensign in the 43rd Regiment on the 29th of March, 1861, and promoted to the rank of Lieutenant on the 30th of June, 1863. He died on service in New Zealand on the 26th of July, 1864.[2]

Lieutenant-Colonel William MacLeod, a son of Major John MacLeod, of the Royal Artillery, and a grandson of Kenneth MacLeod of Scallasaig, was appointed as an Ensign in the 59th Foot on the 29th of March, 1795; Lieutenant on the 31st of October, 1776; Captain on the 5th of December, 1781; Brevet-Major on the 1st of March, 1794; Major on the 1st of September, 1795; Lieutenant-Colonel, brevet, on the 1st of January, 1798; and Lieutenant-Colonel of his regiment on the 25th of November, 1799. Colonel MacLeod retired from the army by the sale of his commission on the 1st of October, 1803.[3]

On the 10th of July, 1795, the 59th Regiment embarked from England for the West Indies, and on the 30th of September landed on the Island of Saint Vincent.[2] On the morning of the 2nd of October an assault was made on a strong post occupied by the enemy. The regiment was ordered to attack in front at a point which proved to be inaccessible, and after holding its ground from daylight till dark it was directed by Major-General Peter Hunter to retire with the whole of the British troops forming the attack. At the same time the enemy retreated from their posts. In this affair the regiment sustained a loss of two captains, one sergeant, and fifteen men killed, and upwards of seventy officers, non-commissioned officers, and private soldiers wounded.

On the 4th of October the regiment advanced, along with the 40th and 54th Regiments, to a stronghold, called Mount Young, twenty miles from Kingston, and remained there over three months. At daybreak of the 8th of January, 1796, the enemy attacked on both flanks of the British front line, drove them back, and they formed behind the 59th Regiment. The whole line was then ordered to fall back by Major-General Stewart, who commanded. The 59th Foot had two officers, one sergeant, and

---

[1] India Office Records. [2] Regimental Depôt Records. [3] War Office Records.

nine private soldiers wounded in this affair. On the day following the regiment marched towards Kingston, and took up a position within a mile of that town. A short time after the enemy attacked the left flank of the 59th, but was repulsed, pursued, and the post, which he held previous to the attack, was taken by a part of the regiment under Major MacLeod. Sir Ralph Abercromby having arrived with troops from England, a general attack was made on the enemy's post on the Vega, in which the 59th took a prominent part. The assault was made in flank and rear; two redoubts were carried, and the remaining posts surrendered. The casualties of the 59th on that occasion were slight (one captain wounded, two men killed, and five wounded); but for its conspicuous gallantry it received the thanks (personally) of the Lieutenant-General Commanding. In July the 59th embarked for St. Kitt's, left four companies there, and the headquarters, with six companies, proceeded to Antigua.[1]

The regiment returned to England in June, 1802, and shortly after its arrival there the following letters were received from the Governor of Antigua, previous to which a sword of the value of 200 guineas had been presented by the House of Assembly of that Island to Lieutenant-Colonel MacLeod:—

" Sir, St. John's, 16th April, 1801.

" I have the happiness to receive the commands of the Assembly to convey to you and to the officers, non-commissioned officers, and privates of His Majesty's 59th Regiment the unanimous vote of thanks of that House for a service of the most distinguished good conduct that we have ever witnessed in any regiment that hath been stationed in this Island. It gives me particular pleasure to be thus employed on the present occasion," &c., &c., &c.

The resolution of the Assembly is as follows:—

"Resolved that the conduct of Lieutenant-Colonel MacLeod and the officers, non-commissioned officers, and privates of His Majesty's 59th Regiment has ever been such as to command our approbation . . . . and that, therefore, the thanks of this House be given to Lieutenant-Colonel MacLeod and the officers, non-commissioned officers, and privates of the 59th Regiment."[1]

A second letter, addressed to Colonel MacLeod, on the 14th of September, 1802, shows the continued interest of the Colony in the regiment. The letter says:—

" And we further entreat that you will have the goodness to express to the officers of the corps the hopes of the Council and Assembly that they will accept the sum of two hundred guineas, to be laid out by the Colony's Agent in London in the purchase of one or two pieces[2] of plate, to be made under the direction of the officers, with an appropriate inscription expressive of the grateful recollection which this Colony will ever entertain," &c.[1]

Referring to the 59th's recent services abroad, an official communication from the Horse Guards, dated the 5th of November, 1802, is full of the highest praise.

---

[1] Regimental Depôt Records.
[2] It may be mentioned that the pieces of plate referred to are not now in the possession of the regiment.

In the summer of 1803, the regiment had the good fortune of being in the brigade which was then under the command of Major-General (afterwards Lieutenant-General) Sir John Moore, at Shorncliffe.

The 59th Regiment owes most of its oldest records to Colonel William MacLeod, who replaced those extending from 1755 to 1782, the originals of which had been either lost or destroyed.

The date of Colonel MacLeod's death does not appear in the official records; but he was living on the 25th of July, 1825.[1]

Lieutenant-Colonel Alexander MacLeod, C.B., 59th Regiment, a son of Major John MacLeod, Royal Artillery, and a grandson of Kenneth MacLeod of Scallasaig, was gazetted as an Ensign on the 23rd of September, 1793; Lieutenant on the 19th of September, 1794; Captain on the 10th of November, 1796; Major on the 1st of October, 1803; Lieutenant-Colonel, brevet, on the 25th July, 1810; Lieutenant-Colonel of his regiment on the 13th of June, 1811; and Colonel, brevet, on the 12th of August, 1819.[2]

The 1st Battalion of the 59th Regiment arrived at Table Bay on the 4th of January, 1806, from England for service at the Cape of Good Hope.[1] On the morning of the 5th the light companies, under Major Alexander MacLeod, were ordered to land and cover the disembarkation of the troops, but owing to the heavy sea this proved to be impossible. The brigade, of which the 59th formed a part, landed on the 7th of January, and on the following day the regiment was ordered to take possession of the passes over the hills, which it did after a smart struggle. The enemy gave way on all sides and retreated towards Cape Town. The troops suffered much on that day from excessive heat and want of water, the ground over which they had marched being deep sand covered with short brushwood, which tore off their shoes and scratched their legs. The troops bivouacked that night near the Salt Pans and moved next morning on Cape Town. The enemy sent an officer with terms of capitulation, which were accepted by General Sir David Baird, who commanded the expedition, and the 59th Regiment was ordered to take possession of the lines and Fort De Knoke. The regiment was then sent in pursuit of General Jansen, the rebel Governor of Cape Town, but he surrendered with his troops to the British Government, and the 59th marched back to Cape Town, where it was publicly thanked by Sir David Baird for its services. The battalion then embarked for India, and arrived at Madras on the 23rd of April, 1806.

On the 20th of June 300 men were detached under Major MacLeod to Wallagabad. The detachment moved suddenly on the evening of the 8th of July to Vellore, where a shocking mutiny of native troops had taken place. The mutineers had murdered their officers and many men of the 69th Regiment who were stationed there. By forced marches the detachment, under Major MacLeod, reached Vellore on the 10th of July, but found that the 19th Dragoons had arrived from Arcot and had taken possession of the place and killed the mutineers.

---

[1] Regimental Depôt Records.   [2] War Office Records.

On the 16th of September, 1810, the 1st Battalion of the 59th Regiment embarked for Mauritius, where it arrived on the 29th of November, landed without opposition, marched eight miles, and halted for the night. The want of water, during the march and the night, was painfully experienced by all ranks, there being only one small well, which was soon emptied. The enemy was driven from a position three miles from Port Louis, and several guns were taken, but fire was opened from the town. Next day the town capitulated.

On the 22nd of December, 1810, the regiment embarked for Madras. On the 13th of April, 1811, it sailed from Madras, and arrived at Rendezvous Island, near the south end of Borneo, in July. On the 20th of the same month the army (four brigades), under Lieutenant-General Sir Samuel Achmuty, sailed for Java, and landed without opposition at Chilling Ching, ten miles from the town of Batavia, on the 4th of August. The 59th Regiment (now under the command of Lieutenant-Colonel MacLeod) took a prominent part, particularly the rifle and light companies, in the storming and capture of Wettevreden.[1] The enemy then retreated to a stronghold called Cornelis.

After several sorties by the enemy had taken place, Sir Samuel Achmuty decided to storm Cornelis. At one a.m., on the 26th of August, the troops commenced the assault, and, in spite of firm opposition, carried four redoubts. "An explosion of "gunpowder, near one of the batteries, took place, occasioning the loss of many men, "among whom were two officers and several men of the 59th. Immediately after "this the 59th Regiment was led to charge a battery of field pieces, which was posted "in front of the enemy's park of artillery. The regiment very gallantly advanced in "the face of a very destructive fire, the men being exposed down to their very feet "the whole time in advancing, and drove the enemy from their guns. The cool and "judicious manner in which Lieutenant-Colonel A. MacLeod led the regiment against "these guns was very conspicuous, and deservedly noticed in the General Orders and "report of the battle." The enemy were finally defeated with great slaughter, and fled, throwing away their arms, accoutrements, &c. The 59th lost on the 26th of August:—killed, seven officers, two sergeants, and forty-two rank and file; wounded, Lieutenant-Colonel MacLeod and nine other officers, three sergeants, and 111 men.[1]

The official report of Colonel Gillespie to the Adjutant-General, dated 27th August, 1811, says:—"The attack of the enemy's park of artillery was effected by "Lieutenant-Colonel MacLeod in a most masterly manner. . . . . "To Lieutenant-Colonel MacLeod of His Majesty's 59th Regiment, who so ably "conducted the attack already noticed, my warmest thanks are due."

In the General Orders issued by the Commander-in-Chief, a like congratulatory mention is made of Colonel MacLeod and his gallant corps.

On the reduction of the island gold medals were conferred by His Royal Highness the Prince Regent on Colonel Gibbs and Lieutenant-Colonel MacLeod (both of the 59th Regiment) for their distinguished services in Java.

---

[1] Regimental Depôt Records.

On the 20th of March, 1812, an expedition was sent from Java to Palambang in the Island of Sumatra, consisting of the flank companies of the 59th Regiment, five companies of the 89th Regiment, and detachments from other corps, under the command of Colonel Gillespie, Lieutenant-Colonel MacLeod being second in command.

Colonel Gillespie, in a letter to the Lieutenant-Governor of Java, dated 28th April, 1812, said:—"The military reputation and gallantry of Lieutenant-Colonel MacLeod "of His Majesty's 59th Regiment are already so well established that any panegyric "of mine would add little to the fame he has so justly earned. I shall, therefore, "content myself, on the present occasion, with returning him my very best thanks "for the activity, anxiety, and attention he has manifested during the progress of the "service."[1]

The troops sailed for Samarang, in Java, on the 16th of May, 1812. Lieutenant-Colonel Macleod was sent with the Grenadier Company to Saltija, and from thence with all available troops to Djokjokarta, the fortified capital of the Sultan of Mataram. On the 20th of May, before daylight, the attack was made, the columns being commanded by Lieutenant-Colonel MacLeod and Colonel Watson of the 14th Regiment. The ladders were placed against the curtain before daybreak, but ere the column of the 59th had ascended the ladders broke and became useless. The column under Colonel MacLeod then went to the principal gate (which was blown open by means of the guns), entered, and cleared the ramparts. The British force amounted to barely 1,000, of whom 100 men were killed or wounded, among the latter being Colonel Gillespie. The enemy were estimated at 15,000; 92 guns were taken. In the General Orders by Colonel Gillespie it is stated that "the prompt and decisive movement of "Lieutenant-Colonel MacLeod to force his passage to the Princes Gate to support "the leading columns was equally daring and meritorious."[1] A like statement appears in the General Orders of the Commander-in-Chief in India.

On the 13th of April, 1814, General Nightingale landed at Sourabaya, with Lieutenant-Colonel MacLeod and the light and rifle companies of the 59th Regiment, and a detachment of artillery. On being joined by the 78th Highlanders, the 59th and the 78th sailed to Poonarookan, a very safe harbour, nearly opposite the Island of Bali, called Boli-Sing. Operations were undertaken against the Rajahs of Bali-Boli-Sing and Boni, who had committed some acts of violence. The 59th, with Lieutenant-Colonel Macleod, had the bad luck, on the passage, to be on board a ship whose captain was very ignorant. From Sourabaya to Poonarookan the ship struck three times—once on a ledge of rock where it was in great danger; but she was got off.

The operations against the Rajah of Boli-Sing ceased without actual fighting. The Rajah of Boni, however, having refused the terms offered to him, General Nightingale gave orders for an attack. In consequence of the dispersion of the ships conveying the troops, and from other causes, the whole force under Lieutenant-Colonel MacLeod is said to have been only 600 men. He, however, put himself at the head of this small party and proceeded to attack the enemy,[1] who were posted behind strong stockades, and who were 4,000 to 4,500 in number, armed with muskets, blunderbusses, and

---

[1] Regimental Depôt Records.

spears. The enemy kept up a heavy fire, but were driven out, and the place was sacked, the palace being burned with immense quantities of valuables. The Rajah fled. The parole given on this occasion was "MacLeod," and the countersign was "Success." With regard to this affair a complimentary letter was addressed by General Nightingall, making particular reference to Lieutenant-Colonel MacLeod.

When the 59th Regiment returned from the Eastern expedition, the state of Colonel MacLeod's health obliged him to leave the country. A number of letters appear in the Regimental Records expressing great regret at the loss of Colonel MacLeod.

For distinguished conduct at the head of the 59th Regiment, Major-General Gibbs was created a Knight Commander of the Bath, and Lieutenant-Colonel MacLeod was on the same occasion (in the year 1815) appointed a Companion of the Order of the Bath.

"On the 12th of August, 1819, Lieutenant-Colonel MacLeod was promoted to the rank of Colonel by brevet of that date.

"On the 29th of March, 1821, Colonel Alexander MacLeod died at Dinapore, a loss to the King's service in India not to be repaired, and an event long and unfeignedly lamented by the 59th Regiment, at the head of which he had so long served with so much distinction."[1]

Lines on the death of Colonel Alexander MacLeod, C.B., of H.M. 59th Regiment. (From "The Calcutta Journal.")

> Hark! the deep muffled drum's low saddening sound,
> The soldiers' heavy footfall wends this way,
> With martial pomp they seek the sacred ground,
> Where they their honoured burden soon must lay.
>
> Halt! Soldiers, halt! Now the dull earth receives
> The cold remains of one beloved and brave,
> With tremulous hand and heart that inly grieves,
> They fire the volley o'er the soldier's grave.
>
> What virtue graced not thy heroic mind?
> In duty, just; in friendship, most sincere;
> Thy name shall leave a soothing charm behind
> To check the tears that friends shed o'er thy bier.
>
> "Son of the Valiant," though no more we view
> Thy manly form, yet shall thy honoured name
> Live in the memory of the brave and true,
> And dark Cornelis Fight record thy fame.
>
> . . . .
>
> Glory shall bind a wreath in days to come,
> And "Brave MacLeod" be sculptured on thy tomb.

---

[1] Regimental Depôt Records.

Superintending Surgeon Bannatyne William MacLeod, M.D., C.B., IX. of Glendale, third son of William MacLeod, VIII. of Glendale, was appointed Assistant Surgeon in the Bengal Medical Department on the 29th of September, 1815; Surgeon on the 5th of May, 1826; and Superintending Surgeon on the 10th of April, 1847. He died on the 3rd of October, 1856.

Dr. MacLeod was employed on miscellaneous duties from 1816 to 1832. He had the medical charge of the 3rd Light Cavalry from the 24th of September, 1832, to the 18th of August, 1843, except that, in 1840, he was temporary Superintending Surgeon to the Sirhind Division, and in 1842 Superintending Surgeon to the Army of Reserve. On the 16th of August, 1843, he was appointed Superintending Surgeon to the Sirhind Division, receiving, in addition, in the following year the medical charge of the Jail at Ferozepore. He was ordered to join the army of the Sutlej as Superintending Surgeon on the 29th of December, 1845; and in the same capacity he did duty in the Dacca Circle in 1847, in the Agra Circle in 1848, and in the Sirhind Circle in 1853.

Dr. MacLeod served in the Punjab Campaign as Superintending Surgeon of the army of the Sutlej; was present at the battle of Sobraon; mentioned in despatches; and created a Companion of the Bath.[2] Dr. MacLeod's only son was Colonel Harry John Bannatyne MacLeod, of the Royal Artillery, whose second son, Harry John MacLeod, was a Lieutenant in the 24th Regiment, or South Wales Borderers.[3]

Lieutenant Donald MacLeod, Royal Scots, was the fourth son of William MacLeod, VIII. of Glendale.

During the years 1815, 1816, and 1817, the Royal Scots (2nd Battalion) continued in the field, traversing the countries of Berar and Candish, at that time in a very unsettled state, and the regiment did not once during that period return to quarters.

The Battle of Mahidpore.

Negotiations were carried on with Holkar till the 19th of December, when the vakeels were dismissed. On the 20th the River Siepa and the enemy's position were reconnoitred, and the army advanced to Hernia preparatory to the attack of the enemy on the following day. On the 21st, half an hour before daybreak, the army was in motion. The banks of the river were 25 feet in height, and there was but one practicable ford. The enemy's line was about 800 yards from the left bank, to which it was nearly parallel.[4]

At twelve o'clock the army began to cross the river, and this was accomplished without any opposition on the part of the enemy, except a powerful cannonade that soon silenced and dismounted the guns of the Horse Artillery which protected the

---

[1] India Office Records.   [2] India Office Records and "London Gazette."
[3] Mackenzie's "History of the MacLeods."   [4] Regimental Depôt Records.

crossing, and which were too light to cope with the heavier pieces opposed to them A smooth glacis of about 700 yards now separated both armies. Sir John Malcolm's Division, led by the flank companies of the Royals, commenced the attack by a rapid and orderly advance on the ruined village which covered the enemy's centre, and the enemy's left was rapidly brought forward to enfilade the British movement. This desperate service was performed by the Royals with great determination. Many men were knocked down by a destructive fire of grape, but the remainder carried the village and the batteries at the point of the bayonet. The enemy's infantry were driven from their position, their artillerymen were cut down at their guns, and the enemy fled, pursued by Sir John Malcolm's Division.[1]

The enemy lost 3,000 men and 63 guns. The British loss was 778 killed and wounded, of these the flank companies of the Royal Scots lost nine killed (including Lieutenant Donald MacLeod) and thirty-three wounded.

The distinguished conduct of the Royal Scots is recorded in an Order by Lieutenant-General Sir Thomas Hislop, Bart., Commander-in-Chief of the Army of the Deccan, dated 23rd December, 1817 :—

"The undaunted heroism displayed by the flank companies of the Royal Scots in storming and carrying, at the point of the bayonet, the enemy's guns, on the right of Lieutenant-Colonel Scott's brigade, was worthy of the high name and reputation of that regiment. Lieutenant Donald MacLeod fell gloriously in the charge, and the conduct of Captains Hulme and MacGregor and every officer and man belonging to it entitles them to His Excellency's most favourable report and warmest commendation."[1]

Thus fell, in the hour of victory, a stalwart son[2] of Skye and a heroic soldier, whose early death was much lamented by his friends (in and out of the service) at the time, and was a great loss to the whole British army.

Major Roderick MacLeod, Bailemeanach, joined the Scots' Brigade in Holland as an Ensign in Captain Dundas's Company of Gordon's Regiment on February 6th, 1757; was promoted to the rank of a Lieutenant on the 3rd of January, 1763; Captain on the 9th of March, 1774; and his name appears in the Dutch Army List with the rank of Major from February, 1783, until 1787.[3]

About 1780, Major MacLeod married Miss Campbell, Ardnamurchan, with issue, several sons (all of whom were doctors, and died young) and a daughter, Margaret, who married MacLean of Ostal, in Skye, whose son was the Reverend Roderick MacLean, minister of South Uist, father of Mrs. Ann MacDonald, late of Eigg, and grandfather of the Reverend D. J. MacDonald, minister of Killean and Kilchenzie, in Argyllshire.

Captain Alexander MacLeod, Stein (a brother of Major Roderick MacLeod of Bailemeanach), was a man of uncommonly fine appearance. The jealousy of a doctor,

---

[1] Regimental Depôt Records.   [2] Lieutenant MacLeod was 6 feet 7 inches in height.
[3] Dutch War Office Records.

at that time resident in Skye, was aroused by the too ardent admiration of his wife for Captain MacLeod, who met his death under tragic circumstances. The story goes that a gentleman called on Captain MacLeod one day whom he asked to stay and dine with him. This his friend, for some reason, declined to do, and MacLeod replied that he felt less disappointed than he otherwise would because he himself was feeling unwell. Thereafter he sent to the doctor's house for medicine. It was brought, put into a cup, and he swallowed it. A little later he said :—" I am a dead man. I am poisoned." So it proved. He died that same night. The doctor's apprentice, who had supplied the medicine, fled to America. In view of the unhappy relations which existed between Captain MacLeod and the doctor, it was suspected that the poisoning was not accidental. The following lines are quoted from an elegy composed for him :—

" 'S ann a mhios gus a bho 'ndè.
Thug an t-eug air na Leodaich an sgrìob."

According to the notions of those days it was believed that his personal attractiveness was owing to " a beauty spot "—" ball seirce "—of which he was the lucky, or, as unfortunately it turned out, the unlucky possessor. At the time of his death he was engaged [1] to be married to Miss Helen MacLeod of Ose, about whom he composed a fine Gaelic song when he was serving with his regiment in foreign lands.

Donald Glas MacLeod, the founder of the Drynoch family (a notable warrior in his day), fell at Carinish, in North Uist, in the fight which took place there between the MacDonalds of Sleat and the MacLeods. His grandson, Alexander MacLeod, was present at the battle of Sheriffmuir, where he saved the life of the Glengarry of the time (Alasdair Dubh) when he was attacked by two English horsemen.[2]

Lieutenant-Colonel Norman Chester MacLeod, Bengal Engineers (son of Norman MacLeod, of the Bengal Civil Service, whose father was the Reverend Roderick MacLeod, D.D., Rector of St. Anne's Church, Soho, London, son of Tormod Mòr, IV. of Drynoch), was born at Calcutta. MacLeod joined the Military Seminary on the 2nd of February, 1830, passed his public examination on the 8th of December, 1831, on which date he received his commission as Second Lieutenant. He went to Chatham on the 2nd of February, 1832, where he remained for about a year. He arrived in India on the 17th of August, 1833, and on the 4th of the following October was directed to do duty with the sappers and miners at Delhi. On the 14th of March of the next year he was appointed to act as Assistant Engineer to the Delhi Division.[3]

In September, 1834, Lieutenant MacLeod applied for leave to join the force which was then assembling for active service, but his application was refused by the Board, as was also a similar application made by him in the following December,

---

[1] Miss Anne Nicolson, Stein, and Miss Helen MacLeod of Ose were first cousins. Miss Nicolson says that Captain MacLeod married Miss MacLeod, left the army, and took the farm of Vatten.
[2] Mackenzie's "History of the MacLeods."   [3] India Office Records.

on the ground that his services at Delhi could not be dispensed with. Regarding these services Captain De Bude, his senior officer on the station, reporting to Colonel Taylor, "Speaks in the highest terms of his assistants, Lieutenants Alcock and MacLeod"; and in another report MacLeod is spoken of as an officer "who is "likely to be a valuable acquisition to the Survey Department." On the 21st of September, 1838, Lieutenant MacLeod was placed at the disposal of the Commander-in-Chief,[1] and appointed to command a company of sappers and miners with the army of the Indus under the command of Sir John (afterwards Lord) Keane, from whose report announcing the capture by storm of the fortress of Ghuznee, on the 23rd of July, 1839, the following extract is taken :—

"Instead of the tedious process of breaching (for which we were ill prepared), "Captain Thompson undertook, with the assistance of Captain Peat, of the Bombay "Engineers, Lieutenants Durand and MacLeod, of the Bengal Engineers, and other "officers under him (Captain Thomson) to blow the Cabool Gate (the weakest point) "with gunpowder. A few minutes before three o'clock in the morning the explosion "took place and proved completely successful." And Sir John Keane added (in a General Order) that "in the execution Captain Thomson reported having been most ably "assisted by Captain Peat and Lieutenants Durand and MacLeod in the daring and "dangerous enterprise of laying down powder in the face of the enemy, and the strong "fire kept upon them, reflects the highest credit on their skill and cool courage, and "His Excellency begged that Captain Thomson and officers named would accept his "cordial thanks."

In a General Order, dated 19th November, 1839, Lieutenant MacLeod was thanked by Government for his services in Afghanistan on the return of a portion of the army of the Indus to the British provinces, and at the same time he received a share of the Ghuznee Prize. On the 3rd of June, 1840, he was appointed Executive Engineer in the Ramgurh Division Department of Public Works; and, on the 3rd of March of the following year, Assistant Secretary to the Military Board. On the 22nd of November, 1843, he received "the Ghuznee medal, 1839," for his services in Afghanistan.[1]

Lieutenant MacLeod was granted a furlough to Europe in December, 1843, and on his arrival in England was placed in charge of certain standard instruments belonging to the great Trigonometrical Survey. He was promoted to the rank of Captain on the 8th of December, 1846. In December, 1848, he returned to India, and was immediately appointed Executive Engineer to the Cuttack Division of the Department of Public Works. From this post he was transferred to act in a similar capacity at Midnapore and Culmeejole on the 1st of March, 1850, and shortly afterwards at Agra. "The energy and judgment evinced by him on discovering "the very unsatisfactory state of the Cuttack Division, and the measures adopted "by him on the occasion, were highly approved of." On the 29th April, 1856, he received the rank of Brevet-Major, was appointed Executive Engineer of the 1st Class

---

[1] India Office Records.

THE MACLEODS OF DRYNOCH.

Captain NORMAN MACLEOD (Drynoch).
(From Colonel Alexander MacDonald, Portree.)

Captain and Paymaster MARTIN MACLEOD (Drynoch).
(From Colonel Alexander MacDonald, Portree.)

Lieutenant DONALD MACDONALD MACLEOD (Drynoch).
(From Colonel Alexander MacDonald, Portree.)

Lieutenant-Colonel JAMES FARQUHARSON MACLEOD, C.M.G.
(Drynoch).
(From Colonel Alexander MacDonald, Portree.)

Lieutenant FORBES MACLEOD (Drynoch).
(From Colonel Alexander MacDonald Portree.)

to the Agra Division on the 19th of May, 1857; Military Secretary to the Lieutenant-Governor of the North-West Provinces on the 9th of June, 1857; promoted to the rank of Brevet Lieutenant-Colonel on the 5th of March, 1858; placed at the disposal of the Public Works Department on the 27th of August, 1858, and advanced to the rank of Lieutenant-Colonel on the 1st of January, 1859.[1] Colonel MacLeod retired from the army on the 1st of July, 1860, and died in 1875.

Two of his brothers were soldiers, viz., George, who was Field Engineer of the Scinde Field Force, and Major-General William Edmonstone MacLeod, of the Bombay army. Another brother, Arthur, served in the Royal Navy.[2]

Major Donald MacLeod (eldest son of Norman MacLeod, VII. of Drynoch, and last of Eileanriach, by his wife, Alexandrina, eldest daughter, by his third marriage, of the famous Donald MacLeod of Bernera) was present with his regiment (the 78th Highlanders) at the battle of Assaye, which, according to General Stewart of Garth, "was the most desperate and the best contested that ever was fought in India," and afterwards commanded the Grenadier company of his corps at the storming of Forts Cornelis and Terquata in Java, for which latter services he was favourably mentioned in Sir Samuel Achmuty's despatches. Major MacLeod married a daughter of Sir Berners Plaistow, of London, with issue, and died at Gravesend in 1824.[2]

Captain Norman MacLeod, 78th Highlanders (second son of Norman MacLeod, VII. of Drynoch, and last of Eileanriach, by his wife, Alexandrina MacLeod), was present at the taking of the Cape of Good Hope, at several actions in India, and at the capture of Java, where he died, unmarried, in 1814.[2]

Major Alexander MacLeod, of the 12th Regiment of Bengal Native Infantry (third son of Norman MacLeod, VII. of Drynoch, and last of Eileanriach, by his wife, Alexandrina MacLeod), commanded the Cuttack Legion, 10,000 strong of all arms, with which he saw much active service in India. As a volunteer he took part in the capture of Java, and subsequently resided for several years at Sourabaya and Bangi-Wangi.

Major MacLeod married Louisa, daughter of Henry Browne (Indian Civil Service), a cadet of the family of Oranmore and Browne, with issue, and died at Forres in 1828.[2]

Captain John MacLeod, 78th Highlanders (fourth son of Norman MacLeod, VII. of Drynoch, and last of Eileanriach, by his wife, Alexandrina MacLeod), served with his regiment in Java, Bengal, and Ceylon, and also with the Royal Scots at Flushing. He died on his way home from Ceylon.[2]

Captain and Paymaster Martin MacLeod (fifth son of Norman MacLeod, VII. of Drynoch, and last of Eileanriach, by his wife, Alexandrina MacLeod) was appointed Ensign in the 27th Foot on the 8th of October, 1812; Lieutenant on the 18th of

---

[1] India Office Records. [2] Mackenzie's "History of the MacLeods."

January, 1815; placed on half-pay on the 25th of March, 1816; transferred to the 79th Highlanders on the 18th of April, 1816; put on half-pay on the 25th of March, 1817; removed to the 25th Foot on the 21st of May, 1818; acted as Adjutant of the same regiment from the 22nd of June, 1820, to the 5th of November, 1823, when he was removed on half-pay to the 22nd Dragoons; was appointed Paymaster of the 25th Foot on the 15th of January, 1824; and placed on half-pay on the 15th of January, 1830.

Martin MacLeod was present with the 27th Regiment at the battles of Nivelle, Nive, Orthes, and Toulouse, for which he received a silver medal with four clasps.[1]

Captain MacLeod married Miss Jane Fry, of Frybrook, County Roscommon, Ireland, with issue. He emigrated to Canada in 1845, and settled near Toronto at a place which he called Drynoch (after the old home in Skye), and there he died on the 18th of December, 1863.

Midshipman Roderick William Keir MacLeod, of the frigate "Belvidere" (sixth son of Norman MacLeod, VII. of Drynoch, and last of Eileanriach, by his wife, Alexandrina MacLeod), was on board his ship on the North American Station in 1812 when she was attacked by the Americans, and received an injury from a part of the falling rigging, from the effects of which he died soon afterwards at Killiegray.[2]

Lieutenant Donald MacDonald MacLeod, 50th Regiment, Madras Native Infantry (seventh son of Norman MacLeod, VII. of Drynoch, and last of Eileanriach by his wife, Alexandrina MacLeod), died, unmarried, at Drynoch, in 1837.[2]

Lieutenant Forbes Brodie MacLeod, 12th Regiment, Madras Native Infantry (ninth son of Norman MacLeod, VII. of Drynoch, and last of Eileanriach, by his wife, Alexandrina MacLeod), died, unmarried, in Madras, in 1828.[2]

Lieutenant-Colonel James Farquharson MacLeod, C.M.G., third son of Captain and Paymaster Martin MacLeod of Drynoch, was born in 1835 at Drynoch, in the Isle of Skye. In 1854, Mr. MacLeod graduated at the Toronto University, with the degree of Bachelor of Arts, and was in due course called to the Bar in 1860. But the military instinct was strong in MacLeod, and, his services having been accepted, he acted as a Brigade-Major under Sir Garnet (now Lord) Wolseley, in the Red River Expedition of 1870. In recognition of the satisfactory manner in which he had performed the duties of his post, he was made a Companion of the Order of St. Michael and St. George. In 1873 he joined the North-West Mounted Police Force which had just been organised, and was appointed Assistant Commissioner in 1874. It was in this year that the force penetrated into the Indian country, and by means of it Colonel MacLeod "saved the situation" at a very critical period. Commissioner French, having retired to Fort Ellis, Colonel MacLeod remained, occupied MacLeod and Calgary, obtained the confidence of the Indians[3] (which he never afterwards lost),

---

[1] War Office Records. Regimental Depôt Records. Mackenzie's "History of the MacLeods."
[2] Mackenzie's "History of the MacLeods." [3] "The Lethbridge News."

put down the whisky traffic (then threatening to assume serious proportions), and was publicly thanked in Parliament for his services. In 1877, Colonel MacLeod was appointed to the Commissionership, and in this position concluded the important treaty with the Blackfeet Indians, which is still in force. In 1880, the powers of a stipendiary magistrate were conferred upon him; and he was created a Puisne Judge of the Supreme Court of the North-West Territory in 1887, which position he filled up to the time of his death, which took place in September, 1894.

Colonel MacLeod was buried at Calgary with full military honours. Among those present were many ex-mounted policemen of the first Red River Expedition, who had gathered from every quarter to do honour to a former chief. At the conclusion of the ceremony the bugles blew the North-West Mounted Police call, followed by " Lights out " ; and, as the crowd dispersed, many a one felt that another worthy soldier had " passed beyond the shadows."[1]

Colonel MacLeod's sound judgment, knowledge of affairs, and uncompromising integrity placed him prominently among the leading men of the North-West, and his death was the subject of universal regret throughout the territories.

The history of the MacLeod District, of which Lethbridge District was formerly a part, practically commenced when Colonel MacLeod and the Mounted Police, after their celebrated expedition to Fort Whoop-Up, established the town on the banks of the Old Man's River, which was named MacLeod after him. From that old town, whose existence ceased about ten years before MacLeod's death, he removed to Pincher Creek, where he continued to reside after his connection with the police was severed until he was required by Government a few years ago to take up his residence in the present town of MacLeod, which occupies a site a little further up the river than its predecessor. His tact and kindly feelings endeared Colonel MacLeod to all his acquaintances, and not only was it among civilised races that this was evidenced, but also among the Indians of the district with whom he was probably the first Government official to come in contact, and over whom he exercised an influence for good that no other white man has ever yet acquired. The old members of the police force who came into the country under his command were unswerving in their attachment to their old Colonel; and his memory is still green in the force although many changes have been made in it, and several Commissioners have commanded it since he exchanged the saddle for the bench. "Few of those who pass away from this world leave such " kindly and warm memories as Judge MacLeod has done, and his widow and children " will have the sympathy of every one in this district for the loss which they have " sustained."[1]

THE MACLEODS OF TALISKER, BERNERA, HAMER, GRISHORNISH, ULINISH, DALVEY, AND ORBOST.

Sir Roderick MacLeod (second son of the famous Rory Mòr, XIII. MacLeod, by his wife, Isabel, daughter of Donald MacDonald, VIII. of Glengarry) was the founder

---

[1] "The Lethbridge News."

of the house of Talisker. He and his brother, Sir Norman MacLeod, I. of Bernera, raised a regiment of 1,000 men, at the head of which they fought at the battle of Worcester, on the side of King Charles II., in 1651, where the MacLeods, fighting with desperate valour, were almost annihilated. Both brothers escaped with their lives, however, and after the Restoration had the honour of knighthood conferred upon them, the only reward which "the Merry Monarch" was able or willing to give to them.

Principal Roderick MacLeod, third son of Donald MacLeod, III. of Talisker, had two sons in the Indian Army, viz., Captain Donald MacLeod, of the Bengal Artillery, who died at sea, off Mauritius, on his way home; and Captain John MacLeod, who served for a time as Aide-de-Camp and Persian Interpreter to the Honourable Mount Stuart Elphinstone, Governor of Bombay, and afterwards acted as Resident and Political Agent at Bushire, where he died, unmarried, in 1824.[1]

Major-General Roderick Bannatyne MacLeod (son of Dr. Roderick MacLeod of London, and grandson of Principal MacLeod of Aberdeen) served for many years in the 21st Hussars, of which he became Lieutenant-Colonel. He died in 1881.

Captain Roderick William MacLeod, of the 29th Punjab Native Infantry and of the Bengal Staff Corps, was a son of Major-General Roderick Bannatyne MacLeod.

Dr. Hugh MacPherson, Sub-Principal and Professor of Greek in King's College, Aberdeen, married Christina, daughter of Principal Roderick MacLeod, and by her had six sons—three of whom were soldiers of high rank, viz., Dr. John MacPherson, Dr. Hugh Martin MacPherson, Inspectors-General of Hospitals, and Major-General Roderick Donald MacPherson—and seven daughters, two of whom became the wives of soldiers—Jessie, wife of Colonel James Young, and Lucy Jane, wife of Lieutenant-General J. J. MacLeod Innes, V.C.

Principal MacLeod's daughter, Isabella, married Colonel Arthur Forbes, of the Craigievar family.[2]

Colonel John MacLeod, IV. of Talisker, after having served in one of the Independent Companies raised by his Chief in 1745, in support of the Government, joined the Scots Brigade in Holland, and served with much distinction, under Prince Ferdinand, in Germany. He was appointed a Captain in Lord Drumlanrig's regiment on the 2nd of June, 1747; Major in the 1st Battalion of Gordon's Regiment on the 6th of February, 1751; and Lieutenant-Colonel in the 2nd Battalion of the same regiment on the 18th of March, 1766. Colonel MacLeod's name continued in the Army List till 1794.[2]

It was remarked of him and of the other gentlemen who accompanied him from Skye to join the Scots Brigade in Holland that they "were particularly successful,"

---

[1] Mackenzie's "History of the MacLeods."   [2] Dutch War Office Records.

and that "they always found a ready supply of young soldiers" from their native island.

At the close of his active service on the Continent, Colonel MacLeod returned to Talisker, where he spent the rest of his days, and there he entertained Dr. Johnson and Mr. Boswell in 1773. Dr. Johnson afterwards wrote from Ostaig: "We passed "two days at Talisker very happily, both by the pleasantness of the place, and the "elegance of our reception."

Colonel MacLeod was married twice, but left no surviving issue. He died at Talisker on the 14th of July, 1798, in the eightieth year of his age.[1]

Lieutenant-Colonel Magnus MacLeod, of Claigean and V. of Talisker, second son of Donald MacLeod, III. of Talisker, succeeded his brother, Colonel John MacLeod, who, as we have just seen, died without surviving issue. Colonel Magnus MacLeod served in Campbell's Highlanders on the continent.

Colonel MacLeod's wife was Margaret Isabella, daughter of MacDonald of Skerrinish, and their two sons adopted the profession of arms, viz., Major Donald MacLeod, VI. of Talisker, who emigrated to Tasmania about 1821, and Colonel Alexander MacLeod, of the Madras Army.

It is said that the lady before their marriage composed a beautiful Gaelic song in honour of her lover. Colonel MacLeod (so the story goes) had been paying Miss MacDonald a good deal of attention for a time, but latterly had shown some coldness towards her. The lady's father gave a ball, to which all the gentlemen of the island were invited. Colonel MacLeod was one of the party, and during an interval in the dancing Miss MacDonald sang her song. That settled the love affair, and the marriage took place soon afterwards.

Captain Norman MacLeod, fourth son of Donald MacLeod, III. of Talisker, served in North America, where he became one of the superintendents of the American Indians.

As may be remembered, we mentioned, when showing the origin of the house of Talisker, that Rory Mòr of Dunvegan's second and third sons were knighted for their gallant services in the Royal cause at the battle of Worcester.

Sir Norman MacLeod, I. of Bernera,[2] "a distinguished Cavalier,"[3] was the third son of Rory Mòr, XIII. Chief, by his wife, Isabel, daughter of Donald MacDonald,

---

[1] "The Edinburgh Magazine."

[2] In 1741, Lieutenant Norman MacLeod registered arms in the Lyon Office, Edinburgh. He is described as "a Lieutenant in Colonel Lamy's Regiment of Foot, in the service of the States-General of the United "Provinces, and eldest lawful son of the deceased Norman MacLeod, Captain in the said regiment when "commanded by Colonel Æneas MacKay, by Alegond Van Brae, his spouse, of a good family in the Province "of Guelderland, which Captain Norman MacLeod was second lawful son of Sir Norman MacLeod of "Berneray, of his second marriage by Dame Katherine MacDonald, daughter to Sir James MacDonald, of "Sleate, Baronet, Chief of the Clan MacDonald, &c."

[3] Mackenzie's "History of the MacLeods."

VIII. of Glengarry. Bernera was taken prisoner at Worcester, and brought to trial, after eighteen months' confinement in jail. He, however, managed to escape out of the hands of his enemies, and to make his way to the Island of Skye, where, of course, he was safe from further molestation by the Ironsides of Cromwell.

William MacLeod, third son of John MacLeod, II. of Bernera and I. of Contullich, had a son in the Dutch service. Probably it was he who joined Murray's Regiment as Ensign on the 12th July, 1712; was appointed Lieutenant on the 23rd of March, 1719; and who served afterwards in Cunningham's regiment at Tournay in 1720, and at Namur in 1723. His name does not appear in the Army List of 1725. This Lieutenant MacLeod married on January 17th, 1717, at Ypre, Antoinetta, daughter of a Lieutenant Stevenson, and they had two sons—John, baptized at Ypre, 22nd November, 1717, and Alexander, baptized at Tournay, 13th October, 1719.

The famous Donald MacLeod of Bernera, "The Old Trojan" (fifth son of John MacLeod, II. of Bernera and I. of Contullich, and therefore, a grandson of Sir Norman MacLeod,[1] I. of Bernera, third son of Rory Mòr, XIII. Chief), was born in 1693.

Donald MacLeod was a staunch Jacobite, and fought for the Stuarts in three pitched battles, viz., at Sheriffmuir, Falkirk, and Culloden.

In 1745, when asked by his Chief (who supported the Government) to attend at Dunvegan on a certain day with the Bernera men, Donald replied:—" I place at your " disposal the twenty men of your tribe who are under my immediate command, and " in any other quarrel would not fail to be at their head, but in the present I must go " where a more imperious duty calls me."[2] "The Old Trojan," accordingly, joined the Highland army, and at the battle of Falkirk "he vanquished a dragoon, hand to hand." After "the dark day of Culloden," Donald was obliged to keep in close hiding until the Act of Indemnity made him once more a free man. In his fugitive days many were the attempts made to capture him, and in this work none of his pursuers was more active than his own son, Norman, who commanded one of the Independent companies in the interests of the reigning dynasty; but, needless to say, the old warrior was never caught.

" Donald MacLeod was married three times, and so numerous were his descendants " that they were known as 'the Bernera tribe.' "[2] His first wife (by whom he had twenty of a family) was Anne, daughter of Roderick MacLeod, XVII. Chief, and his wife, Isabel, daughter of Kenneth MacKenzie, third Earl of Seaforth; his second wife (by whom he had no children) "was a daughter of John MacDonald Gorm of Sleat"; and, when in his seventy-fifth year, he married Margaret,[3] daughter of the Reverend

---

[1] Captain Donald MacDonald, the gallant and accomplished officer who, while leading the successful assault on the stronghold of Quebec in 1759, was able, by his knowledge of the French language, to deceive the French sentinels, and who gloriously fell before that fortress in the following year, was the second son of the Clanranald of the '45, and a great-grandson of Sir Norman MacLeod of Bernera.

[2] Mackenzie's "History of the MacLeods."

[3] At this marriage "the best man" was the bridegroom's grandson, Sir John MacPherson, Baronet, son of the eminent Celtic and classical scholar and writer, the Reverend Doctor John MacPherson, minister of Sleat, whose wife was Janet, daughter of Donald MacLeod.

THE MACLEODS OF BERNERA AND UNISH.

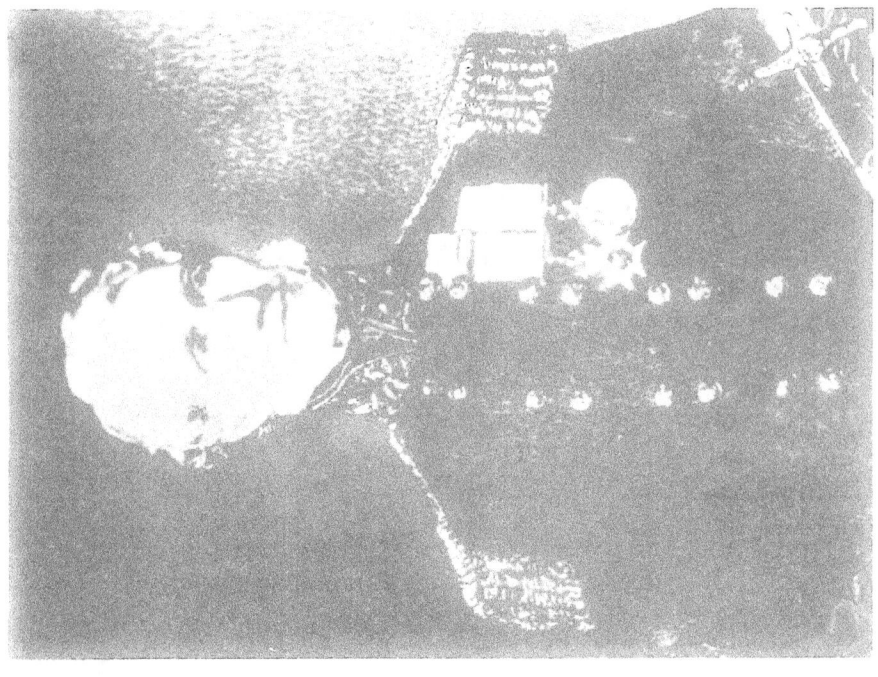

Lieutenant-General Sir CHARLES MACLEOD, K.C.B.
(From Colonel Alexander MacDonald, Portree.)

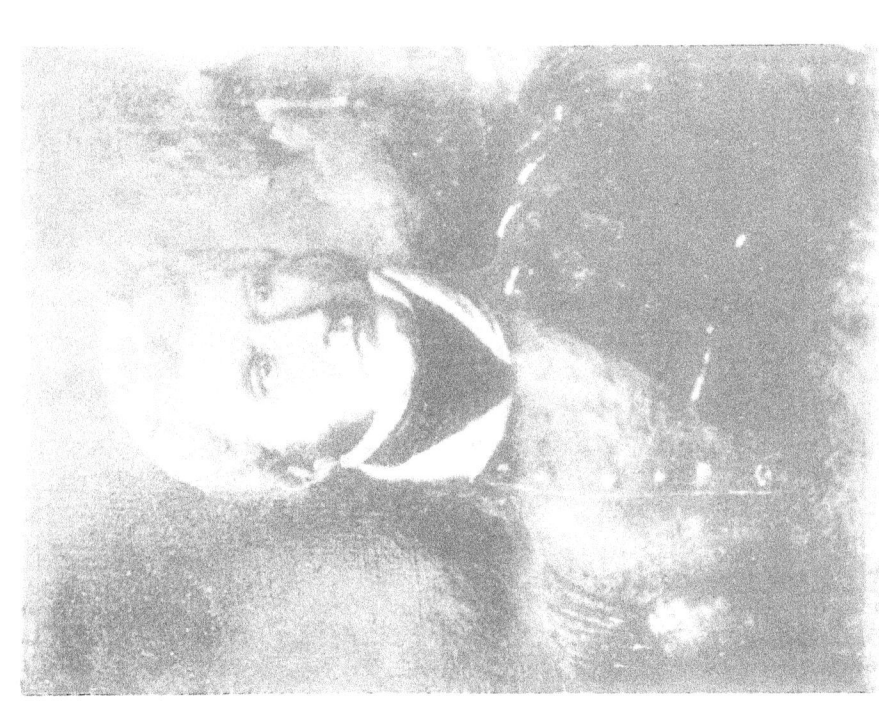

Lieutenant-General Sir JOHN MACLEOD, C.B., K.C.H.
(From Colonel Alexander MacDonald, Portree.)

Donald MacLeod, III. of Grishornish, minister of Duirinish (a young lady of sixteen), with issue, three sons and six daughters.

Donald MacLeod died (at the age of ninety) in 1783, and was buried in the churchyard of Rodel in Harris, the inscription on his tombstone bearing that " in vigour of " body and mind, and in firm adherence to the principles of his ancestors, he resembled " the men of former times."

Lieutenant-General Sir John MacLeod, C.B., K.C.H. (eldest son of the famous Donald MacLeod of Bernera by his third wife, Margaret MacLeod of Grishornish), was born at Unish, Ardmore, Isle of Skye, on the 9th January, 1766, and (because of his birthplace) was known in his native place as " Seochd Unuish." He was appointed Ensign in the 78th Foot on the 9th of March, 1793 ; Lieutenant on the 2nd May, 1794 ; Captain on the 24th of June, 1795 ; Major in the Princess Charlotte of Wales's Fencible Regiment on the 9th of June, 1799 ; Major, half-pay, on the 25th June, 1802 ; Major in the 5th Garrison Battalion on the 14th of September, 1804 ; Major in the 56th Foot on the 21st of February, 1805 ; Brevet-Lieutenant-Colonel on the 1st of January, 1805 ; Lieutenant-Colonel of the 9th Garrison Battalion on the 5th of May, 1808 ; Lieutenant-Colonel of the 78th Foot on the 12th of May, 1808 ; Brevet-Colonel on the 4th of June, 1813 ; Major-General on the 12th of August, 1819 ; Lieutenant-General on the 10th of January, 1837 ; and Colonel of the 77th Foot on the 17th of February, 1840.[1]

In 1794, Lieutenant John MacLeod served in Holland under the Duke of York ; was present in the attack and at the taking of Fort St. Andre ; at the bombardment and sortie of Nimeguen, as well as at the attack and defeat of the enemy at Beirren-Mansel, Gilder-Mansel, and Thuil.

Colonel MacLeod commanded the Brigade (consisting of the 25th (2nd Battalion), 33rd, 56th, and 78th Regiments) which carried the village of Merxem [2] on the 14th of January, 1814, where he was severely wounded.[1]

Sir John MacLeod was particularly successful in recruiting in the Highlands. He had brought 600 gallant men to the colours of the 78th Regiment [2] when the 2nd Battalion was raised by himself and Lord Seaforth.

For his gallant services to his country he was created a Companion of the Bath and a Knight of the Hanoverian Order of the Guelphs.

Sir John MacLeod married a daughter of Colonel Finlayson, with issue, one son, Major Donald John MacLeod, of the Scots Greys—who died just as the regiment was embarking for the Crimea[3]—and two daughters, Bessie, afterwards Mrs. Collins, and Margaret, afterwards Mrs. Cumberland.

Sir John died in London on the 3rd of April, 1851.

---

[1] War Office Records.

[2] It was here that the 78th Highlanders, not quite 300 strong, put to flight upwards of 3,000 Frenchmen ; and Piper Munro, of the same regiment (who was wounded and unable to stand), " sat where he fell and " played ' Johnnie Cope ' and ' The Highland Laddie ' with the spirit of a true Caledonian."

[3] Surgeon-General MacLean's " Memories of a Long Life."

Lieutenant-General Sir Charles MacLeod, K.C.B., Indian Army ("Tearlach Unuish," as he was known in Skye), third son of the famous Donald MacLeod of Bernera and his wife, Margaret MacLeod of Grishornish, was born at Unish, Ardmore, in the Isle of Skye.

Charles MacLeod was appointed Ensign on the 12th of January, 1796; Lieutenant on the 1st of June, 1796; Captain on the 24th of June, 1803; Major on the 4th of June, 1814; Lieutenant-Colonel on the 13th of July, 1821; Colonel on the 5th of June, 1829; Major-General on the 28th of June, 1838; and subsequently Lieutenant-General.

MacLeod landed at Madras on the 5th of January, 1797, and was present at the storming of Seringapatam, for which he received a medal. On the 13th of November, 1804, Captain MacLeod was posted to the 11th Native Infantry Regiment; transferred on the 13th November, 1804, to the 2nd Battalion Native Infantry, and on the 14th May, 1805, was appointed Deputy-Quarter-Master-General to Nizam's Subsidiary Force. On the 1st April, 1815, Major MacLeod was ordered to command the Right Brigade of the Hyderabad Subsidiary Force in Berar. Brigadier-General Doveton, in a report dated 19th December, 1817, said :—"I am quite at a loss "to express how much I feel myself indebted to Major MacLeod, Deputy-Quarter-"Master-General, and to the officers of the General Staff, &c., in the battle of "Nagpore." A return dated 19th to 24th December, 1817, shows that Major MacLeod was wounded at the unsuccessful attack on Nagpore. He is, however, mentioned as having afterwards shared the prize for the capture of that place in 1817, and also that captured in the wars against the Pindarries and certain of the Mahratta States in 1817-18. MacLeod was wounded at the capture of the Pettah of Asserghwe; and in an official letter from Brigadier-General Sir John Doveton,[1] dated 19th March, 1819, he was noticed for "his distinguished merits and services in the attack and capture of the Pettah of Asseer." Lieutenant-Colonel MacLeod was announced as a Companion of the Bath in the "London Gazette" of 26th July, 1823. On the 20th January, 1829, he was appointed to the command of the Field Force in Dooab. In a General Order dated 8th March, 1831, "the Commander-in-Chief gladly avails "himself of the opportunity afforded him by Colonel Charles MacLeod, C.B., having "obtained the permission of Government to return to Europe, thus to record publicly "in General Orders to the army the high sense he entertains of the gallantry, zeal, and "ability which have distinguished that officer during a protracted and honourable "career of nearly thirty-five years of uninterrupted service."[1]

The following extracts from an obituary notice of Sir Charles MacLeod have been furnished by his nephew, Surgeon-General W. C. MacLean, C.B. :—"The remains of a "distinguished Indian officer were on Saturday last consigned to the tomb, amidst "a group of sorrowing relations, friends, and brother officers. The late Lieutenant-"General Sir Charles MacLeod entered the Madras army nearly sixty years ago. He "served with distinction in the Mysore Campaign of 1799 under Lord Harris, and in

---

[1] India Office Records.

"the Mahratta Campaign of 1803-4 under the Duke of Wellington (then Major-
"General Wellesley), with whom he was present at the battle of Argaum. He also
"bore a part with conspicuous merit in the Mahratta War of 1817-18 under Sir John
"Doveton .... and particularly distinguished himself at the battle of Nagpore.
"His professional abilities were considered by good judges to have been of a very high
"class. It is certain that he possessed, in an eminent degree, those qualities and
"virtues which are best fitted to adorn the character of a soldier and a gentleman.
"Brave, frank, gentle, generous, of high and spotless honour, and at the same time of
"a nature singularly disinterested and unassuming, he was the most noble-minded of
"men. His looks and figure, his air and manner, were in harmony with his soul and
"character. In the prime of life he was strikingly handsome, and even to the last he
"continued to be a fine-looking man."[1] Donald MacLeod's second sons—by his first
and third marriages, of course—each commanded an East Indiaman.

Alexander MacLeod, VIII. of Bernera, had two sons, both of whom were killed in the Indian Mutiny, without issue, and with them the male line of the MacLeods of Bernera became extinct.[2]

General Sir Alexander MacLeod, Knight and C.B., Bengal Artillery (youngest son of Alexander MacLeod, II. of Luskintyre, whose father, William MacLeod, I. of that house, was a son of Sir Norman MacLeod, I. of Bernera), was born on the 9th of January, 1766.

Having received his commission, Alexander MacLeod set out for India, arriving there on the 27th of September, 1783. He was promoted to the rank of Lieutenant on the 7th of April, 1793; to that of Captain on the 8th of January, 1798; Major on the 25th of July, 1810; Lieutenant-Colonel on the 15th of February, 1818; Colonel on the 5th of June, 1829; and Brigadier-General on the 3rd of December, 1825.

He held the appointment of Adjutant and Quarter-Master of the 3rd Battery of Artillery from 1797 to 1800, and that of Adjutant from 1801 to 1805.

With regard to the manner in which the duties of this post were discharged, Major-General Cameron, the Inspecting Officer, in a General Order dated 9th May, 1804 (and endorsed by the Governor-General), observes:—"The progress of the
"recruits lately joined is a proof of the assiduity and attention paid by Adjutant
"MacLeod and the drill staff under his direction."

Captain MacLeod was appointed Brigade-Major to Colonel Harford, commanding the reserve in the field, on the 26th of October, 1807. He was directed to proceed from Rewarree, and to command the Artillery at Kurnaul on the 16th of May, 1812.[3]

---

[1] Surgeon-General MacLean says that often, when walking along the streets of London with his uncle, people used to turn round to look at the handsome Skye soldier. Sir Charles MacLeod married a Miss Chinnery, but left no issue.

[2] Mackenzie's "History of the MacLeods."

[3] India Office Records.

Major MacLeod was appointed to the command of the Artillery of the 3rd Division of the Army, for service against Nepaul, on the 15th November, 1814; thanked for his services at the siege of Nalaghur in the detachment orders issued by Brigadier-General Ochterlony on the 15th November, 1814; and also by the Commander-in-Chief through the Adjutant-General's letter in the "London Gazette," dated the 18th of November, 1814.

On the surrender of the Umr Sing Thappa, &c., the Governor-General (in a General Order of date the 21st of May, 1815) "professes his earnest sense of the "meritorious conduct exhibited by Major MacLeod commanding the Artillery."

Colonel MacLeod was made a Companion of the Bath on the 3rd February, 1817, and Brigadier-General Doveton (in a despatch dated the 19th of December following) noticed his good conduct in the action with the Rajah of Berar's troops, as did also the Governor-General, in a General Order dated the 26th September, 1818; MacLeod at the same time sharing the Deccan prize money as a Major-General of Artillery.

Lieutenant-Colonel MacLeod was ordered to proceed on duty to the Presidency on the 27th of September, 1823; was appointed Commandant of Artillery there on the 12th of December, 1823; and to a seat on the Military Board on the 2nd of January, 1824. On the 3rd of December, 1825, he received the general command of the Artillery assembled for service before Bhurtpore, with the rank of a Brigadier-General of the First Class; and the Commander-in-Chief in a General Order, dated 19th January, 1826, reported that he was "greatly indebted to General MacLeod for his "highly creditable exertions in the assault and capture of Bhurtpore," and recommended that "some distinction might be conferred on him for his services to, and at, the assault."[1]

General MacLeod received a Brigadier-General's share of the Bhurtpore prize money, and was thanked by the Governor-General for his "zeal, courage, science, and "patient endurance of fatigue at Bhurtpore." It may be mentioned, in passing, that it was at his suggestion that the famous Laboratory School at Dum Dum (which is now associated in the public mind with the rifle bullet of the same name) was established—under sanction of the Court of Directors—on the 30th of April, 1828. In a General Order dated 17th of February, 1827, General MacLeod was thanked by the Commander-in-Chief " for his zeal as shown in the discipline of the Artillery"; and in the following year he was knighted for his excellent services at the head of the Artillery Department at Bhurtpore.[1]

On the 6th of March, 1830, Sir Alexander MacLeod received the thanks of the Commander-in-Chief "for his attention to the discipline of the Artillery; and the "Court of Directors considered his suggestions for protecting the native inhabitants in "the vicinity of Dum Dum from violence on the part of the European soldiers to be "very judicious."

General Sir Alexander MacLeod died at Dum Dum on the 20th of August, 1831.[1]

---

[1] India Office Records.

THE CAMPBELLS OF STROND AND MACLEANS OF BORERAY.

Colonel CHARLES CAMPBELL OF STROND.
(From Colonel Alexander MacDonald, Portree.)

Lieutenant DONALD CAMPBELL, Royal Navy.
(From Colonel Alexander MacDonald, Portree.)

Surgeon-General WILLIAM CAMPBELL MACLEAN, C.B., &c., &c.
(By kind permission, from his own "Memories of a Long Life.")

THE CAMPBELLS OF STROND.

Colonel Charles Campbell, of the 39th Regiment, was a son of Kenneth Campbell of Strond, in Harris, and Ann, daughter of the famous Donald MacLeod of Bernera ("the Old Trojan").

Colonel Campbell saw much active service under Lord Gough in India, where he behaved with great gallantry, particularly at the battle of Chillianwallah, in which he was severely wounded when successfully charging one of the enemy's batteries, and for which he was specially mentioned in despatches.

Lieutenant Donald Campbell, of the Royal Navy (a brother of Colonel Charles Campbell of Strond), was serving in His Majesty's ship "Bellerophon" when she took the great Napoleon Bonaparte to England. Shortly after this event Lieutenant Campbell died (of cholera, it is said) at Portsmouth. He was a fine type of a British sailor and a most promising officer.

Another brother was killed in an assault on one of the walled towns of Spain at the time of the Peninsular War.

THE MACLEANS OF BORERAY AND DRIMNIN.

Major-General Archibald Neil MacLean, of the Bombay army (a son of John MacLean of Boreray and Drimnin by his wife, Jessie, the youngest daughter of the famous Donald MacLeod of Bernera, and his third wife, Margaret MacLeod of the Grishornish family), was born on the 28th of February, 1805. He received an Ensign's commission on the 21st of February, 1821; and, after serving in various capacities in India, rose to the rank of Major-General.[1] General MacLean was married, but left no issue. He died in London in June, 1875.

Captain Roderick Norman MacLean, a younger brother of Major-General Archibald Neil MacLean, was born on the 2nd of July, 1808.

He joined the Bengal army, and distinguished himself at Kandahar, under General Nott, in the first Afghan War, when serving in the 2nd Bengal Grenadiers. He was made Aide-de-Camp to Lord Ellenborough, Governor-General of India (who had great confidence in him[2]), and afterwards, while on the Staff of Lord Hardinge—who succeeded Lord Ellenborough—he was wounded at the battle of Maharajpore. Captain MacLean married Flora, daughter of Sir Walter Gilbert, but left no issue. He died and was buried at sea off Cape Comorin in 1845.[3]

Surgeon-General William Campbell MacLean, C.B., youngest son of John MacLean of Boreray and Drimnin by his wife, Jessie daughter of the famous Donald MacLeod

---

[1] India Office Records.

[2] His Lordship seldom made a military appointment without consulting Captain MacLean, who never allowed private considerations to influence him when consulted; and those promoted, on his advice, never knew to whom they were indebted for their advancement.

[3] "Memories of a Long Life," by Surgeon-General William Campbell MacLean, C.B.

of Bernera), was born on the 29th November, 1811, at Blackburn House, in Ayr, where his parents were temporaily residing at the time.

When Dr. MacLean was a boy the Highlands of Scotland swarmed with half-pay officers who had served with the Highland Regiments in Spain, Holland, Belgium, and India. The Highland Regiments in those days were something more than Highland in name, and Gaelic was, as much as English, the language of the mess-table. Many Highland officers obtained their commissions by bringing recruits to the service. His uncle, Sir John MacLeod of Unish, had brought in this way 600 gallant men to the colours of the 78th Regiment, when the 2nd Battalion was raised by himself and Lord Seaforth, as we have already seen.

About the year 1820, Dr. MacLean's family went to reside at Drimnin; and at the Manse of Morven, amid its gifted occupants, young MacLean spent the first months[1] of his life in the Highlands, and was well acquainted with all the characters so well described in Norman MacLeod's "Reminiscences." Dr. MacLean remembered seeing his grandmother (the widow of "the Old Trojan"), a stately person, with not a little of the reserve towards young people that was a notable characteristic of Highland manners. Young MacLean was educated at Dollar Academy, Edinburgh Academy, and Edinburgh University. He studied anatomy under the famous Professor Knox, the head of the school to which the notorious murderers Burke and Hare sold the bodies of their victims for dissection. In 1832, MacLean became a Licentiate of the Royal College of Surgeons, and in the session of 1832-33 he obtained his degree of M.D. of the University of Edinburgh.

In the autumn of 1833, Dr. MacLean was enjoying a shooting visit to a friend at Dunans, in Argyllshire, when he received a letter from his uncle, Sir John MacLeod, informing him that Sir John Keene (the Conqueror of Ghuznee, afterwards Lord Keene of Ghuznee) had been appoined Commander-in-Chief[1] of the Bombay army, and was to sail shortly in the "Upton Castle," and that he had been appointed to the surgeoncy of that ship.

During the voyage of the "Upton Castle" Dr. MacLean, having been insulted by one of his fellow passengers—an officer—told the aggressor (with a spirit worthy of "the Old Trojan" himself) "not to twist his moustache at him!" By the way, a moustache in those day was a rare ornament, and in the army was entirely confined to cavalry officers. A challenge followed the quarrel, and was fought with pistols when the ship arrived at Bombay, but, fortunately, without injury to either combatant.

Dr. MacLean returned to London in the "John Stamp."

In the month of June, 1836, he embarked on board the "Marquis Camden," an "Indiaman" of the old East India Company's service, for China, the voyage to and from which was uneventful.

On the 27th of April, 1838, he received an appointment[1] as Assistant-Surgeon in the Madras Army, and was passed by Dr. Hume[2] (the Duke of Wellington's personal physician), then Examiner for the East India Company.

---

[1] "Memories of a Long Life," by Surgeon-General William Campbell MacLean, C.B.

[2] Dr. Hume was well known in the South-West Highlands at one time, his daughter having married the late Captain Archibald Campbell of Glendaruel, afterwards Lieutenant-Colonel of the Argyllshire Rifle Volunteers.

Dr. MacLean landed in India on the 15th of August, 1838, and, after completing two months of probationary duty at a general hospital, he found himself under orders to embark for Masulipatam, there to ship a regiment of native infantry for Moulmein, in Burma, and to return with the relieved regiment to Madras. On this voyage he had to cope with an outbreak of cholera, which, owing to the energetic measures he adopted, was speedily stamped out. Soon after this he was ordered to proceed to Secunderabad to do duty with Her Majesty's 55th Regiment. Surgeon MacLean served with the 55th in the expedition[1] to China (1840-41), for which he received a medal. On Sunday, the 5th of July, 1840, he was present at the attack of Chusan, and at the capture of the town on the following day. On the 22nd of May, 1841, the expedition entered the Canton River for the capture of the city. Having disembarked, the troops were moved on to attack the forts on the heights above Canton. Dr. MacLean was attached to Moore's battery, which engaged the fort to the extreme right within a quarter of a mile or less of the city walls, and witnessed the surrender of the city. This was one of the first occasions (if not the first) on which percussion arms were used in war by British soldiers, to the introduction of which the Duke of Wellington was stoutly opposed, his objection being that the clumsy fingers of the soldiers could not be taught to use such small objects as percussion caps! To please His Grace, the percussion caps first introduced into the Service were made nearly three times larger than those used by sportsmen and shaped like a Dutchman's cap![1]

On the 19th of August, 1841, Dr. MacLean received orders to join the 18th Royal Irish, with which he remained till the end of the war and did all the field surgery.

On the 20th of August, the expedition, of which the 18th Royal Irish formed a part, sailed for Amoy, where it arrived on the 25th. On the following day the men-of-war bombarded the works on the Islands of Kolansoo and Amoy, keeping up a tremendous fire from 1 a.m. till 3.30 p.m., when the troops, consisting of the 18th, 49th, and 55th Regiments, landed and quickly drove the enemy from all their works. Next day the City of Amoy was occupied without further resistance. The fleet sailed for Chusan on the 5th September, and the Island was recaptured on the 1st of October, after a creditable resistance on the part of the Chinese.[2]

Assistant-Surgeon MacLean was present at the attack and capture of Chinhai on the 10th of September, and on the 13th of the same month the City of Ning-Po was entered without opposition. Here the expedition wintered.

On the 10th of March the enemy, who were known throughout the winter to have been making preparations, made their attack on Ning-Po. During the night they attempted, without success, to set fire to the men-of-war by means of blazing rafts and crafts of different kinds fitted up as fire-ships. Towards morning the north and west gates of the city were attacked by large bodies of troops, and the services of a warlike mountain tribe, called the Maoutsee, were brought into play by the enemy. Dr. MacLean accompanied Colonel Montgomerie and Captain Moore, with two

---

[1] All the regiments that took part in the expedition carry the device of "the Dragon" on their regimental colours.

[2] "Memories of a Long Life," by Surgeon-General W. C. MacLean, C.B.

nine-pounder guns and two companies of the 49th Regiment, in a sally made from the west gate, which had been gallantly defended through the night by the 18th Royal Irish under an officer of the name of Armstrong. The result of the sortie was most disastrous to the enemy, who were beaten off, leaving an enormous mass of dead behind them.[1]

Not long after this Assistant-Surgeon MacLean was ordered to Chinhai with a party of the 18th Royal Irish to reinforce that important post. On the 17th of May the fleet and transports assembled at Chapu, and on the following day the force landed at a sandy bay to the left of the enemy's position. At nine a.m. the men-of-war opened fire and soon silenced the batteries opposed to the landing, after which the troops advanced, driving the enemy before them on every side. A body of Tartars had possession of a large building, which, after many efforts, was taken by the 18th and 49th Regiments, and in doing so they lost thirty men killed and wounded, among the former was the brave Colonel Tomlinson, of the 18th Royal Irish.[1]

On the 7th of June the fleet entered the Yang-tse-Kiang River, and anchored opposite the long line of forts defending Woosung. On the 16th, at daylight, the men-of-war cleared for action and stood in to engage the Chinese works. The bombardment was very heavy and lasted about an hour, when the marines and blue-jackets of the fleet landed and cleared the batteries. Shanghai was entered on the 19th without opposition.

On the 6th of July, all the troops having re-embarked, they began the difficult task of working their way up stream, arriving off the City of Chin-Kiang-foo on the 20th, and landing on the following day for the capture of this city—the last military operation of the war. After the western gate of the city had been blown up by the Engineers, the 18th and 49th Regiments rushed in and mounted the ramparts, which they were ordered to clear. Both regiments marched at a rapid pace,[1] driving the enemy before them, under fire from the houses inside below the ramparts. Dr. MacLean had more than one narrow escape, and scarcely was his duty with the attacking column finished, when an order from Sir Hugh Gough called him to another part of the town, in obeying which he was fired at by the enemy all the way, but escaped unhurt.

Thus ended "the Opium War." The treaty of peace was signed on the 29th of August.

Dr. MacLean was Residency Surgeon at the Court of Hyderabad in the Deccan from 1844 till 1856, and while serving there he was also appointed Superintendent of the first Vernacular Medical School in India, which has been the means of training a large number of well-qualified medical men, and which has thus proved to be a great blessing to the country.

In January, 1857—the year of the Mutiny—Dr. MacLean was appointed by Lord Harris to the Third District at the Madras Residency, where he was Sir Patrick Grant's medical adviser, and became his intimate friend. Sir Patrick afterwards gave him the best appointment of the kind which was in his power, viz., the Garrison Surgeoncy of

---

[1] "Memories of a Long Life," by Surgeon-General W. C. MacLean, C.B.

Vizágapatam. Dr. MacLean had an anxious time of it during the Mutiny. He slept every night with revolvers under his pillow. His next appointment was one of the District Surgeoncies at the Presidency, which he held for two years, when he received in 1860 a letter from Mr. Sidney Herbert, then Secretary for War, offering him the Chair of Military Medicine in the Army Medical School, which he accepted, with the rank of Deputy-Inspector-General.[1]

For his eminent services Dr. MacLean was made a Companion of the Bath, appointed Honorary Surgeon to Her Majesty the Queen, and promoted to the rank of Surgeon-General.

Surgeon-General MacLean is the author of many learned articles and pamphlets on tropical diseases, military medicine, and general sanitation.

He married, in 1845, Miss Louisa MacPherson, niece of General Duncan MacPherson, with issue.

Surgeon-General MacLean died at Oakleigh, Sidmouth, Devon, on the 10th of November, 1898, aged 87.[2]

THE MACIVORS.

The following list of officers connected with Skye has been supplied by Mrs. MacIvor, widow of the late Reverend John MacIvor of Kilmuir, in Skye, sister-in-law of the late Mrs. MacIvor of Stein, and a descendant of Donald MacLeod of Bernera, "the Old Trojan," viz. :—Captain John MacIvor, of the 98th Regiment, who died in 1824; Lieutenant Donald MacIvor, of the 70th Regiment, who died in 1844; Lieutenant Norman MacIvor, of the 8th West India Regiment, who died in 1847; and Captain George MacIvor, who joined the 42nd Highlanders as an Ensign on the 31st of March, 1814, retired as a Captain to half-pay on the 5th of April, 1839, and died in July, 1845—all sons of the late Reverend Colin MacIvor of Glenelg.

The MacLeods of Hamer are descended from William (hence they are called "Clann Mhic Uilleim"), fourth son of Sir Roderick Mòr, XIII. MacLeod of Dunvegan.

William MacLeod, III. of Hamer, had two sons in the military service, viz., his eldest son, Captain Norman MacLeod (who commanded one of the Independent companies raised by his Chief in 1745), and his third son, John, a Lieutenant in the army, both of whom died unmarried.

William MacLeod, VI. of Hamer, was a Captain in the army.[3]

---

[1] "Memories of a Long Life," by Surgeon-General W. C. MacLean, C.B.

[2] "The Army and Navy Gazette," in an obituary notice, said:—"With the death of Surgeon-General W. C. "MacLean, M.D., C.B., Q.H.S., the last of the four Professors in the Army Medical School, Chatham and "Netley, during the Sixties and Seventies, has disappeared. The names of Longmore, MacLean, Aitkin, and "Parkes remain household words with the older, and some of the comparatively younger, medical officers. " . . . . They were all able men."

[3] Mackenzie's "History of the MacLeods."

Major-General Norman MacLeod, C.B., son of John MacLeod, of Gillen, in Waternish, Skye—(the last of his family who occupied the farm of Borline, after which this ancient branch—"Clann Mhic Uilleim"—of the MacLeods of Dunvegan, Glenelg, and Harris, was also designated) by his wife, Rachel, daughter of Hector MacLean of Duart[1] was appointed as an Ensign in the 78th Highlanders in 1793; Lieutenant on the 15th of November, 1794; served at the Cape of Good Hope in 1795; was present there in three actions and at many skirmishes, as well as at the capture of the Dutch Squadron in Saldanha Bay—the stratagem that led to which he is credited (in Skye) with having devised and to him fell the honour of planting the British Colours in Cape Town when the Colony was wrested from the Dutch at that time, and temporarily occupied by the British from 1796 to 1803. His regiment having been drafted to other corps, and the officers placed upon half-pay, MacLeod was promoted to the command of a company in the 95th, and he then returned to England.

Norman MacLeod was transferred to the 4th Foot on the 13th of August, 1799; and subsequently served on the staff in England, Ireland, as well as in the Helder Expedition, and fought in the actions of the 2nd and 6th October in Holland.[2] He succeeded to a majority on the 25th of February, 1802; and at the peace was placed on half-pay. In May, 1803, Major MacLeod was restored to full pay, and employed on the staff in England till June of the following year, when he was removed to the 95th Regiment with which he served in South America, where he took part in the capture of Buenos Ayres. In July, 1806, five companies of the 95th Regiment, forming part of the force under General Robert Crawford, sailed from England for Cape Colony, when they arrived in March of the following year, and from whence they were ordered to proceed to South America.[1] "The expedition arrived at La Plata on the 27th of
" April, Monte Video on the 14th of June, and thirty miles from Buenos Ayres on the
" 28th of June—the whole force being then under the command of General Whitelocke.
" Two companies which were detached as an advanced post, under Norcott, were
" furiously attacked. The post was joined by Major MacLeod, who saved the situation
" by his gallantry and judicious arrangements. He was present at the disastrous
" attack on Buenos Ayres, and was the only officer (when the field officers were
" consulted by General Crawford) who was opposed to the unfavourable and disgraceful
" surrender which followed)."

After the battle of Vimiero, MacLeod embarked from England for Portugal in charge of five companies of his regiment, with the 1st Battalion of which he had the honour of covering the retreat of Sir John Moore upon Corunna;[3] they were the last British troops who entered the town, and took part in the ever-memorable battle which was fought there. For these important services Major MacLeod was created a

---

[1] War Office and Family Records.
[2] *See* the Military Record of General Donald MacDonald of Knock.
[3] A general who knows his business (as Sir John Moore did in an eminent degree) selects the best officer in the army to command the rear-guard in a retreat before an enterprising enemy, as the French, under Soult, certainly proved themselves to be in that campaign.

THE MACLEODS OF GILLEN, WATERNISH.

Major-General NORMAN MACLEOD, C.B.

Captain ARTHUR LYTTELTON-MACLEOD.

Lieutenant-General ARTHUR LYTTELTON-ANNESLEY.
(Born a MACLEOD.)

Companion of the Bath. In 1809, he raised the 3rd Battalion of the Rifle Brigade at Shorncliffe;[1] was promoted to the rank of Lieutenant-Colonel, Brevet, on the 4th of May of the same year, and exchanged into the Royals with the rank of Lieutenant-Colonel on the 29th of March, 1810.

After the decisive victory of Mahidpore, the army advanced northward to Mundisore, but before ariving there it joined hands with the Goojerat Division under Sir William Keir. On the 1st and 2nd January, 1817, the combined force arrived at Mundisore where Holkar, having sued for peace, terms were granted to him.

The Royals' Battering Train and Engineer Park, under Colonel MacLeod, marched to Mulkapoor preparatory to the siege of Aperghur. In consequence, however, of the repulse of a part of our troops at Nagpore, General Doveton's Division proceeded by forced marches to that place, and ordered the Royals to join him, which they did, and on the 12th of December they arrived at Nagpore and took up a position in rear of the Residency, but the excessive fatigue which the troops had endured on their march of 230 miles in twelve days rendered it necessary to give them some days' rest previous to their engaging in any further arduous undertakings.

Early on the 15th the troops got into motion and assumed a position on the right of the Residency, and opposite to the enemy, whose most advanced post was distant about a mile and a half.[2] The Royals at this time were the only European force attached to the 2nd Division of the Deccan army. The infantry were divided into three brigades—the 1st, commanded by Colonel MacLeod, headed by five companies of the Royals; the 2nd, commanded by Lieutenant-Colonel N. MacKellar, headed by one company of the Royals. At nine a.m. the action commenced by the storming of the arsenal, which, with a battery of fourteen guns, was carried by the left brigade. The brigades under Colonels MacLeod and MacKellar were ordered to charge the enemy's right battery, and they executed the order with gallantry and success, advancing afterwards against the enemy's right, which retired before them. It was now half-past one, and the enemy had been driven from all their positions. They left their camp standing, and 40 elephants and 41 guns in battery, altogether 64 guns were taken on that day. The force encamped on the Nagah River, fronting it and the City of Nagpore.

Referring to these operations Lieutenant-General Sir Thomas Hislop, Bart., said, in a General Order dated 27th January, 1818:—"The conduct of the 2nd Battalion of His " Majesty's Royal Scots, under the immediate command of Lieutenant-Colonel Norman " MacLeod, has been invariably such as to entitle the valuable corps to my highest " approbation and applause, and more particularly in the action with the enemy's " army at Nagpore on the 16th ultimo their gallantry, steadiness, and good conduct " were most exemplary." An attack made on the 24th had failed in its immediate object, but the determination it evinced on the part of the assailants had made a serious impression on the garrison, and on the following day they offered to evacuate

---

[1] War Office and Family Records.   [2] Regimental Depôt Records.

the city, which they did on the 30th. After the Arabs had left Nagpore there appeared to be no enemy in the city. At Chergur, thirty-six miles to the south-east, a considerable body of predatory troops had assembled, to disperse which Lieutenant-Colonel MacLeod, with three companies of the Royals, under Captain Joseph Wetherell, six guns, four squadrons of cavalry, and a native battalion, marched on the 6th of January, and having dispersed the enemy he returned to camp on the 13th of the same month.[1]

In a General Order dated at Fort St. George, 25th February, 1831, the Governor-General of India also bore testimony to the gallant deeds of the Royal Scots when they served in India. He said:—"The Right Honourable the Governor-General cannot "permit His Majesty's Royal Regiment to quit India after forming a part of the army "of this Presidency for twenty-three years without publicly recording his high sense of "its distinguished services. During the Mahratta War the Royal Regiment was more "than three years in the field. It nobly maintained the character of British soldiers at "the battle of Mahidpore; and after sharing in other conflicts of that eventful period "in the Peninsula it embarked for Rangoon, and assisted in maintaining the honour "of the British arms, and establishing peace with the Ava dynasty. The Right "Honourable the Governor-General has only to add that the conduct of the officers "and men of His Majesty's Royal Regiment when in garrison has been such as to "meet with the entire approbation of Government, and that his best wishes for their "continued welfare and fame will accompany them in whatever part of the world the "national interest and honour may call for their services."

Lieutenant-Colonel MacLeod was promoted to the rank of Colonel in the army on the 12th of August, 1819, and subsequently to that of Major-General. He married, on the 14th of December, 1801, the Lady Hester Annabella Annesley, daughter of Arthur, first Earl of Mount Norris (claiming to be the seventh Earl of Anglesey) by Lucy, daughter and eventual heiress of George, first Lord Lyttelton.

General MacLeod was a very handsome man and of most agreeable manners; but it is said that at first the Lady Hester was (or affected to be) indifferent to his suit until she heard him sing a Gaelic song (of which, by the way, she did not understand a word) and saw him dance a Highland reel, and then she changed her mind and—soon afterwards—her name!

General MacLeod was lost at sea when crossing from England to Ireland in 1831.

Captain Arthur Lyttelton MacLeod, 42nd Regiment, son of General Norman MacLeod, C.B., was appointed Ensign in the 42nd Highlanders on the 12th of December, 1822; placed on half-pay as a Lieutenant on the 9th of June, 1825, and he retired as a Captain from the 86th Regiment on the 12th of March, 1841. Captain MacLeod saw no active service in the field, but was in India for a time. He took the name of Annesley, by Royal Warrant, in accordance with the will of his maternal uncle, George, second Earl of Mount Norris, Viscount Valentia, &c., on succeeding to his property. Captain MacLeod-Annesley died on the 24th of October, 1882.

---

[1] Regimental Depôt Records.

THE MACLEODS OF BORLINE AND BHARKASAIG.

Major-General D. J. S. MacLeod, C.B., D.S.O.

Captain Angus MacLeod, Royal Navy.

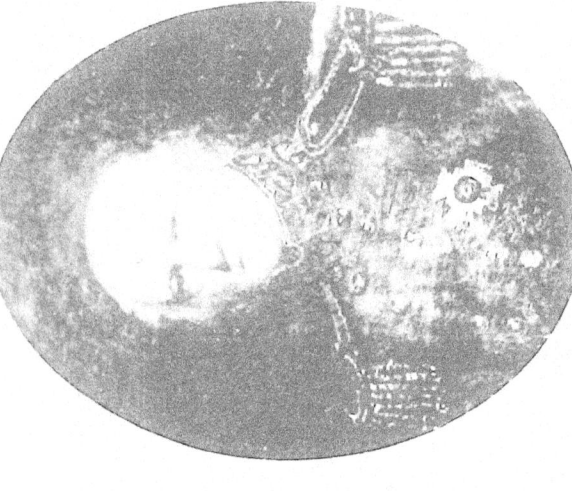

General Sir Donald MacLeod, K.C.B., of Bharkasaig.

Lieutenant-General Lyttelton-Annesley of Craig Lyttelton and Arley Castle, Staffordshire, the eldest son of Captain Arthur Lyttelton-MacLeod, of the 42nd Highlanders, and grandson of General Norman MacLeod, C.B., of Gillen, Waternish, Skye, was born in September, 1837, and bore the surname of MacLeod till 1844, when his father took that of Annesley. He was educated at Harrow, and entered the army in July, 1854; was appointed to the 11th Prince Albert's Own Hussars, and served with that regiment during the Crimean War, including the siege and fall of Sebastopol and the battle of the Tchernaya, for which he received the British medal and clasp and also the Turkish medal. Returning home in 1856, he remained with his regiment in England and Ireland till July, 1866, when he embarked in command of it, and arrived in Bombay on the 25th of October of the same year, the last regiment that went to India by way of the Cape of Good Hope in a sailing vessel. Colonel Lyttelton-Annesley was in India with his regiment for over ten years, only returning home on leave twice during that period, coming to England, the second time, along with His Royal Highness the Prince of Wales, who had taken him on his staff after the Delhi Camp. In 1877 Colonel Lyttelton-Annesley brought his regiment back to England by way of the Suez Canal. Soon after his arrival in England he retired from the command of the 11th Hussars, under the new rules, and was appointed Aide-de-Camp to His Royal Highness the Duke of Cambridge, whom he accompanied to Malta when the Duke went to inspect the Indian contingent. Not long afterwards Colonel Lyttelton-Annesley was appointed Assistant-Adjutant-General at the Horse Guards, which appointment he held for several years, and then went to Bombay as Adjutant-General of the Bombay army, holding that important post for over five years with the approbation of the three Commanders-in-Chief under whom he served. He returned to England in 1881, and after a short time was selected to command the North British District (which embraces the whole of Scotland) for a period of five years with the rank of Major-General. His term of service on the Scottish Station having expired, he received the rank of Lieutenant-General, a year after which he was offered the important command at Portsmouth, which, for private reasons, he was obliged to decline. Since then he has been unemployed, although he has frequently applied for employment. Under the new regulations he was compulsorily retired[1] on the 23rd of February, 1898. At the time of his retirement General Lyttelton-Annesley was in the enjoyment of the annuity for distinguished and meritorious services.

Captain Norman MacLeod, East India Service.

The family to which Captain MacLeod belonged held lands at one time in Glenelg, and afterwards in Bracadale, in Skye, until early in the eighteenth century, the last proprietor, Donald Òg MacLeod, left Skye and took a tack of land in North Uist. His son, the Reverend Angus MacLeod, married Margaret, daughter of Lachlan MacKinnon of Strath, in Skye, with issue, and was minister of St. Kilda from 1774

---

[1] "To the regret of numerous friends in the service who appreciate his sterling merits, which they hoped to find recognised."—"The Army and Navy Gazette."

till 1788, when he was succeeded by his son, the Reverend Lachlan MacLeod, who married, with issue, Marion, daughter of Neil MacLean of Kinloch, near Dunvegan, and who for about forty years attended to the spiritual wants of the people of St. Kilda. The Reverend Lachlan MacLeod had several sons, all of whom died young, except two—Angus, whose wife was the only daughter of General Sir Alexander MacLeod of the Bernera family, and Captain Norman MacLeod, of the East India Service. Captain MacLeod was born on the Island of St. Kilda in 1800, and having gone to sea at an early age, rapidly rose to the rank of Captain, and in later years had command of several well-known East Indiamen. He was employed in the Auxiliary Service during the first China War, and especially at the taking of Chusan,[1] where he met his cousin, Captain Norman MacLean,[2] of the 55th Regiment (afterwards Colonel Norman MacLean, C.B.), from whom he received a handsome silk banner (one of the two flags which had been captured by Captain MacLean from the Chinese), and this trophy he presented to his Chief, who duly added it to the many curiosities that are preserved at Dunvegan Castle. Before retiring on a pension Captain MacLeod held an appointment under the Board of Trade at Liverpool for some time. He married Frances, daughter of Donald MacDonald, a cadet of the Clanranald family, with issue. Captain Norman MacLeod died in Edinburgh in 1877.

Captain Angus MacLeod,[3] Royal Navy (son of Captain Norman MacLeod, of the East India service, by his wife, Frances MacDonald), was born on the 11th of June, 1847, and entered the Royal Navy as a naval cadet on the 10th of December, 1860, at the age of thirteen years and six months. After passing through the usual course of training in the "Britannia" he joined the "Magicienne" (Captain H.S.H. Prince of Leiningen) in April, 1862, and served upon the Mediterranean Station for nearly four years, taking part in that vessel in the cession of the Ionian Islands, the liberation of an English gentleman who had been captured by brigands near Salerno, and many other interesting current events.

Mr. MacLeod completed his time as a subordinate officer in the "Pallas," which was attached during 1866 to the Channel Squadron, and towards the close of that year was actively employed watching the Fenians' movements about Galway and the River Shannon.

Having passed the necessary examinations, he was confirmed in the rank of Sub-Lieutenant, and early in 1867 proceeded to the China Station in the "Rodney" (the flagship of Vice-Admiral the Hon. Sir Henry Keppel, K.C.B.). In 1868 Mr. MacLeod became a Lieutenant in a death vacancy.

The "Rodney" took part in the opening of the Japanese ports of Hiogo and Kobé, and was present during some of the fighting between the naval forces of the Tycoon and the Mikado, in the neighbourhood of Yokohama. To obtain indemnity for a gross attack upon missionaries made by the Chinese, the "Rodney," with a

---

[1] *See* Military Record of Surgeon-General W. C. MacLean, C.B.
[2] Nephew of Major-General Norman MacLeod, C.B., of Gillen, Waternish.
[3] Captain Angus MacLeod's elder brother, Norman Torquil, settled in one of the Western States of America many years ago.

squadron, went up to Nan-king and despatched a naval brigade to Yang-chow, resulting, in a few weeks, in a full apology and satisfactory compensation being given for the outrage.

Upon his return to England in 1870 Lieutenant MacLeod qualified as a Gunnery Officer, and in due course served as such in the "Aurora," training frigate, and afterwards as a Junior Staff Officer in the gunnery ship "Excellent" at Portsmouth.

In the autumn of 1873 he volunteered for employment in the Ashantee War, and was sent out in the "Encounter" to the Gold Coast to join the "Barracouta" (commanded by the present Admiral, the Hon. Sir Edmund Fremantle, K.C.B., C.M.G.) as Senior Lieutenant, and was ordered up country to serve in the Naval Brigade, then co-operating with the land forces under Sir Garnet Wolseley.

Lieutenant MacLeod was thus enabled to participate in the action of Amoaful (where, for the day, he commanded a company of Royal Marines, and was slightly wounded) and in the entry into Coomassie.

Acting as Naval Prize Agent, and assisted by two representatives of the Army, he was officially employed in the looting of the King's Palace, and upon the termination of the expedition rejoined the "Barracouta."

For these services he was mentioned in despatches and received the Ashantee medal with clasp for Coomassie.

After a refit in England and a change of captains the "Barracouta" proceeded to the Australian Station, where she was principally employed in the Fijian and Samoan groups of islands. In the latter she became involved in an extraordinary series of events which culminated in a sharp action at Mulinuu Point, Apia, on the 13th March, 1876.

Under the direct orders of Captain Charles Stevens, R.N., Lieutenant MacLeod commanded an armed body-guard of bluejackets and marines, which was landed to escort the deposed King, Malietoa. Upon attempting to disarm a strong force of Samoans (who were gathered near the council-house to protest against the state of affairs) an engagement ensued. Considerable loss of life occurred on both sides, and the small British force, being quite outnumbered and cut off from the boats, narrowly escaped a serious disaster.

Having returned to England in 1877, a year's experience as Divisional Officer of Coast Guard in County Clare, and three years' senior lieutenancy of the "Assistance," troopship, led to his promotion to Commander's rank in October, 1881.

Commander MacLeod was soon appointed to the "Boadicea," the flagship of Rear Admiral Nowell Salmon, on the Cape of Good Hope and West African Station. In that vessel he remained for more than three years.

In 1883 he was temporarily detached, in command of the "Algerine," as Senior Naval Officer on the West Coast during the Franco-Portuguese complications that arose out of M. de Brazza's activity, in the district between the Congo and Gaboon rivers, which threatened to bring about a breach of the peace. Here Commander MacLeod earned mention " for the very able and judicious manner in which his orders " were carried out, and for the valuable reports made."

Transferred in March, 1885, to the gunnery ship "Excellent," a further period of three years' service ended by his promotion to the rank of Captain, in which grade his turn for first employment came in June, 1891, when he obtained command of the cruiser "Pallas," which was commissioned for service on the China Station.

Captain MacLeod was in 1893 Senior Naval Officer and in charge of the squadron in Siamese waters throughout the Franco-Siamese difficulty. At times the relations existing between Great Britain and France were greatly strained, and, as a matter of fact, a rupture was most narrowly averted. Happily for both countries peace was maintained, and upon the conclusion of an arrangement whereby all danger of hostilities passed away, the Admiralty were pleased to inform him that, "recognising the extreme "difficulty and delicacy of the position," they "appreciated the efforts made to "maintain an attitude of strict impartiality under very trying circumstances."

Later on in the same year Captain MacLeod received the thanks of the French Republic and the approval of the British Admiralty for successfully floating the Messageries Maritimes steamer "Godavéry," when stranded badly on a reef in the Straits of Rhio, near Singapore.

Within a few weeks of paying off the "Pallas" in 1894 he was again ordered to China to strengthen the squadron in view of the progress of the war between China and Japan. In command of the first-class cruiser "Gibraltar," Captain MacLeod witnessed the fighting at Wei-hai-Wei, and was with Admiral Ito's (Japanese) ships when that port capitulated and when Admiral Ting and several of the principal defenders committed suicide.

Upon the cessation of the struggle the "Gibraltar" returned home in June, 1895; and in December Captain MacLeod was appointed to the first-class battleship "Empress of India," one of the Channel Squadron. In June, 1897, he was transferred to the new first-class battleship "Jupiter," a Clyde-built ship of 14,900 tons and 12,000 indicated horse-power, with a complement of 757 officers and men.

During the spring cruise of the Channel Squadron in 1898[1] Captain MacLeod's ship had the honour of being specially selected to carry out "a remarkably useful "series of gunnery experiments" (conducted as nearly as possible under actual service conditions), and the firing is said to have been "exceptionally good."

In October, 1898, Captain Angus MacLeod, having completed his extended period of service in charge of a first-class battleship, was appointed to the command of the "Pembroke," and of the Fleet Reserve at Chatham, for a period of three years—a most important post, involving the responsibility of keeping some forty vessels ready for war mobilisation.

Captain MacLeod married, first, Rose (daughter of the late Robert Hickson and widow of James, son of the Venerable Archdeacon Pollock), who died in 1886; and, secondly, Jane Margaret, only daughter of the late Captain Forster, of the 62nd (Wiltshire) Regiment, an officer who served with distinction in India and fell in the Crimea. Mrs. MacLeod's only brother, Lieutenant-Colonel J. Burton-Forster, now commands the 2nd Battalion of the Royal Irish Regiment.

---

[1] "The Army and Navy Gazette," 30th April, 1898.

Colonel Norman MacLean, C.B., 55th Regiment, son of Donald MacLean, farmer, Dunhalin, Waternish, Skye, by his first wife, a sister of General Norman MacLeod, C.B., of Gillen, Waternish, was appointed Cornet on the 17th of September, 1807; Lieutenant on the 23rd of February, 1809; Captain on the 29th of March, 1827; Major on the 26th of May, 1841; and Lieutenant-Colonel on the 23rd of December, 1842.

"Norman MacLean [1] entered the service at the age of twelve years and eight months. His uncle, the General, bought him his commission. Young MacLean's sword was so long for him at first that it trailed on the ground! He served with distinction in India and China in the 55th, my grandfather's old regiment. In China, at the taking of two forts, he was the officer who hauled down the Chinese flags, one of which he gave to a Captain MacLeod, son of the minister of St. Kilda. It was latterly presented to MacLeod of MacLeod, and is now at Dunvegan Castle; the other he gave to a Major MacLean in Mull . . . . He appears to have exchanged from some other regiment to the 55th in India, preferring to remain out there to coming home, as he would receive higher pay and more rapid promotion. As a recognition of distinguished services, Colonel MacLean was made a C.B., along with other officers of the 55th. The Colonel was married, and had a son who died without issue."

Early in 1839 a wing of the 55th Regiment, under the command of Captain Norman MacLean, was ordered over to Madras. Captain MacLean was then an old officer for his rank. He had no money to purchase his way to a higher grade; and, like hundreds of others in similar circumstances, had to content himself as best he could by the slow steps made for him by death.[2]

On the 20th of August, 1841, the expedition, of which the 55th Regiment formed a part, sailed for Amoy, where it arrived on the 25th. The following day the men-of-war bombarded the works on the Islands of Kolansoo and Amoy, keeping up a tremendous fire from 1 a.m. till 3.30 p.m., when the troops, consisting of the 18th, 49th, and 55th Regiments, landed and quickly drove the enemy from all their works. Next day the City of Amoy was occupied without further resistance.

On the 5th of September the fleet sailed for Chusan, and on the 1st of October the island was recaptured after a creditable resistance on the part of the Chinese.

The troops arrived off the City of Chin-Kiang-foo on the 20th of July, 1842, and on the following day they landed for the capture of the city—the last operation of the war. The western gate of the city was blown up by the Engineers, and was gallantly stormed by the 18th and 49th Regiments, while the 55th was told off to escalade the wall on the east side, in the performance of which duty it greatly distinguished itself.[2]

Major-General William Comperus MacLeod (Indian army), of the ancient Borline family, was born at Pondicherry on the 16th of September, 1805. He was

---

[1] Letter from Mr. A. R. MacDonald, younger, of Waternish, to Doctor Keith Norman MacDonald of Ord.
[2] "Memories of a Long Life," by Surgeon-General W. C. MacLean, C.B.

appointed Ensign on the 27th of April, 1822; Lieutenant on the 8th of September, 1826; Brevet-Captain on the 27th of April, 1837; Captain on the 3rd of June, 1841; Major on the 31st of January, 1845; Lieutenant-Colonel on the 14th of May, 1853, and died a Major-General in 1880.[1]

Major-General MacLeod married Anne, daughter of Dr. Donald MacLeod of the Orbost family, Inspector-General of Army Hospitals,[2] and they had three sons in the army, viz.:—Colonel William Sim MacLeod, of the Madras Staff Corps, who was for several years Superintendent of the Vellore Prison, and who died on the 7th of March, 1888; Major-General Donald James Sim MacLeod, C.B., D.S.O., whose military record is here given after that of his father, and Lieutenant Reginald George MacQueen MacLeod, of the Royal Artillery.

Mr. William Comperus MacLeod arrived in India on the 8th of May, 1822, and was posted to the 15th (now the 30th) Regiment in February, 1823. He was slightly wounded in the attack by Lieutenant-Colonel Elrington's detachment on the Burmese at Syriam on the 14th of January, 1825. MacLeod was appointed a Sub-Assistant-Commissary-General on the 4th of September, 1829, after which he took charge of the Commissariat office at Moulmein, and was promoted to be Deputy-Assistant-Commissary-General on the 20th of August, 1833. Having been deputed to accompany the Burman Commissioners to take part in the negotiations for the settlement of the boundary between Munnypore and Ava, and the work of the Commissioners having been satisfactorily concluded, the part taken in these negotiations by Lieutenant MacLeod on that occasion, and the confidence with which he was regarded by all parties, impressed the Government with a very high opinion of his judgment, temper, and address.

"The Court state that Major Grant, Captain Pemberton, and Lieutenant MacLeod are entitled to commendation for the manner in which they executed this duty."

A Journal which was kept by MacLeod of his route from Ava to the Kubboo Valley gives much interesting information regarding the country and the people.

The Government expressed its approbation of his zeal in having spontaneously compiled a valuable map of the country between the Erawah and Khyendwen Rivers, and of the Kalee district, from materials obtained by him during his visit to that quarter.

The following is an extract from a Report by the Commissions of the Tenasserim Provinces:—"Lieutenant MacLeod is a remarkably intelligent, active young officer, " zealous and attentive in the discharge of his duties, and anxious to render himself " useful beyond the mere routine of his office. Towards the natives his conduct is " unexceptionable, and his knowledge of the Burmese language is very considerable. " He is fluent in Hindoostanee."

On the 4th of September, 1837, Captain MacLeod was selected along with Dr. Richardson to proceed on an important mission to countries bordering on the Tenasserim Provinces, the object of which was to extend the inland trade, and to collect

---

[1] India Office Records.   [2] Mackenzie's "History of the MacLeods."

information relative to countries hitherto unknown. With regard to this mission the Commissioner of the Provinces says:—"Captain MacLeod has executed the duty "entrusted to him with great zeal, prudence, and intelligence. He appears to have "overcome the difficulties placed in his way with much firmness and mildness, and he "made a favourable impression on the Chiefs of those countries hitherto unvisited by "Europeans."

In December, 1846, Major-General (then Major) MacLeod was appointed principal Assistant to the Commissioner of Arracan. In the following year he was actively employed as one of the agents for the suppression of the Mirah sacrifices and female infanticide in the hill tracts of Orissa within the Bengal Presidency. At his own request, he was placed at the disposal of the Commander-in-Chief of the Madras army on the 24th of September, 1847, who reported him to be "a highly estimable "officer in all respects, is zealous and indefatigable in the discharge of his important "duties, possessing all the qualifications necessary for a commanding officer. . . . " . . . His conduct and character are highly exemplary in all respects. He is "a smart, intelligent, and valuable officer, thoroughly acquainted with his duties, and "beloved and respected by all ranks."

Major-General Donald James Sim MacLeod, C.B., D.S.O., is the son of Major-General William Comperus MacLeod, of the Indian Army, by his wife, Anne, daughter of Inspector-General of Army Hospitals, Donald Macleod of the Bernisdale family, and grand-daughter of Norman MacLeod of Bernera.

General MacLeod was born on the 22nd of February, 1845; entered the Indian army (Madras Cavalry) on the 20th July, 1861; was promoted to the rank of Lieutenant on the 20th of July, 1862; Brevet-Captain on the 20th of July, 1873; Captain on the 4th of November, 1874; Major on the 20th of July, 1881; Lieutenant-Colonel on the 20th of July, 1887; and Colonel on the 12th of August, 1893. He served on the Staff as Aide-de-Camp to a General Officer commanding a district from the 24th of May, 1865, to the 28th of April, 1867; as a Deputy-Assistant-Quarter-Master-General from the 6th of November, 1870, to the 25th of April, 1874; Assistant Quarter-Master-General from the 29th of March, 1878, to the 4th of April, 1883; Deputy-Quarter-Master-General in the Madras army from the 5th of April, 1883, to the 28th of November, 1888; commanded the 3rd Madras Lancers from the 11th of July, 1890, to the 11th of August, 1893; served on the Staff as Adjutant-General of a District from the 12th of August, 1893, to the 9th of April, 1894, and again from the 1st of April, 1895, to the 3rd of July, 1895; he officiated as Secretary to the Governor of Madras, Military Department, from the 10th of March, 1894, to the 31st of March, 1895; was appointed Brigadier-General commanding a Second-Class District on the 4th of July, 1895, and transferred to the command of a First-Class District on the 21st of June, 1897. General MacLeod served in the war in Burma in 1886–87, for which he was mentioned in despatches ("London Gazette," 2nd September, 1887), and received the Distinguished Service Order, with a medal and clasp. He was made a Companion of the Order of the Bath on the 11th of July, 1898, and promoted to the rank of Major-General on the 21st of March, 1899.

The MacLeods of Grishornish are descended from Donald, fifth and youngest son of Rory Mòr of Dunvegan.

This Donald was the father of William MacLeod of Claigean, who had two sons in the military service, viz., Captain John MacLeod, who served in the British army, and Colonel Donald MacLeod, of the Indian army.

Colonel Alexander MacLeod of the Madras army (who died in 1805) was the second son of the Reverend Donald MacLeod, III. of Grishornish.[1]

General Sir Donald MacLeod, K.C.B., Bengal army (son of MacLeod of Bharkasaig, near Orbost, Skye), was admitted to the service as a cadet on the 10th of April, 1781; gazetted Ensign 15th September of the same year; Lieutenant on the 23rd of June, 1783; Captain on the 7th of January, 1796; Major on the 25th of April, 1808; Lieutenant-Colonel on the 4th of June 1814; Colonel on the 5th of June, 1829; and Major-General on the 10th of January, 1837. Lieutenant MacLeod served in the war with Tippoo from 1789 to 1792. He was wounded in the battle with the Rohillas on the 26th of October, 1794. On the 22nd April, 1799, Captain MacLeod was appointed Adjutant of the 2nd Battalion of Native Infantry; was severely wounded at the siege of Calpee on the 4th of December, 1803, and was employed in the operations against the fortress of Gohud, for which he was specially mentioned in the following terms in a letter to the Secret Committee of the Court of Directors, dated 14th March, 1806[2]:—"Your Honourable Committee will have the satisfaction to observe that the "first effort of our arms against that place (Gohud) has been completely successful. A "strong entrenchment within two hundred yards of the fort having been gallantly "assaulted and taken by a division of our troops under the command of Captain "MacLeod of the 2nd Battalion, 11th Regiment of Native Infantry. We deem it "probable that the success will have the effect of inducing the insurgents to surrender "the fortress without awaiting an assault. Your Honourable Committee, however, "will observe with satisfaction the sanguine hopes of success entertained by Lieutenant- "Colonel Bowie, even if he should be compelled to proceed to the assault. The "conduct of the officers and troops in the attack of the fortified entrenchment appears "to have been distinguished by a peculiar spirit of gallantry and firmness, and we "sincerely lament the loss that has been unavoidably sustained on the occasion."

MacLeod was appointed Commanding Officer at Moradabad in April, 1809. He was granted a furlough to Europe, on private affairs, in May, 1810, and returned to India in 1813. He served in the Deccan War, and shared the prize money as a Lieutenant-Colonel in the 11th Native Infantry. On the 17th of October, 1818, he was made a Companion of the Bath, and on the 3rd of July of the following year was appointed Commandant of the Fortress of Agra. On the 26th October, 1822, he exchanged from the 2nd Battalion of the 11th to the 2nd Battalion of the 4th Regiment. Colonel MacLeod quitted India on the 24th January, 1826. On the 28th of May, 1838, General MacLeod was created a Knight Commander of the Bath. Sir Donald married

---

[1] "Mackenzie's "History of the MacLeods."   [2] India Office Records.

a daughter of Campbell of Kincraig, and had by her an only daughter, who became the wife of John MacLeod, the last Laird of Raasay. Sir Donald MacLeod died at Montague Square, London, on the 9th of August, 1843.[1]

Captain John MacLeod ("the Veteran"), at one time tacksman of Struan, was a brother of Sir Donald MacLeod, who himself held the farm of Trumpan for some years.

The Family of Ulinish.

Roderick MacLeod, I. of Ulinish, fourth son of Donald MacLeod of Grishornish, was the father of the Reverend William MacLeod, minister at first of Bracadale, and afterwards of Campbeltown, who married Isabella, daughter of Donald MacLeod of Bernera ("the Old Trojan"), and three of whose sons, by her, were officers in the army, and were killed in Indian wars. Another son commanded an East Indiaman, and died at an early age unmarried.[2]

Sergeant Donald MacLeod was the son of John, fourth son of Roderick MacLeod, I. of Ulinish, by his wife, Isabella MacDonald of Sleat. Donald started life as an apprentice stonemason, at Inverness; but finding his work there uncongenial he ran away at the end of two years and went to the town of Perth, where he fell in with a recruiting party, and after some difficulty regarding his youth (he being only thirteen years of age), and his small stature having been overcome through the good offices of a Captain MacDonald from Skye, the future hero was allowed to enlist in the Royal Scots, then commanded by the Earl of Orkney.[3]

Donald's promotion was rapid, for when he was about seventeen he was raised to the rank of sergeant, and sent on a recruiting expedition to Inverness-shire, in which he was most successful. Soon afterwards he went to Flanders with his regiment, and was present at the battles of Schellenberg, Blenheim, Ramilies, and many minor affairs, in all of which he acquitted himself with the bravery of his race. He was by this time considered by his comrades to be the champion swordsman of his regiment, and many wonderful stories are told of his prowess with his "trusty blade." Nor was Donald particular about the question of nationality, provided his foeman was "worthy of his steel." His first duel was with a French sergeant who insulted him, and whom he mortally wounded, his opponent leaving him his watch as a peace offering. He next fought, and disabled, a French officer, who (before engaging in a combat with a man of inferior rank to himself) had to get permission from his commanding officer.[3]

Soon afterwards MacLeod chastised a German officer for taking the part of a fellow countryman with whom the Highlander had quarrelled. "It is enough," said the German, after he had a slice taken off his fat leg and been smartly wounded in the sword arm. After drinking, kissing, and embracing (according to the custom of the Continent) they separated the best of friends.

---

[1] India Office Records.   [2] Mackenzie's "History of the MacLeods."   [3] "Celtic Magazine."

After the peace of Utrecht was concluded the Royal Scots were quartered in Dublin, and there Sergeant MacLeod engaged in a sword match with an Irish giant called MacLean, who, when they formally shook hands before beginning, squeezed Donald's hand so hard that he roared out with the pain; but he made a mortal vow that that squeeze should cost the Irishman his right arm; so it did; and that put an end to the combat.[1]

When the rising of 1715 took place a notable swordsman from Knoydart, named Captain MacDonald, who was in the Highland army, boasted that he could beat any man in the Royal army. The consent of the commanders on both sides having been obtained, the Skyeman was selected to meet the Knoydart man. "I have cut off your sporran," said Donald; "is there anything else I must cut off before you give up?" The Captain was obliged to own that he was beaten, and he left his sporran behind him in token of his defeat. The Earl of Mar and the Duke of Argyll were both so well pleased with Donald's skill that they gave him ten guineas each.

MacLeod behaved with conspicuous bravery at the battle of Sheriffmuir, and towards the close of the action had a desperate encounter with two Frenchmen (both of whom he killed); but he himself received two wounds, one of which (in the head) was dangerous.

About 1730 Sergeant MacLeod was discharged from the Royal Scots (at his urgent request, but against the wishes of his superior officers, who tried to dissuade him from this step) for the purpose of joining the Independent Company, which was then about to be raised by Lord Lovat, who appointed him to the post of Drill Sergeant, the duties of which position he fulfilled to the entire satisfaction of his officers.

One of the principal reasons for raising these Independent Companies was to put down the cattle-lifters or gentlemen-robbers, who were at that time very numerous in the Highlands. On one occasion Donald was sent in command of a small party to Athole to apprehend a notorious horse-dealer named James Robertson. At Aberfeldy "the wine of the country" appears to have been good, and the Sergeant imbibed of it somewhat more freely than the dictates of prudence demanded or the requirements of the service allowed. However, he succeeded in capturing the horsedealer, who was at home. Robertson had four very handsome daughters, with one of whom MacLeod fell in love at first sight, and it was agreed that he should marry her on the spot (after the manner of the Scots) on condition that her father should be allowed to escape. During the night, however, the Sergeant had to fight for his bride, because four men (one of whom was a former suitor for her hand) had come to make her a widow!

There was a short but sharp struggle; MacLeod beat off his assailants, retained possession of his wife, and the marriage, after all, turned out to be a happy one. The six Independent Companies continued to exist as such till May, 1740, when, along with four additional companies, they were embodied as the 43rd (afterwards the 42nd) Regiment of the line.[2]

---

[1] "Celtic Magazine." [2] Brown's "History of the Highlands, &c."

Sergeant MacLeod fought with great valour at Fontenoy, where he was wounded in the leg by a musket ball, but he refused to quit his post. It is related that during the thickest of the fight he—having killed a French colonel—deliberately served himself heir to 175 ducats and a gold watch, which he found on his slaughtered foe. He had scarcely secured his booty when he was fiercely attacked by an Irish Captain of the name of James Ramievie, whom he killed after an obstinate[1] and skilful combat, but next moment he was beset by three or four Frenchmen all at once. Fortune favoured him, however, for a gentleman of the name of Cameron, who (although in the French service), seeing his countryman hard pressed, came to his assistance. History does not record what became of the Frenchmen, but their fate may be imagined.

Sergeant MacLeod, having been transferred as Drill Sergeant from the 42nd Regiment to Fraser's Highlanders, served under General Wolfe in North America; and at the siege of Louisburgh he greatly distinguished himself by volunteering, with a handful of men, to surprise the French outpost, who were cut off to a man, on which occasion he was wounded in the nose by a musket ball. At the battle of Quebec MacLeod was among the foremost of the Grenadiers and Highlanders, who drove the enemy from post to post, and ultimately defeated them. In this action he had his shin bone shattered by grape shot; and a musket ball went through his arm. It was in Donald's plaid that General Wolfe was carried off the field, and he had the honour of being one of the guard that was told off to take charge of the General's body on the journey to Britain in November, 1759. In December of the same year Sergeant MacLeod was admitted as an out-pensioner of Chelsea Hospital, which was the only recognition ever given at head-quarters of the long and arduous services of this hardy veteran, then in his seventy-first year.[1]

After recovering from his wounds he served in Colonel Campbell's Highlanders in Germany, where he was twice wounded. In 1776, hearing that his countrymen had again embarked for the seat of war in America, he could not restrain his longing to be once more actively engaged in the field. The General Commanding (who knew him), struck with the military ardour of the old man, allowed him to remain with the army as a Drill Sergeant; and gave him an allowance out of his own pocket of half a guinea a week; but afterwards, taking pity on him, he made excuse to send him home with despatches. Seeing that he had no further prospect of being employed in the army, MacLeod resolved to return to the Highlands, and settle down quietly for the rest of his life. He accordingly sold his house at Chelsea for about two hundred pounds, but, having been shipwrecked on his way from England to Scotland, he lost everything he had in the world except his gold watch and a ring of some value. And these, too, he soon parted with; so that when he arrived in Edinburgh he was penniless. But what distressed him most was the loss of his trusty sword. Donald MacLeod was married more than once; and of his sixteen sons twelve were in the King's service either as soldiers or sailors. The hardy old fellow said, " I eat when I am hungry and drink " when I am dry, and never go to bed but when I can't help it."[1] Consequently he

---

[1] " Celtic Magazine."

lived (notwithstanding all the hardships which he came through) to be over 103 years of age.

The MacLeods of Dalvey are descended from Donald of Grishornish, fifth and youngest son of Sir Roderick Mòr MacLeod of Dunvegan. Sheriff Alexander MacLeod of Ulinish, grandson of this Donald, had three sons in the military service—viz., Lieutenant Roderick MacLeod, of the British army, who was killed in America; Major Norman MacLeod, of the Bengal army, who fell at Rohilcund; and Major Alexander MacLeod, of the British army, who was I. of Dalvey.

Major Alexander MacLeod married Marion, fourth daughter of the famous Donald MacLeod of Bernera (by his third wife, Margaret MacLeod of Grishornish), and they had two sons in the army—Roderick N. MacLeod, who died abroad, unmarried; and Dr. Donald Alexander MacLeod of the East India Company's Service. Dr. MacLeod's son, Captain Norman MacLeod, succeeded his uncle (who died unmarried), in 1876, in the representation of the family.

Captain Norman MacLeod, III. of Dalvey, joined the Black Watch in 1875; was promoted to the rank of Lieutenant shortly afterwards, and became a Captain in 1886. He served with his regiment in Egypt and in the Soudan from 1882 to 1884; was wounded both at El Teb and Tamai, and was mentioned in despatches for these campaigns.[1]

The MacLeods of Orbost[1] also trace their origin as a branch to Donald, I. of Grishornish, youngest son of Sir Roderick Mòr MacLeod of Dunvegan. This Donald's son, Roderick, had two sons, the second of whom—Captain Norman MacLeod of Bernisdale—married Anne, youngest daughter of Norman MacLeod, of Unish and V. of Bernera, with issue. Their eldest son was—

Dr. Donald MacLeod, Inspector-General of Hospitals.

Donald MacLeod was appointed an hospital mate by warrant dated 10th September, 1799, and was subsequently employed at the Deal General Hospital till he embarked for North Holland, on which station he continued to serve till he was appointed Assistant-Surgeon in the 82nd Regiment of Foot in January, 1800. Dr. MacLeod served with this regiment in Ireland on the coast of France, with the expedition against Belleisle, and afterwards in the Island of Minorca for two years. On the breaking out of the war in 1803[2] he was appointed Surgeon to the 38th Regiment, and was stationed with it in Ireland till August, 1805, when he embarked for the Cape of Good Hope; and from thence he went to South America in January, 1807; was present at the capture of Maldonado, Monte Video, and Buenos Ayres, remaining there during the whole time these places were in possession of the British

---

[1] Mackenzie's "History of the MacLeods."   [2] War Office Records.

army. He returned with the regiment to Ireland in December, 1807. In June, 1808, he embarked for Spain under Sir Arthur Wellesley; landed at Laros; was present in the actions of Roliça and Vimiero, and in the whole of the retreat, through Spain, of Sir John Moore, which ended in the battle of Corunna on the 16th of January, 1809. Dr. MacLeod accompanied the expedition to Walcheren in July, 1809, and remained on the island during the whole period of its occupation. In July, 1810, he went with his regiment to Ireland, and continued on that establishment till May, 1812,[1] when he again embarked for the Peninsula, and joined the army of Lord Wellington on the 20th of June, 1812—the night before the battle of Salamanca. From that time till the final evacuation of France he served continuously with his regiment in the field until he was appointed to the Staff in September, 1813. During this period he was present at the battle of Vittoria, and the siege of San Sebastian. After the battle of Orthes he went to that station, and remained there till the 26th of May, 1814, when he received orders to proceed to Bordeaux, from whence he sailed for Canada, with a brigade under the command of Major-General Robinson; took part in the expedition to Plattsburg in September, 1814; and was stationed on the frontier of Lower Canada till the army returned to England in July, 1815. A few days after he landed he was ordered to join the army in France, which he did,[1] and remained with it at the General Hospital at St. Denis until the reduction of the Staff, in May, 1816, caused his removal to England.

Previous to his joining the regular army, Dr. MacLeod acted as Regimental Mate in the 1st Battalion of the Breadalbane Fencibles; and was Surgeon of the 2nd Battalion from the 25th of January, 1798, to the 24th of August, 1799, with the former in Scotland, and with the latter in Ireland.

Dr. MacLeod served for twenty years and six months on full pay, ten years and five months of which he spent on foreign stations. He was placed upon half-pay on the 24th of April, 1821; but having been restored to full pay on the 15th of March, 1827, he embarked for New South Wales in September of the same year, and on the 27th of November, 1828, was appointed Deputy-Inspector of Hospitals, and ordered to proceed to Bombay, where he arrived on the 15th of April, 1830. He was promoted to the rank of Inspector-General on the 1st of June, 1837; sent to Bengal, and there he died on the 12th of November, 1840.[1]

Lieutenant Roderick MacLeod, a younger brother of Dr. Donald MacLeod, Inspector-General of Hospitals, was appointed an Ensign in the 38th Foot on the 14th of November, 1804, and Lieutenant on the 25th of August, 1807. He died of wounds received at the siege of San Sebastian between the 7th and 27th of July, and was succeeded on the 25th of August, 1813.[1]

William MacLeod, another younger brother of Dr. Donald MacLeod, Inspector-General of Hospitals, was the father of Captain Norman MacLeod of Orbost, who was for a time tacksman of the Island of Rum.

---

[1] War Office Records.

The MacLeods of Colbost, St. Kilda, and Glendale.

Colonel Donald MacLeod of Colbost and Auchgoyle, Madras army, was made an Ensign on the 16th of November, 1767; Lieutenant on the 29th of July, 1769; Captain on the 13th of April, 1777; Major on the 17th of April, 1786; and he resigned with the rank of Colonel on the 16th of October, 1787.

Colonel MacLeod[1] served with great distinction under Sir Eyre Coote in India.[2]

Major-General Donald MacLeod, Madras Cavalry (the second son of Colonel Donald MacLeod of Colbost by his wife, Diana, daughter of Donald MacDonald of Tormore, Sleat, Skye) was born on the 6th of April, 1796; nominated by Charles Grant, Esquire, and admitted to the Establishment on the 20th of August, 1813. He shared the prize for the capture of Mahidpore, in 1817, as a Cornet in the 4th Madras Cavalry, and also the prize captured in the war against the Pindarries and certain of the Mahratta States in 1817-18; was appointed Adjutant to the Governor's Body-Guard by a General Order, dated 5th November, 1824, and Quarter-Master, Interpreter, and Paymaster to his regiment on the 7th of June, 1825. By a General Order of the 11th November of the same year he was promoted to act as Staff Officer to a detachment of the 1st Cavalry remaining at Arcot. On the 23rd October, 1832, Major-General Sleigh reported that "Captain MacLeod, who had been in command of "the regiment since the 2nd of November, 1831, appeared to have discharged his "duties with much zeal."[2]

In December, 1838, Sir Hugh Gough inspected the 4th Light Cavalry at Bangalore, and in his inspection report said :—"Major MacLeod appears to discharge "his duties with much steadiness, zeal, and attention. The interior economy of the "troops and the arrangements of the various departments are most creditable, and "evince Major MacLeod's great attention to his various duties." This high opinion was subsequently confirmed by the inspection report, dated 25th January, 1846, of Colonel Commandant Haleman, who said :—"The state of this regiment is most "creditable to Lieutenant-Colonel MacLeod and the officers under his command for "the efficiency and for the care with which discipline is enforced and maintained." In the following April Colonel MacLeod was appointed a Brigadier-General of the Second Class, and to command Jaalnah, which post he held till the 20th September, 1848, when he was transferred to command the Nagpore Subsidiary Force,[2] which he continued to hold until his "tour of command expired," on the 17th May, 1851. On the 28th of March, 1854, General MacLeod was made a Brigadier-General on the Staff, and put in command of "the Ceded Districts," the limits of which he quitted on the 1st of January 1855.[2]

---

[1] Colonel MacLeod married Diana, daughter of Donald MacDonald, Esq., of Tormore, Sleat, Skye, with issue. Their eldest son was the Right Honourable Sir John MacPherson MacLeod, K.C.S.I., of Glendale, who for his meritorious work in the Civil Service of India was knighted in 1866, and made a Privy Councillor in 1871.

[2] India Office Records.

THE MACLEODS OF COLBOST, ST. KILDA, AND GLENDALE.

Major-General DONALD MACLEOD.
(From Lieutenant John MacLeod.)

Major-General ALEXANDER MACLEOD.
(From Lieutenant John MacLeod.)

Captain DONALD MACLEOD.
(From Lieutenant John MacLeod.)

Lieutenant JOHN MACLEOD.

Lieutenant John MacLeod, General MacLeod's son, says:—"My father served from "1813 to 1858-9 in the Madras Light Cavalry, and during this long period he held "several high commands, his last being that of Major-General Commanding 'the "Ceded Districts, Madras.' He saw active service in India; but had no medal; in "those days medals were not quite so plentiful as they are now. My father was full "Colonel (up to the time of his death) of the 4th Madras Light Cavalry."[1]

Major-General Alexander MacLeod, Madras Cavalry (the third son of Colonel Donald MacLeod of Colbost and his wife, Diana, daughter of Donald MacDonald of Tormore, Sleat, Skye), was born on the 18th of December, 1804. Nominated by Charles Grant, Esquire, at the recommendation of his father, Colonel MacLeod; appointed Cornet in the 5th Regiment of Cavalry on the 13th of February, 1821; Lieutenant on the 1st of May, 1824, and Captain on the 2nd of May, 1835. The dates of General MacLeod's promotion to the higher ranks of his profession do not appear in the Army Services Lists. MacLeod arrived in India on the 23rd October, 1821. On the 24th October, 1825, he was ordered to do duty with the head-quarters of the 1st Regiment of Cavalry, which was under orders for foreign service. On the 16th December, 1825, he was directed, with his regiment, to join the army in the Burman War, Ava; and this he did accordingly. Having returned from foreign service, he was relieved from doing duty with the 1st Cavalry by a General Order dated the 15th of July, 1826.[2]

On the 15th February, 1828, Alexander MacLeod got the post of Riding-Master to his regiment; and on the 8th July, 1831, that of Quarter-Master and Interpreter, as well as that of Adjutant, on the 3rd of the following November, which latter appointment he resigned on the 30th of December, 1833.

His services were placed at the disposal of the Government of India by a General Order, dated the 30th of October, 1835; and on the 23rd of the following month he was appointed to act as an Assistant to the Commissioner in Mysore.

In the narrative of the proceedings connected with the insurrection in Canara, it is stated that "Captain MacLeod and the Honourable Mr. Devereux, with a party of "irregular horse, were of essential service in clearing that part of the district, which "borders on Nuggar, of the insurgents who had invaded it, and in preventing the "extension of disaffection."[2]

The Commissioner for the Government of the territories of the Rajah of Mysore submitted a copy of a communication from the Superintendent of Nuggar, dated 1st May, 1837, containing a detailed report of the services rendered by Captain MacLeod and the Honourable Mr. Devereux in preventing the spread of the late rebellion. To this the Commissioner himself added a short extract from a diary which had been kept

---

[1] War medals for the period from 1793 to 1814 were ordered to be granted on the 1st of June, 1847, to the survivors of the Peninsular heroes. This was after the grant of the Waterloo medals. Before 1847, however, there was a gold medal given for distinguished services to officers not under field rank for Maida, Roleia, Vimiero, and other engagements.

[2] India Office Records.

by Captain MacLeod during these operations, and "which served to display on the "part of that officer a spirit of enterprise and a judgment which, as they have already "been acknowledged by a letter from the Principal Collector of Canara, give to his "services a distinguished place in the suppression of this insurrection." Captain MacLeod was on the 30th of May, 1837, thanked by the Government of Madras "for "the zeal and activity" which he evinced during the recent disturbances.[1]

On the 5th of June following he received the thanks of the Government of India "for the zeal and ability" displayed by him on the occasion of the insurrection in Canara, and "the clear and concise statement submitted by Captain MacLeod of "his sentiments and proceedings in connection with the causes of the late insurrection "is particularly worthy of notice."

On the 14th of February, 1838, Captain MacLeod was appointed to officiate as Superintendent of the Nuggar Division of the Mysore territory, and on the 4th of January, 1839, he was promoted to be Military Assistant to the Commissioner of Mysore. Brigadier Lovell concluded his inspection reports of the 26th July, 1841, on the Mysore Silladar Horse in the following terms :—"The whole arrangement "does great credit to Captain MacLeod and the native officers he employed under "him."[1]

Captain Donald MacLeod, Bengal army, eldest son of Major-General Donald MacLeod, of the Madras Cavalry, was born at Kelledge on the 11th of July, 1827. He was nominated by Major-General Sir J. Lushington, and admitted to the service as an Ensign on the 5th of January, 1845. He arrived at Fort William on the 30th of May in the same year, and was posted to the 12th Native Infantry Regiment. He served in the Sutlej Campaign of 1845-46, and was present at the battle of Ferozeshah (which took place in December, 1846, and which lasted for two days, ending in the rout of the natives and in the capture of their entrenchments), and also at the battle of Sobraon (which was a most obstinate one, fought between a British army, under Sir Hugh Gough, of 15,000 men and a Sikh force numbering 30,000, which was strongly entrenched and made a vigorous resistance, but was defeated with a loss in killed, drowned, and wounded of 13,000 men). For these engagements MacLeod received a medal and a bar. On the 21st of January, 1847, he passed an examination in Hindoostanee; and on the 5th of March, 1850, was ordered to do duty with the Arracan Battalion.[2]

Captain MacLeod served in the Burmese War of 1852-53, for which he got a medal; was appointed to act as second in command of the Arracan Battalion on the 20th of June, 1854, and to take temporary command of the whole battalion on the 28th of April, 1856. From the 6th of September of that year till the 17th of July of the following year he was in charge of the station of Khyouk Phyoo; but he reassumed the command of his regiment on the 21st of October, 1857, and held it until he was placed at the disposal of the Lieutenant-Governor of Bengal

---

[1] India Office Records.

two months afterwards, and appointed junior Assistant to the Commissioner of Arracan.

Captain MacLeod died at Akyab on the 5th of August, 1858.[1] His brother, Lieutenant John MacLeod, says :—"Captain Donald MacLeod served under Lord "Gough through the whole of the Sikh War, and got four medals."

Lieutenant John MacLeod, of the 4th King's Own Royals, youngest son of Major-General Donald MacLeod, served in the Abyssinian Campaign of 1867–68, for which he received a medal. His portrait was taken in the uniform which he wore during that expedition.

The MacLeods of Ferinlea, Ose, and others.

The MacLeods of Ferinlea, Ose, and others were descended from Alexander MacLeod of Minginish, the immediate younger brother of the renowned Ruairidh Mòr of Dunvegan. It was this Alexander who commanded the MacLeods at the battle of Ben-a-Chuilinn, or rather at Coire Na-Crèiche, where they were defeated by the MacDonalds.

Lieutenant Norman MacLeod of Ferinlea, in Bracadale, was appointed as an Ensign in Colville's Regiment of Foot (the 69th) by a commission, signed by His Majesty King George the Second, dated the 19th of May, 1759, and was promoted to the rank of Lieutenant in the same corps, by a commission granted by General Colville, at Belle Isle, on the 2nd of June, 1761, "for the present expedition, or until His Majesty's pleasure is known."

Lieutenant MacLeod died at Grule, in the Island of Skye, on the 19th of August, 1797 :—"A gentleman" (to quote an obituary notice of him which appeared at the time) " possessed of many amiable qualities, and deservedly regarded by all his friends " and acquaintances. A sacred regard to truth, which he was never known to violate, " a solid but unaffected piety, an inflexible integrity from which no motives of interest " could ever induce him to swerve, a generous and manly openness of heart, combined " with a placid serenity of temper ; these principles formed the tenour of his conduct " and were the distinguishing features of his character."

Of the Ose family there were two brothers in the army (nephews of Lieutenant Norman Macleod of Ferinlea), namely, Captain Alexander MacLeod, and his younger brother, Captain Roderick MacLeod, who was killed at the battle of Assaye. He was badly wounded, and was lying helpless on the field of battle when a native woman killed him by striking him on the head with a stone, he having kicked her when she was trying to deprive him of his boots. Another wounded Skyeman, who was lying near at hand, fearing that he might share the same fate, shot the hag dead with a ramrod, not having a bullet left with which to do the deed.

---

[1] India Office Records.

The MacLeods of Swordale and Morven are descended from Donald MacLeod, tacksman of Swordale, near Dunvegan, in Skye. Donald MacLeod's second son, Captain Donald MacLeod, was an officer in the East India Company's service, and died at the Cape of Good Hope in 1774.

Surgeon-Major Sir George Husband Baird MacLeod, Knight.[1]

George Husband Baird MacLeod was born in the manse of Campsie on the 21st of September, 1828, and died in Glasgow on the 31st of August, 1892. He was the son of Norman MacLeod, D.D. (caraide na 'n Gaidheal), at one time minister of St. Columba's Church, Glasgow, who was famed as a Celtic scholar, his writings in the Gaelic language being unrivalled among modern authors. From this cause, added to his eloquence as a preacher, and his unwearied labours for the good of the Highlanders, his memory is still fondly cherished wherever the Gaelic language is spoken. The grandfather of Sir George was Norman MacLeod, minister of Morven, who was the eldest son of Donald MacLeod, of Swordale, in Skye. On his mother's side, Sir George MacLeod was descended partly from a Lowland family (the Maxwells), who achieved no little distinction in their own day and generation, and partly from several well-known Argyllshire families. To the dim but animating memorials of those Highland homes where his parents passed their youth, Sir George attributed much of the success in life which he, with other members of his family, gained; for they were memorials of families revered for their human sympathy, their unswerving rectitude, their kindly solicitude for the people around them, as well as their deep affection for one another.

After attending Mr. Munsie's Academy (then well known) in Nile Street, Glasgow, he entered the University of that city in the beginning of the session of 1843-44. In the Arts course he gained the University prize for an essay, and took high honours in Philosophy. He in due time joined the medical classes, in which he soon made his mark, taking a prize in Anatomy and Materia Medica, and a first in the Institutes of Medicine. But the extra strain and almost incessant work which this implied told upon his health. So he had to give up study for a time and to go abroad for the benefit of his health, but in the spring of 1852 he returned home perfectly restored to health. Dr. MacLeod graduated in medicine in the spring of 1853, and immediately afterwards went to Paris to continue his studies under men of European renown, such as Velpeau, Nèlaton, Bouchardat, Jobert de Lamballe, and Ricord. He returned from Paris in the autumn of 1853, spending some time on his way home in the London hospitals. He then settled down to practise in Glasgow, but it was not long before he was again away. Europe was beginning to echo with the call to arms, the Crimean War was on the tapis, and where better could a young surgeon gain that experience which was so necessary for him in his profession than on the field of battle? But how was he to get there? The opportunity was most unexpectedly put in his way.

---

[1] From a memoir read by his son, the Rev. W. H. MacLeod, B.A., Cantab. B.D., minister of the Parish of Buchanan, before the Royal Society of Edinburgh, on the 16th of January, 1893.

THE MACLEODS OF SWORDALE AND MORVEN, OSE, ETC.

Surgeon-Major Sir GEORGE MACLEOD, Knight.

Captain JOHN NORMAN MACLEOD, Indian Medical Service.

Captain DONALD MACLEAN, 72nd Highlanders.

Captain RODERICK MACLEOD OF OSE.
Killed at the Battle of Assaye.

One evening, at a dance, his host asked him whether he would be willing to go with a friend of his own on a yachting cruise to Constantinople. He jumped at the chance, and on the 23rd of April, 1854, a few days after he had accepted the invitation, he started. He heard at Malta that the war had broken out. He immediately left his yachting friends and pushed on with all speed to Constantinople in the hope of finding employment there; but he only met with disappointment, and was compelled to return home. In November of the same year (1854), however, he was again on the war-path. Colonel George (afterwards Sir George) Campbell of Garscube, who was in the 1st Dragoons, had been severely wounded in the heavy cavalry charge at Balaclava, and his mother, Mrs. Campbell, anxious for his safety, asked MacLeod if he would go out and bring home her son. This request he gladly complied with, and he travelled night and day until he found his patient at Scutari, much in need of some one to tend him. After nursing him for many weeks, he brought him back in safety to London. But, while waiting for his friend to gain sufficient strength for his journey, he worked hard in the English and French hospitals, where he saw and did a great deal of surgery. The experience which he had thus gained led afterwards to his employment at the seat of war. Accordingly, he received his appointment on the 7th of February, 1854, and started three days later for Smyrna, where he arrived on the 25th of the same month, and where, to his surprise, he found himself made senior of the whole staff, and appointed interim superintendent. This piece of good luck came about, partly through his having "so courageously" gone out at once when asked, and partly through the recommendation of the superintendent, who was home on leave, and Major Storks (the Commanding Officer there), who considered him best fitted for the post. There was much need for reorganisation, but he soon had all things in good working order, associated as he was with a band of energetic men, nearly all of whom made their mark afterwards in the world—Spencer Wells, Ranke of Munich, MacDonnell (afterwards Professor of Surgery in Dublin), Rolleston of Oxford, and others. At Smyrna, he remained till the end of May, 1855, when he obtained leave and started for "the front." Dr. (afterwards Sir John) Hall, the Principal Medical Officer in the Crimea, received him most kindly, and he was not long there when, a surgeon attached to the General Hospital having died from cholera, he was placed in orders by Dr. Hall to succeed him, a most responsible position. He was then appointed a first-class Staff-Surgeon in the Army Medical Service, with the rank of Major, and he remained "Senior Surgeon to the General Hospital before Sebastopol" from this time till the Crimea was evacuated in 1856, bearing his share of the hardships of that trying campaign during the whole time he was in the Crimea. He was several times under fire, but he remained at his post until—as the result of all his surroundings combined, bad food, bad water, bad sleeping quarters, and fatigue—he was struck down with erysipelas and camp fever; but he was at his post again before long, remaining there during the winter of 1855-56, until the signing of peace in April 1856.

For his services at the battle of the Tchernaya he got the Sardinian medal, the Turkish medal, and the British medal, with a clasp for Sebastopol, " on account of " having been under fire on several occasions." But he lost the much-coveted Legion of Honour through the carelessness of the Director-General, who, after promising to return his name for it, said he had forgotten to do so. On his return home to Glasgow in the autumn of 1856 Dr. MacLeod settled down to practise, and soon afterwards published his "Notes on the Surgery of the Crimean War, with Remarks upon Gunshot Wounds," a book which at once brought him into notice.

On the death of Dr. Hunter in 1859, Dr. MacLeod was appointed to succeed him in the Chair of Surgery in the Andersonian University; and in 1869 he succeeded Sir Joseph Lister as Professor of Surgery in the University of Glasgow, which important appointment he held till the day of his death.

From the time of his appointment in the University onward (having dropped general practice altogether) his heart was completely bound up in the success of his classes at the College and at the Western Infirmary. Only those who met him there can know the enthusiasm for his work which, even to the very last, possessed him, and which he transferred to his students, who flocked to him in such numbers that every available corner of his large class-room was crowded, many having to content themselves with standing room. It was his desire to help his students to be men of wide sympathy, and to cause them to hate all that was mean and all that was base. Sir George MacLeod was Surgeon-in-Ordinary to Her Majesty the Queen in Scotland, and was a member of many learned societies, both in Great Britain and on the Continent of Europe.

Captain John Norman MacLeod (M.A., M.B., C.M.), of the Indian Medical Service (eldest son of the late Reverend Dr. John MacLeod, minister of Govan, by his wife, Jessie, daughter of General Duncan MacPherson of Burgie), joined the service in January, 1893, in which year he served in Waziristan with the 1st Punjab Cavalry and the 3rd Sikhs; was attached to the 17th Bengal Cavalry at Umballa in 1894; acted as Surgeon on the Staff of His Excellency Sir George White, V.C., G.C.B., &c., Commander-in-Chief in India until the outbreak of the war in Chitral; had the medical charge of the 11th Bengal (P. W. O.) Lancers throughout the Chitral Relief Expedition under General Sir Robert Low, G.C.B.; was present at the taking of Swat River; accompanied the regiment in the charge and pursuit of the enemy on the 7th of April, 1895; and took part in the affairs of Punjkora and Nawagai, for which services he was commended and granted a medal with clasp.

At the end of the Chitral Expedition Captain MacLeod was appointed to the 10th Bengal (D. C. O.) Lancers, and remained with them till hostilities broke out on the North-West Frontier in June 1897, when he went with the Tochi Field Force in command of two sections of No. 29 Native Field Hospital, for which he received a clasp and the Frontier Medal. At the close of this expedition Captain MacLeod was invalided home owing to malarial fever.

Kenneth MacLeod of Swordale, afterwards of Ebost, married Margaret, daughter of Dr. Murdoch MacLeod of Eyre; and their eldest son, Dr. Murdoch MacLeod, served in India in the 11th Native Infantry.[1]

---

[1] Mackenzie's "History of the MacLeods."

Brigade Surgeon-Lieutenant-Colonel Kenneth MacLeod, Bengal Medical Establishment, son of the Reverend Norman MacLeod, Free Church minister of North Uist (a son of Kenneth MacLeod of Swordale and Ebost), and Julia, daughter of Dr. Alexander MacLeod (an Doctair Bàn), was appointed as an Assistant Surgeon on the 31st of March, 1865; Surgeon with the rank of Captain on the same date; Surgeon-Major on the 31st of March, 1877; and Brigade Surgeon-Lieutenant-Colonel on the 26th of June, 1888. He retired on the 16th of April, 1892.

Dr. MacLeod was civil surgeon at Jessore from the 20th of February, 1866, to the 17th of October, 1868; in medical charge of the 6th Bengal Light Infantry and civil surgeon at Julpigweel from the 26th of October, 1868, to the 14th of December, 1869; as well as a member of the Cattle Plague Commission,[1] for his services on which he received the thanks of the Government. He acted as secretary to the Surgeon-General of the Indian Medical Department from the 3rd of January, 1871, to the 2nd of April, 1879; Health Officer in Calcutta from 1879 to 1884; Professor of Anatomy in the Calcutta Medical College from the 1st of April, 1874, to the 14th of June, 1875, and from the 3rd of April, 1879, to the 31st of December, 1879; Professor of Surgery in the same College from the 1st of January, 1880, to the 14th of April, 1892, and he was three times thanked by the Government for his services in connection with veterinary and sanitary affairs.[1]

Private John MacLeod enlisted in Captain Æneas MacIntosh's Company of the 42nd Highlanders in the year 1742, and served abroad for six years and nine months. The regimental records do not show to what part of Skye this soldier belonged.

Private Norman MacLeod, of the 42nd Highlanders.

The Reverend Norman MacLeod, minister of the Free Church, Portree, writing to Mr. A. R. MacDonald, younger, of Waternish, gives the following interesting account of the military services of his gallant grandfather (one of the heroes who made the "Invincibles" of Napoleon bite the dust):—

"My grandfather, I find, was born at Brunal, in Minginish, and died in Waternish. As a youth, being carried away by the warlike spirit which prevailed in the island before the beginning of the present century, he joined the 42nd Regiment. Not long after he landed on March 8th, 1801, under Abercromby, in Egypt, and escaped unhurt in the famous action with the French on the beach. He was so fearless then that he sat in the bow of the boat through a hail of bullets from the shore. He was, however, dangerously wounded on the 21st of the same month at the battle of Alexandria in which the brave Abercromby was mortally wounded, being among those who, carried away by enthusiasm, advanced too far in pursuit of the enemy, and laid themselves open to a cavalry charge. His head was almost cleft in two by the sabre of a dragoon. He soon after left the army, and returned to his native Skye as a soldier in a different field. He lies buried in Dunvegan churchyard. I am sorry I cannot give any photograph or likeness of him. I believe he was over six feet in height, and very handsome even to the last."

---

[1] India Office Records.

After leaving the army Norman MacLeod was well known throughout Skye and the surrounding districts as a catechist and Gaelic school teacher, and for his earnest piety, combined with originality of thought, in conveying to the minds of his hearers the gospel of peace. A tombstone has been erected to his memory in the churchyard of Dunvegan by his grandson, the Reverend Norman MacLeod of Portree, the writer of the letter from which the foregoing quotation is made.

Private Murdoch MacLeod, from the Aird of Sleat, served in the 92nd Highlanders under "the valiant Fassiefern" in the tough fight of Quatre Bras (where the gallant Cameron fell), and in the ever-memorable battle of Waterloo. In both engagements "the Gay Gordons" covered themselves with glory, more especially at Waterloo, where "the regiment, then reduced to less than 250 men, instantly formed and rushed " to the front against a column equal in length to their whole line, which was only " two men in depth, while the column was ten or twelve. The enemy stood as if in " suspense till the Highlanders approached, when, panic struck, they wheeled to the " rear and fled in the utmost confusion."[1] Then arose the shout of "Scotland for ever," followed by the heroic charge of "the Scots Greys."

Private Murdoch MacLeod received the war medal for the Waterloo campaign.

John MacLeod, Royal Navy.

The following information regarding this gallant sailor has been given by his grandson, Mr. Malcolm MacLeod, an eminent mechanical engineer in Los Angeles, California:—

"My grandfather's name was John, and my father's name Angus. I am ashamed I cannot recall their places of abode in Skye. Unfortunately for this purpose, I have been the wanderer of the family, and the family record was entrusted to my father's sister—since dead—and then to her daughter (born in England), who is also dead. This is why, at this distance, I am unable to get or give any further information than this. I know little of my grandfather's history beyond remembering the conversations between my father and grandfather who, being a deeply religious man, was most reluctant to talk of his own experiences, and to his children, never. He was a broad-set, exceptionally powerful man (as was my father), but only about 5 feet 10 inches high. He was, I think, 108 when he died. It appears he entered the navy from Skye. He served for three years under Nelson, but I do not remember in what rank. I have always understood that he was on board the Victory when Nelson was shot."

Corporal John Nicolson, of the 42nd Highlanders, now (1898) residing at Tote, near Skaebost Bridge, by Portree, says that Privates Murdoch MacLeod and Donald MacLeod, both belonging to his neighbourhood, served in the army—the one through the Peninsular Campaign, and the other (in the 74th Regiment) in the Kaffir War.

---

[1] General Stewart of Garth's "Annals of the Highland Regiments."

Private Donald MacLeod, a native of the parish of Strath, was in the 6th and afterwards in the 72nd Foot, and fought in the Indian Mutiny.

Captain Donald MacLean, of the 72nd Highlanders (son of Hector MacLean, tacksman, of Vatten, near Dunvegan, Skye, by his wife, Margaret, daughter of Donald MacLeod of Swordale, Isle of Skye), was born at Vatten, and entered the army at an early age. He was appointed as an Ensign on the 15th of January, 1807; promoted to the rank of Lieutenant on the 13th of October, 1808; and to that of Captain on the 8th of April, 1825. Captain MacLean retired on half-pay on the 14th of June, 1831.

He joined the regiment in South Africa, and did duty with it there till 1810, when it embarked 800 men to take part, along with troops from India, in the expedition which was sent to the Island of Mauritius, and which resulted in the capture of that island.[1]

Having, on the 3rd of December, arrived well to the windward of the Isle of France, it was ascertained that the Indian Army had arrived on the previous morning at Point Cannonnière, and was menacing the enemy's position. The transports carrying the Cape Brigade were, in consequence, ordered to proceed to the mouth of Port Louis Harbour, where the 72nd was held in momentary readiness to land in the rear of the enemy's lines, should he attempt to defend them. The French Captain-General, who affected to despise the Indian sepoys, against whom he had declared he would defend himself, was by this movement placed in a critical position, being exposed to attack in front and rear. This circumstance, to use his own words, "determined the immediate surrender of the Mauritius." Accordingly, on the 5th of December, 1810, the regiment landed and remained on that island for upwards of three years, during which period it won the respect of the inhabitants in a very eminent degree.[2]

In 1815 Lieutenant MacLean went with his regiment to India, and from thence he returned with it to South Africa in 1816; served in the operations against the Kaffirs on the Great Fish River, and took part in the protracted bush-fighting which ensued, and which lasted for nearly three years.[1][3]

Notwithstanding the arduous and toilsome nature of their duties, and their frequent exposure to the inclement weather, the men of the 72nd remained remarkably healthy. The regiment returned from South Africa to England in 1821. At its departure it received the approbation of the Governor-General, Lord Charles Somerset, for the exemplary and steady conduct of the men during their residence at the Cape.[2]

The following interesting information has been furnished by Miss Cameron, of Dunvegan House, Dunedin, New Zealand, a niece of Captain MacLean:—

"My uncle came home occasionally to see his friends, and during his furlough he was very successful in getting many young men to join the army as recruits. As

---

[1] Regimental Records. [2] "Highlands, Highland Clans, &c."
[3] Owing to the unfortunate loss of some of the old Regimental Records about fifteen years ago, the foregoing is all the information that can be gathered from that source about Captain MacLean.

he was handsome and gentlemanly in appearance, and as his looks were further enhanced by his picturesque uniform, he easily induced the young men to follow him as their leader. I remember his retiring on half-pay owing to ill health, and his coming to Skye to live with us for some months. Afterwards he went to visit his uncle's family at Morven, and while there his friends advised him to take Ardincaple House, in Argyllshire. Being a bachelor, he sent for my eldest sister (afterwards Mrs. Ferguson, of Arnisort and mother of Mrs. Watson, of Alness, Ross-shire) to keep house with him, and he remained at Ardincaple for two years, when (his health not improving) his friends persuaded him to remove to Glasgow, where he could have better medical attendance. He was there only a short time when he died, and his remains were buried in Campsie, in the burying-place of his relative, the Rev. Dr. Norman MacLeod, 'Caraide na 'n Gaidheal.'"

The MacCaskills were, for several generations, the Lieutenants of the MacLeods (both by sea and by land), from whom they held large territorial possessions in reward of their services as commanders of their galleys or birlinns; and one of them (clad in full armour) always accompanied the chief as his henchman.[1]

Major-General William MacCaskill, son of John MacCaskill, tacksman, of Rù-an-Dùnain, was appointed as an Ensign in the 71st Foot on the 25th of August, 1776; Lieutenant on the 19th of October, 1778; Lieutenant half-pay 71st Foot (on disbandment) on the 4th of June, 1784; Lieutenant in the 43rd Foot on the 25th of September, 1787; Captain in the Corps of Invalids on the 8th of September, 1790; Captain half-pay, Corps of Invalids (on disbandment), in 1791; Captain in the 92nd Foot on the 31st of December, 1793; Major on the 1st of September, 1795; Major half-pay in 1795; Lieutenant-Colonel, brevet, on the 1st of January, 1801; Colonel on the 25th of July, 1810; and Major-General on the 4th of June, 1813.

General MacCaskill died on the 5th of April, 1815.[2]

He went out to his regiment (the 71st Foot) to North America, in 1778, and served with it till the termination of the war in 1783.[3]

General MacCaskill was for a time Governor of Mauritius; and in 1815 (the year in which he died) was serving on the Staff in the Island of St. Martin, in the West Indies.[3]

He was married to a Miss Shaw of Inverness, and had two sons in the army, —viz., Major Hector MacCaskill, who died of cholera at Varna at the beginning of the Crimean War in 1854 (unmarried); and Major John MacCaskill, who married a daughter of Cluny MacPherson, and left one son, William, who is also in the army.

Captain Kenneth MacCaskill, tacksman, of Rù-an-Dùnain (commonly remembered in Skye as "Old Rù"), eldest son of John MacCaskill of Rù-an-Dùnain, and brother of General William MacCaskill, was a Captain of Militia, and served with

---

[1] "The Scottish Highlander," November 25th, 1897. [2] War Office Records.
[3] The Royal Military Calendar, 1815.

Major-General Sir JOHN MacCASKILL, K.C.B., K.H.
(From Miss F. Tolmie, Oban.)

Dr. WILLIAM TOLMIE, 78th Highlanders.
(From Miss F. Tolmie, Oban.)

Captain NORMAN MacCRIMMON, 74th Highlanders.
(From Lady MacLeod, Wardie Lodge, Edinburgh.)

his regiment in Ireland during the rebellion which broke out in that country in the end of last century. He was a brave and capable officer.

On one occasion, during an action with the rebels, a spent bullet struck him on the forehead, knocking his head-piece round, back to front. He coolly replaced it, and, noticing that the accident had caused some merriment among his men, he said to them (in Gaelic), "Come on quickly, lads; this is no place for loiterers or fools."

One night, after retiring to rest, he was heard roaring "that the devil was under the bed!" His men came and found a rebel concealed below the bed where he had been busily prodding the gallant Captain with his bayonet. The culprit was hauled out, and immediately hanged to a cart. "Old Rù" would face any foe in the field; but of "the powers of darkness" he had (like many Highlanders) a wholesome dread.

Major-General Sir John MacCaskill,[1] K.C.B. and K.H., son of Dr. MacCaskill of Bracadale, was appointed Ensign in the 53rd Foot on the 10th of March, 1797; Lieutenant on the 14th of May, 1801; Captain on the 6th of March, 1806; Major, Brevet, on the 12th of August, 1819; Major of the 53rd Foot on the 11th of March, 1824; Lieutenant-Colonel, unattached, on the 17th of February, 1825; Lieutenant-Colonel of the 86th Foot on the 6th of July, 1826; transferred to the 89th Foot on the 31st of August, 1826; half-pay on the 9th of October, 1831; on particular service, 4th of April, 1833; again on half-pay, 1833; removed to the 98th Foot on the 22nd of October, 1833; to the 9th Foot on the 19th of June, 1835; Colonel, Brevet, on the 28th of June, 1838; and Major-General, when he was killed in action, at Moodkee, in India, on the 18th of December, 1845,[2] after nearly fifty years' service.

Sir John MacCaskill served as an Ensign in the force under Lieutenant-General Sir Ralph Abercromby in the expedition which was sent against Porto Rico in 1797; was present at the landing, and at the unsucessful attack on its strongly-fortified Capital, St. Juan.

As Senior Lieutenant of his regiment he was on passage to India in the fleet under the convoy of Rear-Admiral Sir Thomas Trowbridge when it was attacked by the French Admiral Linois in the "Marengo" (a heavy frigate), and another ship in August, 1805. As Captain in command of the flank companies, of his regiment, and acting Major of a flank battalion of His Majesty's regiments he served throughout the "Mahratta-Pindarrie War of 1817–18," co-operating in the pursuit and expulsion from his territories of the Peshwa and his army, and at the reduction of five of his principal forts:—viz., Sattarah, Singhur, Woossotah, Poorunder, Wyzalghur, and numerous minor ones—and subsequently he was present at the reduction of the strong fortress of Sholapore (commanding the battalion), and the attack and dispersion of 5,000 of the Peshwa's choicest troops, strongly posted with their guns, fifteen of which

---

[1] Sir John MacCaskill and General William MacCaskill were full cousins on the maternal side, their fathers (who were first cousins) having married sisters of the Bethune family. Dr. MacCaskill's mother was a daughter of MacLeod of Bay, a cadet of the family of MacLeod of MacLeod.
[2] War Office Records.

were captured under the walls of the fort on the 11th of May, 1818.[1] This service was conducted by Sir Thomas Munro, and under him was Brigadier-General Pritzler.

Sir John MacCaskill served, with the rank of Major-General as second in command, in the army, under Major-General Pollock throughout the war in Afghanistan in 1842, having been nominated to the command of the Infantry Division of that force at the forcing of the Khyber Pass on the 5th of April, 1842, the affair of the Mamookhail on the 24th of August, and the command of the main column on the occasion of the forcing of the Tezeen Pass, on the 13th of September. He was appointed to the command of a force consisting of two brigades of infantry with a proportion of artillery and cavalry, ordered on service to Kohistan; and with these troops he assaulted, captured, and burnt the strong post of Istalif on the 29th of September, 1842. Here many of the most influential of the Afghan Chiefs with their followers were assembled, and they were dispersed and driven to the higher mountains. The obnoxious forts of Charikar[1] and Oppian were next visited and destroyed, as a just retribution for their previous perfidies and atrocities. General MacCaskill was thanked in public orders for his services before Sholapore; noticed in General Orders for those at the Khyber Pass and at Tezeen; honoured with a vote of thanks from both Houses of Parliament, dated 20th February, 1843, for his services in Afghanistan in 1842; created a Knight of the Royal Hanoverian Guelphic Order by His Majesty King William the Fourth, in 1836, for previous military services; nominated a Knight Commander of the most Honourable Order of the Bath by Her Majesty Queen Victoria on the 27th of December, 1842; and he obtained a medal for his share in the capture of Kabul in September, 1842.

The following is an extract from the official records of the 9th Foot with regard to the battle of Moodkee:—"The 9th Foot sustained the loss of its Lieutenant-"Colonel, Major-General Sir John MacCaskill, K.C.B. and K.H., an officer to whom "his country was indebted for long and valued service, who received a ball through "his chest on the advance of his division (Third Infantry), and immediately "expired."

The Battle of Moodkee.[2]

"On the 16th of December the two British divisions formed a junction at Bussean, and continued their march in the direction of Moodkee. It was reached on the 18th, and as the few Sikh cavalry who occupied it retired as the British advance appeared, it was not supposed that an encounter was at hand. Under this impression the British troops took up their camping ground, and were preparing refreshments, after a fatiguing march of twenty-two miles, when scouts arrived with the intelligence that the enemy were hastening forward, and were only three miles distant. The British mustered 12,350 rank and file and 40 guns, while the Sikh forces amounted to

---

[1] War Office and other Records.
[2] From "The History of India," with the kind permission of Messrs. Blackie & Son, Publishers, Glasgow.

about 30,000 with 40 guns, most of the latter, however, were of much heavier metal than those of the British, which were merely the six-pounders of the Horse Artillery. It was about three in the afternoon when the approach of the enemy was announced, and the British troops, already in a state of great exhaustion, had not more than sufficient time to get under arms and move to their positions when they were ordered to advance to the attack. They had not proceeded above two miles when they found the enemy in position. The battle, which immediately commenced, is thus described in Sir Hugh Gough's Despatch :—' The country is a dead flat, covered at short intervals
' with a low but, in some places, thick jhow jungle, and dotted with sandy hillocks.
' The enemy screened their artillery and infantry behind this jungle, and such
' undulations as the ground afforded, and, whilst our twelve battalions formed from
' echelon of brigade into line, opened a very severe fire upon our advancing troops,
' which was vigorously replied to by the battery of horse artillery under Brigadier
' Brooke, which was soon joined by the two light field batteries. The rapid and
' well-directed fire of our artillery appeared soon to paralyse that of the enemy ; and it
' was necessary to complete our infantry dispositions without advancing the artillery
' too near to the jungle, I directed the cavalry, under Brigadiers White and Gough,
' to make a flank movement on the enemy's left with a view of threatening and
' turning that flank, if possible. With praiseworthy gallantry the 3rd Light Dragoons
' with the second brigade of cavalry, consisting of the body-guard and 5th Light
' Cavalry, with a portion of the 4th Lancers, turned the left of the Sikh army, and,
' sweeping along the whole rear of its infantry and guns, silenced for a time the
' latter, and put their numerous cavalry to flight. Whilst this movement was taking
' place on the enemy's left, I directed the remainder of the 4th Lancers, the
' 9th Irregular Cavalry, under Brigadier Mactier, with a light field battery, to
' threaten their right. This manœuvre was also successful. Had not the infantry
' and guns of the enemy been screened by the jungle, these brilliant charges of the
' cavalry would have been productive of greater effect. When the infantry advanced
' to the attack, Brigadier Brooke rapidly pushed on his horse artillery close to the
' jungle, and the cannonade was resumed on both sides. The infantry, under Major-
' Generals Sir Harry Smith, Gilbert, and Sir John MacCaskill, attacked in echelon
' of lines the enemy's infantry, almost invisible amongst the woods and the
' approaching darkness of the night. The opposition of the enemy was such as might
' have been expected from troops who had everything at stake, and who had long
' vaunted of being irresistible. Their ample and extended line, from their great
' superiority of numbers, far outflanked ours ; but this was counteracted by the flank
' movements of our cavalry. The attack of the infantry now commenced, and the
' roll of fire from this powerful arm soon convinced the Sikh army that they had
' met with a foe they little expected, and their whole force was driven from position
' after position, with great slaughter and the loss of seventeen pieces of artillery,
' some of them of heavy calibre ; our infantry using that never-failing weapon the
' bayonet wherever the enemy stood. Night only saved them from worse disaster,
' for this stout conflict was maintained during an hour and a half of dim starlight,
' amidst a cloud of dust from the sandy plain which yet more obscured every object.'

"The victory, though glorious, was dearly purchased, the British loss amounting to 872, of whom 215 were killed and 657 wounded. Among the former were two officers who had acquired distinction in Afghanistan—Sir John MacCaskill, who was shot dead while gallantly leading his division, and Sir Robert Sale, who was fatally wounded and survived only a few days."

Major-General Sir John MacCaskill had three sons in the army, viz. :—

(1.) Colonel John C. MacCaskill, who served in the 51st Madras Infantry from 1836 to 1863; saw active service with his regiment during the Canarese insurrection, and was with it in the Kurnool Field Force. He died at Bedford on the 12th of November, 1898, aged seventy-nine years.

(2.) Lieutenant Charles MacCaskill, who received his commission in 1843, served for a time as Aide-de-Camp to his father (Sir John MacCaskill), and died at the age of nineteen; and

(3.) Major William MacCaskill.

Lieutenant John MacCaskill (son of Colonel John MacCaskill, and grandson of Sir John MacCaskill) got his commission in the 18th Royal Irish in January, 1892; was promoted to the rank of Lieutenant in the following year, and appointed to the 6th Punjab Infantry—Punjab Frontier Force—in March, 1894.

Lieutenant MacCaskill was present with the 4th Punjab Infantry (Punjab Field Force) in Waziristan in 1894-95, for which he received a medal and clasp. He was transferred to the famous Queen's Own Corps of Guides in January, 1895, and served with it in the Chitral Relief Force in 1895, and for his share in that brilliant campaign he received a medal and clasp. He was also actively employed with his corps in the Malakand Field Force in 1897.

"The infantry [of the Queen's Own Guides] were conspicuous in the assault on the precipitous slopes of the Malakand, while the cavalry [of the Guides] equally distinguished themselves on the following day against the hostile tribesmen in the Swat Valley. But it was in the action on the 13th of April on the banks of the Panjkora River that the conduct of the Guides was most noticeable, reminding those who witnessed it that this was the same corps which had confronted the overwhelming numbers of mutineers at Delhi, which had stormed the heights round Kabul, and of which the name was foremost in a hundred fights on the frontier. The bridge across the Panjkora was carried away by the flood, thus cutting off the retreat of the Guides and preventing reinforcements being sent to them. Yet they steadily fell back on the bridgehead, and inflicted a loss of 500 men on the enemy, probably one for every Guide engaged, their own loss being only three killed and nine wounded." [1]

The celebrated MacCrimmons were for generations family pipers to the MacLeods of MacLeod. The first of these famous musicians of whom we have any notice was Iain Odhar, who lived about the year 1600. The passing of the Heritable Jurisdiction Abolition Act of 1747 put an end to the occupation of hereditary pipers, and the

---

[1] From "Blackwood's Magazine," May, 1897, by kind permission of Messrs. William Blackwood and Sons.

MacCrimmons were consequently obliged to take to other walks of life—notably, the profession of arms, in which several of them gained distinction.

Major MacCrimmon of Glenelg, a distinguished officer, was a Skyeman, and married a Skye lady, Frances, daughter of Norman MacDonald, of Scalpay. Their only son was Captain Norman MacCrimmon, of the 74th Highlanders, who died unmarried in 1874 or 1875.

Captain Peter MacCrimmon, Borreraig, Duirinish, Isle of Skye, afterwards of Cape Coast Castle (known as Padruig Mòr among his own countrymen on account of his great stature), is said to have been in the 42nd Regiment; to have served in Spain under Sir John Moore, and taken part in the famous retreat to Corunna, as well as in the memorable battle which followed. Captain MacCrimmon was a tall, powerful man, and many wonderful stories are told of his prowess. A very large stone, which he is said to have lifted, is still to be seen at Borreraig, a marvellous feat of strength by all accounts. He is also represented as having been the champion pugilist of Great Britain in his own day, having vanquished, after a fierce struggle, an Italian prize-fighter, who was till then considered to be the strongest man in the three kingdoms. Captain MacCrimmon was a grandson, it is said, of the celebrated piper, Donald Bàn MacCrimmon, who was killed in the rout of Moy on the 16th of February, 1746.

Captain Donald MacCrimmon. When General Norman MacLeod of MacLeod returned to the Isle of Skye in 1799, among those that welcomed him to Dunvegan Castle was Captain Donald MacCrimmon (the representative of the famous family of pipers), who earned for himself much renown in the American War, and who, on the occasion of the Chief's return home (above referred to), played the favourite clan salute, "Fàilte Ruairidh Mhòir." The Reverend Dr. Norman MacLeod, "Caraide na 'n Gaidheal," was present, and said afterwards, "I can never forget the impression which " the whole scene made upon my youthful mind."[1]

Lieutenant Donald MacCrimmon, of the 42nd Highlanders, was killed at the battle of Toulouse on the 10th of April, 1814,[2] in which his regiment had the honour allotted to it of leading the attack on the enemy's redoubts, a formidable undertaking, as the result showed. So desperate was the combat that of about 500 of all ranks whom the corps brought into action ninety only reached the fatal goal, to which the blood-stained colour (with broken staff) was borne by a sergeant, three gallant bearers (one of whom was MacCrimmon) having fallen in the advance.

Captain Kenneth Tolmie,[3] a son of William Tolmie, Commissioner to Norman MacLeod, XIX. Chief of MacLeod, was born (probably at Dunvegan) on the 1st of April, 1724. He received an Ensigncy in Lord John Murray's Regiment (as the Black Watch was then designated, after its commanding officer); was promoted to the rank of

---
[1] Memorials of the Rev. Norman MacLeod, Senior.
[2] "History of the Highlands and Highland Clans."
[3] The older spelling was Tolme.

Lieutenant in 1755, and afterwards rose to that of Captain. He served with great distinction on the Continent, in America, and in India. Captain Tolmie died in Ireland in 1809.

Dr. William Tolmie, 78th Highlanders, was a nephew of Captain Kenneth Tolmie, of the Black Watch.

William Tolmie was first appointed as an Ensign in the Skye Northern Battalion of Volunteer infantry in 1804, and afterwards transferred with the same rank to the 78th Regiment. But in order to utilise his medical training he subsequently exchanged his combatant's commission for that of surgeon to his corps. He died in India, unmarried, in 1809.

Dr. Tolmie was a remarkably handsome man. A correspondent, writing about him, said :—" He was born at Duirinish, and brought up soul and body in MacLeod's country,
" where he was much beloved. An old lady once told me that he arrived at one of
" the hospitable houses of his native isle to a gathering, and, being weary, was asleep
" when all the company had assembled. An aged lady discovered him, and lovingly
" called a number of other ladies to come and look at William Tolmie's beautiful
" appearance asleep!"

The following extracts from a letter, written from Goa on the 19th of September, 1809, show in what high estimation Dr. Tolmie was held in his regiment and at the station where he served :—" He was a person for whom I had contracted the highest
" esteem and regard, and whom all his acquaintances at the station most sincerely
" regretted. . . . . . Repeated attacks of a fever during the last twelvemonths
" had very considerably weakened and reduced his constitution. . . . . . . He
" had often, to my own knowledge, intended to have left for Madras, but motives of
" delicacy, in leaving his corps destitute of medical assistance, always induced him to
" defer it, and to that at length he fell a sacrifice . . . . . . one of the finest
" and most sensible of men I ever saw."

Captain William MacKenzie, Royal Navy (who was a native of Duirinish, and who lived at Sgianaidean, in Skye)—another nephew of Captain Kenneth Tolmie—was first Lieutenant of His Majesty's ship "Ajax," and afterwards commanded His Majesty's ship "Magicienne." He was killed in an engagement with the French, which took place off the Lizard early in this century.

Another member of this family, Lieutenant Alexander MacKenzie, also served in the Royal Navy.

Dr. Alexander Morrison, Inspector-General of Hospitals.

Alexander Morrison was the younger of the two sons of Angus Morrison, tacksman, of Sotaran, in Minginish, Isle of Skye, by his wife, Margaret MacLeod of the ancient Borline, or "Clann Mhic Uilleim" family. Dr. Morrison was born at Sotaran some time between the years 1760 and 1765; and, owing to the death of his father, he was, when quite young, left under the guardianship of his brother, Norman Morrison, who succeeded his father as tacksman of Sotaran. After getting the rudiments of his education at Portree, Alexander Morrison was sent to the University of Aberdeen to study medicine, where he had a very successful career as a student, and where he was fortunate in having for companions a number of young gentlemen from Skye. After finishing his studies at college, Dr. Morrison practised for a time in the parish of Bracadale, and afterwards in Edinburgh, until an epidemic of small-pox, having broken out in the parish of Duirinish, with which the local medical men were unable to cope successfully,[1] a messenger was sent for him to Edinburgh on foot. This messenger kept up with the doctor, stage after stage, on the return journey (although the latter was on horseback), and crossed the ferry with him at Kylerea in the same boat. Dr. Morrison was able to stamp out the epidemic in a short time by proper sanitation and other improved methods of treatment.

The amenities of an ordinary medical practice not satisfying his ambition, he went shortly after this to London to pass his examination for the army, the result of which was that he tied with another candidate for first place in the honour list. When he was leaving Skye to join the army a great many of the local gentlemen gathered together at Sconser to give him a farewell dinner, and next morning several of his friends accompanied him on horseback to the place of embarkation at Kyle. Among them were his brother Norman and his cousin, Norman MacLeod of Gillen (afterwards Major-General Norman MacLeod, C.B.).[1]

Shortly after joining the army he was sent to the West Indies, where he met with a serious misfortune, from the effects of which he never fully recovered. While discharging his duty he was severely wounded in the head by a splinter from a shell. He alludes to this accident (in one of the few letters which remain of his correspondence with his brother) as follows :—" We have it from the Duke of York's authority that " we are to embark for the Cape of Good Hope—the first fleet—and from thence to " proceed to the East. I am not yet fully determined with regard to the ship I shall " take in that event. The misfortunes of the West have certainly not rendered me a " very fit subject for an Eastern climate, and yet the situation of first surgeon to a " regiment (the 34th, to which he was gazetted as head surgeon on the 18th of July, " 1796) of such an establishment as ours is too good and profitable to be voluntarily " resigned. I am well assured that my situation (moderately speaking) is worth a " thousand a year, which, you must admit, is rather a tempting inducement to an " ambitious adventurer."

In a subsequent letter he shows signs of impatience at being detained at the Cape during the voyage to which he says (in a letter to his brother) that " in the two " troopships which left in consort over 200 of the soldiers died of fever; and of the " fifteen medical men on board, I am the only one fit for duty. The first Assistant " Surgeon died of the epidemic, and the remainder of the junior surgeons are either " dead or in hospital."

After this Dr. Morrison's promotion was rapid, it having been accelerated by his having had the good fortune to secure the friendship of the Duke of York (a personal friend of whom he had carried through a serious illness) and of General the Honourable

---

[1] Manuscript Memoir by his grand-nephew, Dr. Alexander Morrison, Larkhall.

Arthur Wellesley (afterwards Duke of Wellington), who was the doctor's "best man" when he got married.[1]

Dr. Morrison served throughout the Mahratta War of 1800-1803, and it was probably during this period that he became the intimate friend of General Wellesley.

In consequence of the injury to his head (already mentioned)—a part of the outer table of the skull having been carried away—he was subject to periodic attacks of fever in India, which finally carried him off. After his death a monument was erected to his memory in Calcutta, and his brother officers sent an engraving of it along with an address of condolence to his brother, but both the engraving and the address were unfortunately lost, or destroyed, when the family were removing from Skye to Sollas in North Uist.

Dr. Morrison (who was a man of a very generous nature, and a true Highlander of the old stock) delighted in doing all he could for the welfare of his countrymen, and no Gael (particularly if he was a Skyeman) ever sought his help in vain.[1]

Dr. Morrison appears to have been a man of great force of character. In one of his letters he says:—"I determined I would be something or nothing." This shows the grit he was made of. His widow survived him for several years. They had one son, who was also in the army, and who died in London about the year 1840. Mrs. Morrison visited Skye about 1830, and offered to buy a commission in the army for her nephew, Mr. Alexander Morrison, who was named after her late husband; but the young man's father declined the offer, saying, "The British Army has deprived me of "my only brother, my brother-in-law, and my eldest son, and I am not going to give "it my youngest son also."

Captain Morrison of Sgianaidean, who co-operated with James MacPherson in collecting the poems of Ossian, was a cousin of Dr. Alexander Morrison, Inspector-General of Hospitals. Captain Morrison is said to have served in the field during the American War of Independence, and his name is frequently mentioned in the memorable controversy which arose as to the authenticity of the poems of the Prince of Gaelic Bards.[1]

Captain Donald Stewart was a brother-in-law of Mr. Norman Morrison, and fought in America in the War of Independence. At the close of the war several officers who had been engaged in that campaign were deprived, somehow or other, of their pensions, although they were entitled to them. Captain Stewart immediately applied himself to have their grievances redressed, and at last success crowned his efforts. A number of the officers who had benefited by his exertions in their favour fixed upon a day to give him a public banquet in recognition of his generous services on their behalf. He wrote to his mother asking her to make a plaid of Stewart tartan for him to wear on the occasion; but he never wore it, for the long strain on his mind in advocating the cause of his comrades, acting on a frame already weakened by the hardships which he had endured in active service, brought on an illness from which he

---

[1] Manuscript Memoir by Dr. Alexander Morrison of Larkhall.

died, a few days before the date fixed for the banquet. His mother was Flora MacLeod of the Clann Alasdair Ruaidh, whom MacLeod of MacLeod of the day called "the wise wife." To him she said never to bring an English wife or servant to Dunvegan Castle, as both would alienate the love of his people, and that it would be a bad day for MacLeod when he had only "English Skyemen" about him.[1]

THE NICOLSONS OF SKYE.

Captain Samuel Nicolson.

Corporal John Nicolson, Tote (late of the 42nd Highlanders), says that Captain Samuel Nicolson, who belonged to that neighbourhood, fought in the American War.

Lieutenant Malcolm Nicolson, of the Indian Army, son of Donald Nicolson of Scorrabreck, by his wife, Margaret MacDonald of Scalpay (daughter of Norman MacDonald of Scalpay, and sister of Adjutant-General Sir John MacDonald, G.C.B.), was serving in India when he died of a fever at an early age. He was a remarkably handsome man, and much loved in Skye.

Lieutenant George Elder Nicolson, of the Indian Army, was a brother of Lieutenant Malcolm Nicolson of Scorrabreck. He, too, was an extremely handsome man, and a splendid piper. Like his brother, he was a great favourite in his native isle, and, like him also, he died young in India.

Captain James Nicolson, who died of his wounds at Malta in 1812, was the son of Malcolm, son of Donald of Stenscholl, son of the Reverend Donald Nicolson of Kilmuir, Chief of the Nicolsons of Scorrabreck. Malcolm Nicolson's wife was Jessie MacDonald, sister of Major Allan MacDonald of Knock.

THE BEATONS OR BETHUNES OF SKYE.

The Famous Physicians to the MacDonalds and the MacLeods.

The Beatons or Bethunes of Skye are descended from Archibald Bethune of Pittochy or Capeldray, in Fife, fifth son of John Bethune, V. laird of Balfour of that surname, by Marjory, third daughter of David Boswell of Balmuto, Chief of the Boswells. According to the Chartulary of Glasgow, Archibald Bethune was present with Cardinal Beaton at Dumfries on the 27th of November, 1539, when a solemn protestation was made against his exercising the sacred function as Archbishop of St. Andrews within the Diocese of Glasgow—"coram his testibus nobili et potenti

---

[1] Manuscript Memoir by Dr. Alexander Morrison of Larkhall.

"Domino Hugoni Domino de Somerveile, Roberto Betoun de Creich, Archibaldo "Betoun de Capeldra." The solemnity of the protestation, the grandeur and pomp of his nephew the Cardinal, and the multiplicity of his preferments appear abundantly from the remarks of one John Turner, who acted as Public Notary on the occasion.[1]

Archibald Bethune had a son named Peter, who, being a famous physician, was called to Argyllshire to practise his skill there, and from thence he received an invitation to the Isle of Skye from the lairds of MacDonald and MacLeod, upon condition that he should get as much land rent free as he liked to possess in return for his medical services. It was also promised, on the doctor's side, that one of his posterity—particularly the eldest son of the family, if he had a turn for it—should be educated as a physician, without any expense to him or his successors, while any of them continued in that country and inclined to the study of physic or medicine. It is interesting to note that Dr. Bethune found Skye to be " far from being a disagreeable " place, and that it was fruitful in cattle and victual, and abounded with the best fishes " of all kinds." The doctor married a daughter of MacDonald of Clanranald, with issue, one of whom, Ferquhard, senior, had a son, Angus, a physician, who " wrote " on medicine in the Irish character for the use of Highlanders."

This Angus,[1] we are told, had six sons—Ferquhard, John, Angus (the strong), Ewan, Neil, and Angus (the fair)—all of whom were more inclined to the military than to the medical profession. None of them studied medicine.

John and Angus (the fair) went to Mull; and having there taken part in a fight the former was killed, and it was believed in Skye that the latter also was slain on the same occasion. Angus (the strong) was lost in Glenelg ferry. Ferquhard, the eldest son ("brave and quiet"), along with 700 men from the Island of Skye, fought gallantly at the battle of Worcester on the 3rd of September, 1651, almost all of whom were either killed or taken prisoners. He, however, escaped with his life, and then he fell out with his friends about his marriage, and it is said that " he fought the MacDonalds " frequently and successfully ere agreeing." Ferquhard ("the brave and quiet") had, by his first marriage, a son of the name of Kenneth of " Leabost " in Skye. He married a daughter of " MacLean of Dowart," and by her had five sons and four daughters. John, the second son, occupied the farm of Lourkhill in MacLeod's country. He married Elizabeth Bethune, eldest daughter of Ferquhard Bethune of Trein, with issue, two sons and three daughters. John, the younger son, became tenant of the farm of " Achork in Trotternish."[1]

He served for ten years in the old Highland Regiment (The Black Watch), and was wounded at the battle of Fontenoy on the 30th of April, 1745. John Bethune, senior, a great grandson of Ferquhard, seventh in descent from John Bethune, V. of Balfour, fought at the battle of Sheriffmuir on the 13th of November, 1715. He afterwards died unmarried. The Reverend Duncan Bethune, the eldest son of John, sixth and youngest son of Ferquhard, eldest son of the second Dr. Angus, sixth descendant from John Bethune, V. of Balfour, was a minister in Mull. His only son,

---

[1] "The Bethunes of Skye," by the Rev. Thomas Whyte, minister of Liberton, Mid-Lothian, 1778.

John, married a second cousin of MacLean of Lochbuie, with issue, several sons. This John was "out" in the '45, but returned to Mull.

Hector, the second son of Ferquhard Bethune (tenth in descent from John Bethune, V. of Balfour), who succeeded to Kilellan in Kintyre on the death of his wife's brother, MacEacharn, chief of that surname, we are told, "went to the military."

Of all the physicians of this gifted race perhaps the most notable was Neil, the second son of Neil, fifth son of Ferquhard, who has been mentioned already. This Neil is said to have been a great physician, although he was not well educated. He was forty years old before he appeared as a doctor; judged the various properties of plants and roots by their different tastes; and observed their flowers and learned their qualities thereby.[1] From roots, plants, and flowers he extracted juices in a manner that was peculiar to himself, and these juices he administered to his patients after first carefully studying their constitutions. Martin, in his "Western Isles," refers to the doctor, whose cures he says were attributed to "a compact with the devil"!

Several members of the Bethune family distinguished themselves in other walks of life, notably in the clerical profession. The Rev. John Bethune, eldest son of the 3rd Doctor Angus, eighth descendant from the fifth laird of Balfour, became minister of Bracadale—"an able divine and a learned physician." He was the first who dispensed the sacrament of the Lord's Supper in Skye after the Protestant manner. He died in 1707. His son (by his wife, a daughter of MacLeod of Drynoch), the Rev. Kenneth Bethune, was liberally educated, and was chosen minister of Kilmuir. He died in 1739.

The Rev. Ferquhard Bethune (a famous antiquary and genealogist), third son of Kenneth Bethune of Leabost, was minister of Croy for twenty-seven years. He died on the 5th of February, 1746. His second son, the Rev. Dr. John Bethune (a great pulpit orator), succeeded his uncle as minister of Rosskeen. The learned doctor died on the 14th of April, 1774.[1]

The Rev. John Bethune (the elder son of Angus, third son of John Bethune, of Brebost) was appointed chaplain to Colonel MacLean's Royal Highland Emigrant Regiment.

Captain Malcolm MacLean (Calum Mac an Doctair) was a son of the famous Skye physician, Dr. John MacLean (whose family had, according to Pennant, who met the doctor at Duntulm, in 1772, been physicians to the MacDonalds for centuries) by his wife, Margaret Nicolson.

Captain MacLean, after retiring from the service, settled at Aird, near Duntulm, where he died upwards of fifty years ago. He was a man of great strength, and noted

---

[1] "The Bethunes of Skye," by the Rev. Thomas Whyte.

for some eccentricities. A confirmed bachelor, he had no females among his domestics, and (as a rule) avoided the society of the fair sex. On one occasion (at a Highland ball) a friend called his attention to a fascinating lady, and suggested that she would make a fine wife for the gallant officer. She was of the dark type of Highland beauty, and a somewhat low dress helped to display her charms. The Captain replied, "Ise a phosadh! Co a phosadh ise, 'us craicionn oirre coltach ri craicionn dallaig?"[1]

Superintending Surgeon John Grant, Bengal Medical Department.

Dr. Grant was appointed as an Assistant Surgeon on the 7th of October, 1816; Surgeon on the 17th of August, 1827; and Superintending Surgeon on the 17th of July, 1852. He retired on the 11th of September, 1857, and died on the 14th of April, 1862.

Dr. Grant held the following important appointments in India—viz., Apothecary to the East India Company; Member of a Committee for conducting operations in the Experimental Laboratory; Member of a Committee for the Examination of Senior Students of the Medical College, for which particular service he received the thanks of the Government; Member of the Press Committee; Assay Master of the Calcutta Mint; Visitor to the Medical College, "on account of his high character;" Member of the Council of Education, Calcutta; and Superintending Surgeon of the Dacca and Agra Circles successively.

Captain William Stewart of Ensay was born at Duntulm, Isle of Skye, in 1853. He entered the army in 1875; served for four years as a Lieutenant in the 1st West India Regiment; seven years in the 1st and 2nd Battalions of the 24th Regiment; and ten years as a Captain in the 1st and 2nd Battalions of the Argyll and Sutherland Highlanders.

Captain Stewart retired from the service in December, 1896.

---

[1] "Hereditary Physicians of the Hebrides," by William MacKenzie, "Glasgow Herald," 14th May, 1898.

THE MACLEODS OF RAASAY, RIGG, AND EYRE.

The MacLeods of Raasay derive their Gaelic patronymic ("Clann Mhic Ghille Chaluim") from Malcolm Garbh, I. of Raasay (who possessed that island early in the sixteenth century), second son of Malcolm, IV. of Lewis.

Probably the most remarkable warrior of this gallant race, in the olden times, was John Garbh, the third Chieftain, who succeeded his father in 1648, and who is said to have been the most powerful Highlander of his day. He was, unfortunately, drowned,[1] at the early age of twenty-one, when returning to Skye from Lewis, where he had been visiting his relative, the Earl of Seaforth. Mairi Nighean Alasdair Ruaidh, the famous clan poetess, composed a beautiful Gaelic poem, and Patrick Mòr MacCrimmon, the celebrated piper, made a well-known lament in memory of Iain Garbh Mac Ghille Chaluim.

Malcolm MacLeod, VIII. of Raasay, accompanied by his second son, Dr. Murdoch MacLeod of Eyre, and his nephew Captain Malcolm MacLeod[2] (whose name will always be honourably associated with the hairbreadth escapes of the Prince among the Western Isles, as well as with Johnson and Boswell's visit to Skye and Raasay in 1773) joined Prince Charlie in 1745 at the head of 100 men of their clan. After the battle of Culloden, old Malcolm found his way back in safety to Raasay, where he hid for a time. To escape capture, however, he was obliged eventually to go to the wilds of Knoydart, which were more inaccessible than his own island home. His third son,[3] Norman, was an officer in the service of the States-General.

The Reverend Roderick MacLeod, minister of Snizort, sixth son (by an irregular marriage) of Old Malcolm MacLeod of Raasay, married Mary, daughter of Donald MacLeod, tacksman, of Swordale, and their sons Malcolm, John, Donald, and Charles all served their Sovereign either in the army or in the navy. John was a Captain in the 27th Regiment, Donald an officer in the Royal Navy, and Charles a doctor in the employment of the East India Company.

Dr. Roderick MacLeod, son of the famous Highland divine, the late Reverend Roderick MacLeod, Free Church minister of Snizort ("Maighstir Ruairidh") by his wife, Anne Robertson MacDonald, daughter of Donald MacDonald of Skaebost, joined

---

[1] It is said that the disaster was caused by a witch who, in the form of a hooded crow ("ann an riochd feannaig"), had alighted on the gunwale of the boat near Iain Garbh, who was steering. A stroke of MacLeod's great sword, intended for the unwelcome visitor, missing her, cut through the side of the boat ("sliasaid a bhata") down to below the water's edge, and the galley with its crew went to the bottom of the sea. The emissary of Satan, of course, lived to tell the tale!

[2] It was of "young Malcolm" (who was a son of Dr. Murdoch MacLeod of Eyre) that Boswell said: —"I never saw a figure that gave me a more perfect representation of a Highland gentleman."

[3] Probably the officer of this name who was appointed as an Ensign in Captain Thomson's Company of MacKay's Regiment on the 11th of February, 1745; and Lieutenant in Major MacKay's Company of Marjoribanks' Regiment on the 3rd of November of the same year.—Dutch War Office Records.

the Medical Service in Bengal on the 10th of June, 1868, and served for upwards of twenty-three years at various stations and in several capacities, including those of Superintendent of the Temple Medical School, Health Officer at the Port of Calcutta, and Superintendent of Emigration and Protector of Emigrants.[1]

John MacLeod, IX. of Raasay, married a Miss MacQueen,[2] by whom he had a numerous family. Their eldest son, Colonel James MacLeod, commanded the 1st Isle of Skye Regiment of Volunteers (numbering 517), which was raised in 1803. Another son, Captain Malcolm MacLeod, belonged to the Indian Army, and died unmarried.

Of John MacLeod's many daughters several married military men. The eldest, " an elegant, well-bred woman, and celebrated for her beauty over all those regions by " the name of Miss Flory Raasay," married Colonel James Muir Campbell of Lawers (afterwards fifth Earl of Loudon).

Margaret, the second daughter, was the wife of Martin Martin of Beallach and Duntulm (one of the handsomest and strongest men of his day in Skye), and their daughter became the wife of General Count Maurin, one of the First Napoleon's Brigadier-Generals.

This Martin Martin was uncle of Sir Ranald Martin, Knight and C.B., and granduncle to Field-Marshal Sir Donald Martin Stewart, G.C.B., &c.

Janet, John MacLeod's third daughter, married Archibald MacRa of Ardintoul, in Lochalsh, and they had two sons in the army, Colonel Sir John MacRa, K.C.H., and Dr. James MacRa.

Isabella, daughter of Archibald MacRa and Janet MacLeod, already mentioned, was the wife of Major Colin MacRae of the 75th Highlanders, and their son was the late Dr. Duncan MacRae (Inspector-General of Hospitals, East India Company's service), of Kames Castle, Island of Bute, who served in the Afghan War of 1842 under General Pollock and other campaigns, and who married Grace Stewart, with issue, Major John MacRae-Gilstrap of Ballimore, Argyllshire (who served with "the Black Watch," in the Soudan; fought at the battle of Tamai on the 13th March, 1884; at the battle of Kirbekan on the 10th of the following February, as well as in some minor intervening affairs, for which he was awarded the Egyptian War medal with two clasps, the Khedive's bronze star, and was mentioned in despatches), and Lieutenant Colin MacRae, now of "the Black Watch."

Mary, daughter of Archibald McRa of Ardintoul, and Janet MacLeod of Raasay, married Deputy-Inspector-General of Hospitals Stewart Chisholm, who was present at the battle of Waterloo, the capture of Paris, and took part in the Canadian Campaign of 1838–39. Their eldest son was the late Captain MacRa-Chisholm, a typical Highland gentleman, and their second son, Loudon, was killed in the Burmese War of 1853.

---

[1] India Office Records.
[2] Cameron's "History and Traditions of the Isle of Skye," and Mackenzie's "History of the MacLeods."

Catherine, fourth daughter of John MacLeod, IX. of Raasay, married her cousin, Lieutenant John MacLeod, of the Royal Navy, second son of Dr. Murdoch MacLeod of Eyre.

Isabella, Raasay's fifth daughter, became the wife of Major Thomas Ross, of the Royal Artillery.[1]

Their eldest daughter was the well-known Lady D'Oyly, their second was Lady Gilbert, and another married General Schubrick.

Julia, sixth daughter of John MacLeod, IX. of Raasay, married Olaus MacLeod of Bharkasaig, and this couple's second daughter was the wife of General Farrington, of the Bengal Artillery.[1]

Jane, seventh daughter of John MacLeod, IX. of Raasay, married her cousin, Colonel John MacLeod of Colbecks.[1]

Anne, eighth daughter of John MacLeod, IX. of Raasay, became the wife of Captain Donald MacKenzie of Hartfield, who had served in the 100th Regiment,[1] and two of their daughters became the wives of soldiers—viz., Flora Loudon, wife of General Sir Alexander Lindsay, of the East India Company's service; and Anne, wife of Colonel Christopher Webb Smith.

Mary, ninth daughter of John MacLeod, IX. of Raasay, was the wife of the Reverend Donald Campbell, D.D., minister of Kilninver, Argyllshire,[1] whose daughter, Jean Mary Campbell, married James Munro MacNabb, of the Bengal Civil Service; two of his sons were Sir Donald Campbell MacNabb, K.C.I.E. and C.S.I., and John Campbell Erskine MacNabb, of the 3rd Bengal Cavalry, who was killed during the Indian Mutiny in 1857.

Christiana, Raasay's tenth daughter, married Alexander MacSween, an Indian Judge, whose only son Charles, also an Indian Judge, married his cousin Margaret, daughter of Olaus MacLeod of Bharkasaig, and they had a son, Henry Davidson, an officer in the Bengal Artillery, and another son, Hastings, an officer in the Bengal Engineers.

John MacLeod, XI. and last laird of Raasay, was an officer in the 78th Highlanders. In 1846 the estate was sold to George Rainy.

The MacLeods of Rigg are cadets of the MacLeods of Raasay. John MacLeod, I. of Rigg, was the second son of Alexander MacLeod, VII. of Raasay, by his wife Catherine, third daughter of Sir Norman MacLeod, I. of Bernera. Their eldest son, the gallant Captain Malcolm MacLeod, of the '45, is referred to elsewhere.

Norman MacLeod, II. of Rigg, had two sons in the army—viz., Captain Norman MacLeod, who served in the American War of Independence, and afterwards settled at Camustianavaig, in Skye; and Captain John MacLeod of Ollach, who also served in the American War,[1] and on his return home succeeded his father.

---

[1] Mackenzie's "History of the MacLeods."

Dr. Murdoch MacLeod of Kilpheder, North Uist, third son of Norman MacLeod, II. of Rigg, married Mary, daughter of MacLean of Borreray, and their fifth son was Dr. Alexander MacLeod ("an Doctair Bàn"), who was for many years Chamberlain for Lord MacDonald in Skye and North Uist, and afterwards for Clanranald in South Uist and Benbecula. An Doctair Bàn was probably the most popular man who ever acted as a factor in the Highlands of Scotland.

Dr. Alexander MacLeod married Mary, daughter of Kenneth Campbell of Strond, in Harris (by his wife, Anne, daughter of the famous Donald MacLeod of Bernera and his third wife, Margaret MacLeod of Grishornish). The Doctair Bàn's daughter, Johanna Campbell, married Harry MacDonald of Treaslane. Their eldest son is Colonel Alexander MacDonald, V.D., Portree, and another son,[1] Dr. Thomas Rankin MacDonald, has risen to high rank in the Indian Army, both of whom we have mentioned already.

The first of the MacLeods of Eyre was Dr. Murdoch MacLeod, second son of Malcolm MacLeod, VIII. of Raasay. Mention has already been made of Dr. MacLeod in connection with the rising of "the Forty-Five." The doctor married Anne, daughter of Alexander MacDonald of Boisdale by his wife, Margaret, daughter of John MacDonald, II. of Castleton. Their son John was a Lieutenant in the Royal Navy; saw much active service, and fought in Nelson's ship (the "Victory") at the battle of Trafalgar. Another son, Norman, was a Lieutenant in the 92nd Highlanders, and died in Egypt, in 1801, from the effects of a wound which he had received at the battle of Aboukir.[1]

Colonel Sir John MacRa, K.C.H., son of Archibald MacRa of Ardintoul, Invershiel, and Janet, daughter of John MacLeod, X. of Raasay, was born at Ardintoul. He joined the 79th Highlanders as an Ensign on the 25th of March, 1805; was promoted to the rank of Lieutenant on the 5th of September of the same year; appointed Captain in the 27th Foot on the 23rd of December, 1812; Captain in the 1st Foot on the 28th of January, 1813; Major, Brevet, on the 2nd of June, 1818; Lieutenant-Colonel, Brevet, on the 29th of March, 1821; placed on half-pay on the 4th of May, 1826; Colonel, Brevet, on the 10th of January, 1837; and Deputy-Quarter-Master-General in the East Indies from the 29th of March, 1821, till the 12th of April, 1841.[2] He died at Bruaich, Inverness-shire, on the 9th of August, 1847, and the following obituary notice appeared at the time:—

"COLONEL SIR JOHN MACRA, K.C.H.

"Colonel Sir John MacRa, K.C.H., who died at Bruaich on the 9th inst., was for a long time prior to his death confined to the house by severe indisposition. He joined

---

[1] Mackenzie's "History of the MacLeods."   [2] War Office Records.

THE MACLEODS OF RAASAY, ETC.

Lieutenant JOHN MACLEOD, Royal Navy.
(From Colonel Alexander MacDonald, Portree.)

Colonel Sir JOHN MACRA, K.C.H.
(From Major John MacRae Gilstrap.)

Major JOHN MACRAE GILSTRAP.
(From Mr. John MacKay, Editor of *The Celtic Monthly*.)

CAPTAIN WILLIAM STEWART OF ENSAY.
(See p. 168.)

THE MACLEODS OF RAASAY.

Lieutenant-General Sir JOHN MACLEOD, G.C.H.,
Royal Artillery.

(From Sir Henry Lynedoch-Gardiner, K.C.V.O.)

(The original Portrait, by Hurlstone, along with that of General Sir Robert Gardiner, G.C.B., by the same artist, have recently been presented by Lady Gardiner to the Royal Artillery for the Mess at Woolwich.)

Lieutenant-Colonel CHARLES MACLEOD,
of the 43rd Regiment.

(From Miniature belonging to that Corps.)

General Sir HENRY LYNEDOCH-GARDINER, K.C.V.O.
Equerry to Her Majesty the Queen.

Major NEIL MACLEOD, Royal Artillery.

the 79th Regiment in 1804, when the 2nd Battalion was formed, but was afterwards attached to the 1st Battalion, and served with it in 1807 at the siege and surrender of Copenhagen.

"In 1808 he accompanied the regiment, with the force under Sir John Moore, to Sweden, and afterwards in the same year to Portugal and Spain.

"He was present in the whole of the operations of that campaign, and in the retreat through Galicia to Corunna, taking part in that memorable battle.

"In 1809, with the same regiment, forming a part of the army under the Earl of Chatham, he was present at the siege and capture of Flushing.

"While there Sir John suffered a severe attack of the Walcheren fever, from which he never thoroughly recovered. Towards the end of 1810, he returned to the Peninsula, where he continued to serve with his regiment, and was present in all the engagements in which the regiment took part, down to 1813, including Fuentes d'Onor, Salamanca, the siege of Burgos, and many smaller affairs.

"In 1813 he accompanied the Marquis of Hastings to India as one of the staff, and was with his Lordship during the whole of the operations in that country. At the end of 1818, Sir John was sent home with despatches announcing the successful termination of the Mahratta and Pindarrie war, on which occasion he was strongly recommended to the favour of the Duke of York.

"Returning to India, he rejoined the Marquis of Hastings, and continued to serve during the remaining part of his administration and the command of the army, having filled the situation of Military Secretary to his Lordship for more than two years of the latter period.

"In 1823 Sir John accompanied the Marquis to Europe, and on his appointment to the Government of Malta joined him there in his former capacity of Military Secretary, remaining in that office until the death of the Marquis. From that period Sir John MacRa lived in retirement, the wretched state of his health, partly the effects of the fever caught in the swamps of Holland, rendering seclusion from public life necessary.[1]"

LIEUTENANT-GENERAL SIR JOHN MACLEOD, G.C.H., SENIOR COLONEL COMMANDANT AND FIRST DIRECTOR-GENERAL OF THE ROYAL ARTILLERY.

This distinguished officer was born on the 29th of January, 1752, and was the grandson of Colonel Æneas MacLeod of the Raasay family, who served with great distinction in the campaigns and sieges of the Duke of Marlborough. John MacLeod entered as a cadet into the Royal Military Academy on the 1st of February, 1767.[2]

On obtaining his commission as Lieutenant[3] he was ordered to Gibraltar, where he had an opportunity on a large scale of viewing and practising the garrison duties of his profession. In 1774 he returned to England and solicited leave of absence, with the

---

[1] "The Inverness Courier," 17th August, 1847.

[2] War Office Records.

[3] "Memoir of Sir John MacLeod," by his son-in-law, General Sir Robert Gardiner, G.C.B., K.C.H., published in the "United Service Journal," in 1834.

view of making an extended professional tour on the Continent. He settled, in the first instance, in the College of St. Omer, and was still engaged in general studies there when, in the following year, he was recalled to England, in order to join the forces preparing to suppress the colonial rebellion in North America. He arrived at Portsmouth at the end of the year, the expedition was then daily expected to proceed on its course, assembling previous to its final departure at Cork. Little occurred on his first arrival in America beyond the usual events of ordinary service. His letters are dated in 1776 from South Carolina; in 1777–8, from Philadelphia; in 1779, from Rhode Island; in 1780, from Charles Town. In 1781, he joined the force detached under Earl Cornwallis, which he accompanied into North Carolina during an arduous march of above 600 miles, and he had the good fortune to command the artillery engaged in the signal victory of Guildford over the combined Continental and American forces on the 15th of March. In describing his movements previous to the battle, Lord Cornwallis observes[1]:—"The woods on the right and left were reported to be "impracticable for cannon, but as that on our right appeared to be most open, I "resolved to attack the left wing of the enemy, and whilst my disposition was making "for that purpose, I ordered Lieutenant MacLeod to bring forward the guns and "cannonade their centre."

Again, the despatch, describing a critical period of the battle, states that the 2nd Battalion of Guards, having defeated a corps of continental infantry much superior in number, formed on the open field and captured two six-pounders, but pursuing with too much ardour they became exposed to an attack from Washington's dragoons, with the loss of the six-pounders they had taken. It then mentions that the enemy's cavalry was soon repulsed by a well-directed fire from the guns just brought up by Lieutenant MacLeod; and on the appearance of the Grenadiers of the Guards and the 71st Regiment the guns were soon recaptured. The exertions of the artillery under Lieutenant MacLeod's orders on this service, in overcoming the obstacles opposed to their advance by the difficulties of the country, will be best appreciated by Lord Cornwallis's description of the march of the army previous to the battle of Guildford. His Lordship says:—"Their invincible patience in the hardships and fatigues of a "march of above 600 miles, in which they have forded several large rivers and "numberless creeks, many of which would be reckoned large rivers in any other "country in the world, without tents, and often without provisions, will sufficiently "manifest their ardent zeal for the honour and interests of their Sovereign and of their "country."

Lieutenant MacLeod embarked at New York to return to Europe in November, 1781. In January, 1782, he was promoted to the rank of second Captain. On the return of the army to England, Lord Cornwallis, wishing to mark in a distinguished manner his sense of Captain MacLeod's services while under his orders, more particularly in the battle of Guildford, and in the professional resources he had shown in the previous march of the army, named him to the King, and His Majesty was pleased in

---

[1] Memoir by General Sir Robert Gardiner, G.C.B., K.C.H.

consequence to command his personal attendance and presentation by Lord Cornwallis. In the same year Captain MacLeod was appointed to the Staff of Lord George Lennox. The regiment of artillery had been increased during the American War to four battalions and an invalid battalion; and the Master-General of the Ordnance from so great an augmentation found it necessary to extend its staff, at the head of which he placed Captain MacLeod. In 1790 Lord Cornwallis was appointed Governor-General and Commander-in-Chief in India,[1] and his Lordship immediately expressed a desire that Captain MacLeod should accompany him, but his staff duties, already forming an integral part of the important discipline he was perfecting, compelled him to forego the gratification of attending his commander and friend.

We now approach a period when the peculiar powers and energies of Captain MacLeod's character were to be more conspicuously developed and brought into public notice. The war occasioned by the French Revolution worked rapid changes and improvements in the French army, which it became necessary to meet with corresponding efforts on our part. They had started and matured a system of warfare and celerity of movement peculiarly their own, and the other nations of Europe soon learned the necessity of opposing them on their own system. Their artillery particularly had undergone material change, and facility of movement was of course studied, and adopted. All field artillery was in future to have accelerated activity of movement beyond that of infantry, and a portion of it was trained to rival the movements of cavalry. The first formation of horse artillery [1] in the British army was in the early part of 1793. Two troops were formed in January of that year, others were added in quick succession. The organisation and equipment of this new arm, with the entire change that followed in the nature and system of our field artillery, gave ample scope to the indefatigable mind of Captain MacLeod, and his unremitting attention and exertions were most ably met by the zeal and emulation of the officers appointed to the new commands. At this time there occurred another gratifying instance of the high estimation in which Captain MacLeod's name was held in the army.[1] An expedition was preparing under the command of the Marquis of Hastings with whom he had served in America. His first step in making his arrangements was to offer the command of the artillery to Captain MacLeod; but not only did his staff duties again present an impediment, but his rank in the service at the time precluded the possibility of his appointment to so large a command. The following is an extract from the letter offering the appointment to Captain MacLeod :—" It is probable that I may very " speedily be employed at the head of a considerable force. In such a situation there is " not any person I could so much wish for a commander of my artillery as yourself. " If this cannot be, point out to me somebody upon whom I can rely in such a trust. " Let it be some keen fellow who will laugh in the midst of difficulties as I have seen " you do." The regiment of artillery had now been augmented from a peace establishment to a force of 25,000 men. The staff duties had, of course, increased in proportion both in trust and in importance. The Master-General, in consequence,

---

[1] Memoir by Sir Robert Gardiner, G.C.B., K.C.H.

submitted, with the approval of the Duke of York, Commander-in-Chief, a representation to His Majesty of the indispensable necessity of having a public officer as Deputy-Adjutant-General of Artillery. His Majesty was pleased to approve of the arrangement,[1] and Captain MacLeod was accordingly appointed Deputy-Adjutant-General, with the rank of Lieutenant-Colonel in the army, on March 27, 1795. On the 21st August, 1797, as has been already stated, he was promoted to the regimental rank of Lieutenant-Colonel. In 1798 a rebellion of a most disastrous character broke out in Ireland, and Lord Cornwallis was called on to proceed thither, with extended authority, to suppress it by force of arms. Colonel MacLeod considered the active employment of the Master-General of Ordnance a favourable moment for soliciting permission to accompany him, and he entreated Lord Cornwallis to submit his wishes to the King, and to exert his influence with His Majesty to that effect. He received on this occasion a most gracious and kind assurance of the King's approval of his zeal and motives; but his absence from his responsible duties was considered inadmissible. In addition to the increased extent of the corps, there was added in 1801 the establishment of a riding school on a large and efficient scale, and also a veterinary establishment adequate to the necessities of the cavalry branches of the regiment,[1] now increased by a numerous corps of drivers regularly organised and trained for the service of field brigades of artillery. This corps, which had its first formation in 1793, had grown to the extent of 5,500 of officers and men, and before the conclusion of the war amounted to 7,300 men. The formation and efficiency of these several departments required constant care and watchful superintendence on the part of Colonel MacLeod.

In 1808 Colonel MacLeod was directed to organise a tenth battalion of artillery,[1] and in the same year he was appointed as Master-Gunner of England. In 1809 the Scheldt Expedition was projected, and Lord Chatham being at the time Master-General, Colonel MacLeod again seized the opportunity for soliciting active employment. His Majesty on this occasion was pleased to accede to his request, and he accordingly sailed from the Downs in command of the artillery, under Lord Chatham's orders, in July, 1809. The result of this expedition was unsuccessful, but the arduous and laborious duties of Colonel MacLeod's command throughout the whole of the operations met with uninterrupted success, doing equal honour to the arrangements of the Commanding Officer and the devoted zeal of the corps in surmounting every obstacle as far as the objects of the expedition were persevered in.[1] On the final abandonment of its ulterior views, Colonel MacLeod returned to England, and " at no previous period had the " resources of his mind been more necessarily exerted than in the gigantic outfit of this " expedition." But the war now assumed a character that called for still increasing energy and thought to meet the demands and casualties of the service, multiplied by the extension of our arms throughout every part of the world by a constantly accumulating correspondence from every quarter, and, above all, the hourly increasing importance of the war in the Peninsula, where the vigour of the struggle between the two contending nations seemed actually to grow with its duration. Colonel MacLeod

---

[1] Memoir by Sir Robert Gardiner, G.C.B., K.C.H.

fortunately possessed and knew how to employ a mind devoted to the most arduous undertakings of the service. Before the close of the war the three corps of artillery organised by Colonel MacLeod [1] amounted to upwards of 26,000 men and upwards of 14,000 horses. The recruiting branch of the service alone to keep up such a legion in men and horses had become a source of great and anxious solicitude, and from the commencement of the revolutionary war also there had been an almost constant succession of foreign expeditions, the arrangement and equipment of which devolved upon him. The principal of these were the Continental, in 1793; the West Indies, in 1794; the Cape of Good Hope, in 1795; the Helder, in 1799; Egypt, in 1800; Cape of Good Hope, in 1806; Buenos Ayres, in 1807; the Mediterranean throughout the war; Spain and Portugal, in 1808; Walcheren, in 1809; Holland, in 1813; and, finally, the Netherlands and France, in 1815. On the 25th of October, 1809, he attained the rank of Major-General, and on the 4th of June, 1814, the rank of Lieutenant-General in the army.[1] In 1820, under circumstances of peculiar kindness and distinction, King George the Fourth conferred on him the honour of Knighthood, and appointed him Grand Cross of the Royal Guelphic Order.

The battle of Waterloo at length gave peace to Europe, and on the recall of the British army of occupation from France, Sir John MacLeod was employed in making similar reductions in the artillery to those which took place in all branches of the service. He had now attained a rank which, from the reduced numbers of the corps, would in future prevent his employment in the duties he had fulfilled during the war. It was on this occasion that he received a letter from the Duke of Wellington offering him the situation of Director-General of Artillery.[1] A mind like Sir John MacLeod's could not with indifference quit a post at which he may be said to have formed the corps to whose name and welfare he was in every sense and feeling enthusiastically devoted, and the considerate kindness with which the Duke's proposal was addressed to him was never forgotten by him. He continued to fulfil the duties of Director-General of Artillery to the close of his life, and even throughout his last illness he would never consent to any respite from the details and duties of his trust.

If we revert to the services of Sir John MacLeod throughout the eventful and protracted war, during which he was employed in the most confidential and important duties an officer can fulfil, it would be difficult to distinguish what might properly be termed the most conspicuous period of his career, but it may perhaps be considered to be that between the interval commencing with the chivalrous and enterprising advance of Sir John Moore into Spain, and the brilliant succession of events that followed without intermission till the final close of operations in the Peninsula, at which time the nature and responsibility of the duties be controlled had acquired an extent, variety, and importance quite unequalled in our service.

Sir John MacLeod was married in the year 1783 to Lady Amelia Kerr, second daughter of the fourth Marquis of Lothian, and had had a family of four sons and five daughters.[1] At one time all his sons (of whom more afterwards) were serving

---

[1] Memoir by Sir Robert Gardiner, G.C.B., K.C.H.

together under Lord Wellington in the Peninsula, and when his eldest son, the heroic Colonel Charles MacLeod, of the 43rd Regiment, was killed in the breach at the storming of Badajoz, the patriot father bowed in submission to his affliction, and buried his private griefs for ever in his own bosom.[1]

From the general outline that has been given of Sir John MacLeod's services, some faint impression may be formed of his character, the leading feature of which was the confidence which he inspired in others, and the unbounded trust which they reposed in him. And thus, whether called on for counsel or to act under unforeseen or sudden emergencies of service, he was ever ready and prepared to meet their exigencies. His watchfulness seemed never to sleep, but to be in anticipation of what might occur, and to forestall events by securing means to meet them. His whole soul was in his profession. Of every soldier he made himself the friend. To his equals in rank he was a brother, to those beneath him a father in kindness and in counsel, and to the private soldiers a benefactor, ever watching over their comfort and their welfare. To all he had a ready ear to listen, and a heart and hand to act in their behalf. Throughout his long career he was never known to use the slightest approach to severity, and yet he never failed to maintain discipline, to reprove fault, or to check irregularity. He animated zeal, excited energy, and aimed at perfecting discipline by appealing to the better and nobler feelings that prevail with the soldier's character. His influence extended beyond the branch of the service which he controlled. His name was a passport everywhere, and held in such universal respect that it imposed emulation of good deeds on all who belonged to him, and the conduct and acts of his sons, however they might reflect on him, were thought of but as a matter of course in them.[1] Even at the period of his son's fall at Badajoz, his loss as the son was almost as universally felt as in that of the brilliant officer commanding a distinguished corps. Sir John MacLeod's greatest praises, however, are those which cannot be told to the world. Our private character is best judged of and known by that of our associates and friends; his were among the great and the good. Honoured by his Sovereign, respected by all ranks of the army, loved by his friends, and revered by his family, his private life afforded an example to all who love goodness, honour, and benevolence, while his professional career ever pointed to the highest and noblest attainment by which we can serve our country.[1] Sir John MacLeod died (the father of his corps) at Woolwich on the 26th of January, 1833.

It is most gratifying to find that his eminent services to the Royal Artillery are still valued as they ought to be by that branch of the service. On the 9th of October, 1895, Major-General F. T. Lloyd, Deputy-Adjutant-General, Royal Artillery, visited Weedon to present the Centenary Cup to the 52nd Field Battery, under the command of Major W. N. Lloyd. The occasion was one of great interest to the regiment. General Lloyd, in presenting the Cup, said[2]:—" Major Lloyd, officers, non-commissioned " officers, and men of the 52nd Field Battery, it was with much pleasure that I " accepted Major Lloyd's invitation to come down here to-day to present this Cup. In

---

[1] Memoir by Sir Robert Gardiner, G.C.B., K.C.H.
[2] "The Army and Navy Gazette," 19th October, 1895.

"instituting it there were two motives, one being to do honour to the memory of a "great and gallant soldier of the Royal Artillery, whose centenary, as first Deputy-"Adjutant-General of the Royal Artillery, we celebrate this year, and who, above all "others, was instrumental in raising our regiment to a position of greater importance "and efficiency than it had ever occupied before. A short history[1] of Sir John "MacLeod is contained in an illuminated parchment scroll in the plinth of the cup. ". . . I have the greatest pleasure in congratulating Major Lloyd and the whole "battery on their success in being the first to win this Centenary Cup."[2]

The cup, which was made by Messrs. Lambert, of Coventry Street, London, is in the form of an early hanap, or double gourd, of the sixteenth century, the stem being embellished with a mural crown, chased and pierced, and four chased reliefs. These reliefs are oval medallions in repoussé work representing Horse, Field, Siege, and Garrison Artillery respectively. The cup is 23 inches in height, with a cover surmounted by a figure of an officer of the Royal Artillery in the uniform of 1795, from a design by Lieutenant R. J. MacDonald, Royal Artillery. Round the foot of the cup is engraved the following inscription :—"To the Royal Regiment of Artillery in commemoration "of the Centenary of the appointment of Lieutenant-Colonel John MacLeod as First "Deputy-Adjutant-General, Royal Artillery, 1795, this Cup is dedicated by Major-"General F. T. Lloyd, C.B., Deputy-Adjutant-General, Royal Artillery, 1895."[3]

Lieutenant-Colonel Charles MacLeod, of the 43rd Regiment, eldest son of Lieutenant-General Sir John MacLeod, G.C.H., Royal Artillery, was born on the 20th December, 1784, at Shooter's Hill, Kent, and was therefore $27\tfrac{4}{12}$ years of age when he fell at Badajoz, and not 26, as is inscribed on his monument in Westminster Abbey. Charles MacLeod was appointed Ensign in the 71st Foot on the 5th of September, 1799; Lieutenant in the 62nd Foot on the 21st of March, 1800; Captain in the 3rd West India Regiment on the 22nd of April, 1802; Captain in the 13th Foot on the 25th of May, 1803; Major in the 4th Garrison Battalion on the 26th of November, 1806; Major in the 43rd Foot on the 28th of May, 1807; and Lieutenant-Colonel in the 43rd Foot on the 24th of July, 1810.[4]

On his mother's side (née Lady Emily Kerr, so commonly called, but christened Amelia, after her godmother, Princess Amelia, who was the fourth daughter of the Marquess of Lothian) also—the Kerrs—Charles MacLeod came of a warlike stock, and through his grandmother, Lady Caroline d'Arcy, was fifth in direct descent from the great Marshal Duke Schomberg, who was killed at the battle of the Boyne.[5]

In a letter addressed to his father, dated at Cork, May 16th, 1802, Captain MacLeod says :—"It would be impossible for me, my dearest father, to express my

---

[1] The short history referred to begins by saying that Sir John MacLeod was "of the Raaza clan. and was "a grandson of Colonel Æneas MacLeod, who served with great distinction in the campaigns and sieges of "the Duke of Marlborough."
[2] "The Army and Navy Gazette," 19th October, 1895.
[3] From a memorandum prepared by Major A. J. Abdy, Secretary, Royal Artillery Institution, Woolwich.
[4] War Office Records.
[5] Manuscript Memoir by Lieutenant-General Sir Lynedoch Gardiner, K.C.V.O.

" gratitude to you for your goodness in purchasing me a company; but this I can
" assure you, that I will endeavour to merit it by my conduct. I cannot but be aware
" of the inconvenience it must have put you to, and what an amazing step it is for me
" at my age, and such a period as this."

Captain MacLeod was appointed Aide-de-Camp to the newly-appointed Governor-General of India, Lord Cornwallis, and he arrived at Madras in July, 1805. But his stay in India was soon brought to an end by his Lordship's death (which took place in about two months after his arrival in India), and he was sent home with the despatches announcing that sad event.

In August of 1807 the 43rd Regiment, with MacLeod as one of its Majors, formed part of the force under Lord Cathcart which was despatched to Denmark to prevent the Danish fleet being made over to aid the French under Napoleon. They landed on the 16th of August between Elsinore and Copenhagen, and invested the capital. The 43rd, 52nd, and 95th Regiments (known as Sir John Moore's Brigade of Light Infantry), and the 92nd Highlanders, were detached under Major-General Wellesley to disperse the Danish troops, who were assembling to raise the siege. He attacked them at Kioge on the 19th August, and took 66 officers, 1,100 men, and 10 guns. Copenhagen was then bombarded, and capitulated on the 5th of September, 1807.[1]

Referring to the service of the 43rd at the battle of Kioge, and in following the enemy afterwards under a German General, it is said, in the "Life of Sir William Napier," Vol. I., page 35, " He (Sir William) has left some curious records of German habits on
" this occasion—*e.g.*, the General asked an old gray-haired peasant which way his
" countrymen had fled. The old man proudly answered he would not tell, and the
" General immediately made his orderly shoot him dead. His Brigade-Major had, in
" my hearing two days before, ordered Major MacLeod to shoot all the peasants he
" met with; but he pronounced it *pheasants*, and MacLeod laughingly promised that
" he certainly would obey that order!"

The 1st Battalion of the 43rd, in which Major MacLeod served, sailed from Falmouth for Corunna under Sir David Baird, and joined Sir John Moore at Mayorga in Brigadier-General Crawford's brigade in the end of 1808, and took part in the disastrous retreat to Vigo. Sir William Napier says with regard to this event:—" I had
" marched for several days with bare feet, and with only a jacket and a pair of linen
" trousers for clothes. My feet were swelled, and bled at every step in such a manner
" that General Crawford, who saw me, turned his head away, and I must have perished
" if MacLeod, hearing of my state, had not lent me his spare horse." Major MacLeod says in a letter to his father, dated 27th January, 1809, from Vigo Bay:—" As for
" ourselves, after marching in the most exemplary manner from Benevente to this
" place, over the most abominable roads, and in the most desperate bad weather, we
" arrived and embarked here on the 12th."

On the 20th of May, 1809, the 1st Battalion of the 43rd (1,072 bayonets), with the 1st Battalion of the 52nd and the 95th Regiments, embarked from Harwich for Portugal, and reaching the Tagus on the 28th of June they joined the army.

---

[1] Manuscript Memoir by Lieutenant-General Sir Lynedoch Gardiner, K.C.V.O.

The following is Napier's[1] account of the famous march made by the Light Brigade of which the 43rd Regiment formed a part:—"The 29th, at daybreak, the French
"army quitted its position, and before six o'clock was in order of battle on the heights
"of Salinas behind the Albercke. That day also General Robert Crawford reached
"the English camp with the 43rd, 52nd, and 95th (or Rifle Regiment), and immediately
"took charge of the outposts. These troops, after a march of 20 miles, were in
"bivouac near Malpartida de Plascencia, when the alarm caused by the fugitive
"Spaniards spread to that part. Crawford allowed the men to rest for a few hours,
"and then, withdrawing about 50 of the weakest from the ranks, commenced his march
"with the resolution not to halt till he reached the field of battle. As the brigade
"advanced, crowds of the runaways were met with, and those not all Spaniards,
"spreading the vilest falsehoods—the army was defeated, Sir Arthur Wellesley was
"killed—the French were only a few miles distant, and some, blinded by their fears,
"affected even to point out the enemy's advanced posts on the nearest hills.
"Indignant at this shameful scene the troops hastened rather than slackened the
"impetuosity of their pace, and leaving only 17 stragglers behind, in 26 hours
"they had crossed the field of battle in a close and compact body, having in that time
"passed over 62 English miles, and in the hottest season of the year, each man
"carrying from 50 lbs. to 60 lbs. weight upon his shoulders."

Lord Wellington had now experienced difficulties very similar to those which had hampered Sir John Moore in the mendacity of the Central Government and of the local Juntas, in the stubbornness and incapacity of the Spanish Generals, in the cowardice of their half-trained armies, and in the supineness of the inhabitants. Moreover, he clearly perceived the increased difficulty of his situation. By the victory of Wagram and the peace of Vienna (which was signed on the 14th of October, 1809), Napoleon had overcome in detail the resistance of the Continental Powers, and there was little doubt that his victorious hosts would soon overrun Spain, already held in a firm grasp by some of his Marshals, but his Lordship boldly faced the difficulty and formulated his plans for the defence of Portugal. He had already conceived the idea of maintaining the British army for the defence of Lisbon with the sea and the mouth of the Tagus as his base within the triple line of defence, afterwards known as the lines of Torres Vedras, and as early as October, 1809, he wrote to Colonel Fletcher, the Commanding Engineer, on the subject, and these works were being carried on when he opened the Campaign of 1810. His letters to Brigadier-General Crawford at this juncture show the confidence he reposed in the Light Brigade and the work he expected from them. On the 3rd of January (writing from Coimbra) the Brigadier is desired to obtain all the information possible of the enemy's force and position on the frontier of Portugal, and to employ officers of his division to examine and report upon the course of the Coa, and also, if the enemy's position should admit, of the Agueda.

---

[1] All quotations from Napier's "History of the Peninsular War" are given with the kind sanction of the publishers of that work—viz., Messrs. George Routledge and Sons, Limited, London.

[1]On the 6th of January, 1810, the 43rd crossed the Coa, and were cantoned in villages. Every day, one hour before dawn, they were under arms, and so remained until daylight.

The following amusing extract is from a letter of Major MacLeod's, dated the 10th of February, 1810:—"We are separated in villages. . . . This, of which I am autocrat, "is called Reigada. We are about three leagues from Almeida, which is nearly south "of us, where there are some famous fortifications and some *in*-famous dirty streets, "and some famous Portuguese regiments—without arms—and without breeches; but "do not say anything about this—arms are no use, for they always throw them away— "and breeches do not make the man!"

In April, before it was certain that the investment of Ciudad Rodrigo was a serious siege, Lord Wellington wrote to Brigadier-General Crawford:—"You may depend upon "it that, whatever the arrangement I shall make, I wish your brigade to be in the "advanced guard." The work of the brigade during these months was most arduous. Napier writes, page 273, Vol. III. :—"Meanwhile General Crawford had commenced a "series of remarkable operations with the Light Division. This body of infantry was "composed of three regiments singularly fitted for any difficult service. They had "been for several years under Sir John Moore, and, being carefully disciplined in the "peculiar school of that great man, came to the field with such a knowledge of arms "that in six years of real warfare no weakness could be detected in their system, and in "all that time they were never overborne by courage or skill."

Crawford's force having now been reinforced, Lord Wellington gave him the command of all the outposts, with the view of securing the line of the Coa and succouring Ciudad Rodrigo. As an illustration of the watchfulness required in this situation, Napier mentions that when the Agueda was fordable, as it frequently was, "Crawford always "withdrew his outposts and concentrated his division, and his situation demanded a "quickness and intelligence in the troops, the like of which has seldom been known. "Seven minutes sufficed for the troops to get under arms in the middle of the night, "a quarter of an hour, night or day, to bring them in order of battle to the alarm "posts with the baggage loaded and assembled at a convenient distance in the rear."[1]

We come now to the serious combat of the Coa, and as this is one in which Major MacLeod played a prominent part, it will be necessary again to quote Napier, who also distinguished himself there, and writes as an eye-witness:—"On the 21st the "enemy's cavalry again advancing, Fort Conception was blown up, and Crawford fell "back to Almeida apparently disposed to cross the Coa, but nothing was further from "his thoughts. Braving the whole French army, he had kept a weak division for "three months within two hours' march of 60,000 men, appropriating the resources of "the plains entirely to himself. But this exploit, only to be appreciated by military "men, did not satisfy his feverish thirst for distinction. Hitherto he had safely "affronted a superior power, and forgetting that his stay beyond the Coa was a matter

---

[1] Manuscript Memoir by Sir Lynedoch Gardiner, K.C.V.O., quoting "The Historical Records of the 43rd Regiment." The quotations from the latter work are reproduced by the kind permission of its publishers, Messrs. William Clowes and Sons, Limited, London.

" of sufferance, not real strength, with headstrong ambition he resolved, in defiance of
" reason and of the reiterated orders of his General, to fight on the right bank. His
" British force, under arms, now consisted of 4,000 infantry, 1,100 cavalry, and six
" guns, and his position, 1½ miles in length, extended in an oblique line towards the
" Coa. The cavalry piquets were upon the plain in his front; his right was on some
" broken ground; his left, resting on an unfinished tower 800 yards from Almeida,
" was defended by the guns of that fortress, but his back was on the edge of the
" ravine forming the channel of the Coa, and the bridge was more than a mile distant
" in the bottom of the chasm. A stormy night ushered in the 24th of July. The
" troops, drenched with rain, were under arms before daylight expecting to retire,
" when a few pistol shots in front, followed by an order for the cavalry reserves and
" the guns to advance, gave notice of the enemy's approach. The morning cleared,
" and 24,000 French infantry, 5,000 cavalry, and 30 pieces of artillery were observed
" in march beyond the Turones. The British line was immediately contracted and
" brought under the edge of the ravine; but Ney, observing Crawford's false
" disposition, came down with the swoop of an eagle, 4,000 horsemen and a powerful
" artillery swept the plain, the allied cavalry gave back, and Loisson's infantry, running
" up at a charging pace, made towards the centre and left of the position. While
" the French were thus pouring onward, several ill-judged changes were made on the
" English side. Part of the troops were advanced, others drawn back, and the
" 43rd Regiment was most unaccountably placed within an enclosure of solid masonry
" 10 feet high, situated on the left of the road, about half musket-shot down the ravine,
" and having but one narrow outlet. The firing in front soon became heavy. The
" cavalry, artillery, and the Portuguese caçadores successively passed the enclosure in
" retreat, and the sharp clang of the rifles was heard along the edge of the plain above.
" A few moments later, and the imprisoned regiment would have been surrounded
" without a hope of escape, but here, as in every other part of the field, the quickness
" and knowledge of the battalion officers remedied the faults of the General. One
" minute sufficed to loosen some large stones, a powerful effort burst the wall, and
" the 43rd, reformed in column of companies, was in the next instant up with the
" riflemen. There was no room to array the line, no time for anything but battle,
" every captain carried off his company as an independent body, and, joining as he
" could, with the 95th and 52nd, the whole presented a mass of skirmishers, acting in
" small parties, yet each confident in the courage and discipline of those on his right
" and left. . . . . . Then the British regiments, with singular intelligence and
" discipline, extricated themselves from this perilous position, falling back slowly,
" stopping and fighting wherever opportunity offered, they made their way through a
" rugged country tangled with vineyards in despite of their enemies, who were yet so
" fierce and eager that even the horsemen rode in among the enclosures striking the
" soldiers as they mounted the walls or scrambled over the rocks. The retreating
" troops now approached the river, and the ground became more open, but the left
" wing being the hardest pressed, and having the shortest distance to retreat, arrived
" while the bridge was quite crowded with cavalry and artillery. The right wing was

" still distant, and Major MacLeod of the 43rd, perceiving all the danger, rallied four
" companies of his regiment on a hill covering the line of passage, he was immediately
" joined by some riflemen, and at the same time the Brigade-Major Rowan posted two
" companies on another hill to the left, flanking the road. These two posts were
" maintained for some time, while the right wing filed over the bridge behind them;
" but at last the French gathering in great numbers, and making a serious rush, forced
" the British companies back before the bridge could be cleared, and while a part of
" the 52nd was a considerable distance from it. The danger was imminent, but
" MacLeod, a young man, yet endowed with a natural genius for war, immediately
" turned his horse round, called on the troops to follow, and waving his cap, rode with
" a shout towards the enemy. The suddenness of the thing and the animating
" gestures of the man produced the effect he designed. A mob of soldiers rushed after
" him, cheering and charging as if a whole army had been at their backs; the enemy's
" skirmishers, astonished at this unexpected movement, stopped short, and before they
" could recover from their surprise the 52nd passed the river, MacLeod followed at
" full speed, and the whole gained the other side without a disaster."

The rest of the narrative may be told in the simple words of MacLeod himself. He evidently thought the engagement a military mistake, and it was not till a month later that he wrote about it to his father. He said:—" We made a forward movement
" again to this place (Fraxadas) some days ago, with what object I will not pretend to
" determine, nothing being half so sickening that I know of (barring ipe*cac*uanha wine!)
" as the conjectures of people who cannot possibly possess the information necessary to
" form an opinion of what is likely to happen within a hundred chances of being right;
" yet everybody can guess, and will be more contented with his own guess than
" anybody else's, so I leave it to you to determine the result according to your fancy,
" guarding you simply not to be guided by letters you see in the papers from '*officers*
" *of high rank in the army*' particularly, who always appear to me to be further from
" the mark than anybody else. . . . . . I have never written you an account of
" the affair yet. The truth is I was rather puzzled to give a detailed account. All I
" can tell you is that it was rather tightish work while it lasted, and indeed until it
" ended, and who had the worst of it must be settled between the generals, ...
" so that if they (the French) say they drove us (and I daresay they will) they
" lie in their teeth."

It may be interesting to note in this place that Captain Napier (afterwards Sir William Napier, the historian of the Peninsular War) received on the field the thanks of Lieutenant-Colonel MacLeod, his commanding officer, for rallying his company under a heavy fire, and thereby giving time to gather a few hundred men and to cover the passage of the broken troops over the long narrow bridge, MacLeod having (by the death of Lieutenant-Colonel Hull in the battle) succeeded to the command of the regiment.

The following extract is given from Napier's private correspondence:—"He
" (Crawford) came upon me in the road and seemed overwhelmed with anguish at his
" own rashness in fighting on that side of the river. I have always thought that he was

"going to ride in among the enemy, who were close to us, but that finding me with a
"considerable body of men in command, whom he had given up for lost, he changed
"his design. At all events, he was confused and agitated, and very wild in his
"appearance and manner."

His brother, Captain George MacLeod, Royal Engineers, in a letter to his father, says, referring to the combat of the Coa, "It really was delightful to hear them [some "of his brother officers] speak of Charles."

The 43rd lost on that occasion one lieutenant-colonel, one captain, and one lieutenant killed, and five captains, six lieutenants, and 130 sergeants, drummers, and privates killed, wounded, and missing, all owing to the blunders of the Brigadier-General commanding the division.

MacLeod suffered considerable injustice at the hands of Brigadier-General Crawford. He had commanded the 43rd under the eye of the General for ten months as Senior Major, from early in August, 1810, when the Light Brigade covered the retreat from Arzobispo to Badajoz, then through the ravages of the Guadiana fever at Campo Mayor, afterwards through the hardships of an advanced post, parading every morning before dawn, and on the alert day and night for six months, from the 6th of January to the 23rd of June, when he gave over the command which he prized so dearly to his senior officer, Lieutenant-Colonel Hull, and finally on the death of that officer (who was killed in the middle of the action),[1] he had resumed his command, and it is to be inferred from Captain William Napier's letter that the Brigadier must have been a witness to the exploit of covering the bridge which was so warmly spoken of by others, and yet, while naming the other commanding officers, no mention is made of MacLeod as commanding the regiment in action after Colonel Hull's death. At first MacLeod seems to have taken it for granted (as he well might) that having, as Senior Major, succeeded to the command under fire, he would certainly get the step, but his father seems to have written to him doubting whether somebody might not be put in over his head; and, while labouring under the anxiety of possibly losing a position he so longed for, he wrote to his father as follows:—

"4th September, 1810.

"I find by your letter that you appear to think it not altogether impossible that I shall be superseded again. In my own opinion, which I have only formed upon that of others, it would be an injustice if anybody but myself should be appointed. I very well know how much intriguing, and turning, and twisting of a subject takes place when people wish to gain a point. Black can almost be made white by plausible talkers. The unfortunate business of the 24th, as some of your papers call it, was as sharp and, for those who had any responsibility, as anxious a day as ever was passed, and if the troops had not been really good and unalarmed by the commanding superiority of the enemy under circumstances of position, &c., which from the beginning to the end were advantageous and encouraging to them and the contrary to us—things might have been *bad*. As it happened, we put a face upon it, which prevented anything that could be

---
[1] General Sir Lynedoch Gardiner's manuscript memoir.

called bad. I am going to write to George [his brother] who takes notice of the style of a letter of our Brigadier. It is a correct account, taking it in general, but no despatch gives universal satisfaction. Lord Wellington's embellishment with respect to myself is what I like least in it. Having commanded the regiment for months before, and it having fallen to me again in the middle of the action, besides having commanded the wing of our own and some riflemen on the other side, and maintained the position until everything had crossed, and then took up the forward line again on this side, makes it appear odd to me that I should not have been mentioned as a commanding officer, particularly as our regiment was most concerned from beginning to end, and covered the bridge on both sides directly in front. If General Crawford had said half what he said to me—which I did not want from him, for his opinion is not one I am ambitious of—there could have been no hitch about the matter. I commanded the regiment at least half the action, and five companies during the whole of it. From Lord Wellington I could expect no notice except through the general commanding the division, nor did it ever enter my head until I read the accounts—for recollect that I am writing now my private feelings to you, my father, *only*. Being young and unknown in the army, one cannot help feeling disappointment of this sort, not on my own account as much as on *yours*, whose good opinion I really covet, and whose happiness or satisfaction I should have felt pleasure in adding to in the smallest degree. Do not imagine that I mean to claim any merit above those, the lowest in the regiment, all of whom did their duty, and if they had not been real good of their sort—particularly the officers, all of whom have raised themselves in my opinion and confidence by their zeal, coolness, and gallantry—the trying service we had to perform would have been ticklish work; but it appears to me odd enough where one commanding officer is killed that his successor is not noticed."

Nothing but the apprehension that the omission of his name with the other commanding officers in Lord Wellington's despatch might militate against his being confirmed in the command of the battalion as Lieutenant-Colonel made him break through the reserve which he always observed as to his own services, even to his father. Fortunately the omission was not injurious to him. He was gazetted to the Lieutenant-Colonelcy on the 16th August, 1810, at the early age of twenty-five years and eight months.

On the the 25th of September the Light Division had a slight skirmish with the enemy, and Crawford seemed inclined to repeat his error of making an obstinate stand to no purpose, when Lord Wellington, arriving on the spot, assumed the command in person, covering the retreat with Ross's troop of horse artillery, the cavalry, and light infantry. On the morning of the 27th the position was assailed. Reynier and Ney made a splendid assault, and one division of the enemy actually gained the crest of the height before they where repulsed. When "General Crawford, who had coolly " watched the progress of the advance, called on the 43rd and 52nd to charge, a " cheer that pealed for miles over the sierra answered the order (veterans of the

"British army), and 1,800 British bayonets went sparkling over the brow of the
"hill."[1] The assault was repelled with enormous loss to the enemy.

MacLeod's health broke down so completely in January, 1811, under the hardships and strains to which the Light Division had been exposed during his seventeen months in the field with them, that he was obliged to go home.

Captain William Napier (afterwards Sir William Napier, the Historian of the Peninsular War), in a letter to his mother (Lady Napier), says, with regard to this event :—"I had two friends who could well supply me with sentiments of pleasure to
"reconcile me to my situation, but Lloyd has left the regiment, and MacLeod, whom
"I love as my friend, and admire as the facsimile of General Sir John Moore's
"character, is gone home.[2] I am afraid merely to give his poor father the task of
"putting him in the grave." No higher praise has ever been given to Charles MacLeod, considering the character of the man who gave it, and the veneration in which Sir John Moore was held. MacLeod recovered, however, and rejoined the regiment in Portugal in the following May.

Colonel MacLeod, in a letter to his father dated 3rd September, 1811, says, with regard to his regiment :—"Both my field officers are sick in the rear and several other
"officers, I am sorry to say, but this is the most sickly time of year, and I am
"consoled by the men keeping up better than I expected. We have upwards of
"900 in the field, which is very fair, and as queer a set of looking fellows for anybody
"to choose to pick a quarrel with, as you might wish to see." In another letter, dated

---

[1] Napier's "History of the Peninsular War."

[2] The following note describing the character of the immortal hero of Corunna may be read with interest in this connection :—"Moore's personality.—Moore was, indeed, a great soldier, and with better fortune might
"have anticipated and outshone even the fame of Wellington. He was of Scottish birth ; and perhaps was the
"very finest soldier that martial race has in modern times produced. He had a vivid, commanding personality
"that made him a sort of king amongst men. His eyes were dark and searching, and were set beneath a
"forehead of singular breadth and aspect of power. His mouth had a womanly sweetness about it, while the
"curve of his chin, and the general contour of his face, gave an extraordinary expression of energy. He lacked,
"perhaps, that iron quality of blood and will which augmented Wellington's capacity as a general, while it won
"for him unpleasant reputation for cold-bloodedness as a friend. Moore, in fact, had a strain of womanly
"sweetness in him that made him adored by his own circle. He was generous, high-minded, with a passionate
"scorn of base things and of base men ; a quality which made mean men hate him, and evil men afraid of him.
"Of his signal capacity for war there is no room to doubt. His ideal of soldiership was very noble, and he had
"the art of stamping it on all those around him. 'No man with a spark of enthusiasm,' says Charles Napier,
"afterwards the conqueror of Scinde, 'could resist the influence of Moore's great aspirings, his fine presence,
"his ardent penetrating genius.' Moore did more to create the modern British soldier than any other British
"general that can be named. At Shorncliffe Camp three regiments—the 43rd, the 52nd, and the Rifles—were
"under his hands. Up to that point they were commonplace regiments with no gleam of special fame about
"them. Moore so kindled and fashioned them that afterwards, as Wellington's famous Light Division, they
"were found to be 'soldiers unsurpassable, perhaps never equalled.' From the officers of these three
"regiments, who felt the breath of Moore's quickening genius, there came a longer list of notable men than
"has ever been yielded by any other three regiments of any service in the world. Napier says that in the
"list were four who afterwards commanded armies—three being celebrated as conquerors—above ninety who
"attained the rank of field officer ; sixteen governors of colonies, many generals who commanded districts,
"&c., &c. Half a dozen Moores, in fact, might well have transmuted to gold the whole clay of the British
"army!"—From "Fights for the Flag," in the "Cornhill Magazine," January, 1897. By kind permission of Messrs. Smith, Elder & Co., Publishers, London.

the 20th of November, 1811, he says:—"'Orderly—Sir—you can have just ten minutes
"to write, Sir.' Packet making up for England. We are all rubbing on pretty fairly,
"nothing to do but course, hunt, and act plays, which Colonel Barnard has set going,
"and everybody was inclined to assist in. Half my boys are kings, princes, buffoons,
"&c. To-morrow is to be performed (with variations, no doubt) 'The Most Excellent
"'Conceited, Humorous Play of Shakespeare—Henry the Fourth.' It is not true, as
"the French state, that we are dying of ennui. When they do not amuse us we find
"some way of killing our other enemy—time—with tolerable success. For my own
"part, I confess I am a dull actor, and my time is spent in the more important
"though certainly less profitable or amusing avocation of quarrelling with my general.
"I course and ride, however, as long as the horses can go, but they are, I am sorry
"to say, for want of forage, in a woeful plight. I am glad my friend Bill Napier
"(afterwards Sir William Napier) is improving. If he can get the ball out of his *guts*
"he will do well. If he cannot, he must do well with it in! I hope they will
"make him a Major, but I don't know, I am a little afraid they will put in some
"one else."

With reference to the siege of Ciudad Rodrigo, Colonel MacLeod, writing to his father on the 22nd January, 1812, says:—"I never was more satisfied with the behaviour
"of my own men and officers than on this occasion. I will say for them, in case
"nobody else does, that their conduct was excellent. We entered the breach at the
"same time with the rear of the storming party; and, amidst the confusion and
"irregularity that was going on, every man might have gone his own way (as most
"others did), but we were able to keep them together, and, as a proof of their
"steadiness, there was not a single duty furnished in the town that was not taken by
"our regiment. We got possession of all the gates, and both the breaches, and I do
"not believe a single Frenchman escaped. This is only between you and me, for I do
"not wish to be the trumpeter of my own forces, except to you. I do not think my
"own name will appear, although I think it ought, but this I cannot help. There
"were so many commanding officers of regiments that I daresay they will all be
"clubbed together as usual; but disappointments in this way are numerous. . . .
". . . . . Car's[1] idea of muffatees for the men made me laugh foran
"hour. If she would send them a *chew of baccy* a-piece, they would understand what
"it meant, but the muffatees would puzzle them a good deal."

Referring to the splendid discipline shown by the 43rd during, and after, the assault of Ciudad Rodrigo, the late Sir Lynedoch Gardiner—Colonel Charles MacLeod's nephew—said:—"I have heard much from Peninsular officers, in my young days, of
"the extraordinary control exercised by Charles MacLeod as commanding officer;
"but this is a very astonishing instance of it."

In [2] Captain Cooke's Memoir, Vol. I., page 122, referring to the dreadful excesses which followed this victory, it is said (quoting a remark that "*the soldiers were not to*

---

[1] His sister Caroline, afterwards Lady Gardiner.
[2] Manuscript memoir by Sir Lynedoch Gardiner, K.C.V.O.

be controlled") :—" That excuse will scarcely suffice here, because Colonel MacLeod
" of the 43rd, a young man of a most energetic spirit, placed guards at the breach, and
" did constrain his regiment to keep its ranks for a long time after the disorders
" commenced."

It is a fact well worthy of being added to the records of the regiment that (such was their discipline), after following the storming party into the left breach, and facilitating the storm of the great breach, by taking the enemy in flank, they placed guards at the breaches and gates to prevent the escape of the French who had not surrendered, and preserved order in the midst of general confusion.

With regard to the siege Colonel MacLeod says, in a letter to his friend William Napier, dated January 21st, 1812 :—" The siege of Ciudad was certainly carried on
" with great good management. It was well begun, and well finished. The Governor
" ought to have been killed if he had not preferred his *life to his honour.*" In another letter of the 4th of February, 1812, to Napier, MacLeod says :—" The defence of the
" town as far as it has gone does infinite credit to the military skill and talents of
" *Viscount,* and *Baron,* and *Knight,* and *Condé.* We are in bad quarters, particularly
" for the men, who are obliged to go leagues to cut wood, and bring it home on their
" shoulders, in the worst weather. . . . . . . I hope you are getting well, but
" *sick enough* to keep you quiet for a time."

Marmont gave them no trouble after the fall of Ciudad Rodrigo. MacLeod justly surmised that he would " be somewhat astonished "[1] when he heard of the event, and he certainly had some excuse for his astonishment. The audacity of Lord Wellington's conception, and the extraordinary valour of his army in carrying it out, had triumphed over all established rules of warfare. The storm of a fortress well-provisioned, well-fortified, and garrisoned by some of the best and bravest troops of Europe, after a siege of eleven days, is without a parallel in modern history.

Lord Wellington removed his headquarters to Freneda on the 4th February, and to Elvas on the 9th March. Early in that month the army in Beira were ordered to the Alemtejo, with the exception of one division, which was left on the Agueda. Badajoz was invested on the 16th March by the 3rd, 4th, and Light Divisions. The garrison of Badajoz consisted of 4,700 infantry, under the command of the well-known General Phillipon, who had been governor during the second siege, and who had spared no pains, by improving the works, to render the place as secure as possible.

" On that night (6th April) the great conflict took place."[2] Desperate it was expected to be, and most desperate it proved. The day had been fine ; all the soldiers in high spirits were cleaning themselves and accoutrements as if for a review. At half-past 8 p.m. the ranks were formed and the roll called in an undertone. Before the 43rd joined the division Colonel MacLeod long and earnestly addressed the men, expressing his entire confidence in the result of the attack, and concluded by impressing that he trusted to the honour of all listening to preserve discipline and to refrain from

---

[1] Sir Lynedoch Gardiner's manuscript memoir.
[2] Manuscript memoir by Lieutenant-General Sir Lynedoch Gardiner, K.C.V.O., quoting " The Historical Records of the 43rd."

any species of cruelty on the defenceless inhabitants. In the most profound silence the division drew up behind a large quarry about 300 yards from the breaches made in the bastions of La Trinidad and Santa Maria. A small stream separated the Light from the 4th Division. A voice was suddenly heard giving orders about the ladders in that direction, so loud that it might have reached the ramparts. Everyone was indignant, and MacLeod sent to say that he would report the circumstance to the Commander-in-Chief. Luckily nothing but a croaking of frogs responded to the ill-timed voice. At 10 o'clock a carcass was thrown from the town, which illuminated the ground for many hundred yards. Two or three fireballs followed. Soon after a suppressed whispering announced that the forlorn hope was stealing forward, heading the storming parties, and in two moments more the division followed.[1] One single French musket shot sounded from the breaches. All with great regularity gained ground, leisurely but silently. The 43rd, 52nd, and a part of the Rifle Corps gradually closed to columns of quarter distance. The ladders were placed on the edge of the ditch, and they were descending in rapt stillness when suddenly an explosion took place at the foot of the trenches, and a burst of light disclosed the exact position. The ramparts were crowded with troops who, well prepared, let loose every possible impediment of destruction, while all beneath seemed convulsed. A succession of explosions, with unceasing roar of musketry, soon levelled the party, very few escaping. . . . . . With amazing resolution the whole division rushed to the assault. The soldiers swung themselves down, cheering lustily. The 43rd had to mourn the loss of their chief, the gallant MacLeod, who was killed while trying to force the left corner of the large breach. He received his mortal wound within three yards of the enemy. His character and services are best epitomised in the words of the illustrious commander, who, with the glory of his own deeds, has transmitted to posterity the name of MacLeod.[2] The following is an extract from Lord Wellington's despatch announcing the fall of Badajoz :— ' In ' Lieutenant-Colonel MacLeod, of the 43rd Regiment, who was killed in the breach, ' His Majesty has sustained the loss of an officer who was an ornament to his profession ' and was capable of rendering the most important services to his country.' MacLeod, who had only attained his 27th year, was buried amid springing corn on the slope of a hill opposite to the regimental camp. Six sorrowing hearts, the only officers of the 43rd able to stand, laid him in his grave. His brother officers, desirous of recording their affection and respect, erected a monument to his memory in Westminster Abbey, on which is engraved the preceding extract from Lord Wellington's despatch."[1]

In a letter written by his brother James to his father it is stated that the gallant soldiers of the 43rd (forgetting their own great hardships and privations, and with a devotion that was truly touching) searched for and found the body of their beloved commanding officer on the night of the assault and bore it in grief to the camp.

---

[1] Manuscript memoir by Lieutenant-General Sir Lynedoch Gardiner, K.C.V.O., quoting Sir Richard Levinge's " Historical Records of the 43rd Regiment, 1868."

[2] In this desperate assault the Light Division lost nearly half their number, and the loss of the 43rd exceeded that of any other regiment employed in the operations. They lost twenty officers and 335 sergeants and privates killed and wounded.

At his funeral great was the sorrow manifested, "the very privates who bore him sobbed aloud."

His brother, Sir Henry MacLeod, described him as a remarkably fine rider, active and muscular, with a lithe, graceful figure, and compared the influence which he possessed over the men of his regiment and the way in which he worked them, when skirmishing under fire, to a clever huntsman casting his hounds. Lieutenant Blood, when giving evidence before a Royal Commission with regard to the "influence of "commanding officers," said:—"If he is of experience and of amiable disposition, there "will be harmony and good fellowship; he will be beloved by all ranks, and all will "go on right. Every person assists him in the different duties with delight. All study "his approbation—such was Colonel Charles MacLeod, killed at the head of the 43rd "Regiment at the storming of Badajoz. There was not a man in that corps that night "but would have stood between him and the fatal ball that struck him dead, so "esteemed was he by all."

William Napier was terribly affected by the loss of his friend, and the first letter which he wrote to his young wife betrays the storm of passionate sorrow which swept through his soul. He said:—"MacLeod is dead, and I am grovelling in misery. My "temples ache with the painful images that are passing before me. He was the best, "and will be the last of my friends, for I cannot endure the torture that I feel again,[1] "and where can I find another like him?" In a second letter to his wife he said:— "Everybody says I am the most fortunate of men to have command of such a "regiment; for my part I only find that the recollection of MacLeod comes with "more bitterness to my mind. What comfort or pleasure can I have in filling the "place that belonged to him! The greatest pride I had was to hear him praised, and "see him admired as he deserved, and now I must be content to recollect that he was "everything that was noble and kind, and convince myself that I shall never see him "again."[1] In a third letter to his wife he said:—"I also am in very bad spirits; how "can I be otherwise under so great a loss as I have sustained in the death of that "gallant, noble-minded man, MacLeod? . . . . . Everybody feels his loss as "much as I do. You will have seen by the despatch how highly Lord Wellington "thought of MacLeod's courage and abilities, and yet he only knew half his worth. ". . . . . My poor friend was struck down from the breach twice before he was "killed, once with a stone, once with a bayonet wound in the head. Nevertheless he "persevered in his attempts till a shot went right through his right breast and finished "his career in the only manner that was worthy of his life."[1]

Colonel Charles MacLeod—"the Heroic MacLeod"—received no fewer than three of the much-coveted gold medals, a distinction which was certainly rare, probably unique.

---

[1] Manuscript memoir by Lieutenant-General Sir Lynedoch Gardiner, K.C.V.O., quoting "Life of Sir William Napier."

Colonel George MacLeod, C.B., the second son of Lieutenant-General Sir John MacLeod, G.C.H., Royal Artillery, was born in 1780, and died at his house near Penrith, in 1851. He had a medal and three clasps for the Peninsular War.

Colonel MacLeod began life as a midshipman under Lord Hugh Seymour; afterwards obtained a commission in the Royal Engineers, and distinguished himself at the sieges of Scylla Castle, Ciudad Rodrigo, and Badajoz, where he received a wound from which he never ceased to suffer. He was made a Companion of the Bath for his gallant services.

The following extract is from a letter written by Captain George MacLeod to his father, dated from Elvas, 17th June, 1811:—"You must know that the Engineer
" officers almost invariably posted the covering parties. . . . .
" I never saw Lord Wellington but once, and then he visited the trenches, and that he
" did once during the siege. He was inquiring for Colonel Fletcher (of the Royal
" Engineers). I was not on duty, but went in search of him. At the end of the
" parallel outside I met the Colonel, agreed with him that I should go through the
" batteries, and he should go by the parallel (in case I met His Lordship). When I
" went into the battery I saw a man in a blue great-coat, whom I took to be one of
" Lord Wellington's staff. I addressed him, asking if he was not inquiring for Colonel
" Fletcher, to which he answered 'yes.' I immediately crossed over to the Colonel,
" and, to my great astonishment, this same man was His Lordship, who *was double
" under a traverse*, as one of the men had just called '*Shell!*' This was the custom
" of all officers and men exclusive of the Artillery and Engineers, which I think very
" bad. I don't say people should expose themselves unnecessarily, but if they come as
" amateurs, let them keep right or left of the works, or hold their heads up when
" in them."

Perhaps, in the circumstances, Lord Wellington's conduct was excusable, although it was an infringement of Engineer and Artillery etiquette!

Charles MacLeod, in a letter to his father dated Espeija, 21st May, 1811, says:—
" George is up to his elbows in the trenches at Badajoz, I suppose. He rode like a devil
" all over the position at Lisbon during the few days he stayed there, I am told, and
" was a perfect example in point of complexion in consequence."

" Captain George MacLeod, R.E., was mentioned with other Engineer officers who
" distinguished themselves not less in the storm of the place than they had in the
" performance of their laborious duty during the siege."

The work was very hard for the Engineers—eight hours off and eight hours on—most of the time they were at Ciudad Rodrigo.

After the fall of Ciudad Rodrigo, Charles MacLeod writes to his father from Encina on the 22nd of January, 1812:—" I am in great hopes you will see George's name
" made much of in the despatch. If it is not, it will be the most unjust thing possible.
" He led into the great breach, and the coolness and judgment he showed tended not
" a little to the success of their entry into that gap. Picton and Fletcher paid him the

" most gratifying compliments, and assured him that the most distinct mention of his
" conduct should be made to the Commander of the Forces."

A characteristic letter from George MacLeod to his father may find a place here :—

"Ciudad Rodrigo,
"22nd January, 1812.

"My Dear Father,

"I cannot pretend to give you a detailed account of the siege of this place; *because for why*, we are now as hard at work repairing, as we were before destroying, the works. .... I had the honour to lead the way to the breach, but, what is better, I had the singularly good fortune to escape unhurt. .... I have been told that I behaved as I ought to do. I don't wish to boast, and most especially to you, as I have an idea that you already fancy I think too much of myself. For your sake as well as mine, I will relate to my credit the approbation I have met with. When I say 'your sake,' I think you must feel any son having by some fortunate genius distinguished himself. I was walking on the then melancholy scene, next morning, before the poor fellows were buried, and I met General Picton who commanded in the trenches. He stopped and said, as nearly as I can recollect, 'Captain MacLeod, I ' have made known to the Commander of the Forces the great obligations we were ' under to you last night.' I pulled off my hat and looked like 'Lady Mary's fool,'[1] upon which he turned and paused, and said, 'Captain MacLeod, the *very* great ' obligations we were under to you.' I don't care whether you think I boast or not, but I tell it to you that you may esteem me 'a chip of the old block.' When I returned to camp I called on Colonel Fletcher. He shook hands with me and congratulated me on my escape; but the next morning (I suppose, from some fellow embellishing my actions) he addressed me in the midst of all the officers of all regiments, and then shook hands with me for a long time—told me my conduct as to gallantry and judgment was beyond what he had thought of (I suppose somebody who had escaped in the fray had told him)—that he should make a point of writing home about me—in short, his speech was as overpowering as General Picton's. My friends think that I ought to get rank for it. I was in front of the forlorn-hope whose getting rank is understood."

Captain James MacLeod, third son of Lieutenant-General Sir John MacLeod, G.C.H., Royal Artillery, was born in 1788, and served in the Royal Artillery at Copenhagen, in the Walcheren Expedition, and through the greater part of the Peninsular War, both before and after the death of his brother Charles. In 1823 he was transferred (through his father's influence) to the 41st Regiment, as promotion was more rapid in the line than in the Royal Artillery. Captain MacLeod was on active service with his regiment in the Burmese War, when he died at Rangoon, from the effects of the climate, in 1824.

---

[1] "Lady Mary's fool" probably alludes to some story of his cousin's, Lady Mary Lennox, which was known to the house-party.

Colonel Sir Henry MacLeod, Knight, the fourth son of Lieutenant-General Sir John MacLeod, G.C.H., Royal Artillery, was born in 1791. He began his military career in the Royal Artillery, in which arm of the service he was present at the battle of Talavera, but, on the death of his brother Charles, the Commander-in-Chief (the Duke of York) offered him a commission in the line, which he accepted, and with his new corps took part in the battle of Quatre Bras, at which he was wounded. It is not certain, although it is probable, that he received the Peninsular War medal; but he was awarded that for the battle of Waterloo. He went as Deputy-Adjutant-General to Jamaica after the peace of Waterloo, and was subsequently Governor of St. Christopher or St. Kitts and of Trinidad. At the close of his government there he came back to England, and settled down in a house bordering on Windsor Park, where he died in 1847. Colonel MacLeod had been knighted when he was Governor of St. Kitts. He married a daughter of Sir John Robinson, Baronet, but left no issue.

The following is an extract from a letter written by his brother Charles to his father, dated at Fraxadas, August 22nd, 1810:—"I must not leave off without telling " you that Henry did me the honour to dine with me about a week ago at a village " near Celerico, where we were quartered about ten days at our ease. He is quite " recovered from his ague, but has seen service enough for a boy of his age. He looks " thinnish, but eats like a *devil!* and says he is quite well."

General Sir Henry Lynedoch Gardiner, K.C.V.O., C.B., Royal Artillery (son of General Sir Robert Gardiner,[1] G.C.B., K.C.H., and Caroline, daughter of Lieutenant-General Sir John MacLeod, G.C.H., Royal Artillery), was born in 1820. He served during the Canadian rebellion of 1838, under Colonel Dundas (afterwards Lord Melville), and was in command of two field guns, under fire, at the action which took place at Prescott.

With regard to his subsequent services, Sir Lynedoch Gardiner, in a letter dated 18th July, 1897, said:—"At the outbreak of the Crimean War I was Assistant Military

---

[1] Sir Robert Gardiner was a most distinguished soldier. He served at Gibraltar during the blockade of that fortress by the French and Spanish fleets in 1797-98; was present at the capture of Minorca; was engaged at Roleia on the 17th and in the crowning success against Junot on the 21st of August, 1808; acted as Brigade-Major of Artillery under Sir John Moore in the retreat to Corunna, where he witnessed the death of his much-loved friend and General; was Brigade-Major of the Artillery commanded by Brigadier-General John MacLeod (afterwards Lieutenant-General Sir John MacLeod, G.C.H.) with Lord Chatham's army of the Scheldt, and took part in the capture of Middleburg and Flushing; joined the Peninsular army under Sir Thomas Graham for the defence of Cadiz; was mentioned in despatches by Lord Wellington for his services in the trenches at the siege of Badajoz; commanded a field battery at the battle of Salamanca, capture of Madrid, siege of Burgos, and minor affairs; was engaged at the battle of Vittoria; the affairs in the Pyrenees; the battles of Orthes, Tarbes, and Toulouse; his troop was most severely pressed in covering the left of the army on the retreat from Quatre Bras to Waterloo on the 17th of June, and took part in the great battle of the 18th of June, 1815, as well as in the capture and occupation of Paris; was military Aide-de-Camp to George IV., William IV., and to Her Majesty the Queen, until he attained General's rank in 1841; Governor and Commander-in-Chief of Gibraltar, 1848-55; was awarded the Grand Cross of the Bath in 1855; and subsequently the Guelphic Order, the Russian Order of St. Anne, a distinguished service pension, and the gold medal and clasps for Barossa, Badajoz, Salamanca, Vittoria, Orthes, and Toulouse, and the silver war medal for Roleia, Vimiero, and Corunna.—From manuscript memoir by General Sir Henry Lynedoch Gardiner, K.C.V.O., C.B.

"Secretary to my father, who was Governor of Gibraltar from 1849 to 1856. I volunteered for the Crimea, and Sir Hew Ross, who was Lieutenant-General of the Ordnance, acting for the Master-General (Lord Raglan), appointed me to the command of a battery of Royal Horse Artillery *in the Crimea*. I hastened home, preparing to go out immediately, but, unluckily for me, another vacancy occurred shortly afterwards in *England* in the command of the battery next for the Crimea, and Lord Raglan, on receiving news of this, posted another officer *who was on the spot* to the battery to which I had been appointed, and transferred me to the battery next for service. No doubt he was right, but it lost me service for the Crimea. For though I took out the other battery and landed at Scutari, the armistice was declared shortly after, and the battery never got to the Crimea. Mine was the only battery of the large reinforcement sent out at the beginning of 1856 which disembarked; the others sailed straight back again. The consequence of this was that when I went up to the Horse Guards at the outbreak of the Indian Mutiny, and claimed to be first for service, the reply was that I *was the last*, because I had disembarked. I did eventually get out there, in command of the very battery of Royal Horse Artillery which my father had commanded in the Peninsula and at Waterloo; but the neck of the rebellion was then broken. I was employed in Central India, in a flying column, consisting of my battery of Royal Horse Artillery, the 17th Lancers, and the 72nd on camels, in pursuit of Tantia Topee; but the enemy were then fugitives rather than combatants. We had some very hard marching, and got the India War medal.

"At the close of 1858, or beginning of 1859, I was ordered home, having been promoted to Regimental Lieutenant-Colonel, and was in command of two field batteries at Shorncliffe, and shortly afterwards appointed Assistant-Adjutant-General, Royal Artillery, in Ireland, in succession to Sir Collingwood Dickson. Just then the Trent affair occurred, and war with the Northerners seemed certain. I threw up the Staff appointment and volunteered for Canada, and went out there in command of two field batteries, arriving in December, 1861. The Northerners knocked under, and I was placed then on a Royal Commission for reporting on the defence of Canada. As soon as this duty was concluded, I returned to England, the Duke of Cambridge having kept Sir Collingwood Dickson on until my return, when I took up the duty in Ireland, and a few months later was removed to become Assistant-Adjutant-General at the Horse Guards Headquarters. At the end of my term of Staff service I was appointed to the Queen's household as Groom-in-Waiting, and shortly afterwards became Equerry. I remained in these active duties for twenty-four years, and in January, 1896, thinking it was time to make room for a younger man as Equerry, I resigned that responsible post, and Her Majesty has graciously kept me on as Groom-in-Waiting and Extra Equerry. Her Majesty knighted me last January as Knight Commander of the Royal Victorian Order, and I have received, by Her Majesty's permission, the Grand Cordon of the Order of Leopold of Belgium."

Sir Lynedoch Gardiner died on the 15th December, 1897, at his residence, Thatched House Lodge, Richmond Park, Kingston-on-Thames.

The following quotation is from an obituary notice of him which appeared in "The Army and Navy Gazette" of the 18th of December, 1897:—

"His commanding officer, General Michel, writing from Mhow, writes:—'I shall 'be rejoiced to have you again some future day under my command in any post where 'activity, energy, and zeal are required. The D Troop, Royal Horse Artillery, while 'under your command, serving in my division in the field, were in the most perfect 'state of equipment, discipline, and order. It is impossible to speak too highly of 'them in every respect, and their efficiency, after some of the most rapid marches on 'record in this country, I attribute to the excellent spirit infused into the troops, and 'the unwearied pains taken by you to render them perfect in every respect.' . . . . Sir Henry received the Indian Mutiny medal, and was awarded a good service pension. The late General was universally popular. . . . . The remains of the deceased will be interred at Esher Churchyard, and by command of the Queen will be accorded full military honours. The Court Circular contained this notification:—'The Queen received last 'night, with deep regret, the news of the death of Lieut.-General Sir Lynedoch 'Gardiner after a short illness. Her Majesty is much grieved at the loss of one of her 'oldest friends who had served her for many years, and whom she had known from 'their mutual childhood. He was in his 78th year, greatly respected and esteemed.'"

Sir Henry was the last male representative of this distinguished branch of the MacLeods of Raasay. None of his four uncles left issue. His mother was the eldest of Sir John MacLeod's three married daughters, each of whom had two sons and two or three daughters, but (as has been already stated) the male issue is now extinct. Sir Henry Lynedoch Gardiner was a born soldier, and had eagerly sought for more active employment than what fell to his lot, but this was unluckily denied to him.

It cannot fail to be interesting to note that before his death he presented to the 43rd Regiment the blade of the sword which had been worn by Sir John Moore in his last campaign, and at the battle of Corunna, as he thought that this corps (particularly as it now forms one regiment along with the 52nd, both of which had been so closely associated with that immortal hero) would be its most fitting custodiers. After Sir John's death the sword passed to his brother, the distinguished Admiral (Sir Graham Moore), who had the blade mounted for his own wear, according to the pattern of the Royal Navy. The remounted sword was given to Sir Henry Lynedoch Gardiner by the Admiral's widow, Lady Moore, after the death of her only son, John, a naval officer, who had been Sir Henry's schoolfellow and intimate friend.

General Harry MacLeod,[1] Royal Artillery (Madras), served in the Afghan War of 1878–79, and became a General in 1895.[2]

---

[1] General MacLeod, in a letter dated 9th December, 1896, says:—"I do not come from Skye, but from the *adjacent* island of Raasay!"

[2] Hart's Army List, 1897.

General Macleod acted as British Consular Agent at Pondicherry and Kari Kal from July, 1895, to September, 1896. In March, 1898, he was appointed Vice-Consul at Granville, in the Consular District of Cherbourg, in France.

Major Neil MacLeod, Royal Artillery, was born on the 20th of August, 1825, in the district of Waternish, Skye, where his father, John MacLeod (a descendant of the Chiefs of Raasay) occupied a small farm. Major MacLeod's mother, Marion MacLeod, was of the Gesto family, and both his parents were noted for their piety. Born just when the religious movement which culminated in the Disruption was beginning to assume vast proportions, and to have a mighty influence over the minds of the great body of the people of Scotland, Neil MacLeod, being naturally of a religious cast of mind, early took a deep interest in spiritual affairs. The parental example no doubt tended to increase this interest, and, like many eminent men, he owed much to his mother's wise training and to her assiduous efforts to bring him to a knowledge of the truth as it is found in the Gospel.

Educational facilities at Waternish were not numerous in those days, but between the parish school and self-instruction the embryo Major soon managed to acquire a large stock of knowledge which he afterwards turned to good account. At the age of eighteen he left Skye, and was employed for a time as a contractor on agricultural works in the Island of Lewis, in Aberdeenshire, and in other places. But, finding this employment to be both uncongenial and unprofitable, he threw it up in disgust, and enlisted in the Royal Artillery at Aberdeen [1] in the year 1850, and induced several other young men also to join the service. Having now discovered his proper vocation, and having passed through the usual course of training, he soon gave evidence of the excellence of the stuff he was made of, and as fast as the Army Regulations which were then in vogue would allow he was advanced step by step until " in 1869 he received " Her Majesty's commission to do the very heavy duties of Quarter-Master at the " Royal Military Academy at Woolwich," and finally he retired from the army with the honorary rank of Major.

In July, 1854, MacLeod embarked for the Crimea. On the 19th of September he reached Callamatta Bay, and was sent in charge of the first two British guns which were landed there. He fought at the battles of Alma, Balaclava, and Inkerman, and took a prominent part in the siege of Sebastopol. At the battle of the Alma " it was arranged that the French should first attack the Russian left on the sea side, " and, when they reached a certain point, we were to attack the Russian right and " centre. So we halted and remained inactive for some time under a galling fire from " the Russian batteries to which we were not allowed to reply. The first I noticed " knocked over were some of our Highlanders, and the sight of their feather bonnets " lying on the ground kindled in me such a spirit of retaliation that I felt I could " rush upon the enemy alone for revenge.[2] The longed-for order to advance came

---

[1] " The Highland News " and Major MacLeod's Reminiscences.
[2] Major MacLeod's Reminiscences.

"at last, and the Russians were soon broken up, and in full retreat to Sebastopol,
"mowed down by our artillery fire until out of reach, leaving their line of march
"thickly marked with their dead."

At the battle of Balaclava MacLeod succeeded in blowing up a Russian field magazine by means of a well-directed shell, a feat which immediately turned the tide of battle in favour of the British, the lack of ammunition effectually preventing the Russian advance. "The Russians ceased firing and began to retire, but we followed
"them with shot and shell to the ground of the Light Brigade disaster, where we
"peppered them until Lord Raglan came in the evening and ordered us to cease firing,
"the Russians having done so previously. My gun was loaded when the order to
"cease firing was given, and I asked permission to fire, as a loaded gun cannot be
"moved. Lord Raglan gave me permission, and all glasses were up to see its effect.
"I laid it on the thickest column at the bottom of the valley, and I saw clearly the
"lane it made through it, for which I got a cheer and several shots in return. During
"the action a large shell passed so near my cheek that I fancied it took some of my
"whiskers with it, and, knowing that my horses were in its line, I cast a glance behind.
"It entered the chest of the near leading gun horse and blew him to pieces. Driver
"MacKibben sat still in the saddle over the dead horse under the impression that he
"was blown up with the horse. . . . He was carried to the doctor who had some
"difficulty in assuring him that he was unhurt."[1]

The Battle of Inkerman.

"At daybreak on Sunday, the 5th of November, 1854, I finished the replacing of ammunition for day service, when I heard heavy firing on the right, through a thick fog and rain, and, judging its seriousness, I hooked in my horses so as to be ready when called upon, which I felt sure would soon be, from the heavy firing. Orders came to despatch every gun got ready without waiting for the rest. So, mine being ready, I trotted off to the right through the mud, and as soon as I got into the line of the Russian fire a shot carried away a piece of my gun wheel, which almost disabled it, but on I went, and when ascending the hill in a shower of shot, shell, and bullets, I observed a little confusion among the men and shouted, 'Fear not; none shall fall here to-day without God's permission.' This had the desired effect, and we came quickly into action with diminished numbers. . . . . My gun and another were ordered to advance 200 yards in front of our line to take the Russian columns in flank, not knowing that one of these columns was advancing in front of us. We were without infantry support, and found ourselves surrounded. The other gun was taken at once, but I tried to get a cannister shot into them before I fell (as it was my firm resolve never to retreat nor be taken prisoner, but to fight it out). I found myself alone as the last man, an English lad named Gaston, fell with three shots in his forehead. I quickly turned the empty gun upon them which they supposed to be loaded. In this

---

[1] Major MacLeod's Reminiscences.

way I kept a circle clear for a few seconds, when a Russian officer on the other side levelled his revolver at my left ear, when a private of the 57th Regiment shot the officer before he had time to fire. . . . . At this juncture a dreadful shower of bullets rushed through the wood like hail from our side. It was the 88th Regiment, I think, sent to recover the guns (not knowing that I was there), which they did with bullet and bayonet. I got another detachment, but they were soon killed or wounded, and I was again left alone, and ended the battle with one instead of ten."

During an engagement which resulted in the capture of the Russian rifle-pits before Sebastopol, the brave MacLeod volunteered to bring in the wounded, when only a sailor from one of the war-ships could be persuaded to man the stretcher along with him. Through this noble action the whole of the wounded were safely carried in amidst a perfect storm of shot and shell, the gallant bearers escaping without a scratch. MacLeod afterwards remarked, " Our escape was of God."

One night a shot from Sebastopol came and ploughed the ground close to his stone pillow on Cathcart's Hill.

He also had a miraculous escape in 1855, when engaged in charge of a squad of twelve men roofing a house. He had sent ten of them away for wood when a terrific explosion took place. MacLeod's two companions were burned to death, and he himself was struck by some of the débris, but was not seriously injured. It was found that 250,000 lbs. of gunpowder had been blown into the air. In the beginning of the following year he was nearly shipwrecked on the voyage from the Crimea to England.

In September, 1857, Neil MacLeod sailed for India to engage in the suppression of the Indian Mutiny, but by the time he reached that country the rising had been quelled.

In 1860, he left India for service in the China War, and took part in the capture of the Taku Forts, the town of Sinho, and the City of Pekin.[1]

In 1870, he was again sent to India, and served at Peshawur, Meerut, Lucknow, and Bombay, returning to England in 1877. Two years after that he was in Ireland during the agrarian troubles in that country. In 1881 he retired from the service. For his distinguished services Major MacLeod received the Crimean War medal with four clasps, the Turkish medal, and the Chinese medal with two clasps. It was said that, if his good friend and commander Colonel Townsend (who was killed at Inkerman) had lived, the gallant Skyeman would have been recommended for, and would probably have received, the ribbon of the French Legion of Honour and the Victoria Cross, but " another king arose who knew not Joseph."

To those religious principles which Major MacLeod held so dear he consistently adhered during his whole career in the army, notwithstanding the many obstacles and difficulties that came in his way. He was a member of the first military Bible class ever organised. His work in this connection was singularly blessed, many of the members of his own Bible classes being themselves well fitted to conduct religious services, and, being a thorough believer in total abstinence, he did much to

---

[1] Major MacLeod's Reminiscences.

induce large companies[1] of soldiers to become total abstainers, forming many military temperance societies. He served on a large number of committees in connection with the Free Church, doing excellent work in them all, especially in the Committee on Religion and Morals.

Major MacLeod died at Dalkeith on the 3rd of December, 1898, and (in accordance with his own long-cherished wish) his remains were buried (on the 7th of the same month) in the churchyard of Trumpan, in Waternish, Skye.

IN MEMORIAM.

Major Neil Macleod, Waternish, Isle of Skye, late Royal Artillery.

Isle of the Mist, let thy wild pibroch sound
In mournful notes o'er thy lone winding vales,
And round the crags of thy loud murmuring shores,
E'en to the summits of thy cloud-clothed bens:
Since that, alas! one of thy greatest sons
Sleeps his last lonely sleep; who nevermore
Will speak in glowing words thy matchless praise
As was his wont in the dim years agone.

Ah, Neil MacLeod! I knew thee in thy prime
Upon the plains of Ind! Thou wert a man!
That is thy fair, full record, thy proud meed,
And on the brightest page—with eager hand—
Of our world's history I'll write it down.
Thou wert a man with bearing stern and bold
When thy loved country's foemen fiercely frowned;
Yet mild and gentle as a tender child
When reigned the peaceful hours. Thy nature yearned
To benefit thy fellows. In God's house
(Like great King David) 'twas thy chief delight
To meditate upon that great goodwill
Which Jesus came to bring from God to man.

Nor vanity, nor pride, nor love of fame
E'er swayed thy soul throughout life's pilgrimage;
The impulse of high duty could alone
Lead thee to act, and all thine actions speak
The story of a heart which pulsed to live
The life unselfish, manly, noble, true.
And that thou hast thus lived Skye speaks to-day,
For all her sons and daughters drop the tear
Of sweet affection o'er thy silent tomb.

---

[1] "The Highland News."

THE MACKINNONS OF STRATH.

Major-General HENRY MACKINNON.

(From Colonel Lionel Dudley MacKinnon.)

Colonel DANIEL MACKINNON.

(From Colonel Lionel Dudley MacKinnon.)

Lieutenant-Colonel DANIEL LIONEL MACKINNON,
who was killed at the Battle of Inkerman.

(From his son, Colonel Lionel Dudley MacKinnon.)

Lieutenant-Colonel LIONEL DUDLEY MACKINNON.

> Farewell, MacLeod! I mourn thee as my friend;
> Nay, more—my leader, teacher, faithful guide.
> Thou hast not lived in vain, for through the years
> Thy presence shall go forth to nerve our race
> To higher, nobler, purer, loftier aims;
> And thus the "Misty Isle" shall yet sing high acclaims.
>
> A. MacPherson,
> Late Lance-Corporal 15th (The King's) Hussars.

"From the Highland News."

THE MACKINNONS OF SKYE AND OTHER CLANS.

> " Gabhaidh pàirt do t-iorghails',
> " Clann Ionmhuinn's oirdheirc càil;
> " Mar thuinn ri tìr a sior-bhualadh;
> " No bile lasrach dian-loisgeach;
> " Nan treudan luatha, fior-chonfach,
> " Thoirt griosaich air an nàmh;
> " An dream chathach, Mhuileach, Shrathach,
> " 'S math gu sgathadh chnàmh."
>
> Alasdair Mac Mhaighstir Alasdair.

The MacKinnons are descended from Fingon, a brother of Andrew, the ancestor of the MacGregors, and are thus a branch of the Siol Alpin. The MacKinnons had their seats in the Islands of Skye and Mull, and held their lands of the Lords of the Isles. Fingon, the founder of the clan, is mentioned as such in a manuscript dated 1450, and the chiefs usually took their style from Strathswordale, in Skye—"the Strath of the MacKinnons."

Major-General Henry MacKinnon.

Major-General Henry MacKinnon, the youngest son of William, 32nd Chief[1] of Clan MacKinnon, was born in 1773. He got his first commission as an Ensign in the 43rd Regiment on the 31st of May, 1790; was promoted to the rank of Lieutenant on the 30th of November, 1792; transferred to the Coldstream Guards with the rank of Lieutenant and Captain on the 9th of October, 1793; promoted to the rank of Captain and Lieutenant-Colonel in the same battalion on the 18th of October, 1799; received the post of Lieutenant-Colonel on the 25th of October, 1809; the local rank of Major-General in Spain and Portugal on the 26th of October, 1811; and the full rank of Major-General on the 1st of January, 1812. Henry MacKinnon was educated at a lycée in France along with the Great Napoleon, whose esteem and regard he then won, and never lost. He served as a Major on the staff in Ireland during the Rebellion of 1798, and was there distinguished for his courage and humanity. He took part in the Helder Expedition, under the Duke of York, in 1799, and was present at all the four actions (on September 19th, October 2nd, 3rd, and 6th) there,

---
[1] The chiefship is also claimed for the family of Lachlan MacKinnon of Letterfearn.

where he gained much credit for his skilful handling of a detachment of the Coldstream Guards during these disastrous operations. In 1801, Colonel MacKinnon commanded the 1st Battalion of the Coldstream Guards in Egypt, and fought at Aboukir Bay and at Alexandria. He went with his regiment to Bremen in 1805, and Copenhagen in 1807. In 1809 he proceeded to Portugal; was present at the passage of the Douro, and was the victor of Salamonde with the Coldstream Guards and some guns. At the battle of Talavera in July, 1809, he had two horses shot under him, and received five balls in his cloak, which he found after the action. To him was given the charge of the wounded (5,000 men) in the town after the British retreat; and having been basely deserted by the Spanish General, Cuesta, he commended to the generosity of the French those of the wounded who could not move, and marched with the rest for 180 miles to rejoin Wellington at Elvas, where he was appointed Commandant. In October, Colonel MacKinnon rejoined the Guards at Badajoz,[1] and was then made Brigadier-General, his brigade consisting of the 45th, 60th, and 88th Regiments. At Busaco General MacKinnon commanded a division owing to the temporary absence of the Lieutenant-General; and with the 74th, 79th, and 88th Regiments, and some Portuguese, so gallantly repulsed the French, and turned the fortunes of the day that Wellington visited his tent after the battle to thank him in person. He led the Light Brigade of the 3rd, or "Fighting Division," after Torres Vedras, at Fuentes d'Onor, where he held the key of the position with the 71st, 74th, and 79th Highlanders, supported by the 24th and 88th Regiments, and practically saved the day, for which he was specially mentioned by Wellington in his despatches. With regard to the battle of Fuentes d'Onor, Sergeant Joseph Donaldson says in his "Recollections of the eventful Life of a Soldier":—"The 88th Regiment (Connaught Rangers), being "detached from our division, led on by the heroic MacKinnon (who commanded our "right brigade), charged them [the French] furiously and drove them back through "the village with great slaughter." Taken ill in the trenches at Badajoz, General MacKinnon had to go home on sick leave,[2] but was back in time to lead the 45th, 74th, and 88th Regiments against the principal breach in the walls of Ciudad Rodrigo. Having secured possession of the breach, on clambering over the parapet a magazine belonging to the enemy blew up, and the heroic MacKinnon fell in the hour of victory. "The last time he was seen alive was when addressing a young officer who "had displayed much courage, 'Come,' said he, 'you are a fine lad, you and I will go "together.' The next moment the mine sprung."[3]

The country raised a monument to him and to General Crawford (who fell at the head of the Light Division) in St. Paul's Cathedral. Napoleon is said to have shed tears at the news of his old schoolfellow's death, and issued orders that every member

---

[1] He started on leave for home, but, hearing outside the bar of the Tagus of Napoleon's peace with Austria after Austerlitz, he threw up his leave and returned to Badajoz.

[2] On this occasion his wife, walking with him in the garden one evening, led him to a spot where she had planted a laurel tree to commemorate each of his victories. The gallant soldier, much affected by this loving tribute, could only whisper, "Alas! love, the cypress will be the next." And so it was.—From memoir of Field-Marshal the Duke of Wellington. "Printed for the author by W. G. Blackie & Co., Glasgow, 1845."

[3] "The eventful Life of a Soldier."

of the General's family was to have a free pass during the war throughout France. Wellington respected General MacKinnon very greatly for his refusal of Napoleon's offer of a Marshal's bâton if he would join the French army. He was buried where he fell, but the Coldstream Guards exhumed his body and carried it to their headquarters at Espeija, where it was re-interred, amid the greatest feelings of sorrow, in presence of the whole regiment. In those days, medals, decorations, and orders were not so plentiful as they are nowadays. In fact, it was only to senior officers that these honours were given at all. For specially gallant services there were gold medals bestowed, which, as a matter of course, were highly prized by the recipients. General MacKinnon (who was one of Wellington's "hard-fighting dandy captains") received one of these coveted gold medals. He was blown to pieces by the explosion of the mine; and when search was being made for his remains, a leg with a boot on was found, and identified as his by the *gold spur* on the boot.

In a Divisional Order, dated January 10th, 1812, General Picton said:—"Every "officer and soldier of the division will join the Lieutenant-General in heartfelt sorrow "for the loss of that able, gallant, and illustrious officer, Major-General MacKinnon, "who fell in the moment of victory covered with laurels." And it was of him the poet Southey wrote:—"Perhaps this country has never sustained so great a loss since "the death of Sir Philip Sydney in 1586."

General George Henry MacKinnon, C.B.

Major-General Henry MacKinnon married, in 1804, Catherine, daughter of Sir John Coll, Baronet, county Cornwall, and left two sons, to whom, for their father's gallant services, were given commissions without purchase. The eldest, General George Henry MacKinnon, entered the Grenadier Guards in 1824; was promoted to the rank of Captain in 1828, and to that of Lieutenant-Colonel in 1840. He served as Assistant-Quarter-Master-General at the Cape of Good Hope, in the Kaffir War in 1846-7; and as a Colonel on the Staff in command of the Second Division of the Forces in the field in the Kaffir War of 1851-2. For these services he was made a Companion of the Bath. He became a full General in 1873, and at present is Colonel of the 26th Cameronians, and is (in 1898) the oldest living officer in the British army.

Colonel Daniel MacKinnon, Coldstream Guards, was appointed Ensign in that regiment on the 16th of January, 1804; Lieutenant and Captain on the 25th of March, 1806; Captain and Lieutenant-Colonel on the 25th of July, 1814; Major on the 22nd of June, 1826; and Lieutenant-Colonel on the 22nd of July, 1830. He received the Waterloo medal,[1] and probably also the Peninsular War medal with several clasps.

---

[1] War Office Records.

Colonel Daniel MacKinnon.[1]

This brave soldier, who acquired a high military reputation in the Peninsular War and at Waterloo, was born in 1790, and was the second son of William MacKinnon, eldest son of William, the thirty-second Chief of the ancient clan of that name in the Western Highlands of Scotland. This chiefship, however, had dwindled into a mere lairdship, in consequence of the abolition of the patriarchal system of government in the Highlands; and Daniel, whose energies, a century earlier, might have been wasted in some petty feud or creach, was reserved to be one of the honoured heroes in a great European warfare. At the early age of fourteen he entered the army as Ensign in the Coldstream Guards, and quickly won the esteem of his brother officers by his activity, cheerfulness, and kind disposition, which was further increased when he had an opportunity of showing his valour in the field. His first service, however, was nothing more than a little harmless marching and countermarching; for his regiment, which was ordered to proceed to Bremen in 1805 to co-operate with the Prussians and their allies, never came in sight of the enemy. After their return home the Coldstreams, in 1807, were sent with the armament against Copenhagen. MacKinnon arrived at Elsinore Roads with his corps on the 9th of August, landed at Welbeck on the 16th, and marched at once to Copenhagen. Upon the surrender of this city he returned to England with his regiment. Two years more elapsed of mere parade and warlike demonstration, which, however, were brought to an end when Lieutenant MacKinnon embarked with his regiment for the Peninsula in 1809. The military life of a subordinate young officer can be nothing else than a record of personal daring and hairbreadth escapes. He obeys the commands and fulfils the wishes of his superiors through every difficulty and at whatever risk, thus establishing his claim to promotion to the higher grades of his profession in his turn. Such was the case with Dan MacKinnon. He was appointed Aide-de-Camp to Brigadier-General Stopford, who commanded the Guards, and had thus an opportunity of distinguishing himself through the whole course of that terrible and eventful war from 1809 to 1814. And these opportunities were neither shunned nor neglected, so that the bivouac and the mess-table were enlivened with tales of his personal prowess and daring. On one occasion his supreme contempt of danger partook of the ludicrous. While our army was passing a defile, and debouching from it, there was one spot in which part of the troops were exposed to a very heavy fire. But, in this post of peculiar peril, Captain MacKinnon was found performing the duties of the toilet and lathering and shaving his chin as coolly as if he had been fifty miles from the scene of action. No sight was better calculated to animate the dispirited troops, who rushed immediately to the onset and drove the French before them. No wonder that the soldiers loved, and were ready to follow, an officer who, let the risk be what it might, was ready to encounter or abide his full share of it. But he was equally endeared to his brother officers by his

---

[1] From Chambers' Biographical Dictionary of Eminent Scotsmen, by kind permission of Messrs. Blackie & Sons, Publishers, Glasgow.

overflowing kindness and invincible goodnature, so that, during the whole of these trying campaigns, in which patience was tried to the uttermost, he never gave offence or caused quarrel. Long after his own death the amiable qualities of the gallant Celt were affectionately remembered by his surviving veteran comrades. After having taken part in every battle from Talavera to Toulouse, the peace of 1814 released MacKinnon from active military duty. It is pleasing also to add that his services had been appreciated at the headquarters of the army, for he was at once raised from the rank of Captain to that of Lieutenant-Colonel in the Coldstream Regiment. Relying upon the promise of a lasting peace, he returned to England, but was suddenly roused, like many of his brethren upon leave of absence, by the escape of Bonaparte from Elba, and the astounding events that followed in quick succession. Napoleon was once more upon the throne of France, and a fresh war was inevitable. Knowing this, Colonel MacKinnon hurried to Ramsgate to join his regiment, now quartered in Brussels, but, not finding the expected vessel ready to sail, he threw himself, with another officer, into an open boat, and reached Ostend in time to join in the engagements of the 16th and 17th of June,[1] and finally in the great battle of Waterloo. Of the many hundreds of episodes that constitute this "great military assize of the nations," out of which so many volumes of history and biography have been constructed, and amidst the mêlée of wonderful charges and brave deeds that occurred every moment, over every part of the field, we must confine our attention to a limited portion of the great drama, and attend exclusively to the movements of MacKinnon. Amidst the fire he had three horses shot under him. One of these volleys, by which he was successively brought down, wounded him in the knee, his sword flew from his hand, and in falling he alighted upon a prostrate French officer, who was wounded like himself. MacKinnon immediately took possession of the Frenchman's sword, with an apology for using it, as he had lost his own, mounted a fresh horse, and continued to charge at the head of his regiment, until he was detached, in the afternoon, with 250 of his Coldstreams and the 1st Regiment of Guards for the defence of the farm of Hougoumont.[2] This was the key of Wellington's position, and MacKinnon was ordered to defend it to the last extremity. And well do the records of Waterloo testify how faithfully this command was obeyed. For a considerable period the whole interest of the conflict was converged round this farm and its outhouses, the possession of which was of the utmost importance to Napoleon, so that mass after mass of French Grenadiers was hurled against it in rapid succession, with golden promises to the first who entered; but, as fast as they approached the walls, the close, steady fire from within tore their ranks into shreds and strewed the ground with the dead and wounded; and as fast as they fell back,

---

[1] His repulse of Marshal Kellerman's superior force with four companies of the Coldstream Guards at Quatre Bras was considered one of his best military achievements.

[2] We must mention that another gallant Highlander, Colonel (afterwards General Sir James) MacDonell of Glengarry, greatly distinguished himself also in defending this most important post. It is worthy of note, too, that Sir James was descended, in the female line, from two Skye families—the MacDonalds of Sleat and the MacLeods of Dunvegan—having been sixth in descent from a chief of the one house, and seventh in descent from a chief of the other.

MacKinnon and his little band sallied from their defences, piled up the dead bodies in front of the doors as a rampart, and hurried back to their posts, as soon as a fresh inundation of fire and steel came sweeping down upon them. Again and again was this manœuvre successfully performed, but in the midst of imminent peril by which the brave band of defenders was reduced to a mere handful. Still the utmost efforts of Napoleon upon this point were defeated and Hougoumont was saved. At last the farmhouse was relieved, and MacKinnon, with his party, joined the British army, now assailants in their turn. But the wound which he had previously received in his knee from a musket shot, and which he had disregarded during the whole of the action, now occasioned such pain, accompanied by loss of blood, that he became delirious, fainted, and was carried off the field in a litter to Brussels, where he was treated with the utmost courtesy and kindness. The wound healed after a time, but the buoyant activity which had hitherto made exercise a necessary of life to him was broken.[1] As for the sword which he had appropriated to his own use at such a curious crisis, he not only fulfilled his promise by using it gallantly in the defence of Hougoumont and through the whole action, but ever afterwards wore it on field days and parades as a fair trophy of Waterloo. Thus, at the early age of twenty-four, the military career of this intrepid soldier was closed by the return of universal peace, after ten years' arduous service, and having won by his merits a rank which few soldiers so young are privileged to occupy. He still continued to hold his commission in the army, and a majority in the Coldstreams having become vacant he was induced to purchase it, by which he obtained the rank of a full Colonel in the service, and the ultimate command of the regiment.

From the foregoing account it could scarcely be expected that Colonel MacKinnon should also obtain distinction in the field of literature. Entering the army at the raw age of fourteen, when a stripling's education is still imperfect, and returning to domestic life at a period when few are willing to resume their half-conned lessons and become schoolboys anew, we are apt to ask how and where he could have acquired those capacities that enabled him to produce a well-written book? But this (by no means the easiest or least glorious of his achievements) he has certainly accomplished. Soon after the accession of William IV., His Majesty was desirous that a full history of the Coldstream Guards should be written, and he selected no other than the gallant Colonel of the regiment to be its historian. Such a choice, and the able manner in which it was fulfilled, show that MacKinnon also possessed literary qualities of a high order, and that he must have carefully cultivated them after his final return to England. In this task indeed he found congenial occupation and recreation. The effects of his wound

---

[1] The Rev. Donald D. MacKinnon of Speldhurst Rectory, Tunbridge Wells, says:—"Colonel Daniel "MacKinnon's marvellous agility was known throughout the army, and he was the only man who was ever "permitted to take liberties with Wellington. His coolness in action was remarkable. It would be impossible "to record his many marvellous feats and escapades at Copenhagen and in the Peninsula . . . . After the "wound in the knee, which he received at Hougoumont, he never performed any more of his startling "feats."

which he received at Waterloo, having debarred him from the more active enjoyments to which he had been accustomed. Although such an undertaking required no small amount of historical and antiquarian research, the origin of the Coldstreams dating so far back as the year 1650, he ably discharged it by his work in two volumes, entitled "The Origin and Services of the Coldstream Guards," which was published in 1833, and dedicated, by permission, to His Majesty. In this work he has traced the actions of this distinguished brigade, in England and Scotland, during the wars of the Commonwealth, Restoration, and Revolution; its services in Ireland, in Holland, and upon the Continent; and, finally, in the Peninsula and at Waterloo. While he has shown a thorough acquaintanceship with the history of these various wars, his work is pervaded throughout not only with the high chivalrous magnanimity of a British soldier, but the exactness of a careful thinker, and the taste of a correct and elegant writer. The rest of Colonel MacKinnon's life may be briefly summed up, as it was, one of peace and domestic enjoyment. After he had settled in England he married Miss Dent, the eldest daughter of Mr. Dent, M.P. for Pool, a young lady of great attractions, but who brought him no family. With her he led a happy and retired life, surrounded by the society of those who loved him; and cheered, as we may well think, by those studies which he turned to such an honourable account. It was thought that, from his strong robust frame and healthy constitution, he would have survived to a good old age; but the sedentary life to which his wound confined him proved too much for a system so dependent upon active and exciting exercise. After having scarcely ever felt a day's illness he died at Hertford Street, Mayfair, London, on the 22nd of June, 1836, being only forty-six years old.

Major-General Daniel Henry MacKinnon.

Major-General Daniel Henry MacKinnon, son of John Daniel, second son of William, 32nd Chief of MacKinnon, entered the 16th Lancers in 1836 (having previously taken his B.A. degree with high honours at Trinity College, Dublin). He served with the regiment through the Afghan Campaign of 1838–39, and was present at Ghuznee. In the army of the Sutlej he was present at the battles of Buddiwall, Sobraon, and Aliwal (a victory which is said to have been "without a fault"), at which latter he had his horse shot under him, and commanded the third squadron throughout the day. He received two medals with clasps for Ghuznee, Sobraon, and Aliwal. MacKinnon returned with his regiment to England in 1847, and exchanged into the Carabineers for service in the Irish Rebellion of 1848. He again exchanged into the 43rd Regiment of Light Infantry, and, after serving a short time in it, was appointed a staff officer of pensioners in Enniskillen, Leicester, Woolwich, and finally in the North London division. He wrote a history of the campaigns in the far East, and was the author of many lectures. He married, in 1847, Caroline, daughter of Thomas Robert, Baron Dimsdale, with issue. General MacKinnon had the reputation of being one of the strongest men in the army, and was a noted sportsman.

Lieutenant-Colonel Daniel Lionel MacKinnon, Coldstream Guards, youngest son of the late, and brother of the present, Chief (William Alexander) of MacKinnon, was born in 1825, and in 1843 was gazetted to the Coldstream Guards. He became a Captain in 1848; a Lieutenant-Colonel in 1854; accompanied the 1st Battalion of the Coldstream Guards to the Crimea; and, after taking his share of camp life before the enemy's position, took part in the battle of Inkerman, where he fell, near the Sand-bag Battery, with seven of his brother officers, in the discharge of his duty.[1] The country erected a monument to his memory and to that of those seven officers in St. Paul's Cathedral, London.

Lieutenant-Colonel Lionel Dudley MacKinnon, son of Lieutenant-Colonel Daniel Lionel MacKinnon, who fell at Inkerman, was born in 1850. He entered the Coldstream Guards in January, 1871; became a Captain in 1875; was Musketry Instructor to the 2nd Battalion from 1877 till 1883; promoted to the rank of Lieutenant-Colonel in 1884; and was Commandant of the Guards' Depôt at Caterham in 1884 and till February, 1885. He accompanied the 2nd Battalion to Egypt in 1882, and served with it throughout the campaign. He went with the 1st Battalion to the Soudan in 1885, serving with it until the close of the war in that country, including the engagement at Hasheen, the attack on the convoy, and the destruction of Tamai. Colonel MacKinnon retired in 1887 on retired pay, and his name is at present on the list of the reserve of officers.

Surgeon-Major-General Sir William Alexander MacKinnon, K.C.B.

The Director-Generalship of the Army Medical Department is a post which is traditionally exposed to a good deal of hostile criticism, but it is one, at any rate, which has hitherto been filled by signally competent men. Indeed the attainment to that position is in itself a guarantee of exceptional services and distinction both at home and abroad. The career of Sir William Alexander MacKinnon is no exception to the rule, either from the standpoint of the criticism which was levelled at him during his term of office, or from the brilliant services which fitted him to occupy it, and the impartiality and thoroughness with which he exercised his power.

Sir William[2] was born in the Isle of Skye in 1830. His father was the Rev. John MacKinnon of Strath, a cadet of the ancient MacKinnons of Strathswordale and Strathaird, in that island; whilst his mother—the eldest daughter of Lachlan MacKinnon[3] of Corry, Isle of Skye—was also a descendant of the old line. He was educated at Glasgow and Edinburgh Universities, taking his diploma M.R.C.S., Edinburgh, in 1851;

---

[1] Colonel MacKinnon proceeded to Varna with his regiment, was invalided; but when orders came to select those who were fit to go to the Crimea, he being Senior Officer in command, at once selected himself, against the advice of the Medical Board, and reached the front in time to take part in the bloody battle of Inkerman.

[2] Mr. Charles Fraser-MacKintosh, writing about Sir William MacKinnon in "The Celtic Monthly" for August, 1896, says:—"The subject of this sketch is one of the best types of Islanders of the age. Every real Highlander, or Islander, being naturally a gentleman, defined and distinct from his fellows, if it were asked to mention any locality in pre-eminence where this is true, the island of Skye would be certainly named."

[3] Lachlan MacKinnon, son of Lachlan MacKinnon, VI. of Corry, was an officer (a Captain or a Major) in the East India Company's service.

THE MACKINNONS OF STRATH.
THE MACKINNONS OF KYLE.

Captain NEIL MACKINNON OF KYLE.
(From his grand-daughter, Miss Scobie, Keoldale, Sutherlandshire.)

Captain DONALD WILLIAM MACKINNON OF KYLE.
(From his son, Colonel Donald William MacKinnon.)

Lieutenant-Colonel WILLIAM ALEXANDER MACKINNON, C.B., R.A.
(From Colonel Donald William MacKinnon.)

Colonel DONALD WILLIAM MACKINNON.
(From a photograph given by himself.)

THE MACKINNONS OF SKIATH.
THE MACKINNONS OF KILBRIDE AND CORRY.

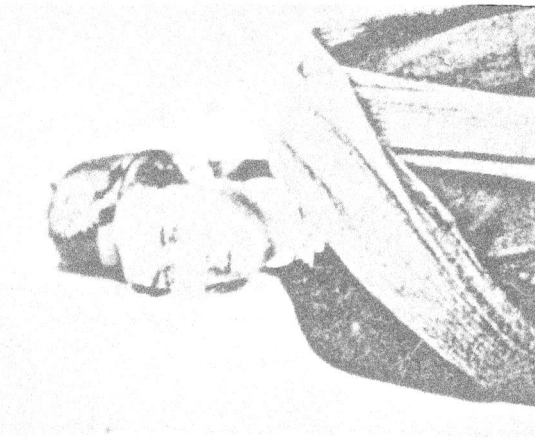

Lieutenant-Colonel CHARLES KENNETH MACKINNON
(From Miss F. MacKinnon, Duisdale.)

Colonel WALTER HENRY MACKINNON, Grenadier Guards, Assistant-Adjutant-General, Horse Guards, London.
(Clann Dhonnachaidh 'Ic Iain.)
(From a photograph given by himself.)

Surgeon-Major-General Sir WILLIAM ALEXANDER MACKINNON, K.C.B.
(From a photograph given by himself.)

F.R.C.S., Edinburgh, in 1872; LL.D., Glasgow, and Hon. F.R.C.S., Ireland, in 1891. He entered the Army Medical Department as Assistant-Surgeon on February 18th, 1853.

His first active service was in the Crimea, where he acted as Assistant-Surgeon of the 42nd Highlanders at Alma and Balaclava, the expedition to Kertch and Yenikale, the siege and fall of Sebastopol, and the assault of the outworks on June 18th and September 8th. For his part in the war he received a medal with three clasps, and was made a Knight of the Legion of Honour, receiving also a Turkish medal.

During the Indian Mutiny he served on the personal staff of Lord Clyde from April, 1858, to the close of the Mutiny. Referring to this part of his life, Sir Owen Tudor Burne writes in a footnote to his work on Lords Clyde and Strathnairn :—" Lord Clyde " was warmly attached to his friend MacKinnon, who served on his personal staff " during the campaign, after a distinguished training in the Crimea. 'Mac' was well " known in the Crimea, India, New Zealand, and Ashanti for his combative qualities, " and for his coolness and gallantry in the field."

Sir William, though, was less a combative man than a courageous one, but the former quality was never lacking, as we shall presently see, when he had to defend his wounded as well as attend to their injuries.

He next served throughout the New Zealand War of 1863-66 with the 57th Regiment. There, for his personal bravery no less than for his valuable professional services, he obtained the recognition of the General Commanding in that country and the Principal Medical Officer, Sir James Mouat, K.C.B., whose representations, contained in despatches, procured from the Government his promotion to be Companion of the Most Honourable Order of the Bath. The " Medical Times and Gazette" for 1864, commenting upon this appointment, says :—" We can safely assert that no officer in Her Majesty's service " has ever won the Companionship of the Bath by more gallant conduct than Surgeon " MacKinnon. The occasion of his exploits was the unfortunate assault on the Gate " Pah, in New Zealand, on April 29th, 1864, when so many valuable English lives were " sacrificed. He not only attended the wounded under fire, but personally protected " them by keeping the natives at bay. He rallied the soldiers, fired several shots in " defence of the wounded with his own hand, and shot down a native chief who was " in the act of tomahawking a wounded Englishman."

We may add to this that Sir William afterwards tended the wounds of the native chief, whom he had disabled, with as great assiduity as he bestowed upon his own men.

His last field service was in Ashanti, 1873 to 1874, when he served as Principal Medical Officer in the second phase of the campaign, including the capture of Kumasi.[1]

---

[1] "As an example of what is done by medical officers it may be permitted to tell of an incident in the " Ashanti War of 1874. The English force was hotly engaged at Amooful, and the 42nd were gallantly " making their way through the dense bush. Several men had fallen, and every surgeon on duty with the " fighting line was fully occupied, when two Highlanders were seen coming into the open space, where were " collected the Brigadier and other officers, supporting between them the Regimental Sergeant-Major, a " magnificent old soldier wearing the medals of the Crimea and Mutiny. He had been shot through the neck,

For his services there he was several times mentioned in despatches and afterwards promoted to the rank of Deputy-Surgeon-General.

In the intervening years, 1867 to 1873, Sir William was Assistant Professor of Military Surgery at Netley Hospital. From 1879 to 1880 he was Principal Medical Officer in China, 1880 to 1882 in Malta, 1882 to 1883 in the War Office, and from 1888 to 1889 at Gibraltar.

In the different stations abroad where he was placed, Sir William always exercised a vigilant surveillance over sanitary matters, and insisted upon a rational compliance with such measures as would ensure the protection of the public health. Quick to observe, he was no less ready and forceful in expressing his views, and his trenchant criticism, which appeared in the "China Mail" of 1882, upon Sir John Pope Hennessy having adopted Chinese views in the matter of sanitation at Hong Kong, drew instant attention to the danger threatened by this departure from the hygienic rules of Western life.

On the subject of hospital work he was also keenly interested, and whilst at Gibraltar he aided in the complete reorganisation of the civil hospital there, on a perfectly new basis, with English nurses and the most approved methods in vogue at home.

In 1889 Sir William was appointed Director-General to the Army Medical Department, and held that post until he retired in the spring of the year 1896.

The late Secretary of State for War, Mr. (now Sir Henry) Campbell Bannerman, in his speech of July 3rd, 1894, on the Army Estimates in the House of Commons, said :—
" As to the headquarters of the Medical Department of the Army, I have observed
" in the criticisms in the newspapers something like personal feeling against those at
" present at the head of that department. I am anxious to say that there could be no
" more efficient or just chief of that great department than Sir William MacKinnon."

When, in 1891, the distinction of Knight Commandership of the Bath was conferred upon him, the announcement was received both abroad and at home with unanimous approval.

After forty-three years of meritorious service, distinguished often by deeds of conspicuous bravery, and always by characteristic unselfishness and devotion to his work, Sir William could proudly look back upon the vicissitudes of his long and honourable career with the gratifying assurance that he gained the implicit confidence and maintained the friendliest relations with the chiefs under whom he served, and enjoyed

---

" and the arterial blood was spurting like a fountain from the wound. The gallant Principal Medical Officer,
" who had pushed to the front to watch the progress of the action and superintend the work of his
" subordinates, saw the wounded man approaching, and saying, ' If that man is not attended to he will be
" dead in five minutes,' at once set himself to the task, to perform which there was no other officer available.
" He extemporised a support for the poor fellow's head and laid him down. Then, while the ugly ' phit, phit,'
" of bullets sounded all around, he tied the carotid artery with as steady a hand and as unshaken a nerve as if
" he had been in the best appointed operating room in England. A brave and skilful man acted with courage
" and skill, and the life of another brave man was saved to his country. The medical officer was Surgeon-
" Major (now Sir W. A.) MacKinnon, until lately the Director-General."—From "Blackwood's Magazine" of December, 1896, by kind permission of the Publishers.

the respect and admiration of all his brother officers. Essentially a soldier, he regarded his own profession with the greatest pride, and looked back on the innumerable benefits he had been enabled to confer on his patients by his surgical and operative skill with the utmost complacency. Wherever he had served, in the colonies or at home, Sir William was ever ready to give the civil population the benefit of his surgical knowledge, and to aid his medical brethren in the profession with his advice and assistance when called upon.

He was a Governor of Wellington College, a Member of Committee of the Patriotic Fund Commission, and Honorary Surgeon to the Queen.

Sir William MacKinnon died at his residence in London on the 28th of October, 1897. His remains were cremated at Woking, and his ashes were finally deposited in the family burying-ground at Kilchrist, in "Strath of the MacKinnons."

Sir W. H. Russell on the late Sir W. A. MacKinnon.

In a letter to the "Times" of yesterday (1st of November, 1897), Sir W. H. Russell, the veteran war correspondent, writes:—

"The obituary notice of Sir W. A. MacKinnon in the 'Times' of last Saturday was a succinct record of the services of one of the best and bravest soldiers that ever wore the uniform of the Queen, but it conveyed no idea of the man himself, who was an embodiment of some of the finest traits of the Celtic Highlander—a dour, tender-hearted man, stern and kind, imaginative in all that related to clan and country, loyal to his Sovereign, but full of sentimental affection for 'the lost cause' of the Stuarts, which still lives in poetry and song north of Perth, and is not altogether ignored in high places along the valley of the Dee; keen in maintenance of the rights of the profession to which he belonged, and highly sensitive on the point of honour, but practical enough to recognise that there were broad lines of demarkation between the combatant and the medical officer in relation to military duties, and it must be confessed promptly pugnacious in vindication of his views against all comers. After the repulse of the Russian detachment by the 93rd, his own loved regiment, on October 25, he became so full of warlike ardour that he resigned his appointment as Assistant-Surgeon, and applied to Sir Colin Campbell to obtain him a commission as Ensign, which, I believe, he actually received, although his 'Chief,' as he called the General, endeavoured to divert him from his purpose by the remark, 'My good man, why, if you want to kill 'people, depend upon it you'll be more deadly with the lancet than you'll be with your 'sword.' The link that was forged between him and Sir Colin in the fire of battle was never broken, and MacKinnon was wont to rage at large when he spoke of the repulse at the Redan. 'We' (meaning the Highland Brigade) 'would have just driven them 'like chaff before the wind if Sir Colin had had the word.' When Campbell took the command of the army in India he selected MacKinnon as his personal Staff Surgeon. 'And an awful time I have of it,' the doctor said. 'He is not amenable to advice, and ' is more difficult to look after than a whole hospital!' When Sir Colin, riding furiously to check a troop R.H.A. that were galloping after some flying Sepoys, was thrown from his horse and broke his collar-bone, MacKinnon exclaimed, 'Well! He will have to 'be quiet for a time now at all events.' It was a short while before this that there was a temporary coolness between the chief and his body surgeon. MacKinnon rushed into the tent of a friend one morning with staring eyes and every symptom of bodily suffering, exclaiming, 'I am poisoned! I am dying! The apothecary gave me a deadly 'dose of belladonna in mistake. Heaven have mercy on me!' His friend rushed off to the tent of Dr. Tice, the P.M.O., who hastily caught up some specifics, and both made for the tent where MacKinnon lay in agony on a charpoy, which they reached just as Lord Clyde was entering it with the brusque demand, 'What's all this noise about?' 'I am dying! Sir, I am dying! That's all,' exclaimed MacKinnon in great agony. 'Dying! Then why can't you die quietly like a gentleman, Sir, and not make such a row?' And so retired. But peace was soon restored, and when MacKinnon set the mess tent on fire in the course of his execution of a strathspey on the table to enliven our Christmas dinner on the borders of the Ruptee (1859), Sir Colin merely observed that 'he must not do it again.' Sir William had not a trace of the Puritan about him; he loved a Gaelic song, and he pitied the folk who did not understand it; and he has been known in moments of social relaxation to exhibit to his intimates his skill in the various dances, steps, and measures which were in vogue when he was a boy in his well-beloved Isle of Skye, the traditions and tales of which were familiar and most dear to him. He was too sensible to deny to the races which were not fortunate enough to be born in the Western Isles a share in the virtues of manhood and in a proper development of fighting qualities, but he believed in his heart and soul that the warlike and other virtues of the human race obtain their highest pitch among his own people and their congeners. Whatever touched the fame or good name of the clans touched him to the quick, and it was as though he had suffered a personal outrage that he read the damning proofs of the treachery of Glengarry to his unfortunate master, and denounced the miscreant as though he was there standing before him as a villain who had brought eternal dishonour upon the country. When he was speaking of a medical officer with whom he had quarrelled in rather severe terms, he was reminded by a friend that the other was his countryman and that Scotchmen should hang together. 'Scotchmen!' exclaimed MacKinnon, 'Don't you understand the 'difference between a Glasgow body like that and a Highland gentleman? God forbid 'we should be considered the same!' By all the officers he served under he was held in friendly esteem and regard, by Lord Clyde, by Cameron, and by Lord Wolseley, and it is not to the credit of some of his own particular department of the army that MacKinnon was subjected to bitter attacks in the press when he was Director-General, for his assailants knew well that he could not reply to them; but he was sustained by his sense of duty and by the consciousness that he was actuated by devotion to the public service—'Tam Marte quam Mercurio'—he was a soldier-surgeon indeed, and he set a bright example which perhaps will be followed when the medical officers of the army are content to be so."[1]

---

[1] This letter and also all quotations from the "Army and Navy Gazette" are given with the kind permission of Sir W. H. Russell.

A memorial tablet (designed in white statuary marble on a black background) has been erected in the Chapel of the Royal Victoria Hospital, Netley, to the memory of the great Surgeon-General, with the following inscription :—

"Sacred to the memory of Surgeon-Major-General Sir William Alexander MacKinnon, K.C.B., Q.H.S., A.M.S., born at Strath, Isle of Skye, June 27th, 1830; died in London, October 28th, 1897. He served in the Crimea with the 42nd Royal Highlanders, and through the Indian Mutiny on the personal Staff of Lord Clyde; he also took part in the New Zealand and Ashanti (1873-74) Campaigns, and closed as Director-General of the Army Medical Staff an honourable and active career, which extended over forty-three years. This tablet is erected by his brother officers and several old comrades and friends."

Among the subscribers were H.R.H. the Duke of Cambridge, Generals C. J. Russell and Sir John MacNeill; Surgeon-Generals J. Jameson, Sir J. Mouat, J. B. Reade, and W. R. Hooper; Colonel A. Davidson, Sir W. Howard Russell, the Duke and Duchess of Somerset, Surgeon-Colonel K. MacLeod, &c.[1]

Dr. Kenneth MacKinnon (of Corry), Bengal Medical Department, was appointed Assistant-Surgeon on the 19th of November, 1826; Surgeon on the 1st of March, 1843; retired on the 5th of January, 1857; and died on the 13th of February, 1861. Dr. MacKinnon prepared a medico-topographical report of the Tirhoot District, in 1836, for which he received the approbation of the Governor-General. He was appointed medical officer to the staff at Dinapore on the 21st of March, 1844; to the medical charge of the 1st Bengal Native Infantry on the 17th of August, 1844; transferred to that of the Cawnpore Depôt on the 7th of December; was chosen to be secretary to the Medical Board at Calcutta on the 20th of September, 1852; and was apothecary to the East India Company from 1853 to 1857.[2]

Lieutenant-Colonel Charles Kenneth MacKinnon, of the Bengal Staff Corps, son of Dr. Kenneth MacKinnon of Corry, was born in India on the 15th of December, 1840. He was nominated by Sir F. Currie, Baronet, and arrived in India on the 26th of August, 1858. He was posted to Her Majesty's 73rd Regiment on the 10th of September, 1858; and soon afterwards to Her Majesty's 52nd Regiment; joined the 63rd Native Infantry Regiment in February, 1860, and the 3rd Punjab Infantry on the 6th of December, 1861; transferred to the 6th Punjab Infantry in 1863; and made Adjutant of the same corps on the 22nd of February, 1864.[1]

MacKinnon served with Her Majesty's 73rd Regiment against the mutineers on the Nepaul Frontier in 1858, for which he received a medal. He acted as Adjutant of the 6th Punjab Infantry through the Umbeyla Expedition of 1863-64, and his name was brought especially to the notice of the Punjab Government by His Excellency the Commander-in-Chief for the good service which he had rendered at the Umbeyla Pass,

---

[1] "The Army and Navy Gazette." [2] India Office Records.

as was notified in the Staff Office Memorandum, dated May 15, 1865. He was severely wounded in a skirmish near Kohat with the Bezoti Afridis on the 11th of March, 1868, for which his name was mentioned by the Officer commanding there in his report on the subject to the Brigadier-General in command of the Frontier Force, and for which he received the thanks of the Punjab Government ("for gallant conduct in the field"),[1] as well as those of the Governor-General in Council ("for gallantry before the enemy"),[2] and also a medal with a clasp.[3] Colonel MacKinnon died on the 8th of March, 1887, near Edwardsabad.

Major Alexander MacKinnon, East India Company's service, son of John MacKinnon of Kyle, was born on the 20th of March, 1788. He was nominated by C. Grant, Esq., at the recommendation of Major MacDonald, and was appointed Ensign in the 21st Native Infantry on the 21st of November, 1809; Lieutenant on the 16th of December, 1814; Captain on the 24th of April, 1824; was transferred to the 39th Native Infantry on the 13th of April, 1825; served for a time as Second Officer of the Nagpore Auxiliary Horse; and received the rank of Major on the 28th of June, 1838. He retired on the 6th of July, 1838. "The activity and zeal displayed by Lieutenant "MacKinnon in causing the dispersion of the followers of a dacoit, the Governor- "General considers to be highly creditable to him."[4]

Captain Neil MacKinnon, 93rd Highlanders, brother of Major Alexander MacKinnon, was appointed Ensign on the 24th of June, 1802; Lieutenant on the 14th of May, 1804; and Captain on the 25th of May, 1813. Lieutenant MacKinnon commanded a company of his regiment at the taking of Cape Town, under General Sir David Baird in January, 1806. The Highland Brigade, consisting of the 71st, 72nd, and 79th Regiments, landed at Lospard Bay, experiencing a slight opposition from a light corps of the enemy, which was scattered along the heights bordering on the shore, and thirty-five men of the 93rd Highlanders were lost when disembarking by the upsetting of a boat.[5] The British troops advanced on the 8th, and, ascending to the summit of the Blue Mountains, perceived the enemy drawn up on a plain in two lines of about 5,000 men, with twenty-three pieces of cannon. Sir David Baird quickly formed his troops in two columns, and directed the first brigade towards the right, while the Highland Brigade, thrown forward on the high road, advanced on the enemy, who opened a heavy fire of grape, round shot, and musketry, seemingly determined to retain their position, the enemy kept up a smart fire as the British troops advanced till General Ferguson (who commanded the Highland Brigade) gave the word to charge. The order was instantly obeyed, and the charge was so impetuous and so irresistible that the enemy, appalled and panic-struck, gave way at all points, and fled in great confusion, having sustained a loss of 600 men killed and wounded, while the casualties on

---

[1] India Office Records.
[2] Military Secretary's Report, dated 31st March, 1868.
[3] Brigade Order, dated 5th May, 1868.
[4] India Office Records, 31st May, 1816.
[5] Regimental Records.

the British side were only sixteen men killed and 191 wounded. The enemy made no further resistance, and thus easily was the important colony of the Cape of Good Hope acquired. The 93rd remained in the colony till it embarked for England in 1814, and was consequently denied a share of the triumphs that were gained by many other corps on the Continent of Europe. In the spring of 1814 Captain MacKinnon accompanied the 2nd Battalion (which was raised in the previous year) to Newfoundland, where it was stationed till the beginning of October, 1815; but did not take part in the expedition to New Orleans in 1814, and in the disastrous operations which took place there in 1814 and 1815, after which the weakened state of the regiment prevented its employment in the Waterloo Campaign in 1815. Captain MacKinnon retired from the service in 1823.

Captain Donald William MacKinnon, of the East India Company's Service (Madras Staff Corps), second son of Dr. Farquhar MacKinnon of Kyle, Isle of Skye, received the rank of Ensign on the 2nd of January, 1836; Lieutenant on the 26th of May, 1840; and that of Captain on the 2nd of July, 1851. He served in China, on the River Yangtse-Kiang, in 1841-42, for which he received a medal; in the operations against the Rohillas in 1858-59; and was present in the action of Chichumbah, where he was severely wounded and died (of wounds received in action), on the 16th of January, 1859.

Colonel Donald William MacKinnon, son of Captain Donald William MacKinnon of Kyle, was appointed Ensign in the 109th (late 3rd Bombay (European) Infantry) on the 27th of July, 1861; Lieutenant on the 22nd of April, 1864; Captain on the 6th of December, 1873; Major in the Prince of Wales' Royal Canadian (Leinster) Regiment (late 109th Regiment); Lieutenant-Colonel on the 1st of December, 1885; Lieutenant-Colonel commanding the 1st Battalion, September, 1886. He retired on a special pension in April, 1889. In addition to the posts already mentioned, he held those of Regimental Interpreter, Acting Quarter-Master, and Adjutant, as well as the following appointments on the Army Staff, viz.:—Brigade-Major, Deputy-Adjutant-General for Musketry, and Deputy-Assistant-Commissary-General.

In 1865 Colonel MacKinnon (then a Lieutenant) served as a volunteer in the expedition against the Arabs from Aden, and in the Abyssinian Campaign of 1867-68, for which he received a medal.

Lieutenant-Colonel William Alexander MacKinnon, C.B., Royal (late Bengal) Artillery, fourth son of Dr. Farquhar MacKinnon of Kyle, Isle of Skye, was born on the 20th of April, 1822. He was appointed 2nd Lieutenant on the 10th of December, 1841; 1st Lieutenant on the 1st of July, 1845; Captain on the 22nd of August, 1855; Major (army rank) on the 20th of July, 1858; Commander of the Bath on the 16th of November, 1858; and Lieutenant-Colonel on the the 20th of February, 1862. Colonel MacKinnon died (unmarried) at Beechwood, Stirling, on the 30th of September, 1867.

MacKinnon, as we have seen, entered the army in 1841. He served with "the army of the Sutlej," under Lord Gough, throughout the campaign of 1845-46; was present at the battles of Moodkee, Ferozeshah, and Sobraon; commanded 2nd Troop, 1st Brigade Horse Artillery, throughout the engagements of the 21st and 22nd December, 1845, at Ferozeshah, subsequent to the death of Major Todd, who was killed during the advance upon the enemy on the 21st, for which he received a medal and clasps. He served with the force under Brigadier Sir Hugh Massey Wheeler, K.C.B., which formed part of the army of the Punjab, during the Punjab Campaign in 1848-49; was present at the capture of the Forts of Runganungle, Kulallwalla, and Moraree, and in the several affairs in which the force was engaged. MacKinnon commanded the 3rd Troop, 1st Brigade, Horse Artillery, during a great part of the time. For this service he got a medal also.

His next service was with the force under Sir Colin Campbell, G.C.B. (the late Lord Clyde), employed against the Momunds and Hill Tribes west of Peshawur in 1851-52. He commanded two guns under Sir Colin in the affair against the Hill Tribes on the height of the "Punj Pao" in April, 1852. Also had command of the 2nd Troop, 3rd Brigade, Horse Artillery, with the army under Lord Clyde in 1857-58, and was present at the action in the "Kala Nuddee," the taking of Futtezhar, and final siege and capture of Lucknow. With the column under Sir Hope Grant, K.C.B., he served throughout the operations in Oudh in the hot season of 1858; was present at the affairs of Koorsee, Baree, and Simree; commanded the Horse Artillery at the battle of "Nuwabgunge Burra Banke," and in the affair at Selimpore under Colonel Pratt, C.B. MacKinnon was employed with the column under Sir George Barker, K.C.B., during the remainder of the operations in 1858-59. He was very honourably mentioned in all the despatches connected with the above operations, and received his Brevet Majority, C.B., medal and clasp.

Annexed is a copy of a Memorandum in support of a memorial for a Brevet Majority by the unsolicited desire of Lord Clyde (then Sir Colin Campbell, G.C.B.) in 1856, which was approved of by General Anson, the Commander-in-Chief in India, and forwarded by him for the sanction of the Government in May, 1857, but, owing to the breaking out of the Mutiny, was lost in transit from Simla to Calcutta, and therefore never reached its destination.

"MEMORANDUM BY LIEUTENANT-GENERAL SIR COLIN CAMPBELL, G.C.B., IN SUPPORT OF THE MEMORIAL OF CAPTAIN MACKINNON, BENGAL ARTILLERY, FOR PROMOTION.

"In the month of April, 1853, while in command of the Peshawur Field Force, I heard that the Momund Tribes were assembling in the hills to the north and west of Muttah, with a view to plunder the rich villages in that neighbourhood, as well as the Doaba between the Caubul and Swat rivers. Although this report was disbelieved by the civil authorities, I thought it prudent to go and judge for myself, and I accordingly moved from Peshawur with two guns under Lieutenant MacKinnon, and about 200 cavalry, and came to Shubkuddur on the evening of the 16th April. On the following morning I observed large masses of the hillmen on the hills to the north and west of Shubkudder. I wanted to see them develop their plans. One body came down and occupied the heights of "Punj Pao," about a mile west of Shubkuddur, with a view to hold the garrison in check, while the remainder, in great force (upwards of 6,000 men), moved towards their left in the direction of Muttah.

"As I had no infantry except the small garrison of Shubkuddur, I could not fight a battle with such a force; but I saw that if I could carry these heights (Punj Pao) I should threaten the retreat of the hillmen, and probably succeed in driving them back. Accordingly I advanced, Lieutenant MacKinnon's guns covered by 200 cavalry, and drove the enemy from the heights above "Punj Pao," by the fire of the artillery, and after crowning them, immediately turned the guns on the masses of the enemy then moving upon Muttah. The fire of these guns broke their order, and forced them to retire into the hills, abandoning the enterprise. When sunset approached it became necessary to regain Shubkuddur, but as soon as the guns were limbered up, the Momunds rallied, and attempted to take them, and now Lieutenant MacKinnon showed the *firmness* and *dash* which I have attributed to him in my report. I ordered him to unlimber, and to open with grape, and he continued his retreat unlimbering and opening fire at 300 yards, covered by the cavalry, not only securing his retreat, but inflicting such a loss on the enemy that they dispersed on the next day, and thus the rich villages of Muttah, as well as the whole Doaba, were preserved from being plundered and destroyed, and the object of the enemy completely frustrated. I can, therefore, recommend Captain MacKinnon very strongly as a gallant and skilful officer, and as truly deserving of any reward which the service will admit of being extended to him.

"(Signed)   C. CAMPBELL, Lt.-General,
"Late Brigadier, Commanding Peshawur Field Force.

"London, Dec. 2nd, 1856."[1]

The present Chief of Clanranald, Admiral Sir Reginald MacDonald, K.C.B., K.C.S.I., is connected with Skye. His great-grandmother was the celebrated Flora, daughter of MacKinnon of MacKinnon.

MACKINNONS.
(CLANN DHONNACHAIDH 'IC IAIN.)

Brigade-Surgeon-Lieutenant-Colonel H. W. A. MacKinnon, D.S.O. (son of the late Dr. Charles MacKinnon, of the Indian Army, who was descended from a branch of the MacKinnons of Strath, Clann Dhonnachaidh 'Ic Iain) was appointed Assistant Surgeon on the 2nd of October, 1865; Surgeon on the 1st of March, 1873; Surgeon-Major on the 2nd of October, 1877; Surgeon-Major (Lieutenant-Colonel) on the 2nd of October, 1885; and Brigade-Surgeon (Lieutenant-Colonel) on the 10th of March, 1892.

---

[1] Extracts from Sir Colin Campbell's report to the Adjutant-General of the Army in India:—"I beg "particularly to dwell on the gallantry and steadiness of the Artillery under the command of Lieutenant "MacKinnon and Lieutenant Blunt, who had accompanied his brother officer as a volunteer. It was owing "to the *firmness* and *dash* of this very slender detachment that I was enabled to drive back 6,000 men, and to "retreat, when it became necessary, without loss."

He served in the Egyptian Expedition of 1882; was present at the battle of Tel-el-Kebir, where he was slightly wounded, and for which he was mentioned in despatches, received a medal with a clasp, and the Khedive's bronze star.

Dr. MacKinnon served also in the Burmese Expedition of 1885-86-87; was named in despatches in the "London Gazette" of the 2nd September, 1887, and got the Distinguished Service Order.[1]

Colonel Walter Henry MacKinnon, Grenadier Guards, Assistant-Adjutant-General, brother of Brigade-Surgeon-Lieutenant-Colonel H. W. A. MacKinnon, D.S.O., joined the army as Ensign and Lieutenant in the Grenadier Guards on the 22nd of June, 1870; was promoted to be Lieutenant and Captain on the 3rd of August, 1872; Adjutant of the 2nd Battalion from July, 1876, to January, 1881; Captain and Lieutenant-Colonel on the 1st of January, 1881, and Colonel on the 10th of February, 1889.

He was Assistant Military Secretary to the Governor and Commander-in-Chief in Malta from the 8th of June, 1884, to the 26th of July, 1885; Private Secretary to the Governor of Madras from the 27th of July, 1885, to the 8th of December, 1886, and Assistant-Adjutant-General of the Home District from the 26th of July, 1893, to the present time.

Bombardier Peter MacKinnon.

Bombardier Peter MacKinnon was born at Glendale, in the parish of Duirinish, Skye, in the year 1828. His grandfather, Roderick MacKinnon, was born in Glendale, Skye, in 1750. He joined the 2nd Battalion of the Black Watch (now the 73rd Regiment) in the year 1780, and served with it under Colonel (afterwards General) Norman MacLeod of MacLeod in the campaigns of those days in India. Bombardier Peter MacKinnon says:—" I have heard my grandfather relating various stories about
" his battles, especially with Tipoo Sahib, and I have a good recollection of seeing many
" marks of wounds upon his body. He died in 1834, aged eighty-four years.[2] I had a
" grand uncle, Big Allan MacCaskill, also in the Black Watch, who was counted a great
" hero. He saved his own life and the lives of two of his comrades when seventeen of
" his party perished, having been caught in a terrible snowstorm on a moor near Fort
" Augustus. The cairns of these unfortunate men are still visible upon the said moor.
" Big Allan was a pensioner and died (unmarried) when he was ninety years old. I had
" two uncles as sailors in the Royal Navy along with the famous Nelson. I have a
" nephew a pensioner in England, having served his twenty-one years in the army; and a
" son for six years in 'the Thin Red Line,' and with the Indian Frontier Force since
" July last (1897); and besides I have six other sons who are quite passable for facing
" a foe either by sea or by land."

---

[1] War Office Records.
[2] This veteran retained his agility and vigour almost to the last. It is said that he danced "Gille Calum" when he was eighty years of age!

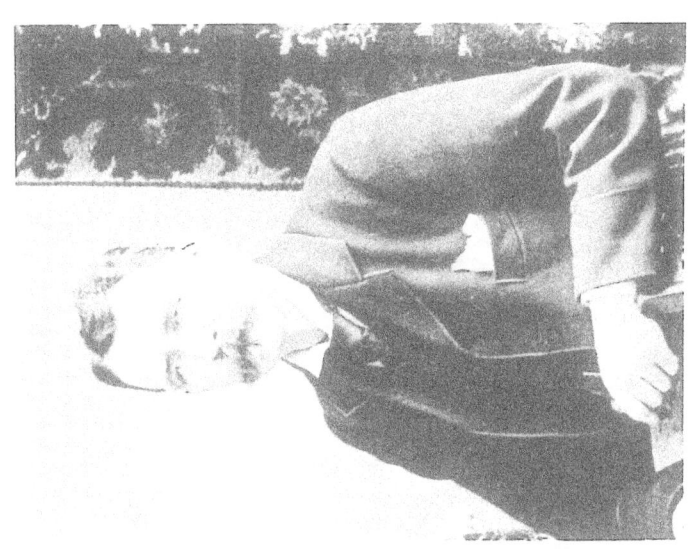

Lance-Corporal ALEXANDER MACPHERSON, 15th Hussars.
(From a photograph given by himself.)
(See p. 227.)

Corporal JOHN NICOLSON, 42nd Highlanders.
(From a photograph taken by Dr. Charles MacDonald of Skaebost.)
(See p. 228.)

Bombardier PETER MACKINNON, Royal Marine Artillery.
(From a photograph taken by Mr. A. R. MacDonald, Younger, of Waternish.)
(See p. 218.)

Peter MacKinnon at the age of twenty-three joined the Chatham Division of Royal Marines in the year 1851, but was soon after transferred to the Royal Marine Artillery, and in 1853 he was sent on board the "Royal George," then fitting out at Sheerness for the Baltic. In September, 1854, he was ordered to proceed from the Baltic to the Black Sea in Her Majesty's ship "Spiteful," commanded by Captain Kidston. MacKinnon was present at the taking of Kinburn Fort and of Sebastopol. In the first action the "Spiteful" having been disabled, her crew were landed and took part on shore in several engagements with the Cossacks. On joining the "Spiteful," MacKinnon was promoted to the rank of Bombardier, and at the capture of Kinburn Fort was Second Captain of the after pivot gun; but the First Captain having been killed during the action, MacKinnon was advanced to the vacant post.

When the "Spiteful" returned to England in 1857 it was found that there were only nine survivors of the 160 officers and men who left home with her in 1854. Bombardier MacKinnon then went to the American coast. In 1859 the vessel was overtaken by a tremendous storm on the banks of Newfoundland. MacKinnon was one of those who saved the ship, and when they returned home they were personally thanked by Her Majesty the Queen for their brave conduct. Owing to the severe injuries which he received on that occasion he was discharged with a pension in 1860. Bombardier MacKinnon has two medals, viz., the British Crimean War medal with a bar for Sebastopol, and the Turkish medal for the same service.

The gallant old man says:—"I have at present a son in the army in India, and "my other six sons would be there too, if they had taken my advice."

Private Norman MacKinnon, Strath. Miss MacKinnon of Duisdale mentions that this man saw some service in the 42nd Highlanders.

THE ELDERS OF ISLEORNSAY AND KNOCK IN THE PARISH OF SLEAT.

"These men had the fear of God in their hearts, and were upright and honourable in their lives."—A Friend's Loving Tribute.

MAJOR-GENERAL SIR GEORGE ELDER, K.C.B.

Although Sir George Elder was not born in "Eilean a Cheo," he is claimed as a Skye soldier, because of the long and honourable connection of his family with the parish of Sleat, and because it was from Skye he joined the army, his inherent military genius having doubtless received not a little stimulus from the warlike spirit which prevailed in the island at that time.

The Elders had fighting blood in their veins from both sides of the house, ancestors of theirs (Stuart and Elder) having fought at Culloden on the side of the Prince.

Sir George Elder was a soldier born, and efforts which were made to prevent his going to the army were in vain.

He was appointed as an Ensign in the 46th Foot on the 27th of November, 1799; Second Lieutenant in the 95th Foot on the 5th of November, 1800; Lieutenant on the 24th of March, 1803; Captain on the 23rd of May, 1805; Major in the Portuguese army on the 13th of April, 1809; Major, half-pay, in the same army, on the 25th of December, 1816; Lieutenant-Colonel, Brevet, on the 30th of May, 1811; Colonel, Brevet, on the 19th of July, 1821; Major-General on the 22nd of July, 1830; Lieutenant-Governor of Newfoundland on the 4th of October, 1826; and Commander-in-Chief in Madras in August, 1836.[1]

While stationed at Shorncliffe in 1805, under the command of Sir John Moore, Lieutenant Elder's assiduity in the performance of his duties, and the excellent state of discipline to which he had brought his company, so attracted the notice of that distinguished General that, on the occasion of the Militia being allowed to volunteer for the line, he was pleased to say he would recommend Lieutenant Elder to the Commander-in-Chief for a company, if he were successful in obtaining men (for which duty he was detached), and on his return with the prescribed number he was promoted to a company in the 2nd Battalion of the 95th Foot.

Captain Elder's company formed part of the detachment from the Rifle Corps which was employed in the expedition that was sent to South America in 1806.[2]

An interesting communication in the "Naval and Military Gazette" alludes to Captain Elder's services at Monte Video in the following terms:—"In 1806 he
" embarked with a detachment of three companies on the secret expedition which
" terminated in the assault and capture of Monte Video, the troops on which occasion
" were under the command of Brigadier-General Achmuty. In this affair the conduct
" of Captain Elder was particularly conspicuous, he having led his company to the
" breach, and established himself on the ramparts, in defiance of a numerous body of
" the enemy then pressing hard upon him. In the confusion the vigilant eye of
" Captain Elder saw the importance of occupying the tower of the Cathedral, and he
" at once took possession of it, and, by his flanking fire, succeeded in driving the
" enemy from their guns, and enabling our troops to clear the ramparts. For this
" eminent service he received the thanks of the officer commanding. In 1807, on the
" arrival of the force under Brigadier-General Crawford, Captain Elder moved on with
" his corps to the attack of Buenos Ayres, and on the march, being with the advanced
" guard, he had an opportunity of distinguishing himself by throwing a bridge across
" a small river in two hours, which enabled the artillery to pass over rapidly, and
" which led to the total discomfiture of a force of Spaniards consisting of 5,000 men, by
" the light brigade, only amounting to fourteen companies of riflemen and artillery.
" On this occasion eleven pieces of artillery were taken from the enemy, principally
" owing to a charge of Captain Elder's company on the flank, aided by a bold advance
" of the line."[1]

Captain Elder further had the good fortune to be most favourably noticed for his zeal and ability by Brigadier-General Robert Crawford, who, on the disembarkation of the troops in the Bay of Barragon, personally inspected the manner in which the sentries had been posted, and declared that he could not have done it better himself.[2]

---

[1] War Office Records.

[2] "Short Memoir of Major-General Sir George Elder, K.C.B." Kindly lent by Miss Maggie M. Elder, late of Knock, Sleat, Skye.

On the pursuit of the enemy by Brigadier-General Crawford, Captain Elder was requested to reconnoitre a position, and while engaged on this service a party of the enemy, who had concealed themselves in a trench, fired on Captain Elder and wounded him dangerously in the groin. He fell instantly, when the Brigadier-General, seeing it, and believing him killed, exclaimed, "There falls as brave and gallant a fellow as ever lived!" He was carried off the field, and for a considerable time doubts were entertained of his ever recovering. He had lost entirely the use of his limbs, but the strength of his iron constitution brought him through. The ball was never extracted, but was supposed to have lodged near the spine, from the effects of which he often suffered great pain.

In 1808 Captain Elder joined the army under Sir John Moore in the Peninsula and was almost daily engaged with the enemy while covering the retreat of the British troops upon Corunna. In this service his activity and the excessive fatigue he surmounted were remarkable.[1]

He embarked for England after the battle of Corunna (in which he was engaged) with the remains of his corps, and in April, 1809, being one of the twenty officers originally chosen, he was promoted to a Majority, and appointed by Marshal Beresford to the command of the 3rd Battalion of Caçadores in the Portuguese army, with the rank of Lieutenant-Colonel in that service.

On leaving his old corps (the 95th) the company he had commanded presented Major Elder with a silver-mounted sabre, suitably inscribed, as a memorial of their respect and gratitude.

Lieutenant-Colonel Elder was indefatigable in training and disciplining his battalion. Lord Wellington and His Excellency Marshal Beresford reviewed them, when his Lordship said:—"Colonel Elder, the Marshal and myself are under great " obligations to you for the fine state of discipline to which you have brought your " battalion, and to your country you have rendered a most essential service."

At the commencement of the Portuguese Campaign the 3rd Battalion of Caçadores was attached to the light division in advance of the Allied Army.[1]

On the 18th of July, 1810, in the affair of Almeida, Lieutenant-Colonel Elder received the congratulations of Major-General Robert Crawford for the gallant conduct of his battalion in an attack of two squadrons of French cavalry who were nearly destroyed. During this affair the remainder of the light division cheered the Caçadores from an eminence in the rear.

On the 24th of July, in the severe action of the Coa, the 3rd Battalion was particularly mentioned in orders by Marshal Beresford, who, in thanking the commanding officer and corps, observed that "their brilliant conduct on that occasion " was equal in every respect to that of British troops."

On the evening preceding the battle of Busaco Lieutenant-Colonel Elder had his horse shot under him in a sharp engagement with the enemy's advance in front of the position.

---

[1] "Short Memoir of Major-General Sir George Elder, K.C.B."

At the battle of Busaco, the 3rd Caçadores were engaged during the whole of the 27th and the morning of the 28th, and, incited by the energy and intrepidity of their commanding officer, behaved with a spirit worthy of older soldiers, and fully justified the encomiums passed on the Portuguese troops by Lord Wellington and by Marshal Beresford, the former of whom in his orders was pleased to say that "the 3rd "Caçadores, under the command of Lieutenant-Colonel Elder, have added to their "former reputation by their gallant behaviour, which was admired not only by his "Excellency, but by the army in general."

The 3rd Caçadores distinguished themselves particularly at Alenguer, where, owing to a heavy rain and thick fog, the enemy succeeded in taking the village unobserved. The Caçadores promptly formed on a height commanding the bridge, and held it against a division of the enemy until the part of the army occupying Alenguer had time to form and retreat to their respective stations.

From the arrival of the allied army in the lines of Torres Vedras, Lieutenant-Colonel Elder's corps occupied the outposts of the famous Light Division; and on Massena's retreat to the position of Santarem it covered the advance of the army, and was on several occasions closely engaged with the rear-guard of the enemy.[1]

Whilst the French army were in the position of Santarem (upwards of three months), Lieutenant-Colonel Elder was entrusted with the occupation of the bridge and two forts of Ponte Solario, the most advanced point of the allied army, and to which the greatest responsibility was attached. During this service the corps quite equalled the expectations that had been formed of it.

On the retreat of the enemy from Santarem, Lieutenant-Colonel Elder, always in advance, had repeatedly the honour of being opposed to the heroic Ney (the great master of rear-guard actions, who succeeded in outwitting even Wellington himself at the Redinha), and, while thus employed, took and kept possession of the Castle of Pombal until the arrival of the allied army. Here he maintained his position for upwards of ten hours against the rear-guard of the enemy, consisting of at least 10,000 men, and the loss sustained by the 3rd Caçadores was very considerable; but Lieutenant-Colonel Elder and his corps received the thanks of the Commander-in-Chief and the praise of the whole army. On the day following he was engaged with the right of the enemy's advanced posts, and Lord Wellington was pleased to state, in General Orders, "that he had never witnessed a more brilliant attack than "that made by the 52nd Regiment and Lieutenant-Colonel Elder's Caçadores in "driving the enemy from the heights of Redinha."[1]

On the 13th of March his battalion was ordered to turn the enemy's right flank on the position of the Sierra d'Estrella; and, falling in with them at Choa da Lama (whilst they were attacked in front by the Light Division), he participated in the glory of driving them from the heights. On the following evening the Caçadores composed a part of the troops which attacked the enemy with such rapidity at Foz d'Aronse that they were thrown into confusion; and in crossing the river they lost an eagle and a number of men and officers were drowned.

---

[1] "Short Memoir of Major-General Sir George Elder, K.C.B."

The Caçadores were again engaged in the skirmish at Guarda, and in the attack at Sabugal they forded the river in two places in front of the Light Division, driving in the enemy's advanced piquets. Lieutenant-Colonel Elder received the thanks of Lord Wellington on the field, and afterwards in orders, for his conduct on this occasion.[1]

The allied army having gone into quarters on the frontiers of Portugal, the Caçadores were sent in advance to the village of Espeja, in Spain, and they distinguished themselves by repulsing, in square, an attack of seven squadrons of the enemy's cavalry, who suffered severely in killed and wounded. The corps was publicly thanked by General Robert Crawford for their steady and determined conduct on that day.

In the battle of Fuentes d'Onor, on the morning of the 5th May, Lieutenant-Colonel Elder was engaged in covering the Light Division in the wood on the right of the line, from whence they were obliged to retire in square, being attacked by nearly the whole of the enemy's cavalry. After the battle Lieutenant-Colonel Elder was appointed, in May, 1811, to a British Lieutenant-Colonelcy as a remuneration for his services.[1]

From this period until the investment of Ciudad Rodrigo, the corps was constantly in the advance, and had many opportunities of attracting the notice of the commander of the forces. The 3rd Caçadores was the first corps that broke ground before that fortress, and, in the storming and capture, it had the honour of leading the Light Division to the assault, under a tremendous fire, carrying, besides their arms, 300 sacks of hay, which they placed in the ditch and immediately mounted the breach. On their gaining the square they were publicly thanked by General Picton (who commanded the attack) for their gallant conduct, which, besides being praised by Marshal Beresford in orders, was also particularly mentioned in Lord Wellington's despatch of the 28th of January, 1812, wherein, after recording the merits of various officers, his Lordship says:—"Lieutenant-Colonel Elder and the 3rd Caçadores were likewise distinguished on this occasion." At the storming of Badajoz, Lieutenant-Colonel Elder, with his usual daring, led a brigade composed of the 1st and 3rd Caçadores, and five companies of his old and favourite regiment, the 95th, to the great breach, where he fell desperately wounded. He was left on the spot for dead, the troops passing over his body. Returning animation, and the blaze of fire around him, enabled Colonel Elder to distinguish his old beloved regiment, the 95th, and he had just strength to exclaim, "Elder! Elder!" when two men of his former company lifted him up and carried him into Badajoz, where he was for a considerable time confined by his wounds, which brought on lockjaw. In his despatch of the 7th April, 1812, Lord Wellington again records his opinion of Colonel Elder's gallant conduct.

Being in a precarious state of health, owing to the severe nature of his wounds, he was obliged to return to England; but previously to his departure from the Peninsula he was made Knight Commander of the Order of the Tower and Sword

---

[1] "Short Memoir of Major-General Sir George Elder, K.C.B."

by the Regency of Portugal; and His Royal Highness the Regent of England was pleased to confer the honour of Knighthood on him soon after his arrival.

In July, 1813, while yet in a state of convalescence, Sir George Elder rejoined the army. On his arrival in France he was promoted to the rank of Colonel and appointed to the command of the 7th Regiment of Portuguese Infantry. He was engaged after this in several skirmishes and affairs of outposts. At the head of a body of troops, upwards of 3,000, he captured the Castle of Blois.[1]

At the peace of 1814 Sir George Elder accompanied the Portuguese army on their return to their own country, where he was, in 1816, promoted to the rank of Brigadier in that service, with the command of the 5th Brigade in the Alemtejo.

At the distribution of honours by His Royal Highness the Prince Regent of England, Sir George Elder was decorated with the much-coveted Gold Cross for the general actions and assaults of Busaco, Fuentes d'Onor, Ciudad Rodrigo, and Badajoz. He had received nine wounds in battle, eight of which were considered dangerous; and his Sovereign, in consideration of his sufferings, conferred on him the appointment of Lieutenant-Governor of St. John's, Newfoundland. In 1830 he was promoted to the rank of Major-General, and at the same time was nominated a Knight Commander of the Order of the Bath; received the star of a Spanish Order from Ferdinand VII.; and, finally, was appointed Commander-in-Chief in Madras in August, 1836, an appointment which was as highly gratifying to his many friends among the bravest and most distinguished in the British and Portuguese armies as it was to his relatives and to himself.[1]

Sir George Elder was accidentally killed at Madras on the 3rd of December, 1836.

His indomitable courage, tempered with prudence, his unswerving adherence to his duty when under command, and his quick perception and determined exertions when command devolved upon himself, characterised his career as a soldier; and his strict honour, his kindly feelings, forgiving temper, quiet manners, and propriety of conduct under all circumstances,—his life as a man. He was consequently favoured with the esteem and confidence of those under whom he served, and beloved by his men, into whom he infused courage. Thus honoured and distinguished by the favour of his Sovereign, the praise of a Wellington, the approbation of his superiors, and the kind wishes, respect, and friendship of all who had served under him or who had known him intimately, he terminated his career.[1]

Lieutenant-Colonel Alexander MacDonald Elder, of the Bombay Fusiliers, who had the honour of being described by the leading military men in India as "a most reliable officer," was born in the parish of Sleat, as was also his brother, Commander Benjamin John Elder, a highly capable officer in the East India Company's naval service. Both were nephews of Sir George Elder, K.C.B.

---

[1] "Short Memoir of Major-General Sir George Elder, K.C.B."

Captain MacLean of Kilmaree, in the Parish of Strath.

Of this soldier very little information can now be obtained. He was a bachelor, and was an uncle of the late Mrs. MacInnes of Camuscross, in Sleat. The gallant Captain had many curiosities which he collected when he was abroad, among them was a mysterious-looking box, "shaped somewhat like the case of an Egyptian mummy." The box and its contents the veteran guarded with jealous care, and not even the blandishments of his young lady friends (who, with the curiosity inherited from mother Eve, were keenly anxious to see what was inside of it) would induce him to open it. What became of the wonderful box and of "a rare illustrated history" which the veteran possessed no one seems now to know. The old soldier is said to have been buried with military honours by the officers and crew of a British gunboat which happened to be lying in the Sound of Scalpay when he died.

Sergeant John MacBeth,[1] Cameron Highlanders.

Sergeant John MacBeth (eldest son of the late Donald MacBeth, teacher, Applecross, Ross-shire, and grandson of the late John MacLeod, Gaelic teacher in the Torran district of the Island of Raasay, and of "Mairi Laghach," about whom the beautiful and ever popular Gaelic song of that name was composed by her father, Murdo MacKenzie, "Murachadh Ruadh Na 'm Bò") joined " the Cameron Highlanders" at Inverness on the 18th of December, 1890; and having gone abroad with his regiment, was stationed for a time at Malta and Gibraltar. Sergeant MacBeth went through the recent Soudan Campaign with " the Cameron Highlanders," including the battles of Atbara and Omdurman, at the former of which he was wounded, " a Dervish bullet, " after hitting and bending the buckle of his belt, entered his flesh, knocking him down " unconscious." He soon regained consciousness, however, and having succeeded in extracting the bullet, at once joined again in the fight. "This happened as the " regiment was pulling away Mahmoud's Zareba." Before returning home on furlough, after a severe attack of enteric fever, Sergeant MacBeth received the Khartoum medal from the hands of the Sirdar himself, now Lord Kitchener.

Sergeant Archibald MacSween, Duisdale-beg, Sleat, served in the 42nd Highlanders in the Peninsular War and at the battle of Waterloo, for which he obtained the Peninsular War medal and the Waterloo medal.

Private John MacIntosh, Isleornsay, Sleat, served in the 42nd Highlanders in the Peninsula, for which he received the war medal (with clasps for Corunna, Salamanca, Pyrenees, Nive, and Orthes) and also at Waterloo, for which he was awarded the Waterloo medal.

---

[1] " I claim to belong to the Island of Raasay, where the most of my relatives stay, including brothers and " sisters, although I was born at Applecross, which place I left quite young."—Letter from Sergeant John MacBeth, dated 10th February, 1899.

The following private soldiers all served in the 92nd Highlanders, and fought at the battle of Waterloo, for which they each got the Waterloo medal:—viz., William MacLure, Stonefield, Sleat; Donald Nicolson, Calgarry, Sleat; James Nicolson, Calgarry, Sleat; and James Fraser, Aird, Sleat. It is probable that all these men went also through a part, if not the whole, of the Peninsular Campaign, but there is no reliable information now to be obtained on this point.

Private Donald Campbell,[1] Teangue, Sleat.

Private Donald Campbell, Teangue, Sleat, served with the 92nd Highlanders throughout the Peninsular War, and was present at the battle of Waterloo, for which he got the Peninsular War medal (with clasps for Corunna and other engagements) and the Waterloo medal.

It is related of this veteran that in one battle he was wounded in the forearm, in another a bullet went through the bridge of his nose, while in a third he received a bullet in the forehead which travelled round and came out at the back of his head.

Private Murdoch Macintyre and Private Alexander MacGilvray, both of Aird, Sleat, served in the 42nd Highlanders in the Peninsular Campaign and at Waterloo, for which they got the Peninsular and Waterloo War medals. Macintyre was wounded at the battle of Corunna.

Private Murdoch MacLeod of Aird, Sleat, served in the 42nd Highlanders in the Peninsula, was wounded at the battle of Corunna, and received the Peninsular War medal.

Private Malcolm MacPherson, late of the 1st Battalion of the Scots Fusilier Guards, writes, saying:—

"Four MacPhersons from your native parish (Sleat) were present in the Crimea, viz.:—Privates Alexander MacPherson (James's son), who served in the 42nd Highlanders, and afterwards was through the Indian Mutiny (since dead); Angus MacPherson (Martin's son), 92nd Regiment, who went through the Indian Mutiny; Donald MacPherson (Miles's son), 71st Highlanders; and the writer, 1st Battalion Scots Fusilier Guards, in which battalion there served in the Crimea several others from various parts of Skye. Nicol Nicolson from Portree was present at all the engagements, and attained to the rank of Sergeant; Hugh Ferguson, Edinbane, was also present at all the engagements, and was discharged a private; Alexander Nicolson, Portree (medal and one clasp), attained to the rank of Sergeant, and died in the service; Angus MacLean, private (medal and clasp), and Donald MacKenzie, Tarskavaig, enlisted in the 92nd Highlanders, transferred to the 44th Regiment, present at all the engagements; severely wounded in the head at the attack on the Quarries.

---

[1] After his final return home from the wars, nothing pleased good old Donald Campbell more than to make kilts "of regulation pattern" for the little boys of Mid Sleat (including the writer), and to show them how to wear them with the dignity becoming the dress of the Gael.

Private Hugh Robertson.

The following information is quoted from "The Highland News," dated 22nd May, 1897:—

"Death of a Crimean Veteran.—The remains of Hugh Robertson, pensioner, King Street, Inverness, were interred in the Churchyard, Inverness, on Saturday. Deceased who was a native of Sleat, Skye, enlisted in the 92nd Regiment in the Forties, and was present in the Crimea and Indian Mutiny, and took part in the various engagements during these campaigns, for which he held the medals and clasps. Deceased was, like his brother Skyemen, a well-behaved soldier, and wore five good conduct badges. On retiring from the army in 1862 he came to Inverness, where he acted as groom to Colonel Stuart, Millburn, and was afterwards with Colonel Sutherland, Huntly Lodge, and latterly with Dr. Macnee. Captain Wimberley took a great interest in the old soldier, and many tokens of respect were shown at the funeral—wreaths being sent by Dr. and Mrs. Macnee and other friends."

Lance-Corporal Alexander MacPherson, a son of Neil MacPherson (Niall Ruadh), Knock, in Sleat, served for eight years (over seven years of which were abroad) in the 15th Hussars. He joined the service on the 24th of June, 1869; and on the 1st of December, 1874, passed as a telegraphist at Meerut, in India. He earned one good conduct stripe, and a first-class certificate of education. Like his gifted uncle, the late John MacPherson, Knock (Iain Mòr Buachaille), Corporal MacPherson is a poet of considerable merit.

Private Angus MacPherson enlisted in Captain Æneas MacIntosh's company of the 42nd Highlanders in 1745, and served abroad for three years and six months.[1]

Private Murdoch MacKenzie enlisted in Captain Æneas MacIntosh's company of the 42nd Highlanders in 1751, and served abroad for six months.[1]

The following list has been supplied by Corporal John Nicolson, late of the 42nd Highlanders (now residing at Tote, Skaebost Bridge, Skye), of veterans who belonged to his own neighbourhood, viz.:—John MacLean, who fought in the American War; Neil Ross, Neil Gillies, and Angus Beaton, who fought in Egypt under Sir Ralph Abercromby; Murdoch Nicolson, Angus Nicolson, and Malcolm Nicolson (Calum Na Rightaig), who served in the Peninsular War; Duncan Munro, who served in the Crimea for which he received a medal with three clasps, and in the Indian Mutiny, for which he got a medal and one clasp; Donald MacLean, 79th, Donald Beaton, Sergeant Roderick Matheson, John Nicolson, 92nd Highlanders, who served for

---

[1] The Regimental Records do not show to what part of Skye these two soldiers belonged.

21 years in India; Roderick Matheson, John MacFarlane, and Corporal John Nicolson himself, who was present at Bulganock on the 19th of September, 1854; the battle of the Alma on the 20th September, 1854; the battle of Balaclava on the 25th of October, 1854; the siege of Sebastopol from the 2nd to the 25th of October, 1854; the expedition to Kertch and Yenikale, and subsequently at the siege and capture of Sebastopol, for which he received the Crimean medal with three clasps. Corporal Nicolson served also in the Indian Mutiny, including the siege of Lucknow, battle and capture of Bareilly, and various minor affairs, for which services he was awarded the Indian Mutiny medal and one clasp. Nicolson has had an army service of twenty-four years and two months.

Private Samuel MacKay, Borve, by Portree, writing on the 13th of February, 1897, said:—" I will send you the names of pensioners in my own part of the parish " of Snizort. For myself I went to India in 1849, left it in 1860, was at the siege " and capture of Delhi, and all through the Mutiny. John Nicolson, 93rd, who is " living yet, had twenty-four years' service, was in the Crimea and in the Indian " Mutiny."

Colonel Alexander MacDonald, V.D., of Portree, Isle of Skye, writing on the 29th of January, 1898, said:—

"I heard a story the other day (from his daughter) of an old pensioner whom I knew well (Murdoch Nicolson, of the 79th Highlanders). When I was a small boy I used to gaze at him in silent awe. He was a very fine-looking old man, of magnificent physique, over six feet in height and broad-shouldered. He was severely wounded at Corunna, and fell near one of the Majors of the battalion whom he knew well. While they were both lying wounded, and almost helpless, on the field, a marauding or pillaging French party came round and at once seized on the Major, expecting money, his watch, &c. Murdoch, however, got up on his elbow and gave the man who had seized the Major a good thrust with his bayonet, which he was able to do, although he himself was suffering and scarcely able to move. Almost immediately after an ambulance party came round and took the Major—they could not at the time take both him and Murdoch. When being carried away the Major called back to Murdoch that he would not be left long there, and thanked him for what he had done. Soon after the ambulance people came round again for Murdoch and took him to the hospital. When recovered, to his surprise, he was taken before Wellington, who told him that he had heard of his gallantry, and said that he would be glad to do anything for him that he could, and asked him if he could read and write. There were no school boards in those days, and Murdoch was obliged to reply that he could do neither. Wellington then said 'poor man,' and added that he was sorry that he could do nothing for him, but that he appreciated his gallantry. This is an old story, but I knew the man myself, and he should not be forgotten. The old man was a fine specimen of the soldier, and quite erect and well set up, although he was between seventy and eighty when I knew him.

"I told you that about fifty years ago the village of Portree, on the day on which the pensioners were paid, used to be like a market day almost. The veterans used to turn out then in force, and, according to 'use and wont' with old soldiers, they had a good glass together, and the boys of the place used to gather around them and listen to the stirring stories of the veterans' sufferings and campaigns. One pensioner named MacQueen ('Wallace,' we used to call him) told the most sensational tales, and our delight was to make him fight his battles over again. This, with the aid of a little 'Talisker,' he was unfailingly delighted to do. I also told you how an old soldier from Broadford (MacKinnon or MacInnes) had carried, or helped to carry, one of the MacDonalds (a gallant artillery officer[1]) from Scalpay in his plaid off the field of Waterloo. The man had been a herd-boy at Scalpay, and the first meeting of the pair was when MacKinnon or MacInnes found his friend lying wounded. They had been boys together. You may fancy their feelings!"

Private Malcolm Nicolson (Calum Na Rightaig), of the 92nd Highlanders, formerly mentioned:—

Mr. D. Nicolson, retired teacher, Uig, Skye, writing to Miss Susan Martin of Glendale, on the 20th of January, 1898, said:—"I knew Calum Na Rightaig personally. "When I came to Uig in 1852 he was a tenant in Edrigil, Uig, and many a day he "was 'Ceilidh' or visiting in my house, and very jolly he was. When I left Uig for "Kilmuir he removed to Tote in Snizort, and there he died." Calum Na Rightaig had five clasps to his Peninsular War medal—viz., those for Corunna, Vittoria, Pyrenees, Nive, and Orthes. It was at Orthes he lost his arm.—Extract from letter from Secretary of the Royal United Service Institution, London, dated 6th December, 1897.

The following paragraph, which went the round of the newspapers recently, contains a reference to Calum's War medal, and may be of interest.

Interesting Medals, 1898.

"Visitors to the Royal United Service Institution, Whitehall, just now have the opportunity to see a representative and extensive collection of war medals—certainly one of the best in existence—gathered together by Colonel the Hon. H. F. Eaton, Grenadier Guards. Among others is the clasp won by M. Nicolson, 92nd Foot, for his courage at Orthes, on 27th February, 1814. Nicolson spent the evening of his life in the Isle of Skye, where, at the age of ninety, he died in 1863. In the West he was known as 'Calum na ritaig,' Malcolm with the stump arm. J. Maclean, 42nd Foot, was one of the men who carried Sir John Moore to his grave, and the clasp given to him bears the significant names Corunna, Salamanca, Pyrenees, and Toulouse. Among other medals awarded to Scotsmen is that of A. Munro, Sergeant, 42nd Royal Highlanders, the Black Watch, the obverse showing troops filing through a mountainous district, the figure of St. Andrew, with a motto, 'Nemo me impune lacessit,' and the thistle; on

---

[1] Captain (afterwards Lieutenant-General) Alexander MacDonald.

the reverse side, Corunna, Orthes, &c., the flying figure of Victory, and the 'Forty-second,' surrounded by laurel leaves. That, again, awarded to J. Munro, 93rd Highlanders, for the relief of Lucknow, is an interesting remembrancer."—"The Highland News."

Private Donald Matheson (already mentioned), 93rd Highlanders—"a Thin Red Line" Hero—enlisted in the 93rd Highlanders on the 30th of July, 1851, at Inverness, and was discharged at Netley, on pension, on the 27th of July, 1869. He was born at Stenscholl, near Portree, and joined the army at the age of twenty years. He served in the Eastern Campaign, including Bulgaria and the Crimea, from the 27th of February, 1854, to the 16th of February, 1856; in the East Indies from the 20th of September, 1857, to the 22nd of January, 1869; has the Crimean medal with clasps for Alma, Balaclava, and Sebastopol, and also the Turkish medal, and the Indian medal, and clasp for the capture of Lucknow.

www.ingramcontent.com/pod-product-compliance
Lightning Source LLC
Chambersburg PA
CBHW080543230426

43663CB00015B/2697